SEVEN SEAS ENTERTAINMENT PRESENTS

DAI DARK

story and art by Q HAYASHIDA   VOLUME 3

TRANSLATION
Daniel Komen

ADAPTATION
Casey Lucas

LETTERING
Phil Christie

ORIGINAL COVER DESIGN
**Shun SASAKI +
Yoko NAKANISHI(AYOND)**

COVER DESIGN
Nicky Lim

PROOFREADER
Kurestin Armada

COPY EDITOR
Dawn Davis

EDITOR
J.P. Sullivan

PRINT MANAGER
Rhiannon Rasmussen-Silverstein

PRODUCTION ASSOCIATE
Christa Miesner

PRODUCTION MANAGER
Lissa Pattillo

MANAGING EDITOR
Julie Davis

ASSOCIATE PUBLISHER
Adam Arnold

PUBLISHER
Jason DeAngelis

DAI DARK Vol. 3
by Q HAYASHIDA
© 2019 Q HAYASHIDA
All rights reserved.
Original Japanese edition published by SHOGAKUKAN.
English translation rights in the United States of America, Canada and the
United Kingdom arranged with SHOGAKUKAN through Tuttle-Mori Agency, Inc.

Seven Seas press and purchase enquiries can be sent to Marketing Manager Lianne
Sentar at press@gomanga.com. Information regarding the distribution and purchase of
digital editions is available from Digital Manager CK Russell at digital@gomanga.com.

Seven Seas and the Seven Seas logo are trademarks of
Seven Seas Entertainment. All rights reserved.

ISBN: 978-1-64827-367-4
Printed in Canada
First Printing: December 2021
10 9 8 7 6 5 4 3 2 1

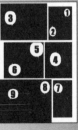

//// READING DIRECTIONS ////

This book reads from *right to left*,
Japanese style. If this is your first time
reading manga, you start reading from
the top right panel on each page and
take it from there. If you get lost, just
follow the numbered diagram here.
It may seem backwards at first,
but you'll get the hang of it! Have fun!!

Follow us online: www.SevenSeasEntertainment.com

DAI DARK ③

Q HAYASHIDA

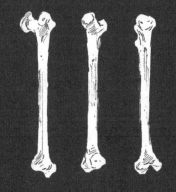

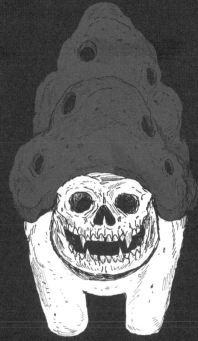

CAST

DARK PAGGY AVAKIAN

A dark paggy even more special than the paggies most spacelings carry. Always concerned for Sanko's safety, and rarely on good terms with Death.

ZAHA SANKO

An ever-journeying boy who maintains a cheerful and friendly disposition despite everyone trying to kill him all the time. Loses it under Damemaru's mind control. Now his dark hide's in tatters and his body's gushing blood!

The Four Little Shits

Hated all over the galaxy!!

HAJIME DAMEMARU

The last of the Four Little Shits. Blown to smithereens by Photostere, shipped in pieces through space, and now in contact with Sanko's crew...?

SHIMADA DEATH

Sanko's friend, an enigmatic life-form born of the world of darkness. Immortal, as far as we know, and quite powerful indeed. A free spirit. Sanko's only friend.

MISETANI BOX

Arms dealer on Darknest, world of darkness. Sells all kinds of things in exchange for bones. Can be summoned to any planet by ringing Misetani's Toll.

MOJA

Support minibot of Sanko's spaceship, the *Moja*. Performs useful functions such as adjusting the cabin environment and helping Sanko make meapswiches.

The Story So Far

Somewhere in the endless darkness of space... Fourteen-year-old Zaha Sanko, whose bones are said to grant any wish to those who acquire them, was fleeing for his life with both his faithful dark paggy Avakian and the grim reaper Shimada Death. Pursuing them is spacewide megacorporation Photosfere, which labels them the "Four Little Shits"! As Sanko and company infiltrate a spaceship belonging to Photosfere's Purge Crew, they come upon the fourth Little Shit, Hajime Damemaru.
It looks as if he's already dead, until his eyes glint with menace...

Dai Dark, vol. 3

Bone 13
Inside Lighthead
007

Bone 14
Lighthead's Dark Side
041

Bone 15
How Much for That Damemaru
071

Bone 16
Bone Improvement
105

Bone 17
Ow Ticka Ow Ow
139

Bone 18
Fear of Failure
171

Bonus Bone
203

Bone 13: Inside Lighthead

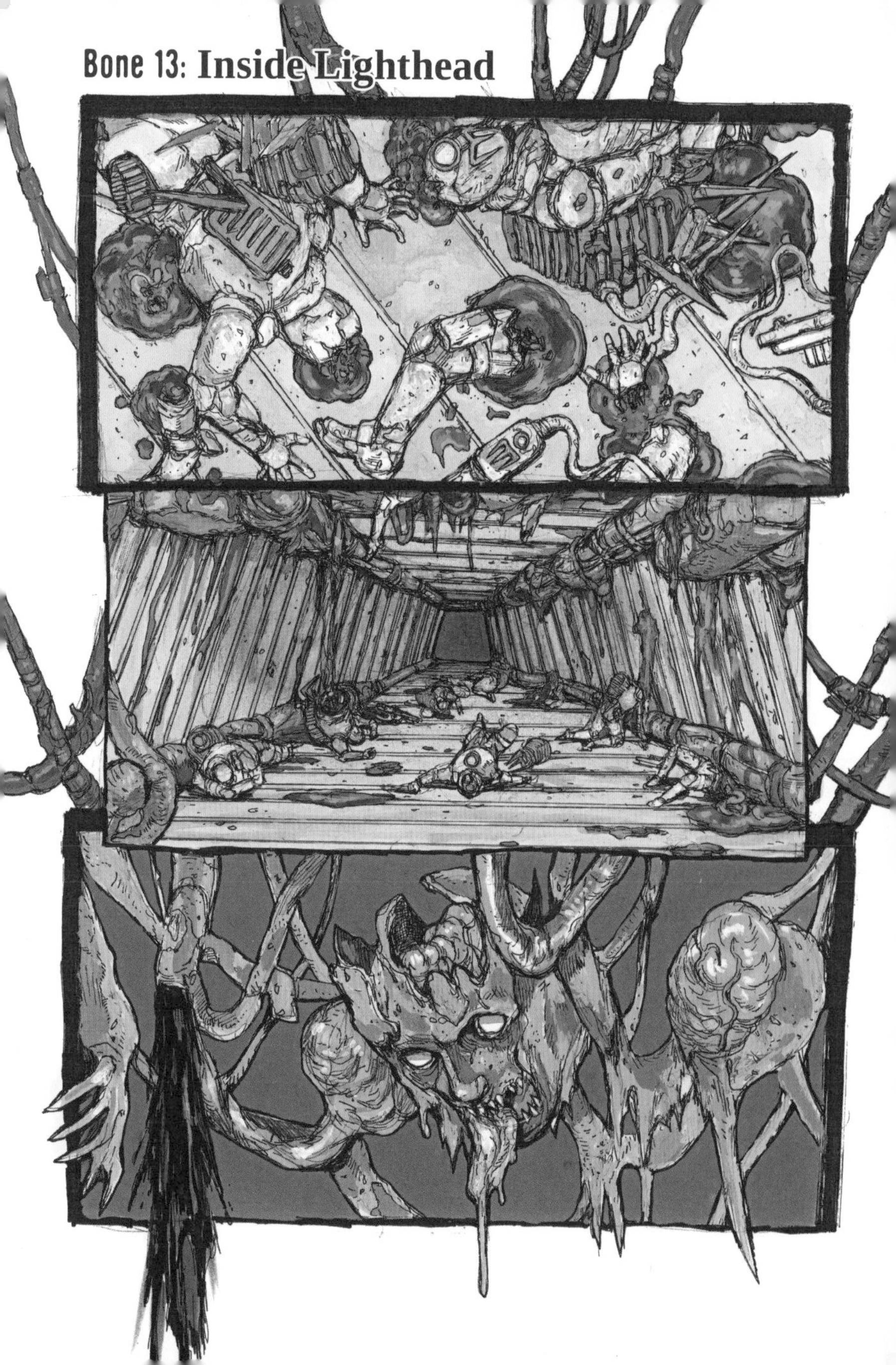

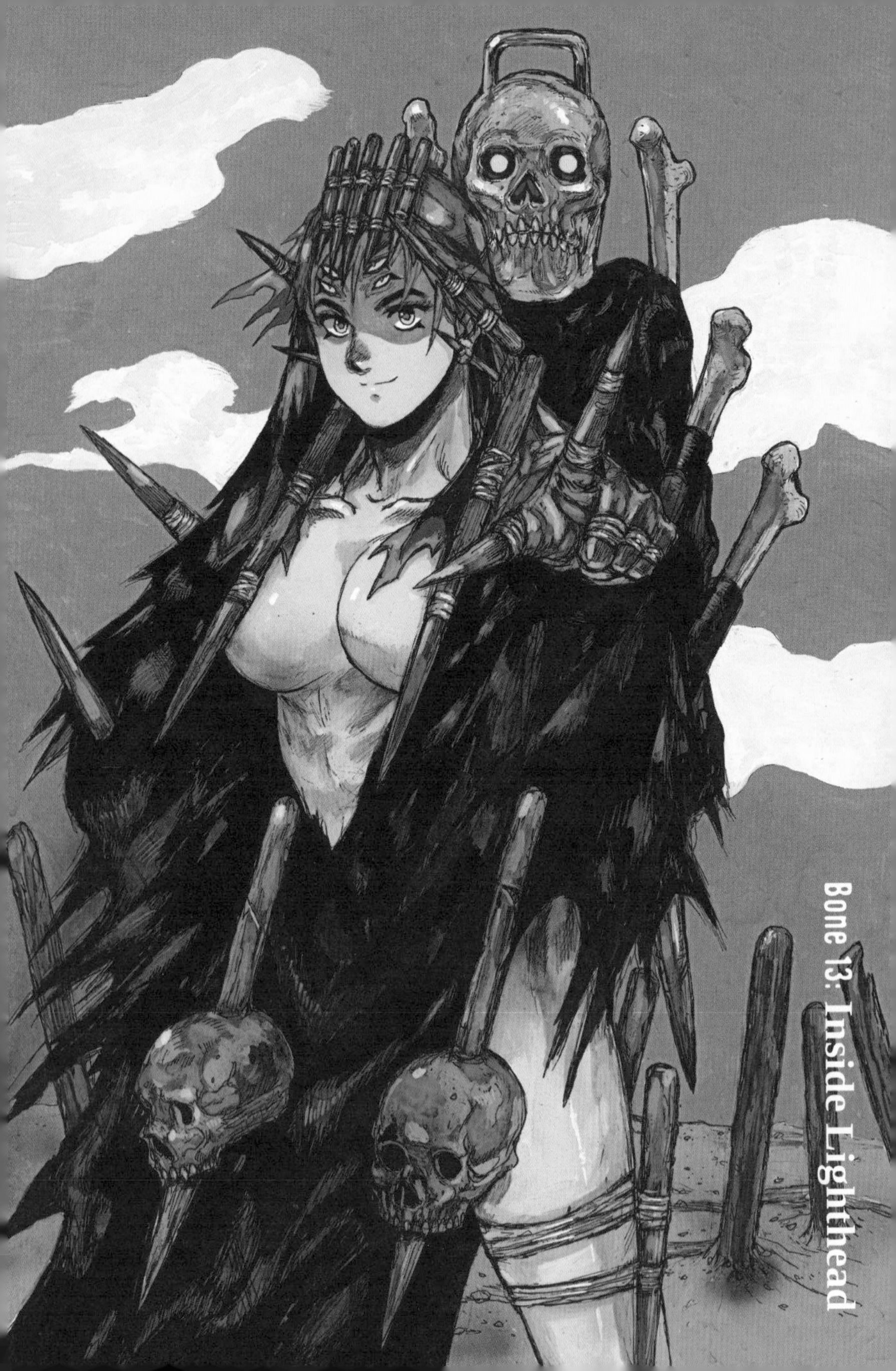

Bone 13: Inside Lighthead

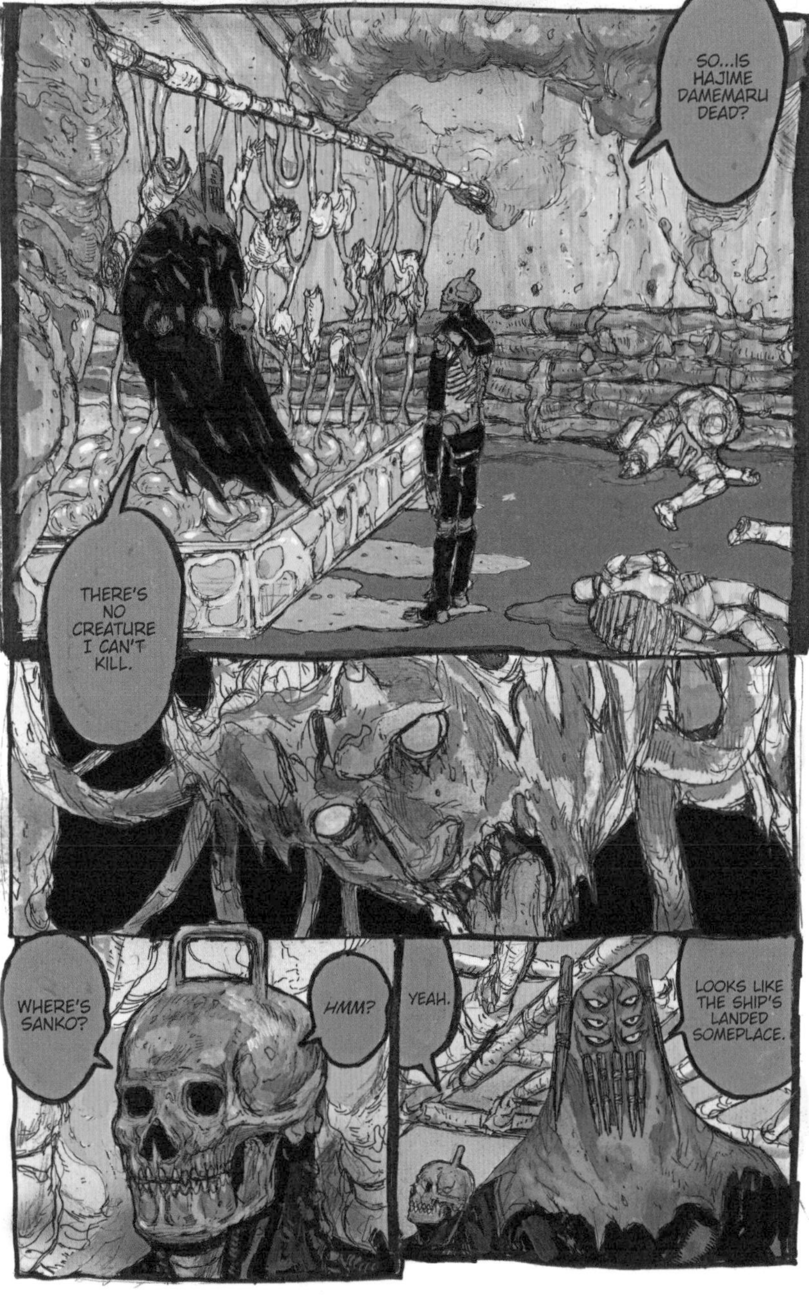
SO...IS HAJIME DAMEMARU DEAD?
THERE'S NO CREATURE I CAN'T KILL.
LOOKS LIKE THE SHIP'S LANDED SOMEPLACE.
YEAH.
HMM?
WHERE'S SANKO?

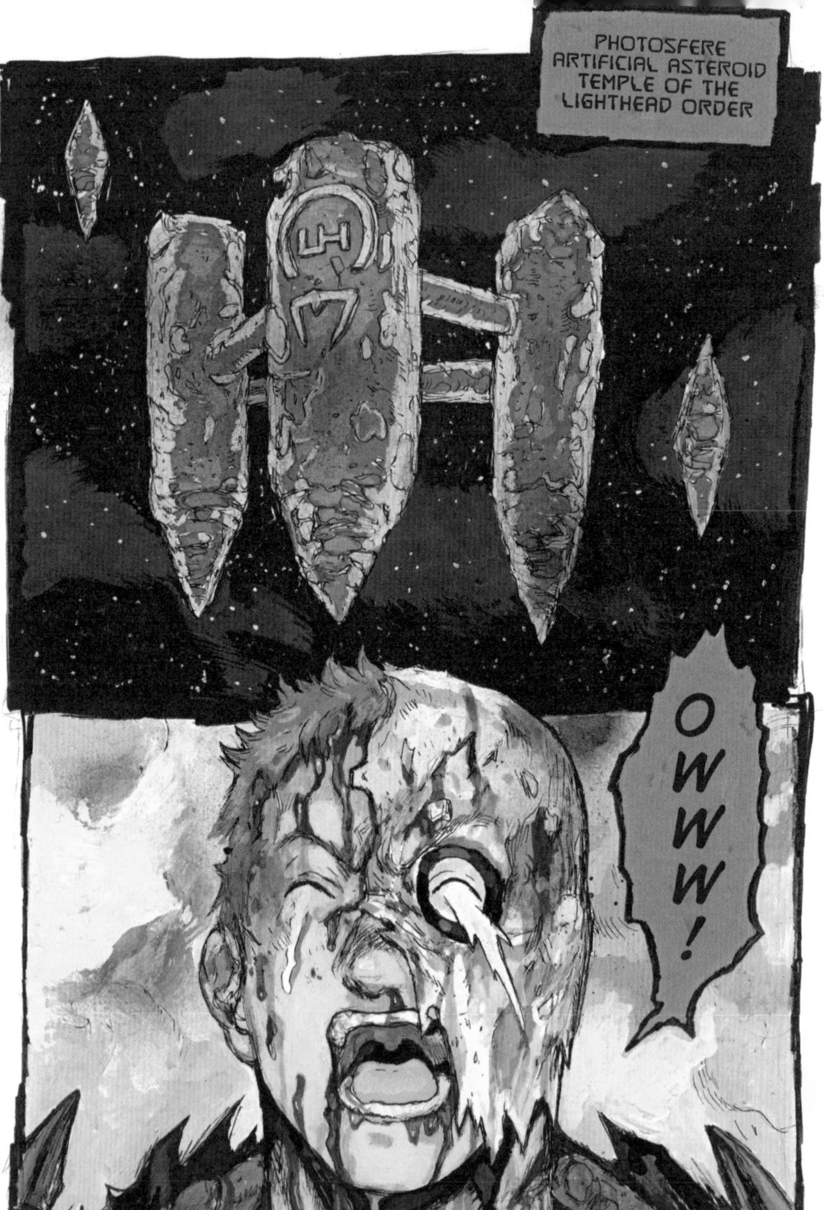
PHOTOSFERE ARTIFICIAL ASTEROID TEMPLE OF THE LIGHTHEAD ORDER
OWWW!

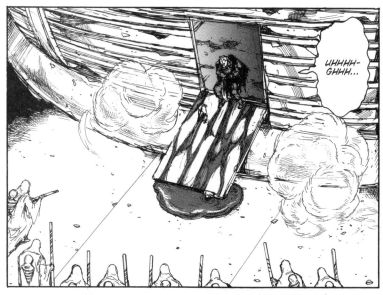

UHHHH-GHHH...

SHIMA-AADA!

AVA-KIAN!

UHHH... WHO ARE YOU GUYS?

WH... WHERE AM I?

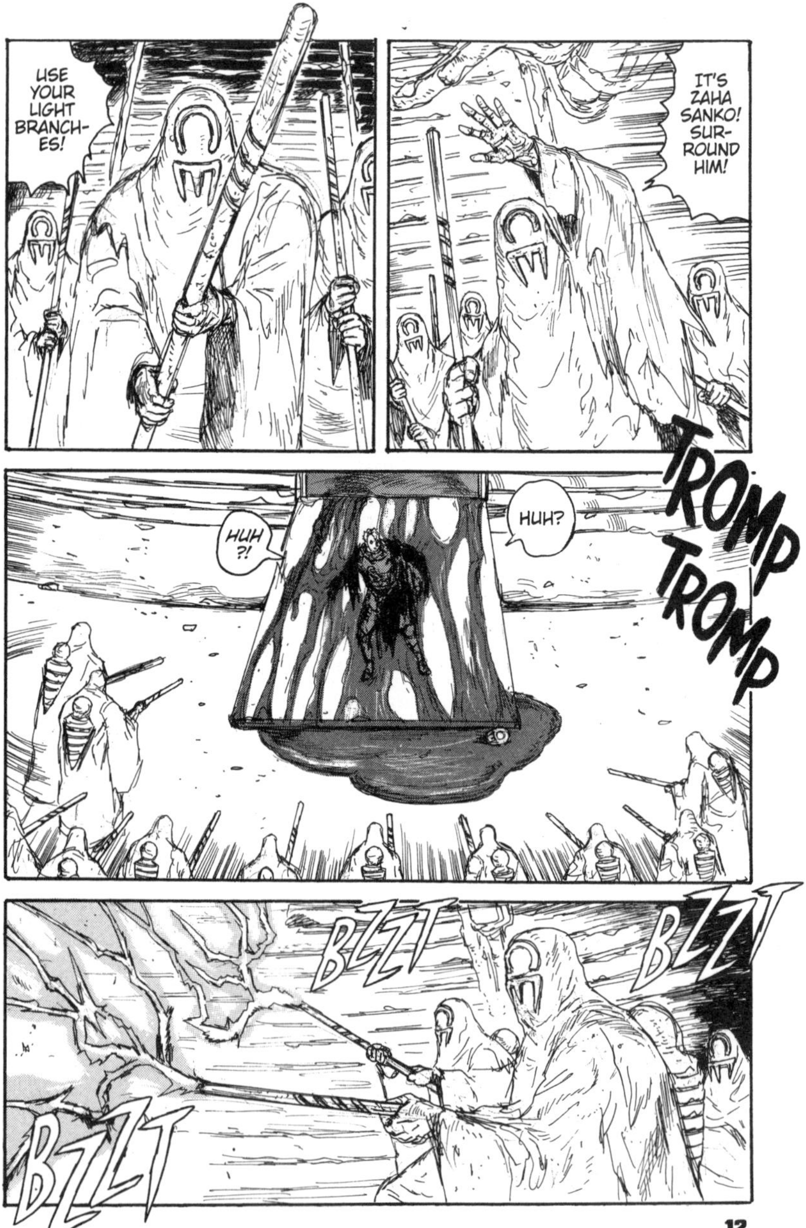
IT'S ZAHA SANKO! SUR-ROUND HIM!
USE YOUR LIGHT BRANCH-ES!
TROMP TROMP
HUH?
HUH ?!
BZZT
BZZT
BZZT

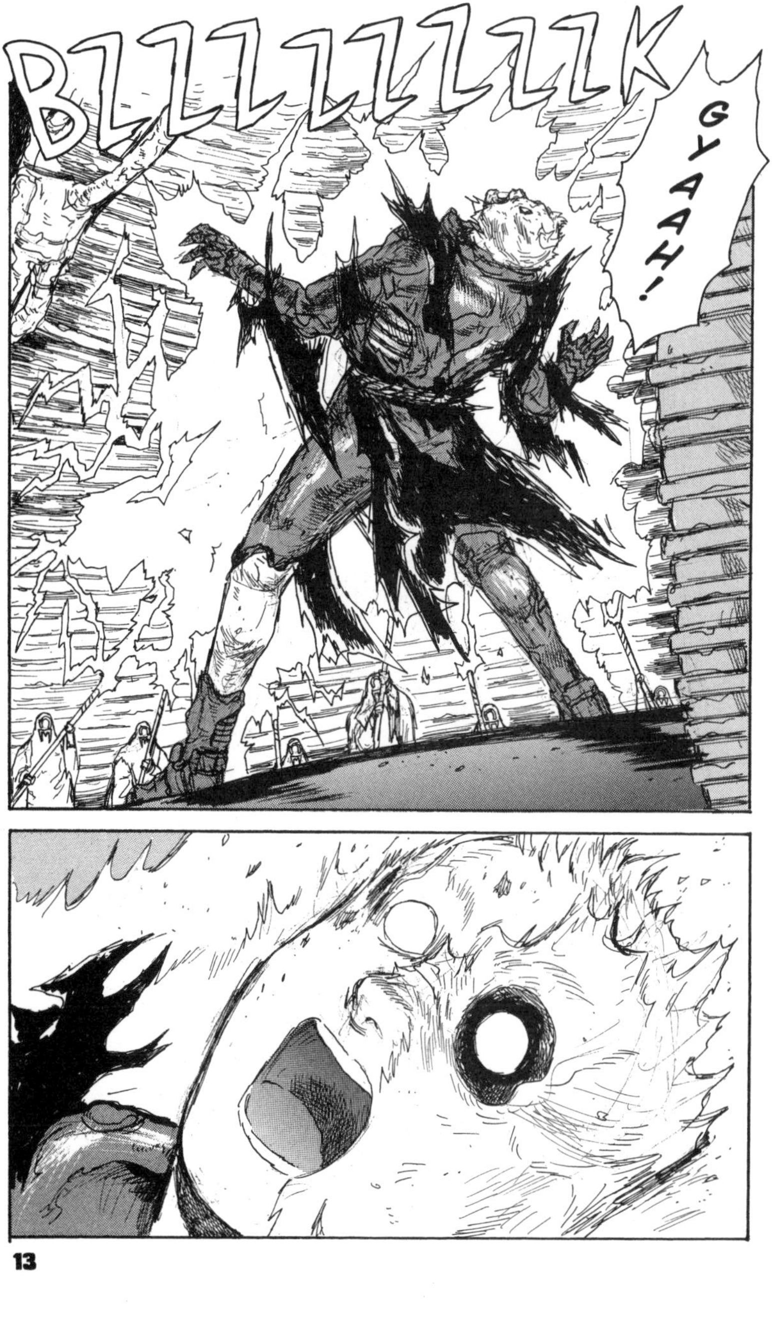
BZZZZZZZZZK
GYAAAH!

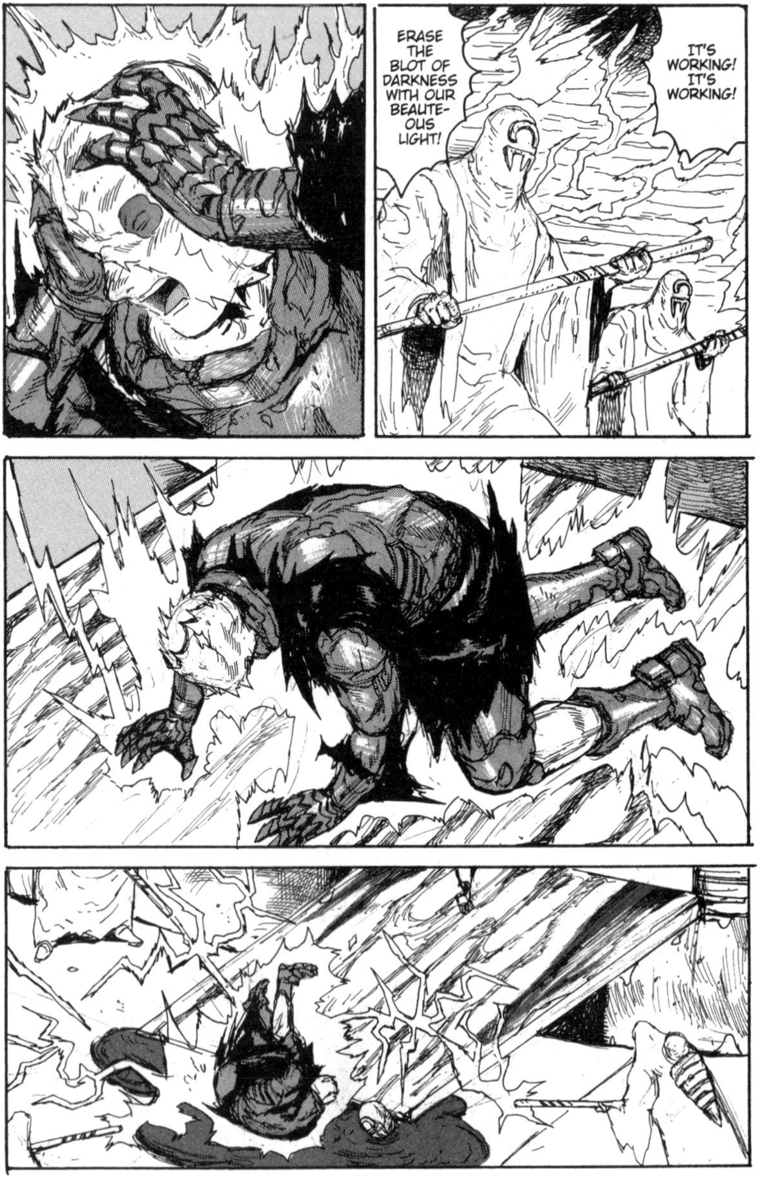
IT'S WORKING! IT'S WORKING!
ERASE THE BLOT OF DARKNESS WITH OUR BEAUTE-OUS LIGHT!

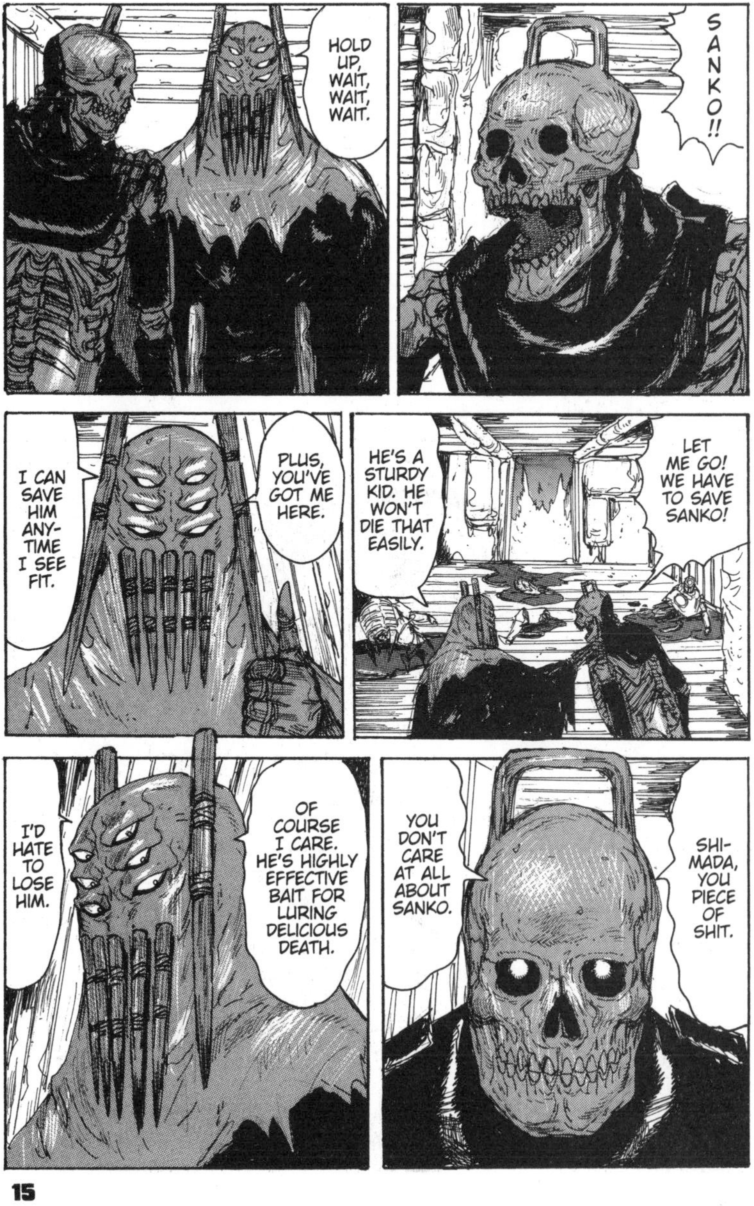
SANKO!!
HOLD UP, WAIT, WAIT, WAIT.
LET ME GO! WE HAVE TO SAVE SANKO!
HE'S A STURDY KID. HE WON'T DIE THAT EASILY.
PLUS, YOU'VE GOT ME HERE.
I CAN SAVE HIM ANYTIME I SEE FIT.
SHIMADA, YOU PIECE OF SHIT.
YOU DON'T CARE AT ALL ABOUT SANKO.
OF COURSE I CARE. HE'S HIGHLY EFFECTIVE BAIT FOR LURING DELICIOUS DEATH.
I'D HATE TO LOSE HIM.

AND YOU NEED MORE BONES, DON'T YOU?
YOU NEED ME AS WELL, MY LITTLE FRIEND.
NGH...
I THINK YOU OUGHT TO ASK ME NICELY.
I **AM** THE MOST POWERFUL BEING IN THE UNIVERSE, AFTER ALL.

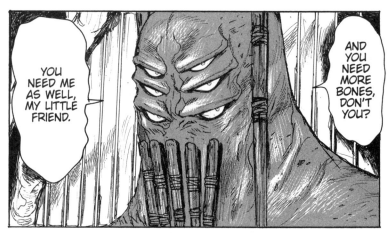

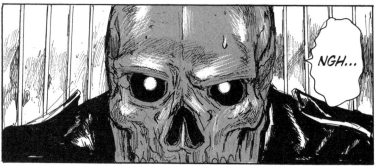

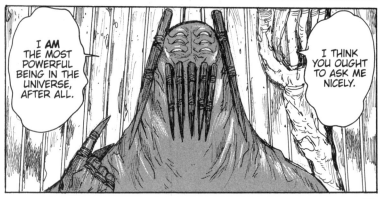

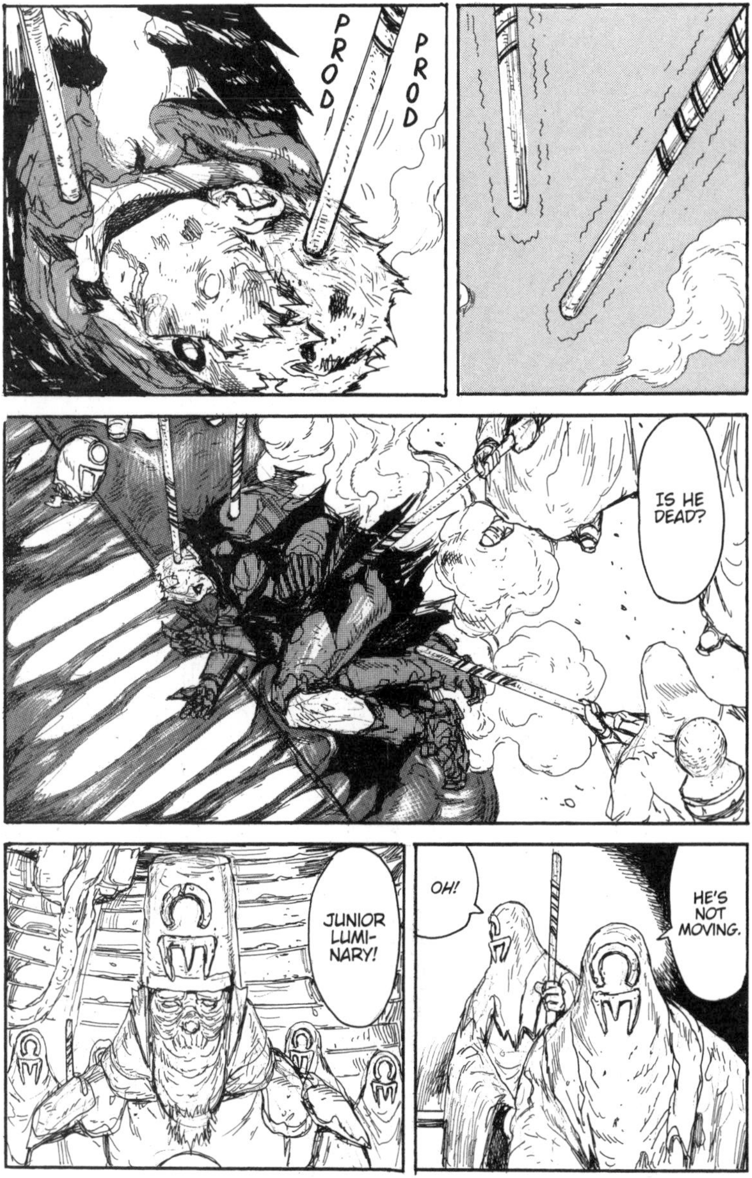
PROD
PROD
IS HE DEAD?
HE'S NOT MOVING.
OH!
JUNIOR LUMINARY!

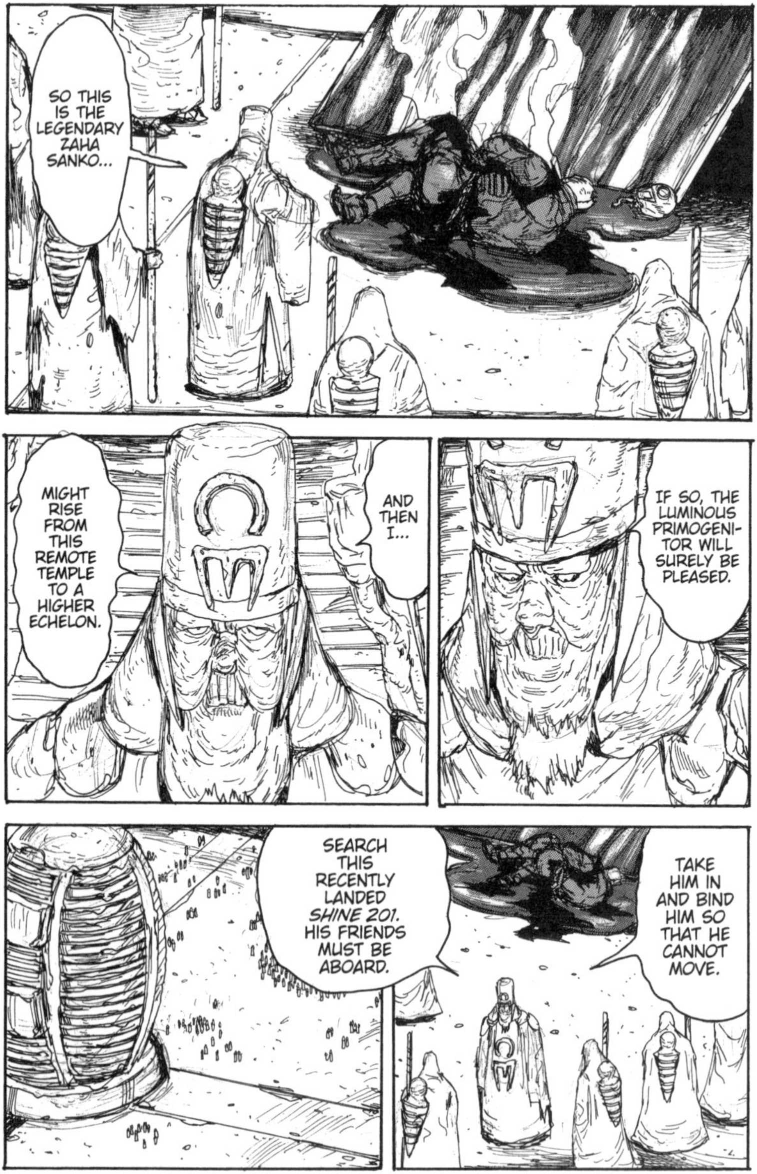
SO THIS IS THE LEGENDARY ZAHA SANKO...
IF SO, THE LUMINOUS PRIMOGENITOR WILL SURELY BE PLEASED.
AND THEN I...
MIGHT RISE FROM THIS REMOTE TEMPLE TO A HIGHER ECHELON.
TAKE HIM IN AND BIND HIM SO THAT HE CANNOT MOVE.
SEARCH THIS RECENTLY LANDED *SHINE 201*. HIS FRIENDS MUST BE ABOARD.

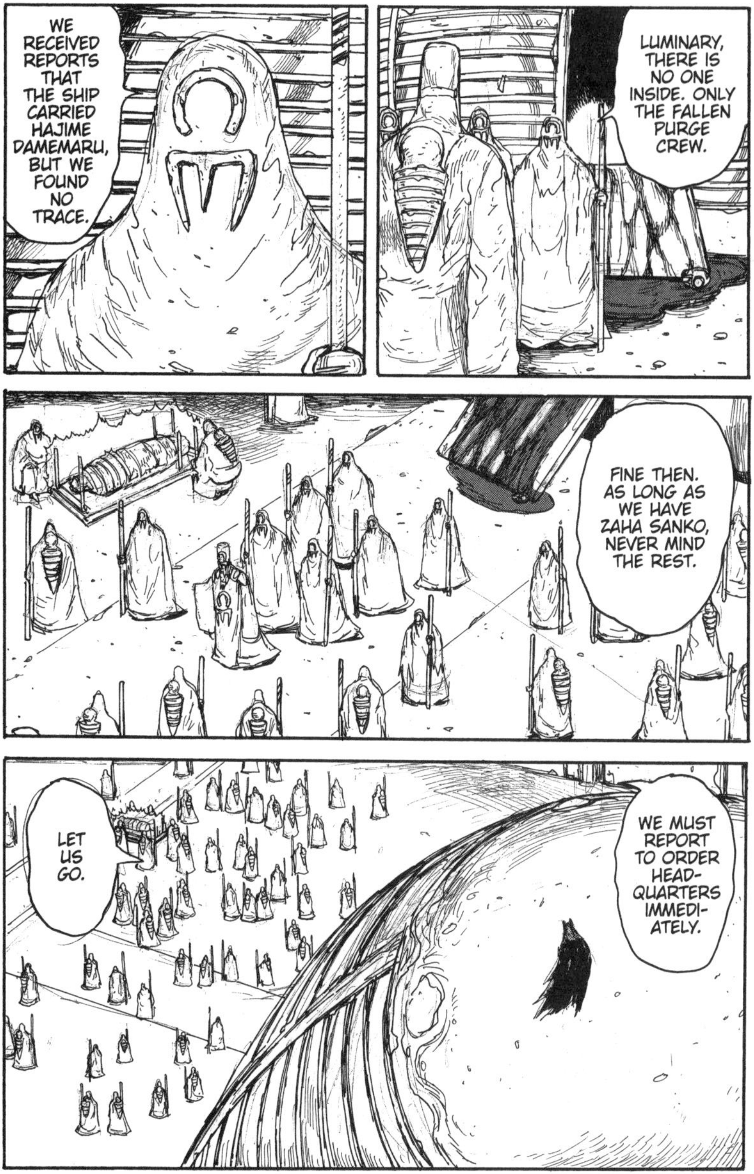
LUMINARY, THERE IS NO ONE INSIDE. ONLY THE FALLEN PURGE CREW.
WE RECEIVED REPORTS THAT THE SHIP CARRIED HAJIME DAMEMARU, BUT WE FOUND NO TRACE.
FINE THEN. AS LONG AS WE HAVE ZAHA SANKO, NEVER MIND THE REST.
WE MUST REPORT TO ORDER HEAD-QUARTERS IMMEDI-ATELY.
LET US GO.

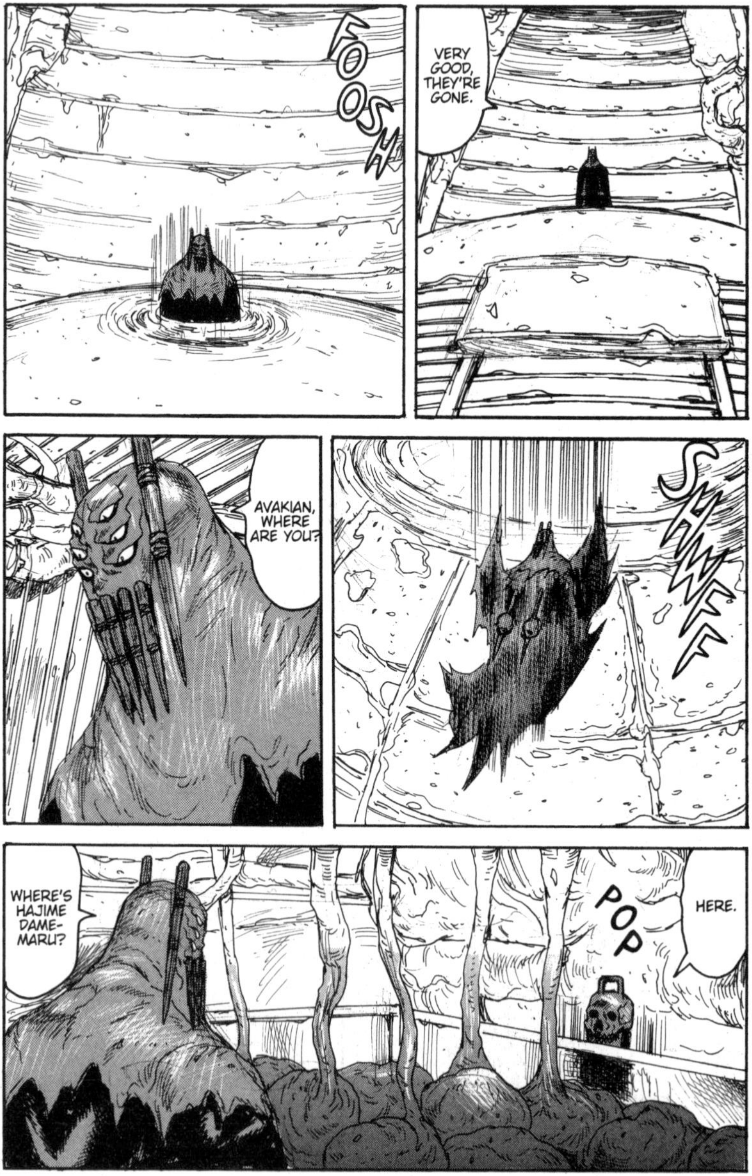
VERY GOOD, THEY'RE GONE.
FOSH
AVAKIAN, WHERE ARE YOU?
HERE.
POP
WHERE'S HAJIME DAME-MARU?

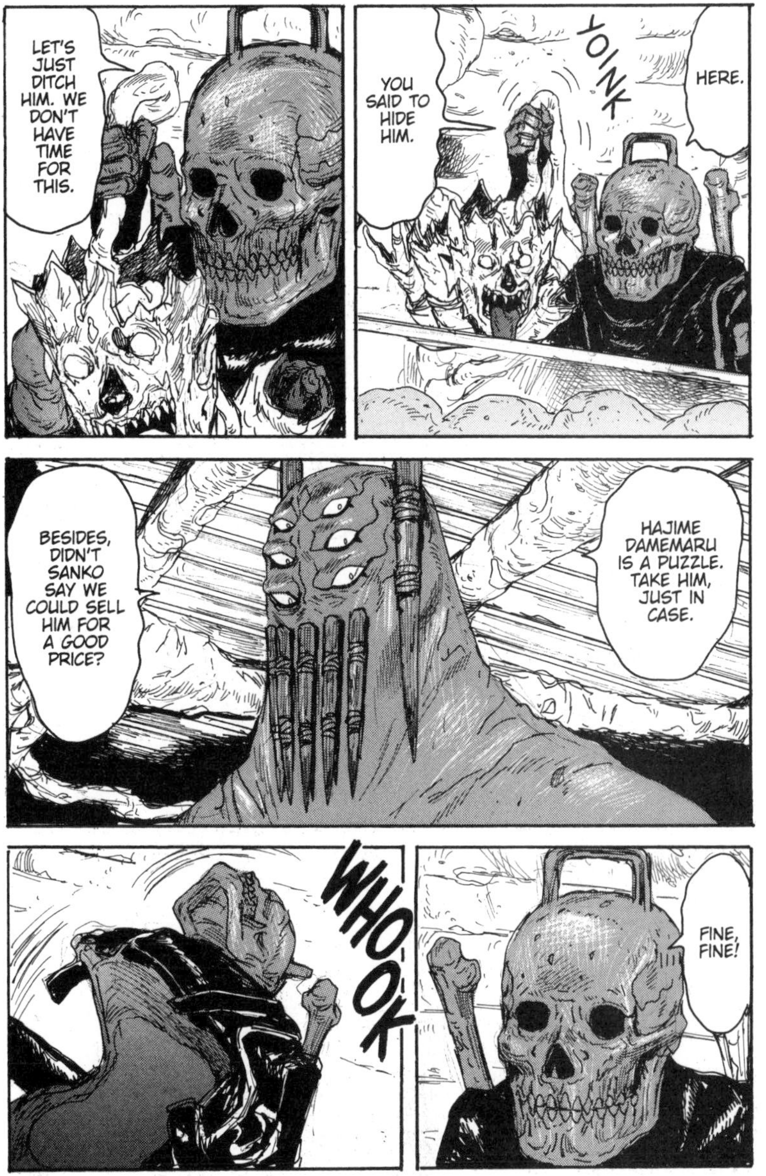
HERE.
YOINK
YOU SAID TO HIDE HIM.
LET'S JUST DITCH HIM. WE DON'T HAVE TIME FOR THIS.
HAJIME DAMEMARU IS A PUZZLE. TAKE HIM, JUST IN CASE.
BESIDES, DIDN'T SANKO SAY WE COULD SELL HIM FOR A GOOD PRICE?
FINE, FINE!
WHOOOK

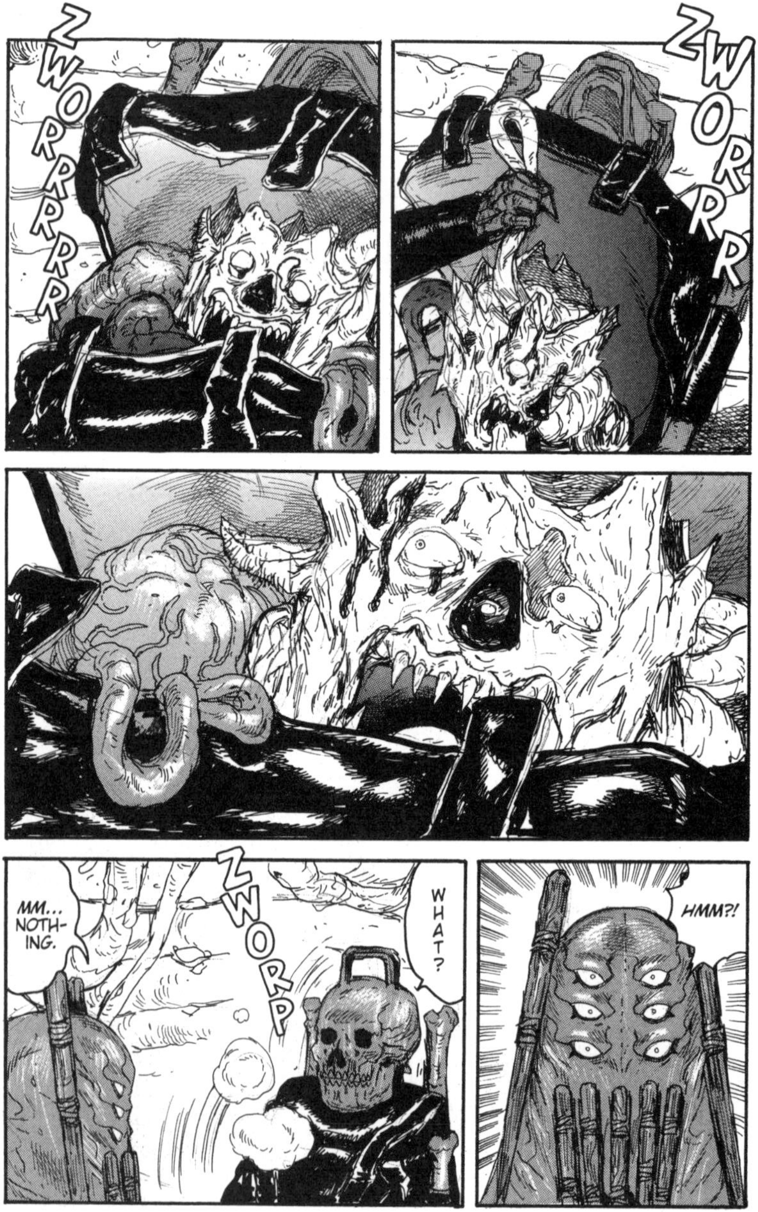
ZWORRR
ZWORRRRR
HMM?!
WHAT?
ZWORP
MM... NOTHING.

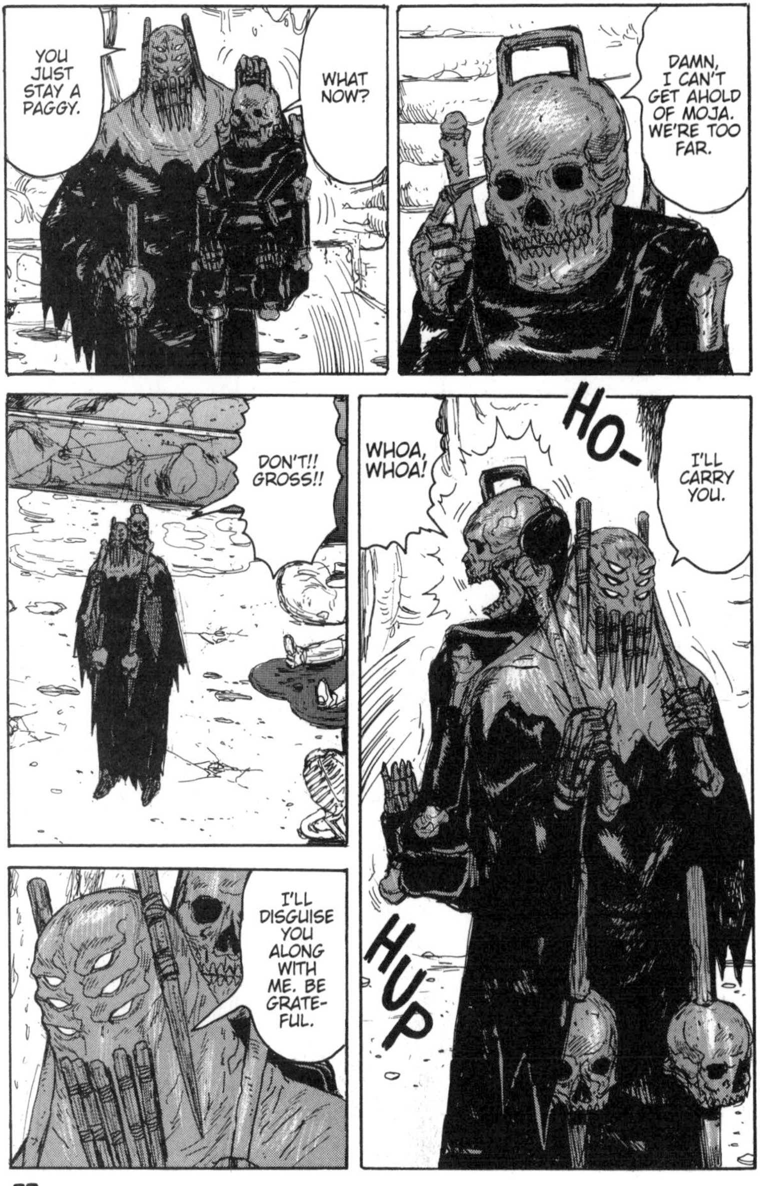
DAMN, I CAN'T GET AHOLD OF MOJA. WE'RE TOO FAR.
WHAT NOW?
YOU JUST STAY A PAGGY.
HO-
I'LL CARRY YOU.
WHOA, WHOA!
HUP
DON'T!! GROSS!!
I'LL DISGUISE YOU ALONG WITH ME. BE GRATEFUL.

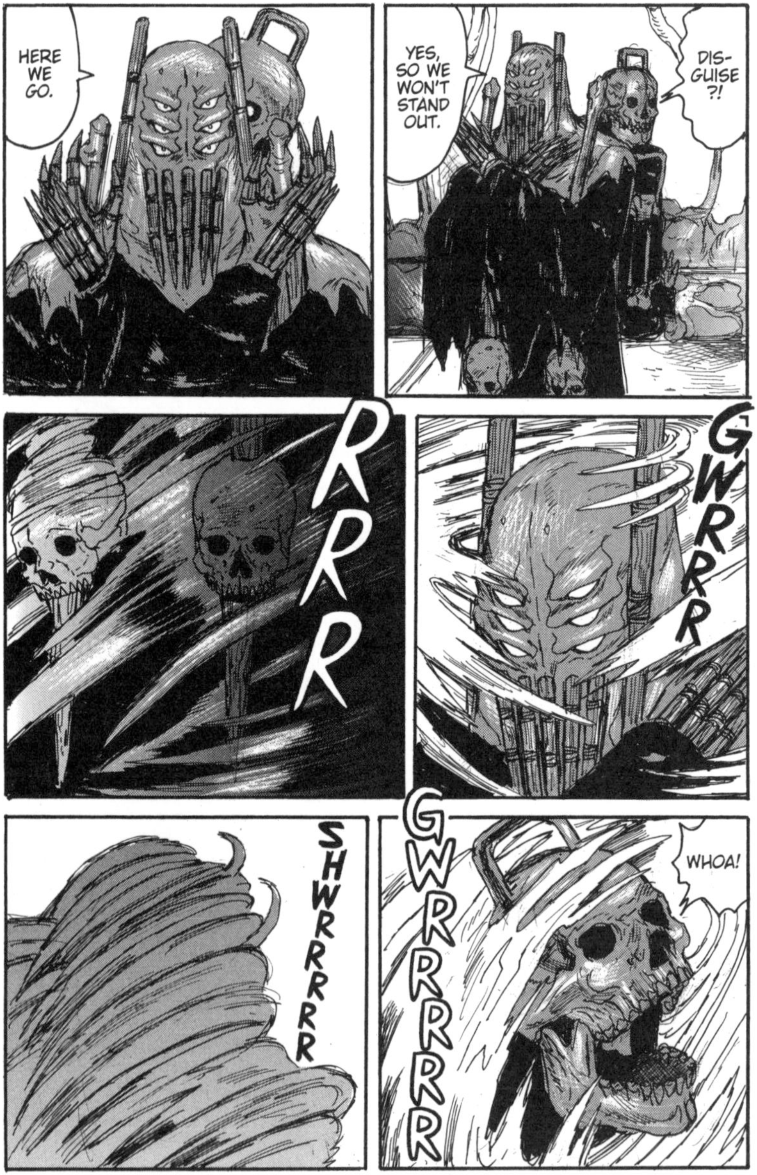
DIS-GUISE?!
YES, SO WE WON'T STAND OUT.
HERE WE GO.
GWRRRR
RRRR
WHOA!
GWRRRRRR
SHWRRRRRR

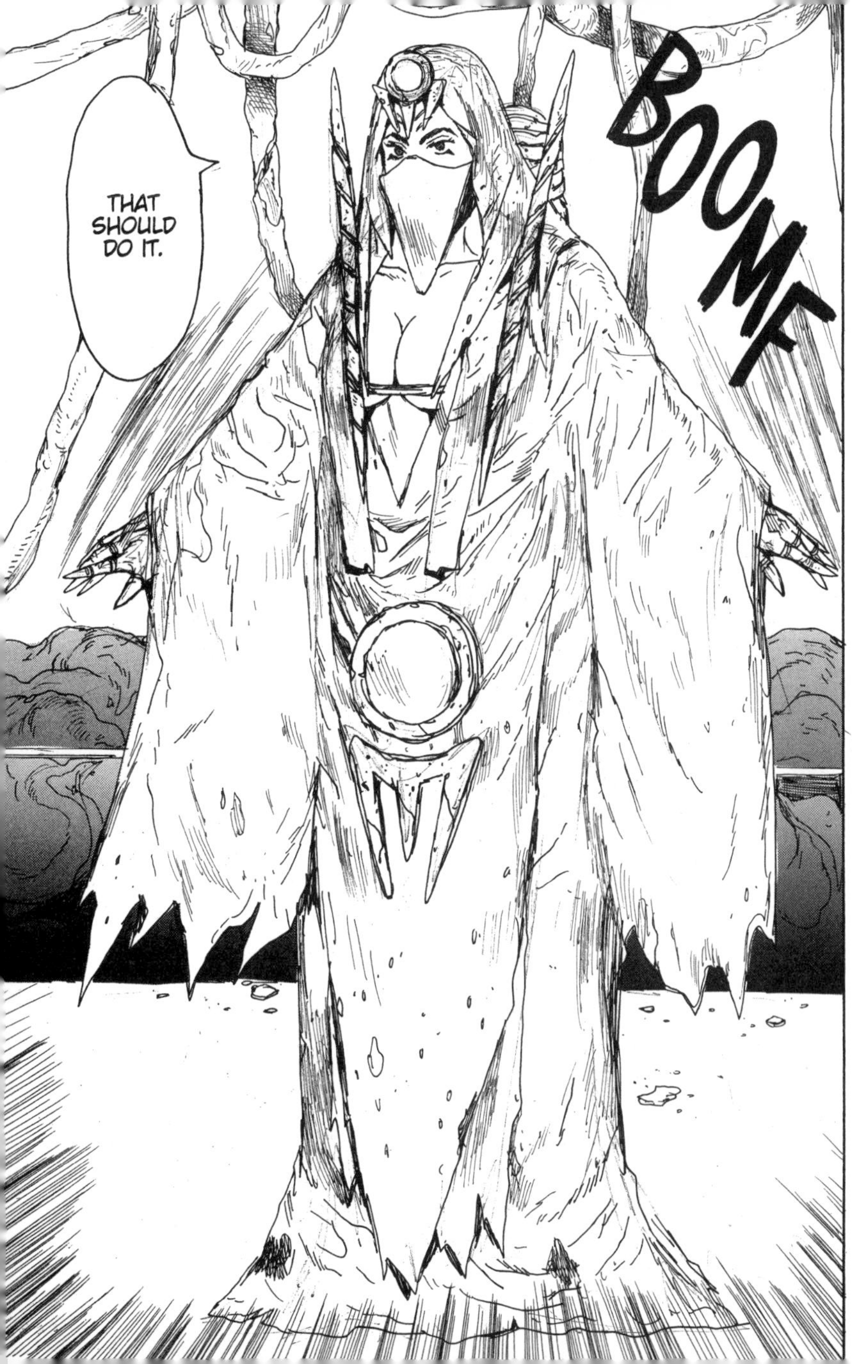
BOOMF
THAT SHOULD DO IT.

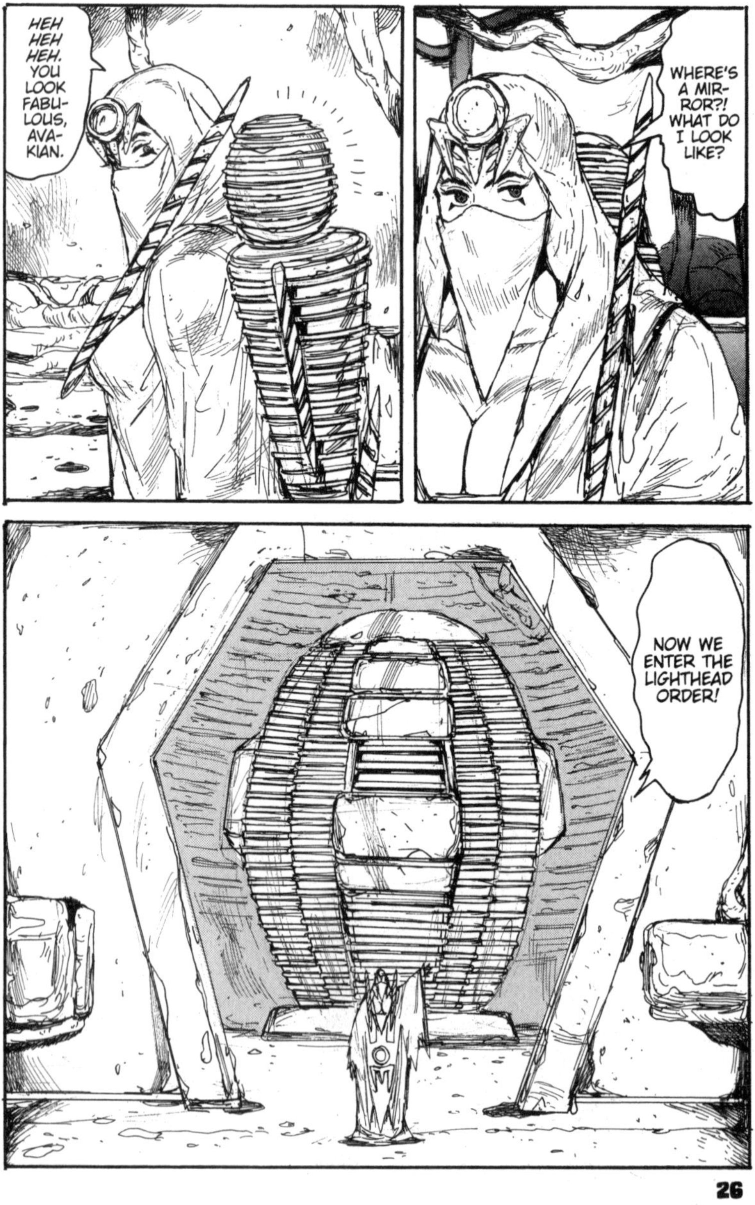
WHERE'S A MIRROR?! WHAT DO I LOOK LIKE?
HEH HEH HEH. YOU LOOK FABULOUS, AVAKIAN.
NOW WE ENTER THE LIGHTHEAD ORDER!

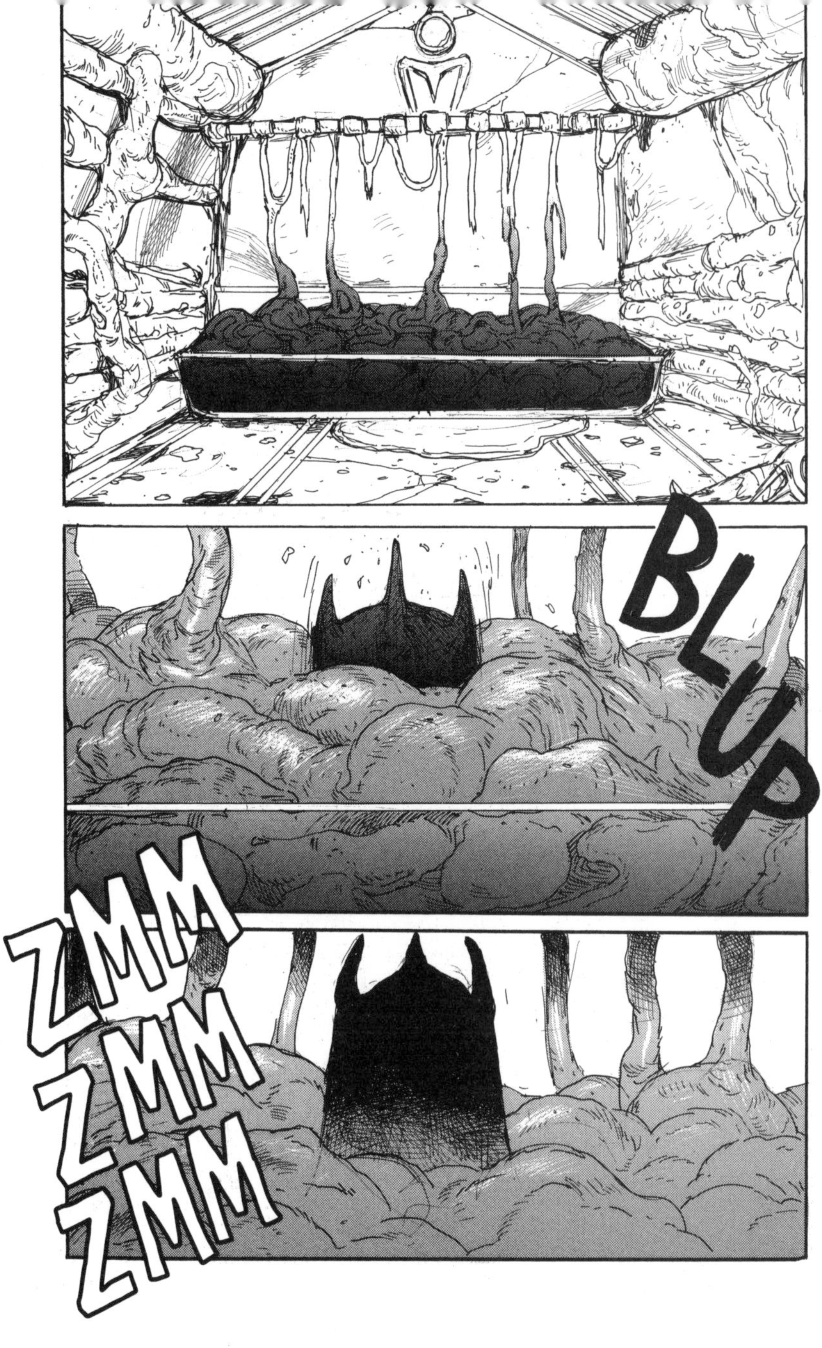
BLUP
ZMM ZMM ZMM ZMM

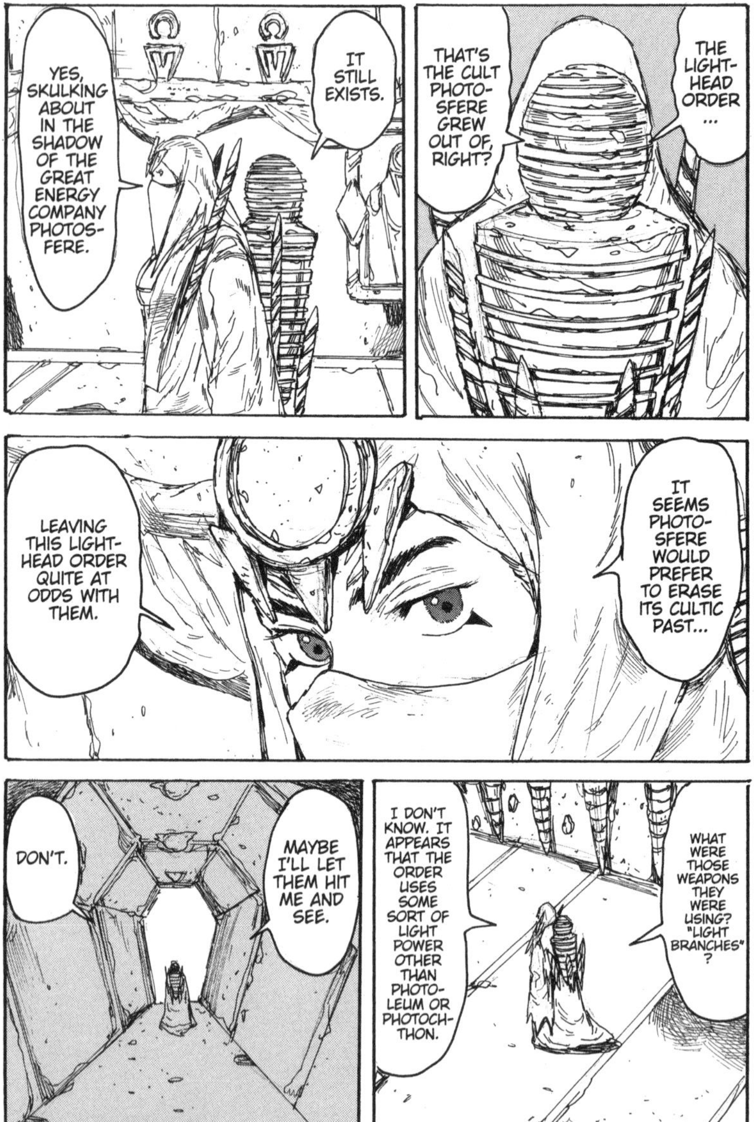
THE LIGHT-HEAD ORDER ...
THAT'S THE CULT PHOTOSFERE GREW OUT OF, RIGHT?
IT STILL EXISTS.
YES, SKULKING ABOUT IN THE SHADOW OF THE GREAT ENERGY COMPANY PHOTOSFERE.
IT SEEMS PHOTOSFERE WOULD PREFER TO ERASE ITS CULTIC PAST...
LEAVING THIS LIGHT-HEAD ORDER QUITE AT ODDS WITH THEM.
WHAT WERE THOSE WEAPONS THEY WERE USING? "LIGHT BRANCHES"?
I DON'T KNOW. IT APPEARS THAT THE ORDER USES SOME SORT OF LIGHT POWER OTHER THAN PHOTOLEUM OR PHOTOCHTHON.
MAYBE I'LL LET THEM HIT ME AND SEE.
DON'T.

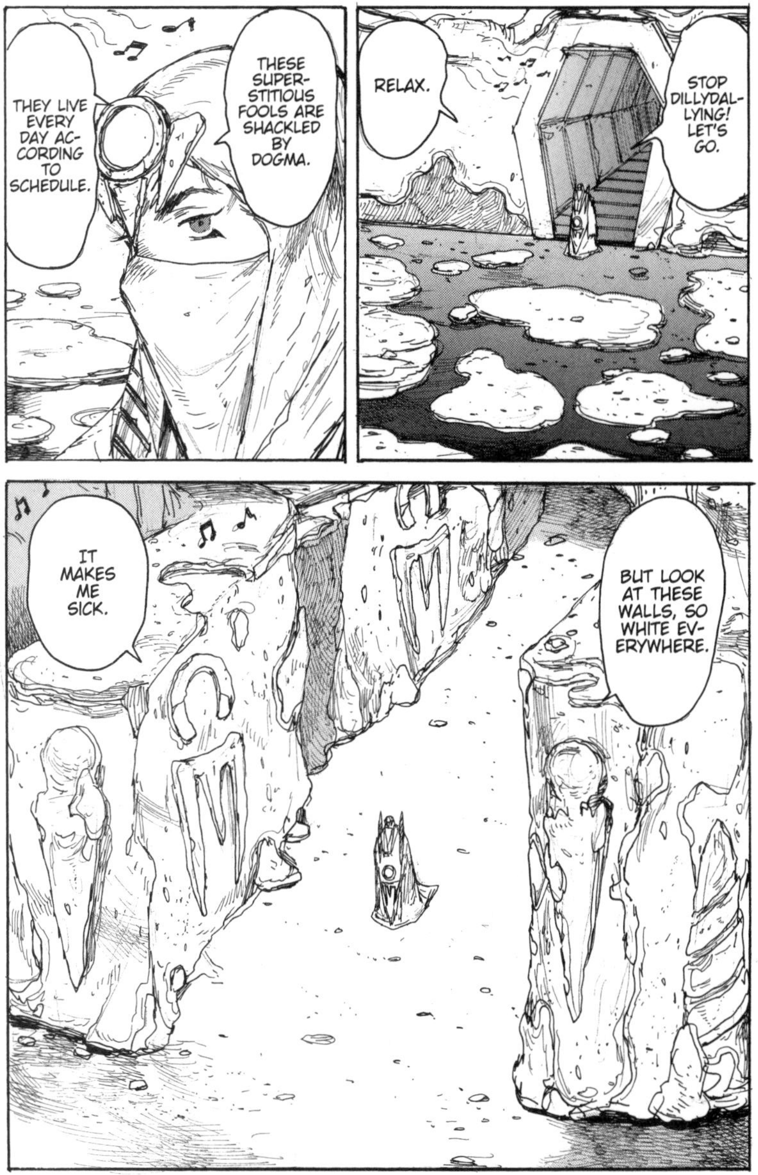
STOP DILLYDALLYING! LET'S GO.
RELAX.
THESE SUPERSTITIOUS FOOLS ARE SHACKLED BY DOGMA.
THEY LIVE EVERY DAY ACCORDING TO SCHEDULE.
BUT LOOK AT THESE WALLS, SO WHITE EVERYWHERE.
IT MAKES ME SICK.

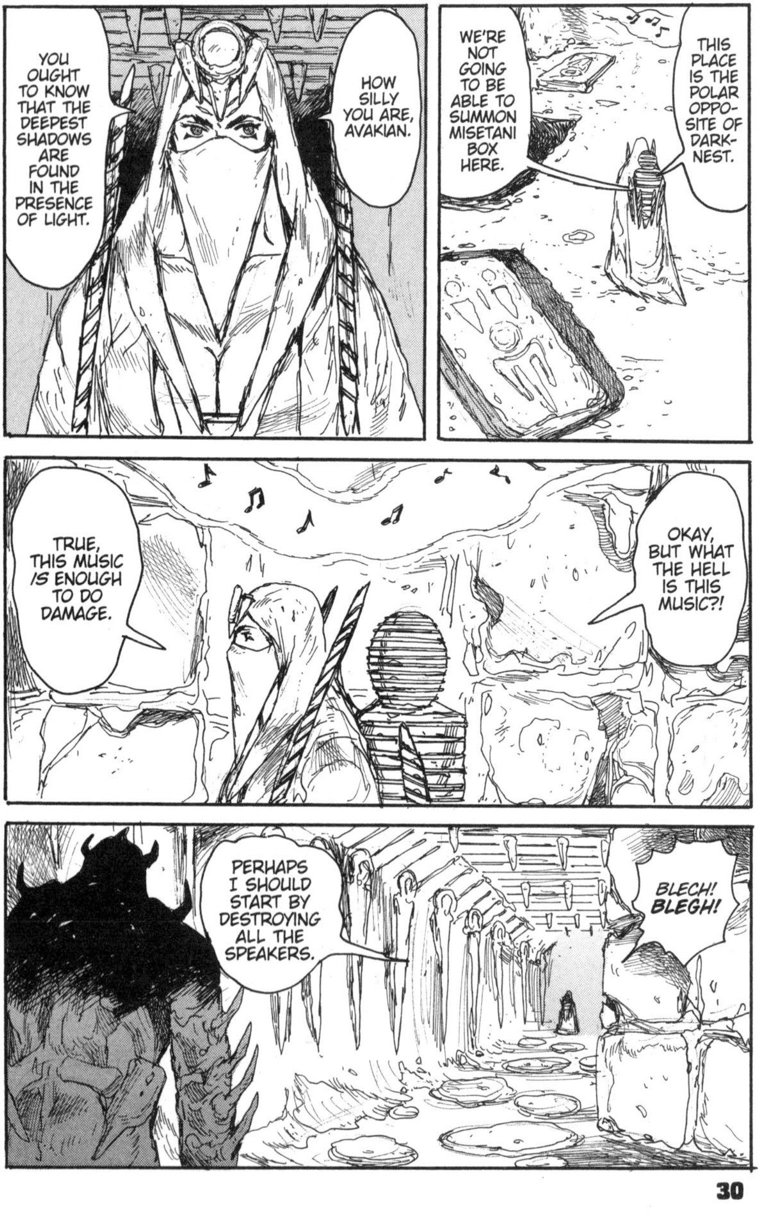
THIS PLACE IS THE POLAR OPPOSITE OF DARKNEST.
WE'RE NOT GOING TO BE ABLE TO SUMMON MISETANI BOX HERE.
HOW SILLY YOU ARE, AVAKIAN.
YOU OUGHT TO KNOW THAT THE DEEPEST SHADOWS ARE FOUND IN THE PRESENCE OF LIGHT.
OKAY, BUT WHAT THE HELL IS THIS MUSIC?!
TRUE, THIS MUSIC *IS* ENOUGH TO DO DAMAGE.
BLECH! BLEGH!
PERHAPS I SHOULD START BY DESTROYING ALL THE SPEAKERS.

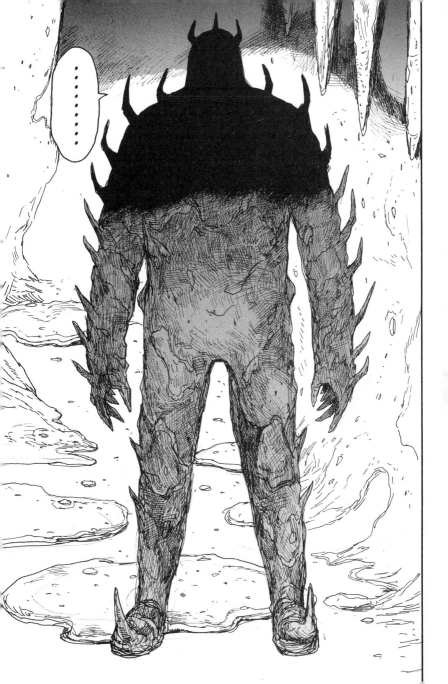

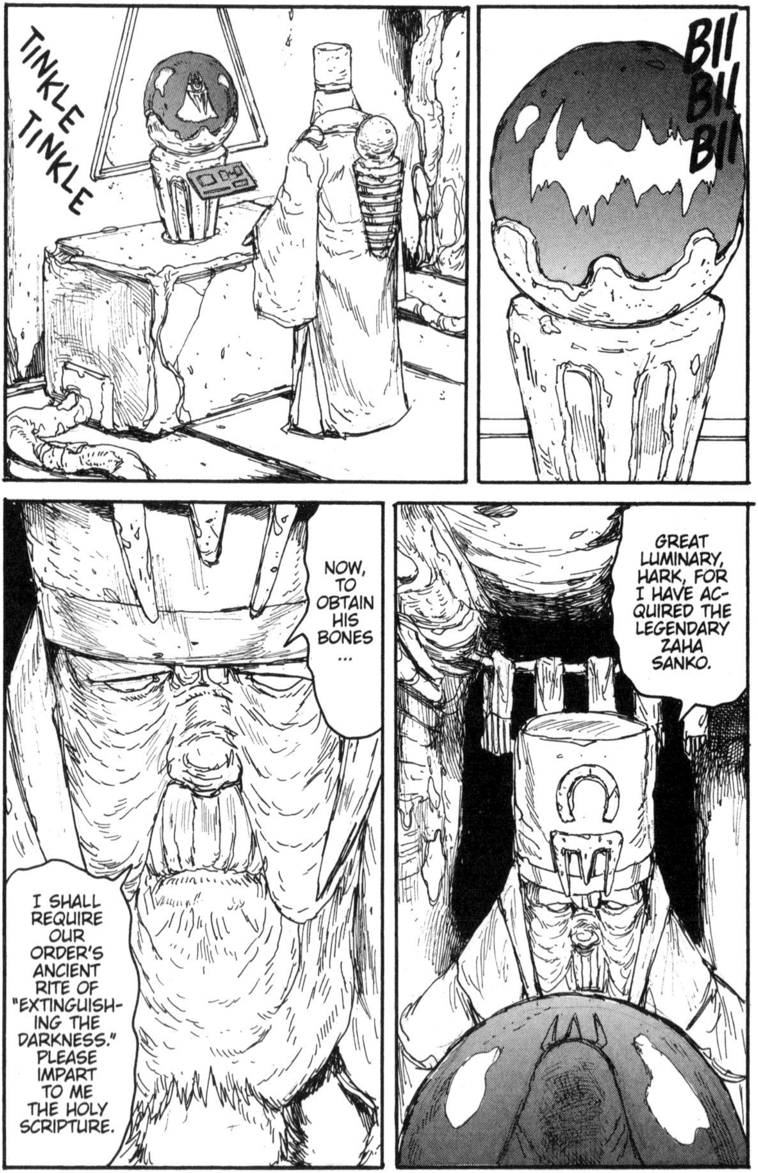
BII BII BII
TINKLE TINKLE
GREAT LUMINARY, HARK, FOR I HAVE AC-QUIRED THE LEGENDARY ZAHA SANKO.
NOW, TO OBTAIN HIS BONES ...
I SHALL REQUIRE OUR ORDER'S ANCIENT RITE OF "EXTINGUISH-ING THE DARKNESS." PLEASE IMPART TO ME THE HOLY SCRIPTURE.

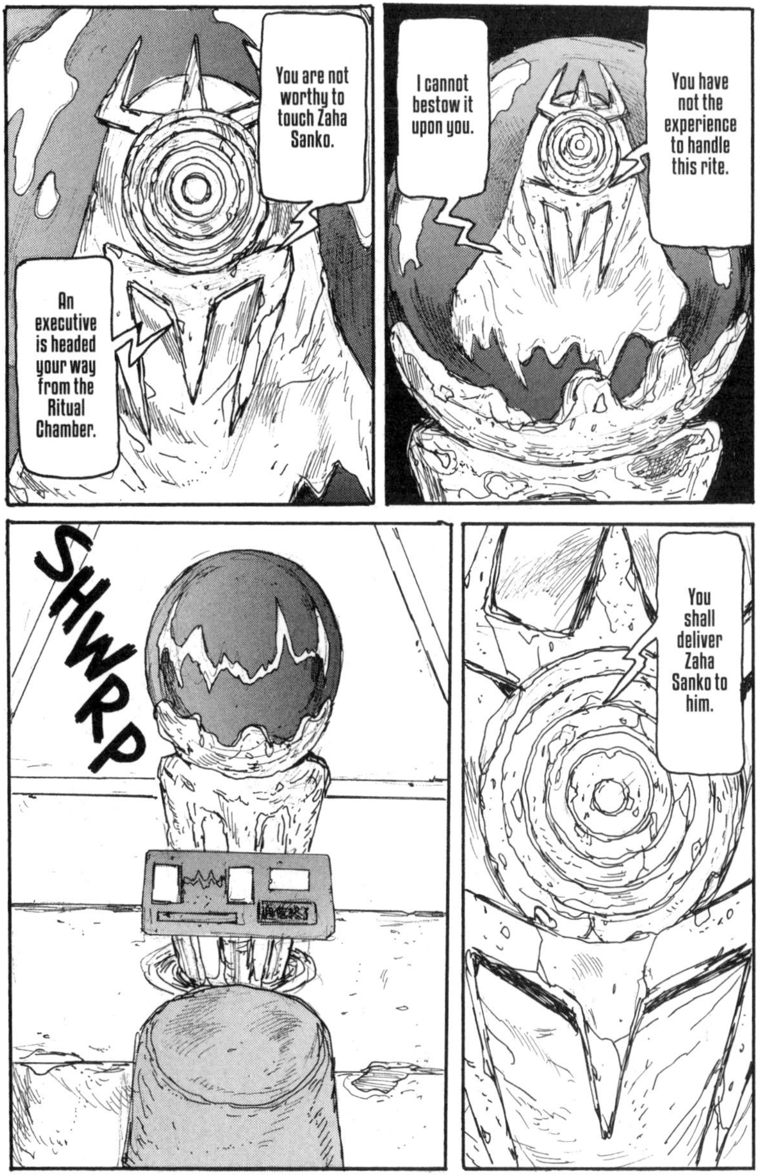
You have not the experience to handle this rite.
I cannot bestow it upon you.
You are not worthy to touch Zaha Sanko.
An executive is headed your way from the Ritual Chamber.
You shall deliver Zaha Sanko to him.
SHWRP

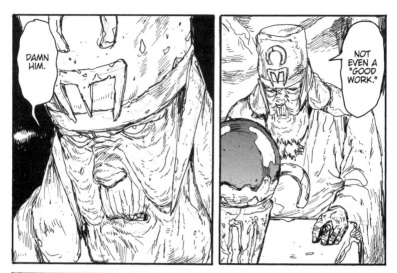

DAMN HIM.

NOT EVEN A "GOOD WORK."

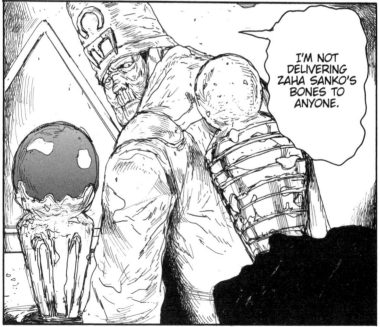

I'M NOT DELIVERING ZAHA SANKO'S BONES TO ANYONE.

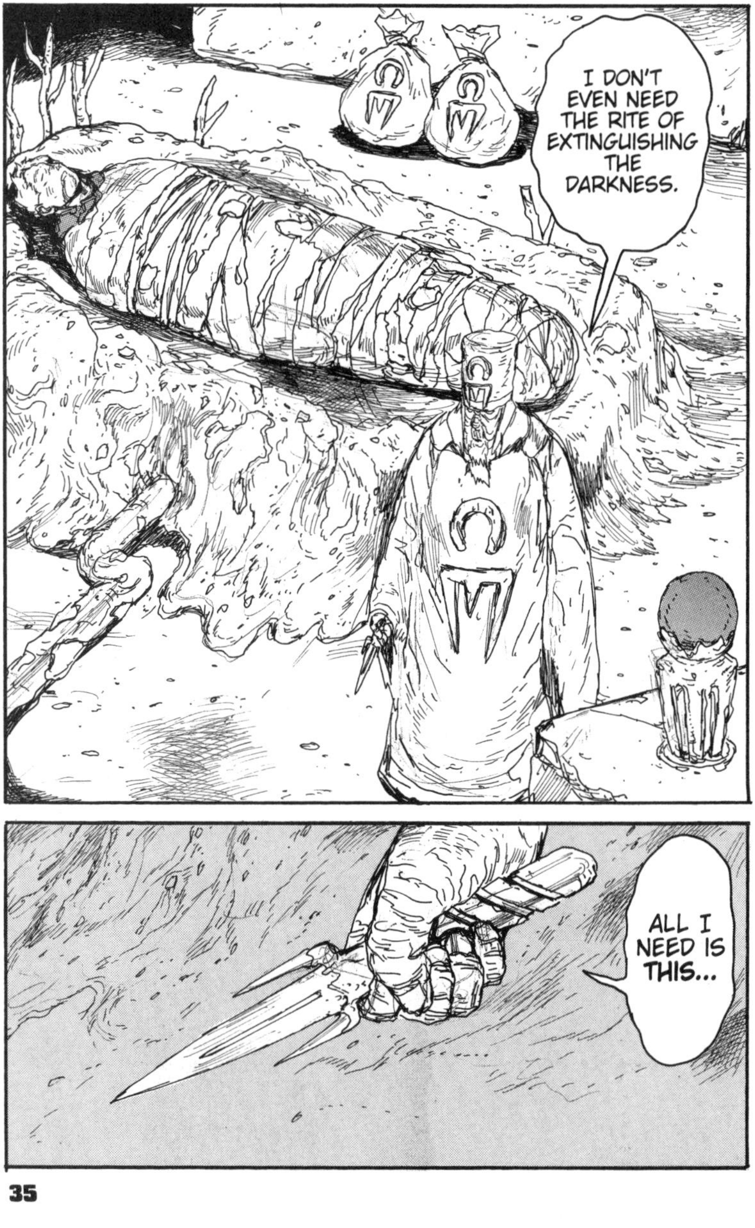
I DON'T EVEN NEED THE RITE OF EXTINGUISHING THE DARKNESS.
ALL I NEED IS THIS...

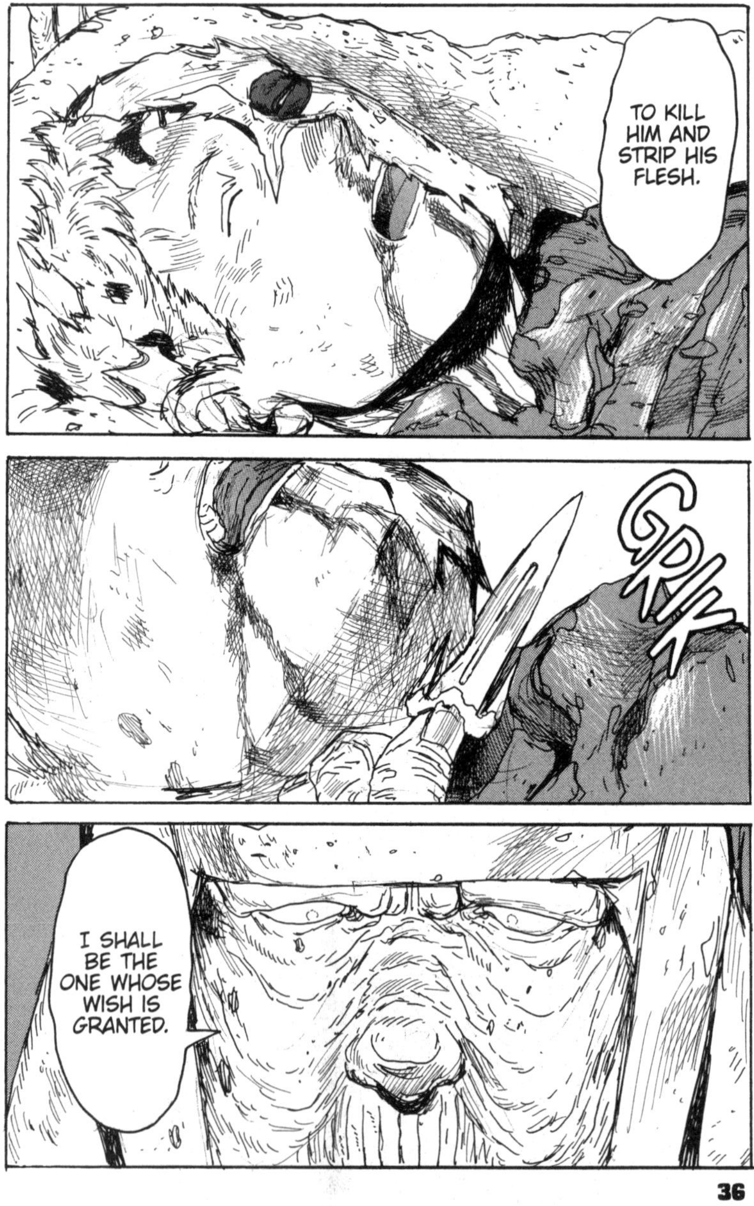
TO KILL HIM AND STRIP HIS FLESH.
GRIK
I SHALL BE THE ONE WHOSE WISH IS GRANTED.

★ *Dai Dark* vol. 1 store special sheet, black-and-white version

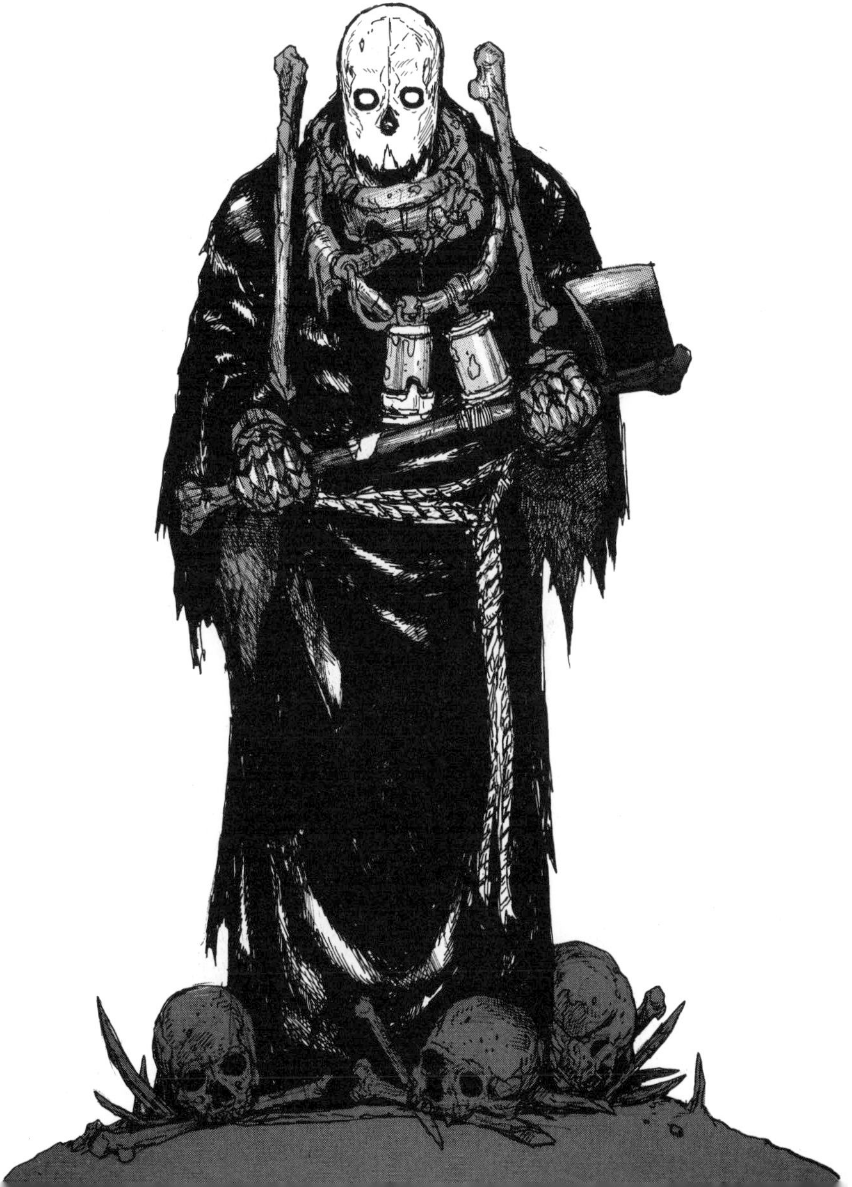

★ *Dai Dark* vol. 2 store special sheet, black-and-white version

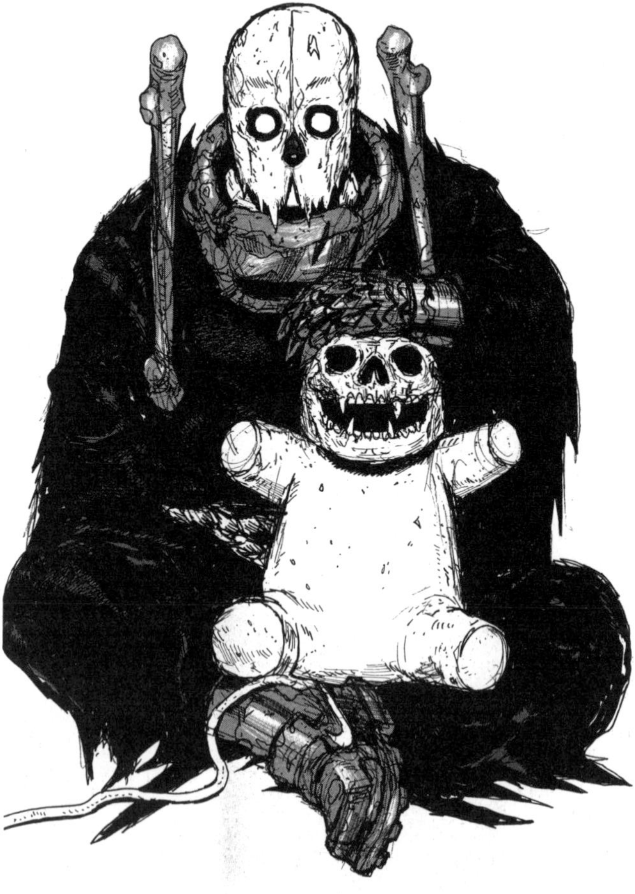

DAI DARK

DAI DARK

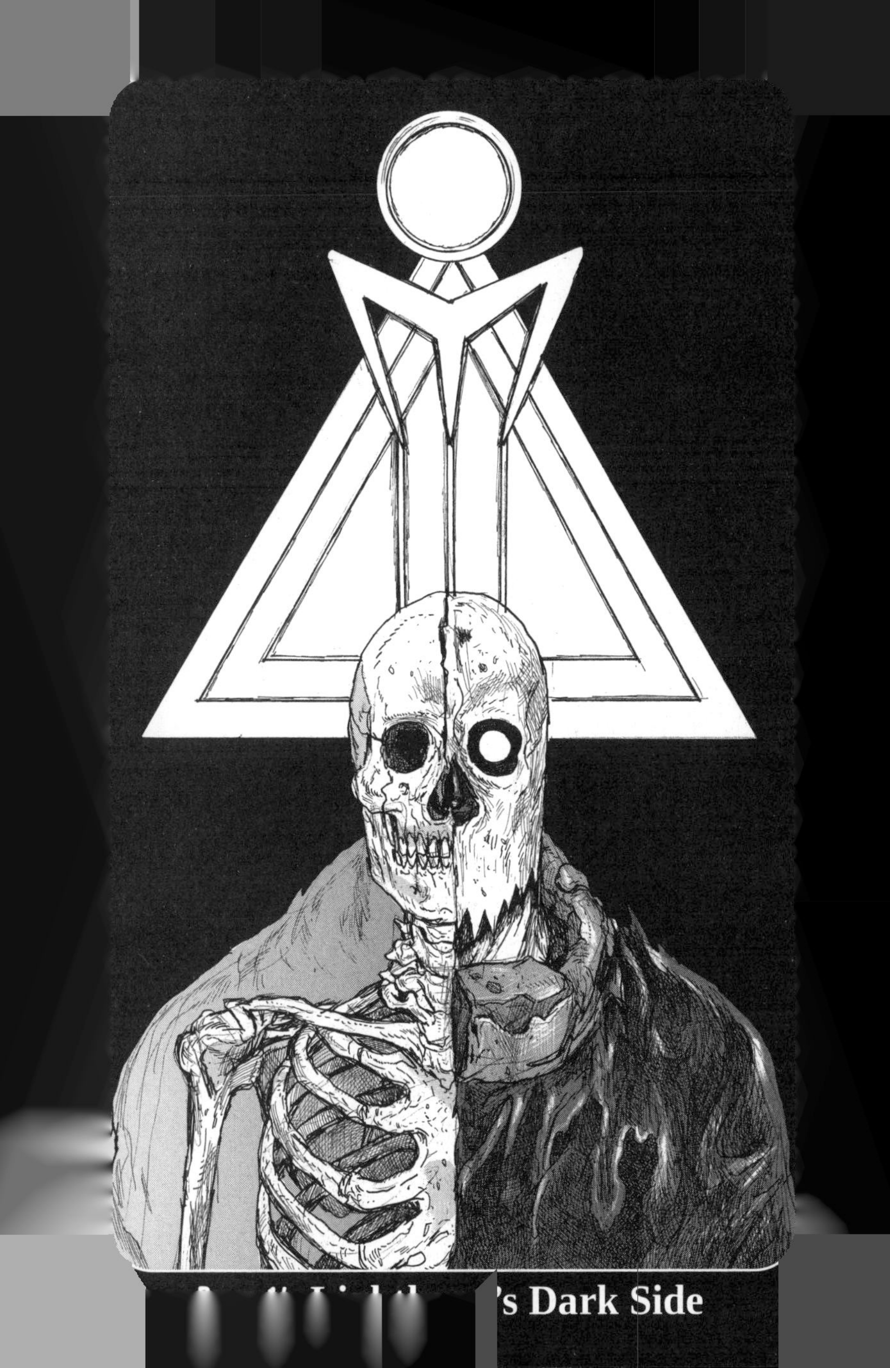

[illegible]’s Dark Side

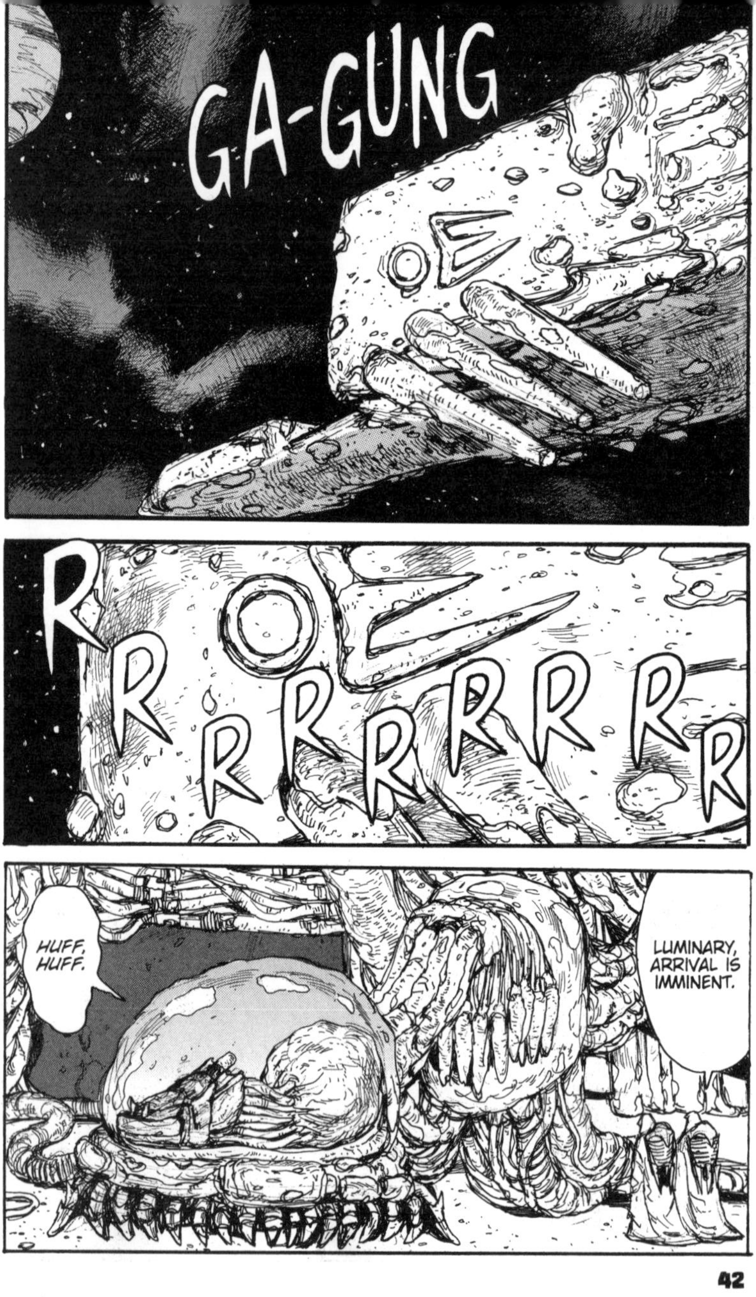
GA-GUNG
RRRRRRRRR
LUMINARY, ARRIVAL IS IMMINENT.
HUFF, HUFF.

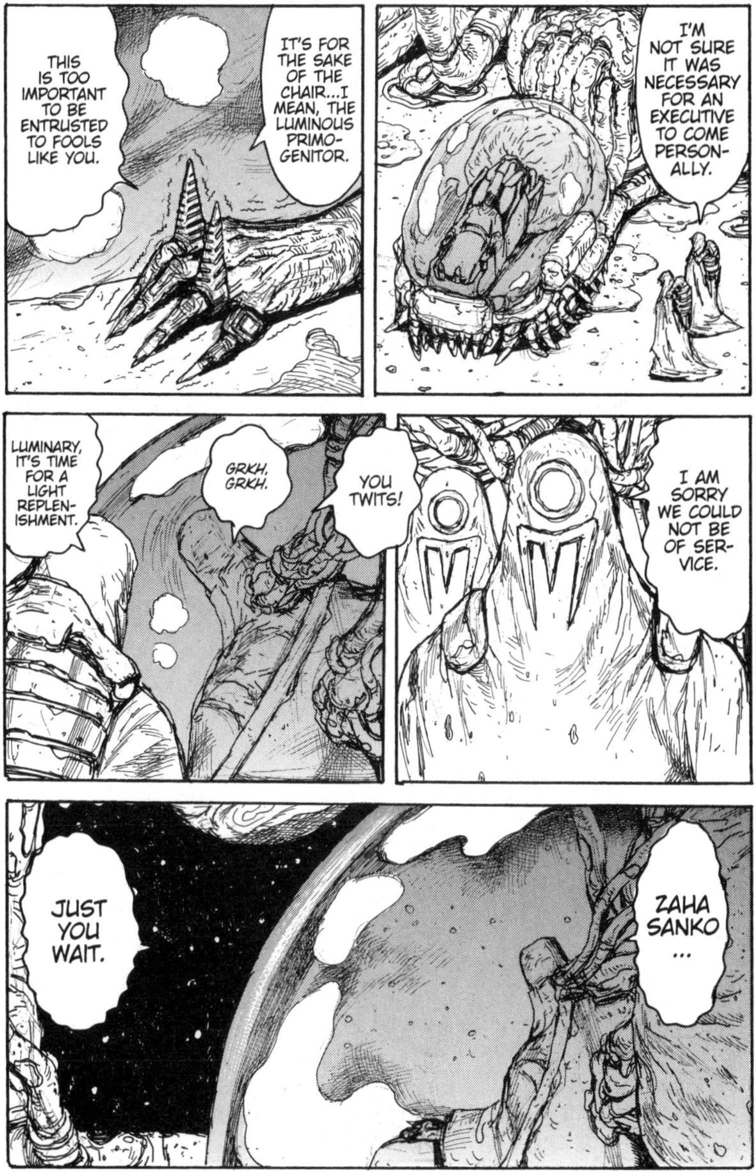
I'M NOT SURE IT WAS NECESSARY FOR AN EXECUTIVE TO COME PERSONALLY.
IT'S FOR THE SAKE OF THE CHAIR...I MEAN, THE LUMINOUS PRIMOGENITOR.
THIS IS TOO IMPORTANT TO BE ENTRUSTED TO FOOLS LIKE YOU.
I AM SORRY WE COULD NOT BE OF SERVICE.
YOU TWITS!
GRKH, GRKH.
LUMINARY, IT'S TIME FOR A LIGHT REPLENISHMENT.
ZAHA SANKO ...
JUST YOU WAIT.

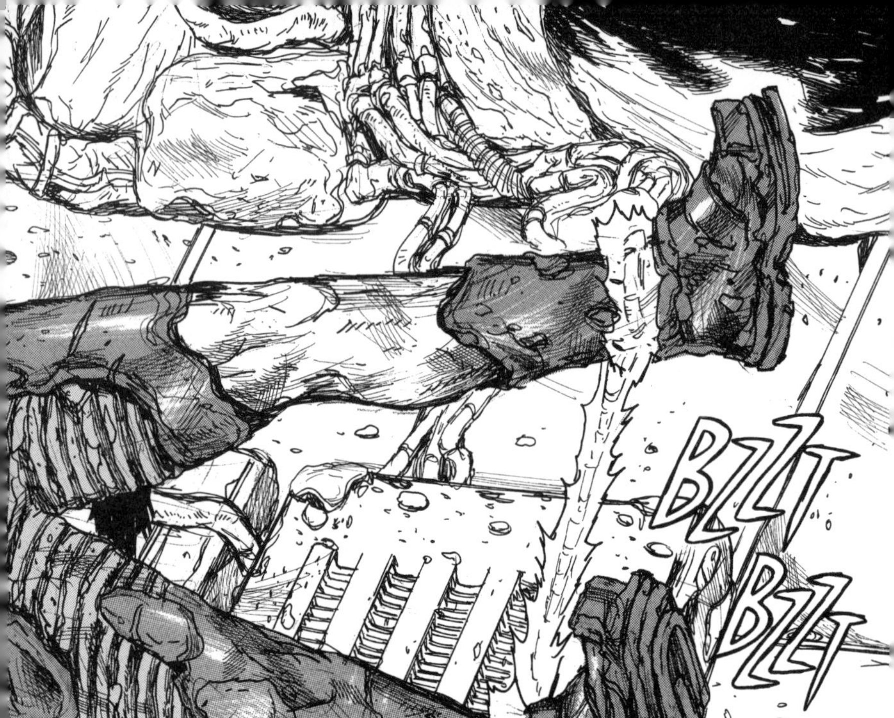
BZZT
BZZT
BZZT

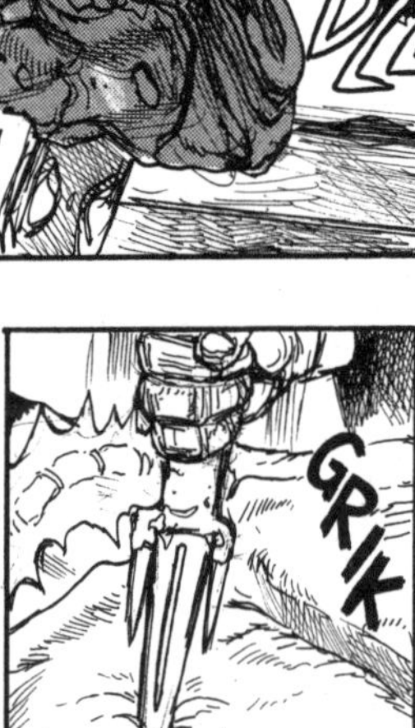
GRIK

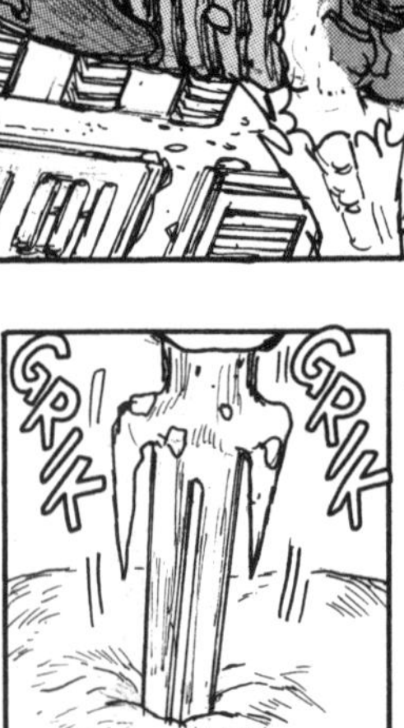
GRIK
GRIK

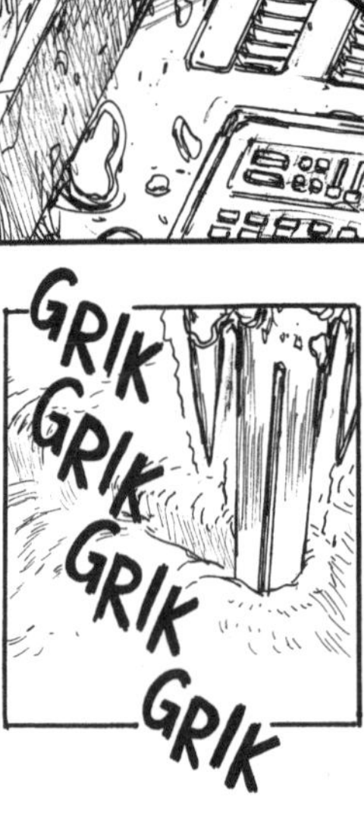
GRIK
GRIK
GRIK
GRIK
GRIK

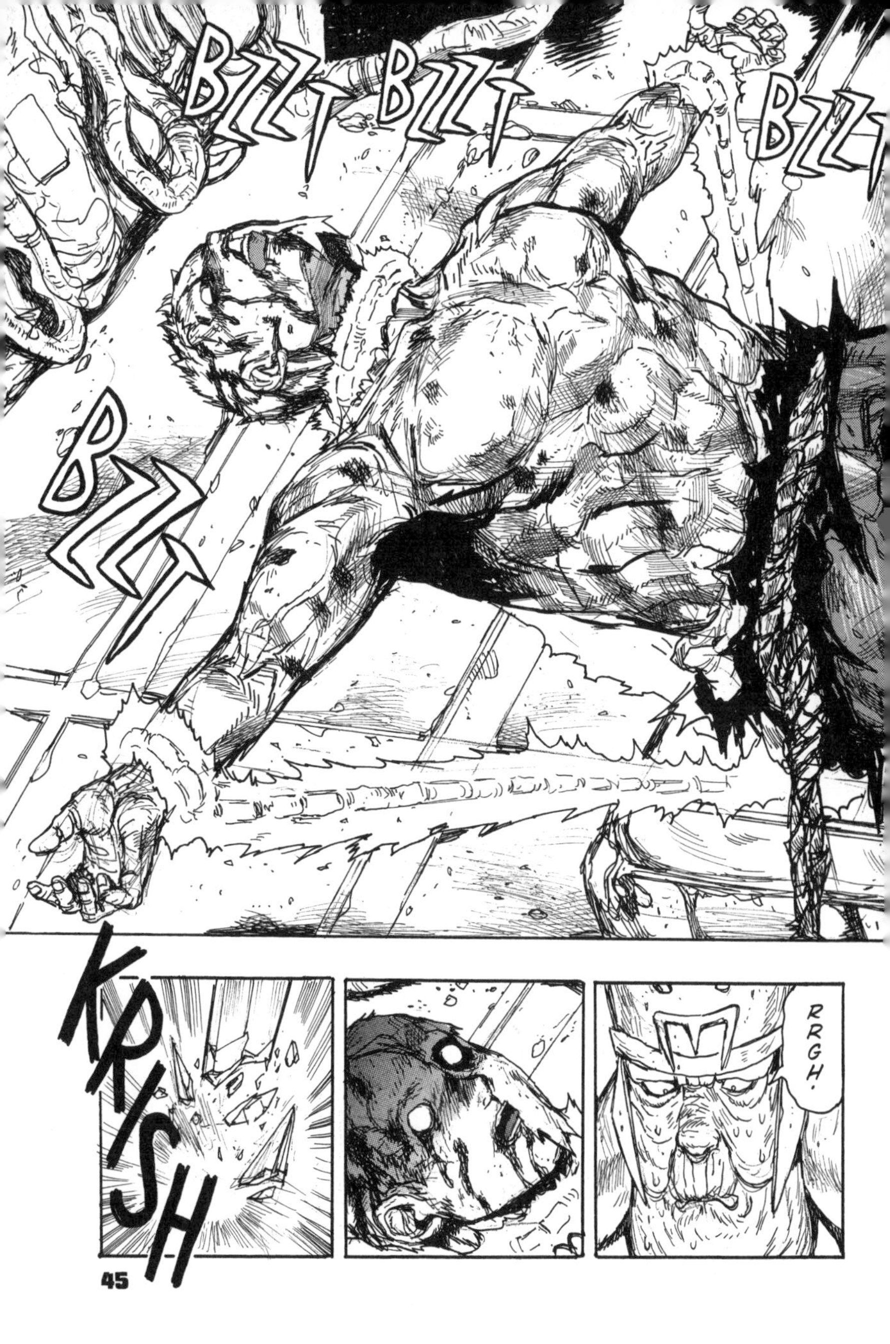
BZZ
BZZT
BZZT
BZZT
RRGH!
KRISH

IT'S-- IT'S HOPE-LESS!
GAAH!
DAMN IT ALL.
KA-TANG
THAT'S THE TENTH KNIFE I'VE RUINED.
THIS BOY LOOKS JUST LIKE ANY OTHER SPACELING...
BUT A RITUAL DAGGER WON'T BE ENOUGH TO LAY A SCRATCH ON HIM.
THAT MONSTER!

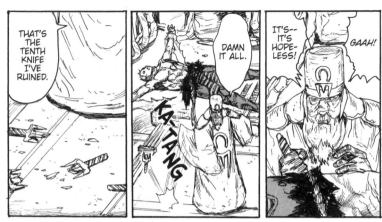

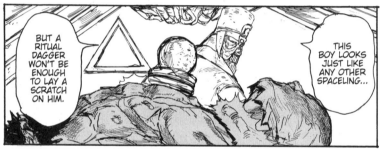

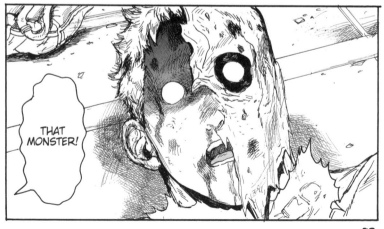

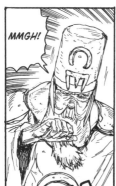

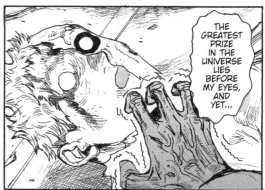

THE GREATEST PRIZE IN THE UNIVERSE LIES BEFORE MY EYES, AND YET...
MMGH!
ZMM ZMM ZMM ZMM
ZMM ZMM ZMM
BEING THIS CLOSE TO A CREATURE OF DARKNESS MAKES ME FEEL ILL...
NNGH... M-MY BACK ...!!
THIS IS TOO MUCH LABOR FOR AN OLD MAN OF A HUNDRED FIFTY-THREE.

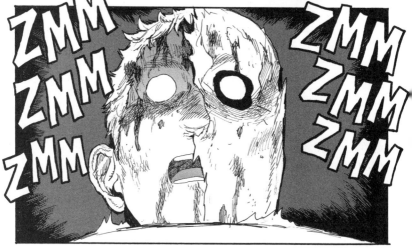

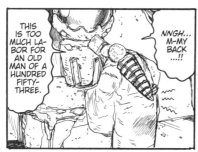

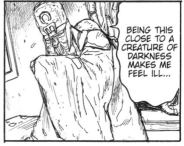

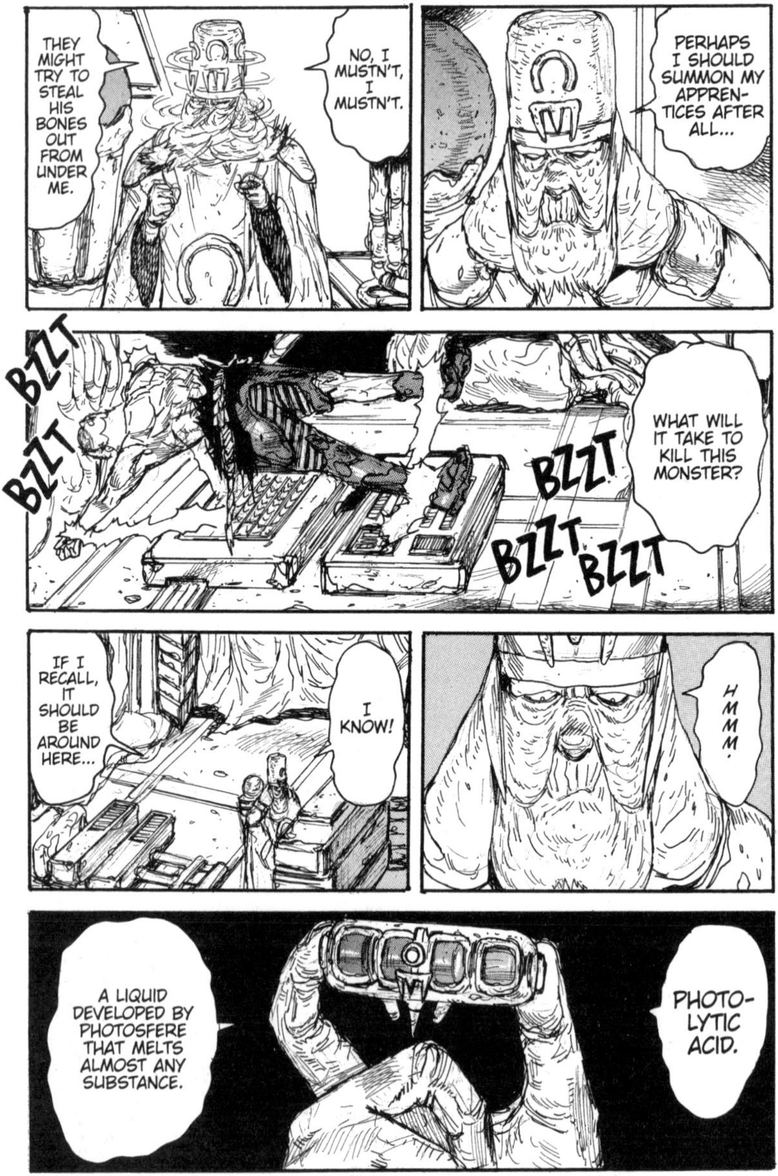
PERHAPS I SHOULD SUMMON MY APPREN-TICES AFTER ALL...
NO, I MUSTN'T, I MUSTN'T.
THEY MIGHT TRY TO STEAL HIS BONES OUT FROM UNDER ME.
WHAT WILL IT TAKE TO KILL THIS MONSTER?
BZZT
BZZT
BZZT
BZZT
BZZT
HMMM.
I KNOW!
IF I RECALL, IT SHOULD BE AROUND HERE...
PHOTO-LYTIC ACID.
A LIQUID DEVELOPED BY PHOTOSFERE THAT MELTS ALMOST ANY SUBSTANCE.

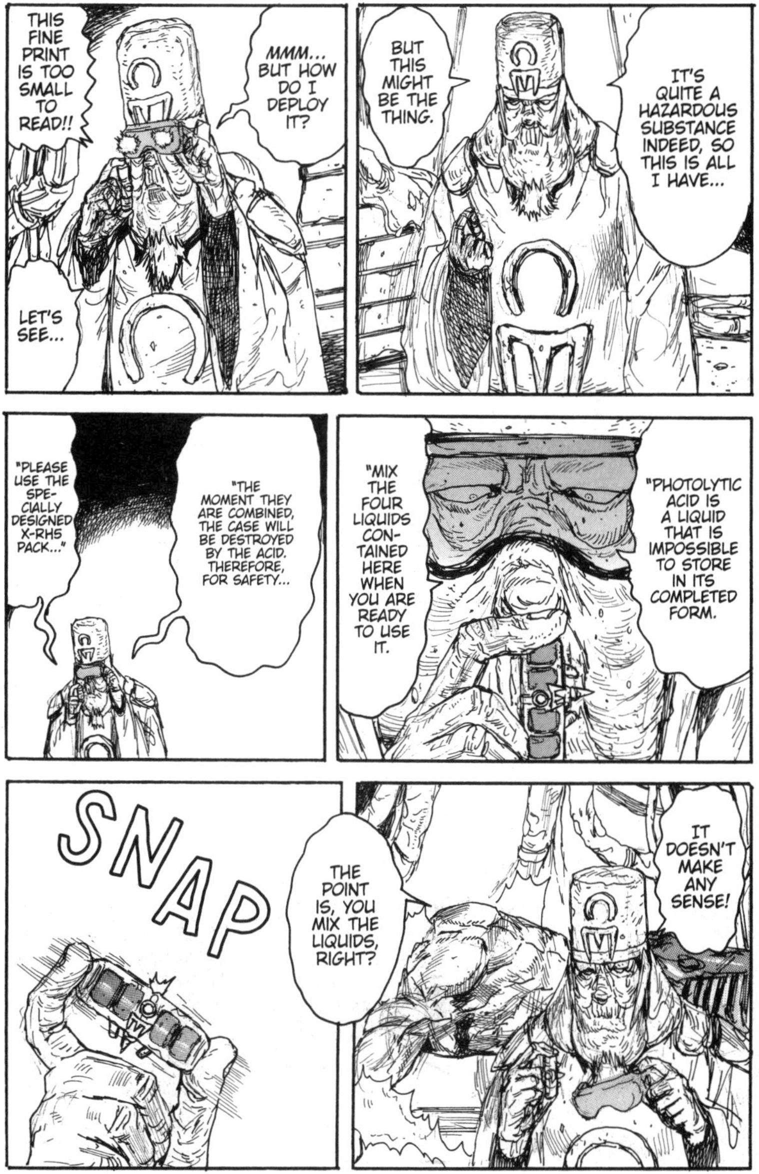
IT'S QUITE A HAZARDOUS SUBSTANCE INDEED, SO THIS IS ALL I HAVE...
BUT THIS MIGHT BE THE THING.
MMM... BUT HOW DO I DEPLOY IT?
THIS FINE PRINT IS TOO SMALL TO READ!!
LET'S SEE...
"PHOTOLYTIC ACID IS A LIQUID THAT IS IMPOSSIBLE TO STORE IN ITS COMPLETED FORM.
"MIX THE FOUR LIQUIDS CONTAINED HERE WHEN YOU ARE READY TO USE IT.
"THE MOMENT THEY ARE COMBINED, THE CASE WILL BE DESTROYED BY THE ACID. THEREFORE, FOR SAFETY...
"PLEASE USE THE SPECIALLY DESIGNED X-RHS PACK..."
IT DOESN'T MAKE ANY SENSE!
THE POINT IS, YOU MIX THE LIQUIDS, RIGHT?
SNAP

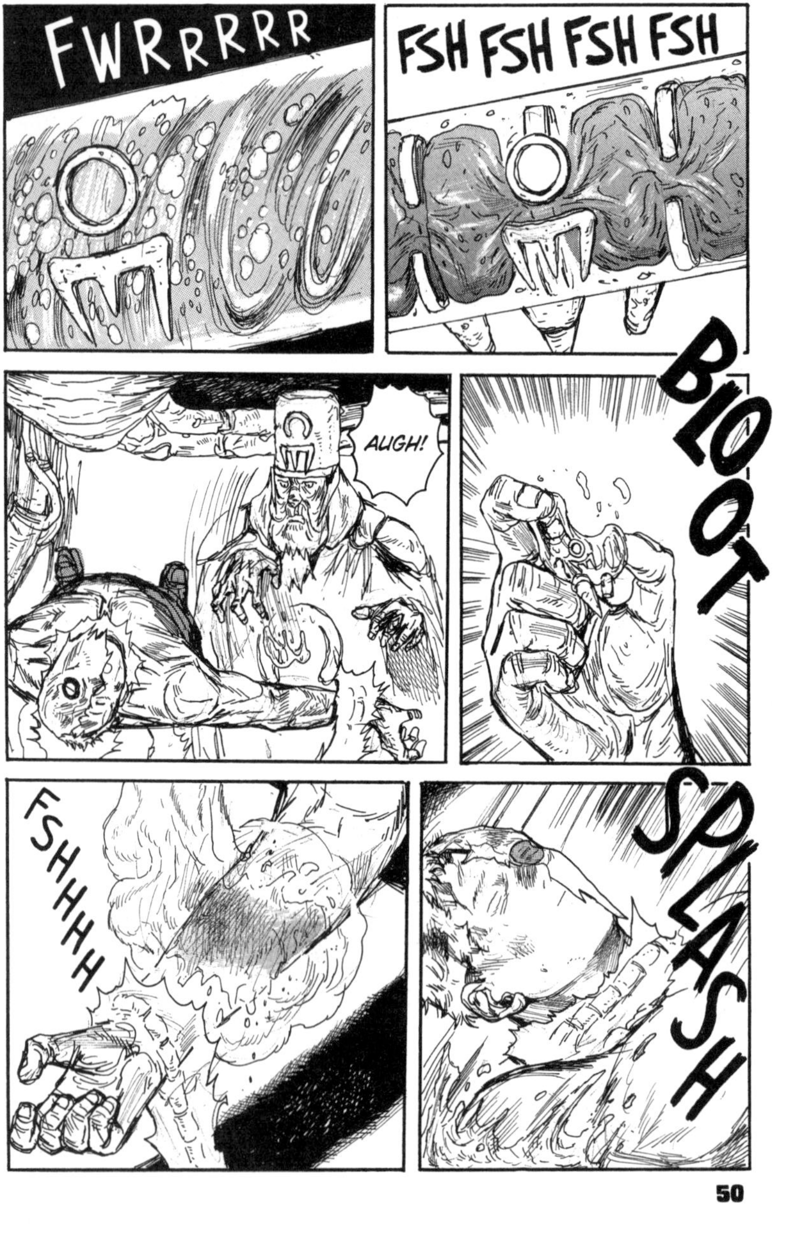
FSH FSH FSH FSH
FWRRRRR
BLOOT
AUGH!
SPLASH
FSHHHH

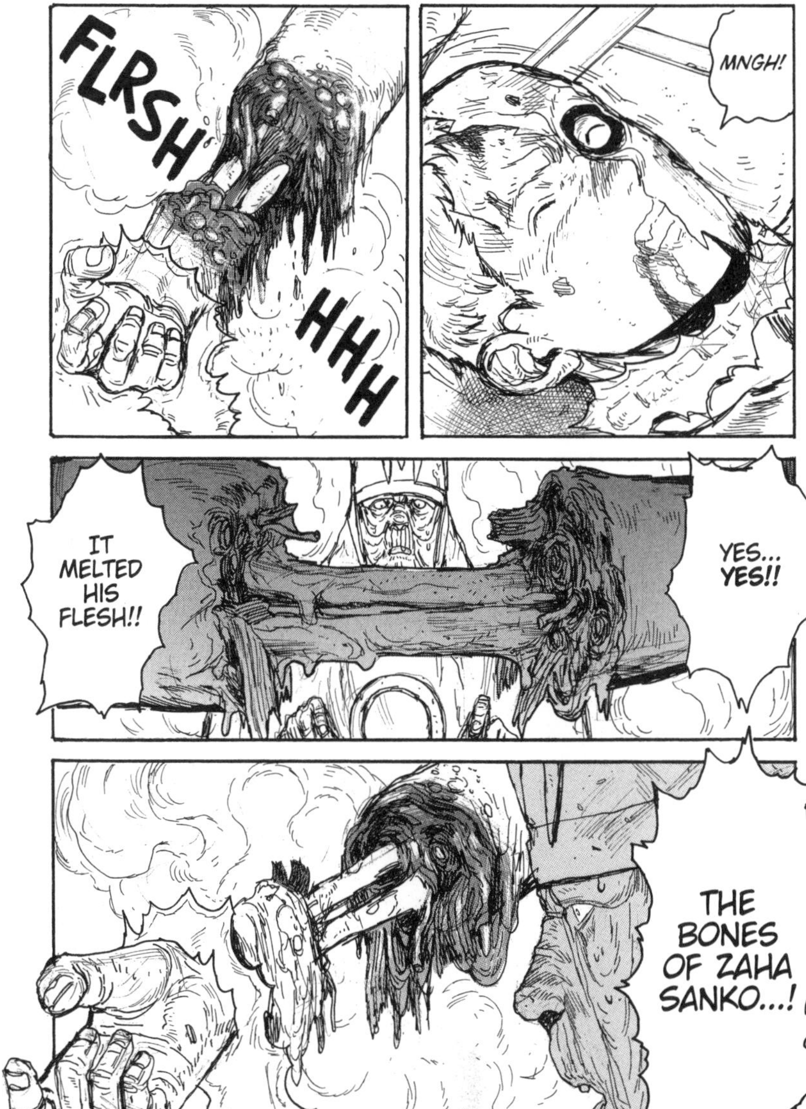
MNGH!
FLRSH
HHH
YES... YES!!
IT MELTED HIS FLESH!!
THE BONES OF ZAHA SANKO...!

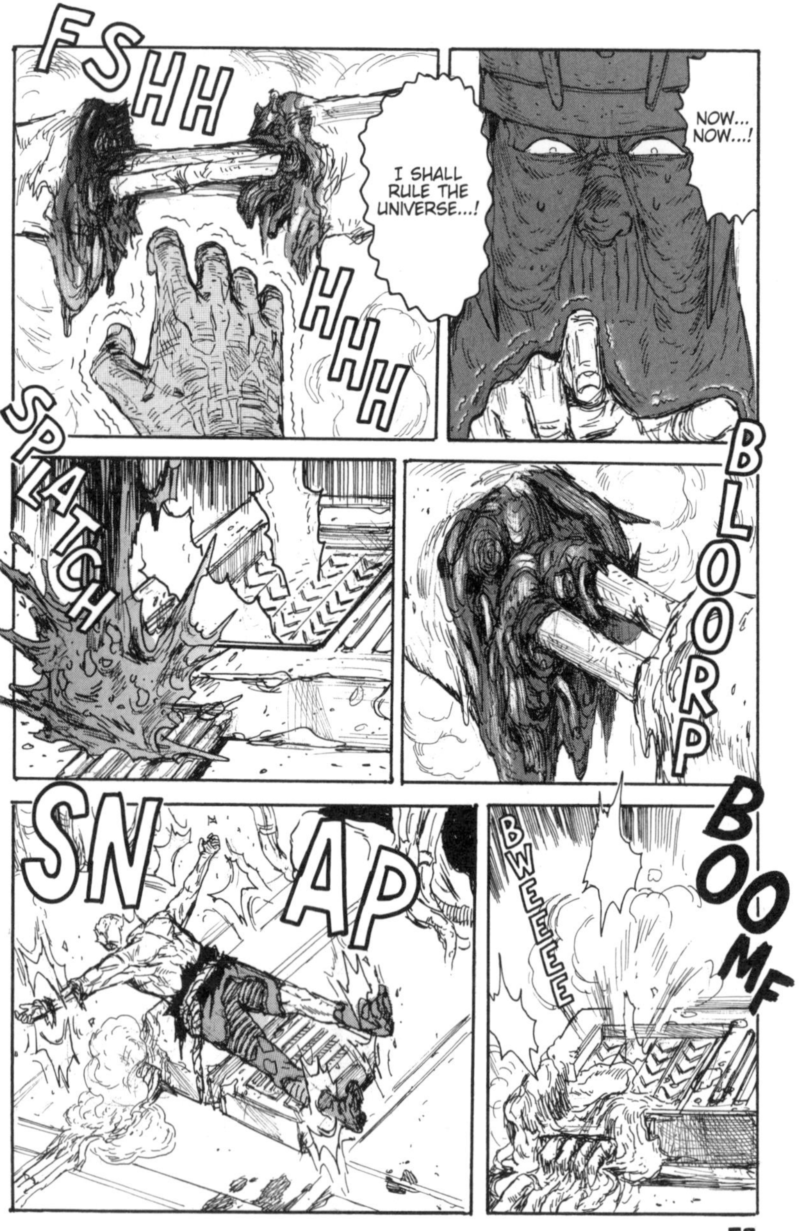
NOW... NOW...!
I SHALL RULE THE UNIVERSE...!
FSHH
HHH
BLOORP
SPLATCH
BOOOMF
BWEEEE
SNAP

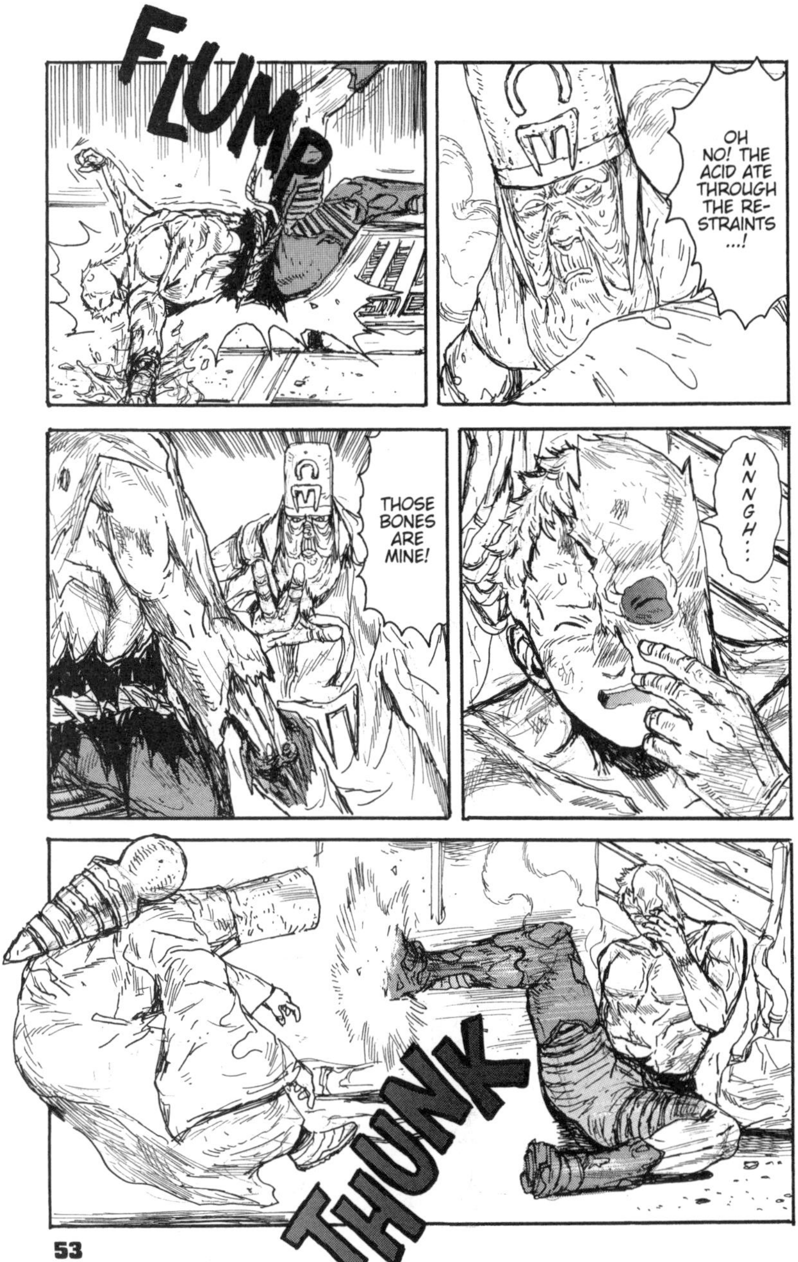
OH NO! THE ACID ATE THROUGH THE RE-STRAINTS ...!
FLUMP
NNNGH...
THOSE BONES ARE MINE!
THUNK

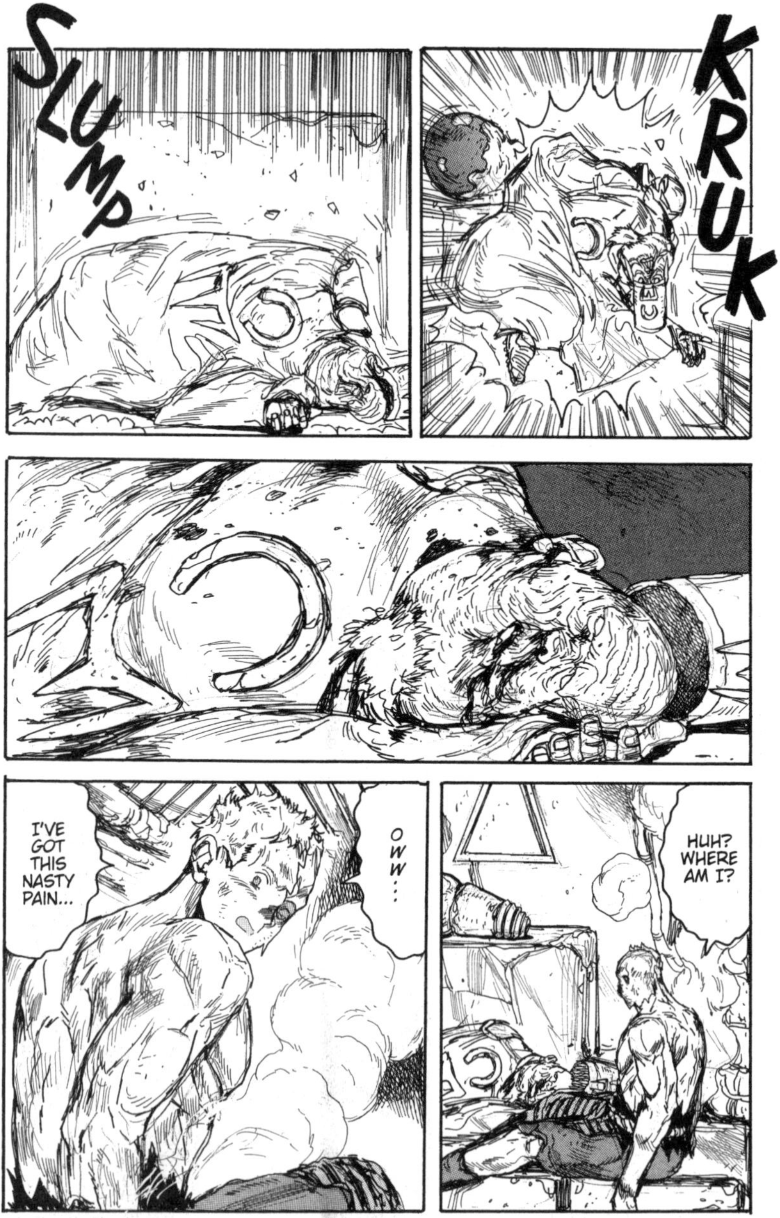
KRUK
SLUMP
HUH? WHERE AM I?
OWW...
I'VE GOT THIS NASTY PAIN...

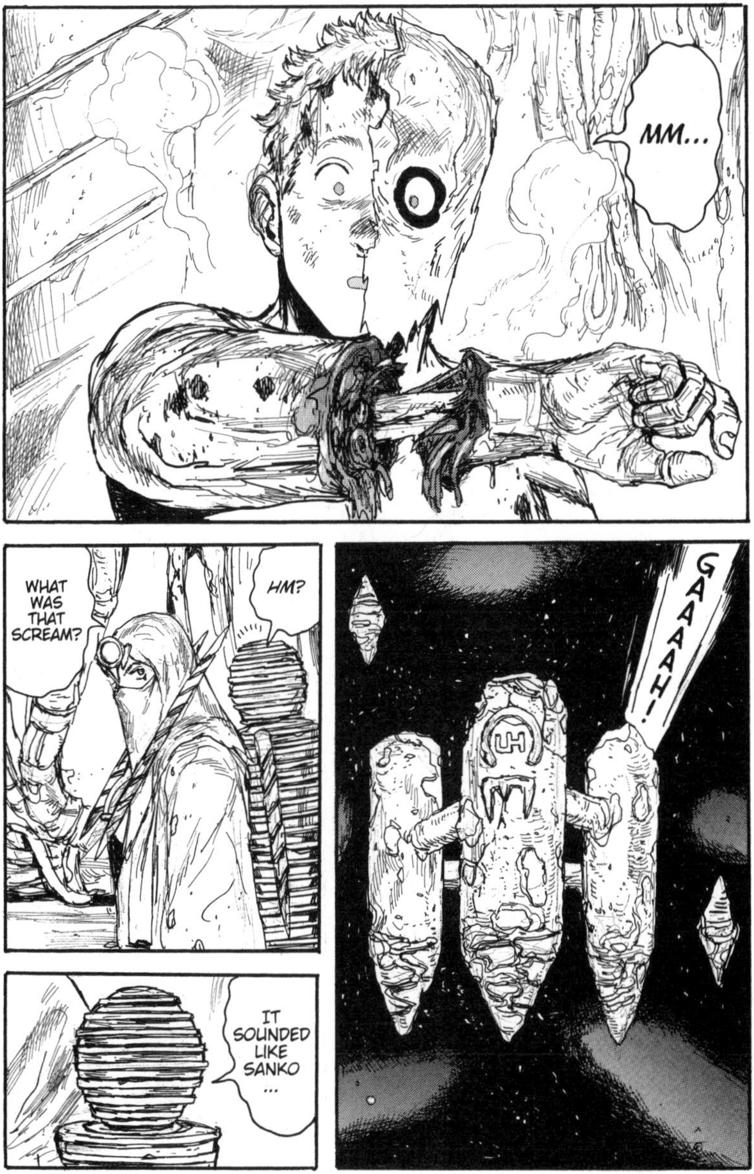
MM...
GAAAAAH!
HM?
WHAT WAS THAT SCREAM?
IT SOUNDED LIKE SANKO ...

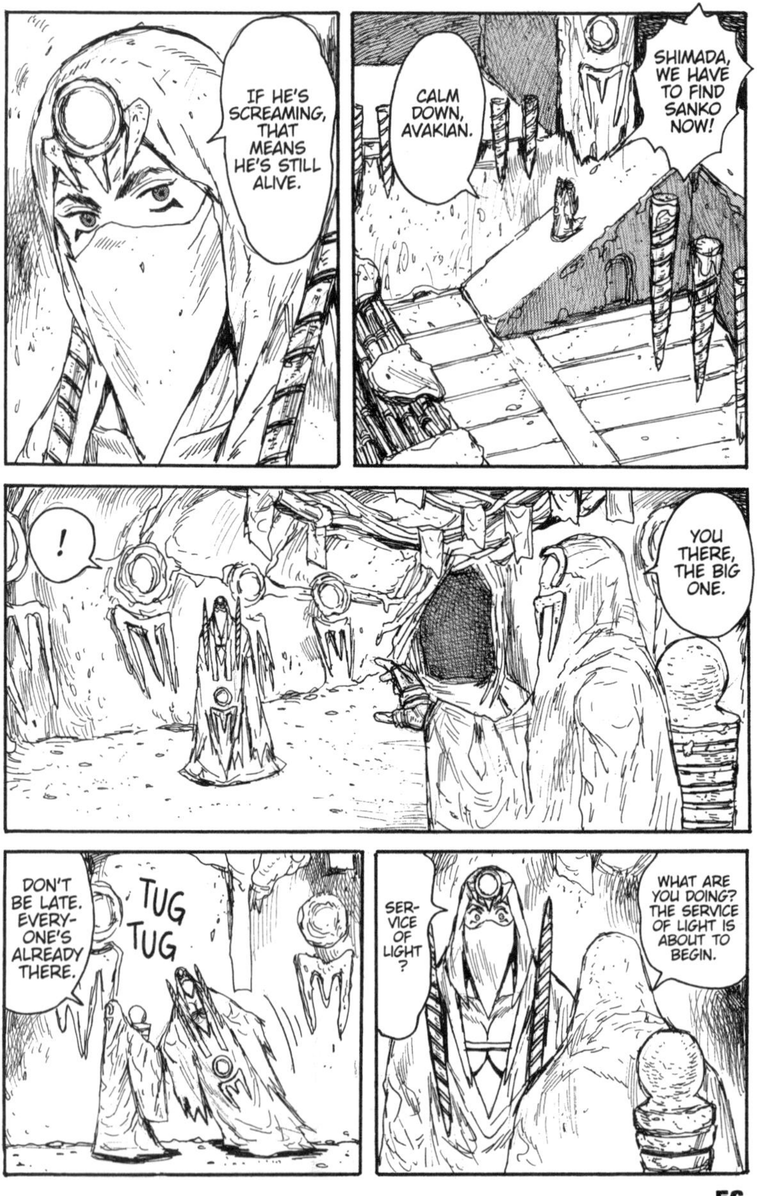
SHIMADA, WE HAVE TO FIND SANKO NOW!
CALM DOWN, AVAKIAN.
IF HE'S SCREAMING, THAT MEANS HE'S STILL ALIVE.
YOU THERE, THE BIG ONE.
!
WHAT ARE YOU DOING? THE SERVICE OF LIGHT IS ABOUT TO BEGIN.
SER-VICE OF LIGHT?
TUG TUG
DON'T BE LATE. EVERY-ONE'S ALREADY THERE.

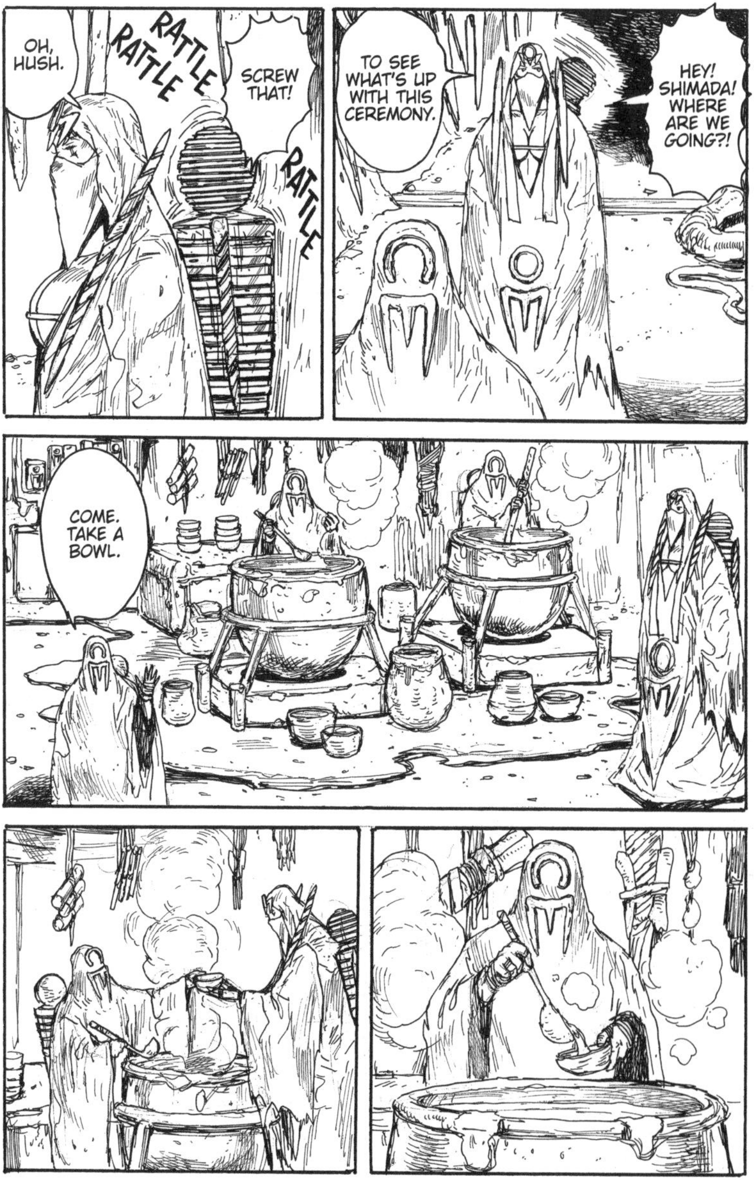
HEY! SHIMADA! WHERE ARE WE GOING?!
TO SEE WHAT'S UP WITH THIS CEREMONY.
RATTLE
SCREW THAT!
RATTLE RATTLE
OH, HUSH.
COME. TAKE A BOWL.

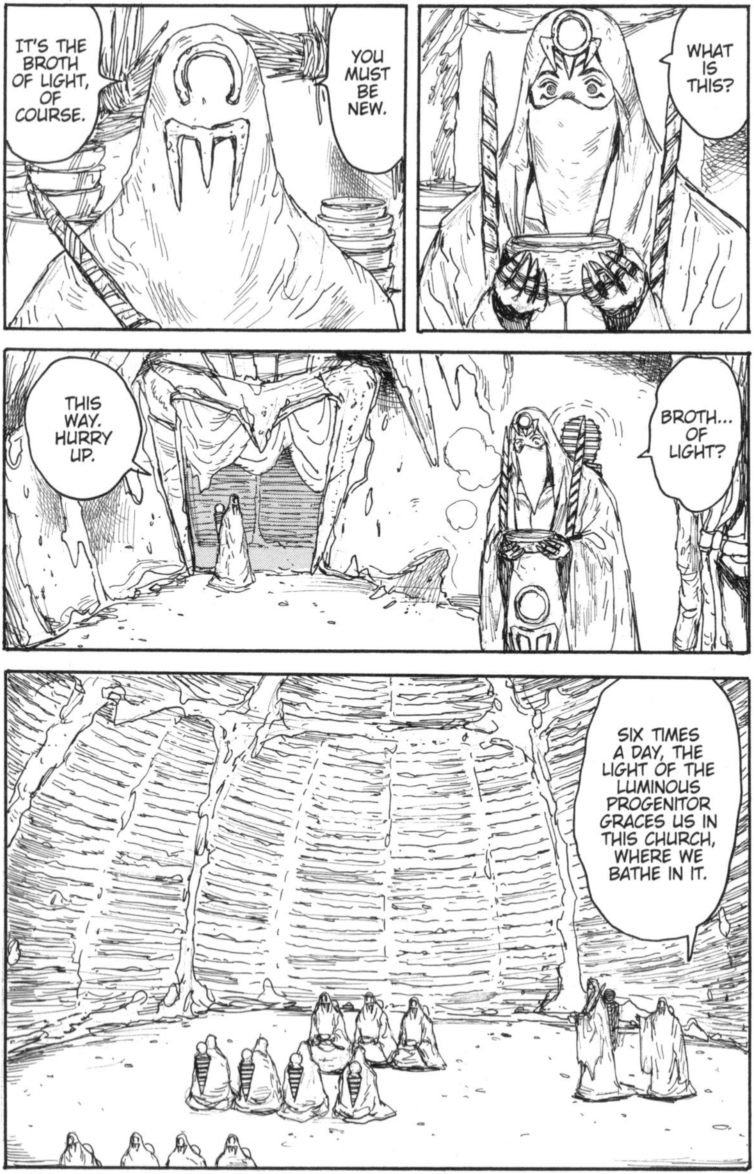
WHAT IS THIS?
YOU MUST BE NEW.
IT'S THE BROTH OF LIGHT, OF COURSE.
BROTH... OF LIGHT?
THIS WAY. HURRY UP.
SIX TIMES A DAY, THE LIGHT OF THE LUMINOUS PROGENITOR GRACES US IN THIS CHURCH, WHERE WE BATHE IN IT.

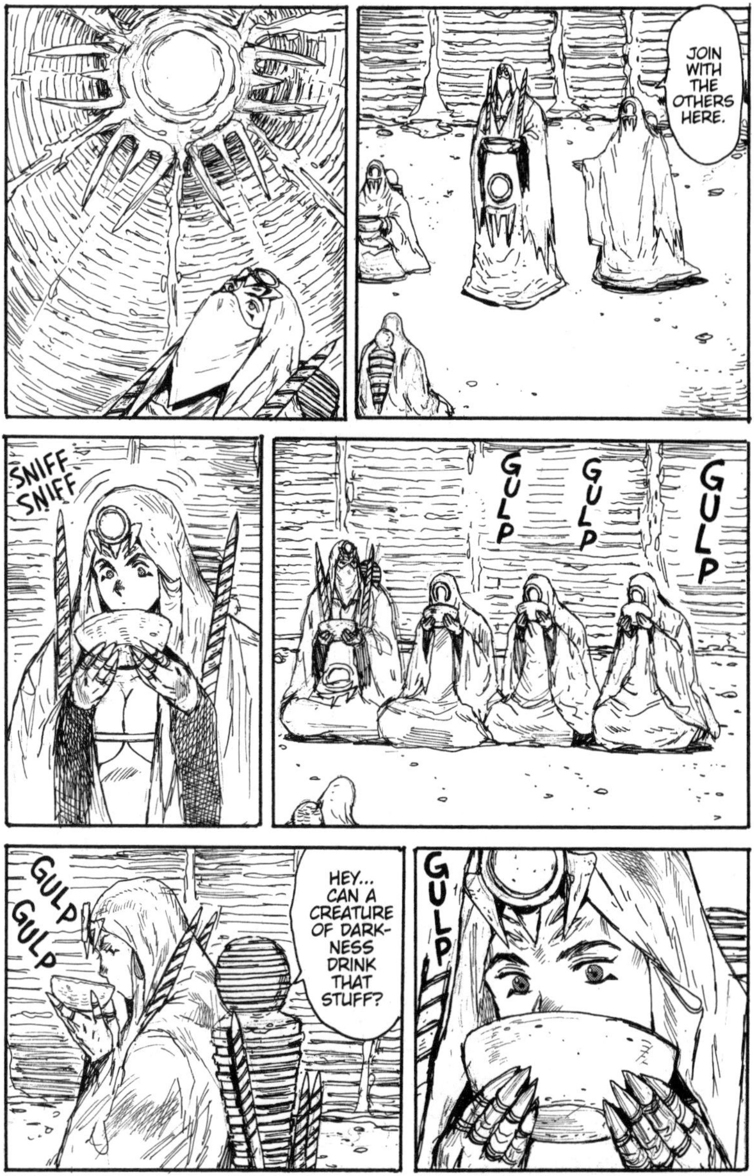
JOIN WITH THE OTHERS HERE.
GULP
GULP
GULP
SNIFF SNIFF
GULP
HEY... CAN A CREATURE OF DARKNESS DRINK THAT STUFF?
GULP GULP

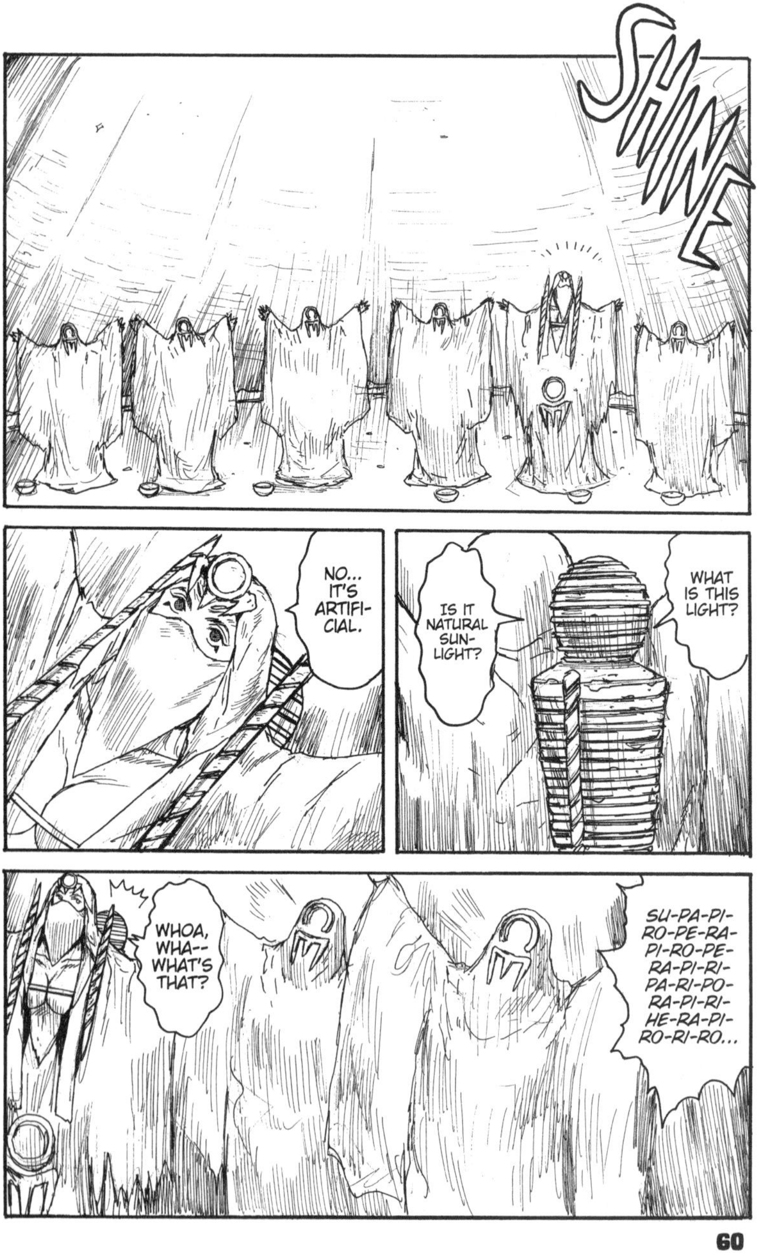
SHINE
WHAT IS THIS LIGHT?
IS IT NATURAL SUN-LIGHT?
NO... IT'S ARTIFI-CIAL.
SU-PA-PI-RO-PE-RA-PI-RO-PE-RA-PI-RI-PA-RI-PO-RA-PI-RI-HE-RA-PI-RO-RI-RO...
WHOA, WHA-- WHAT'S THAT?

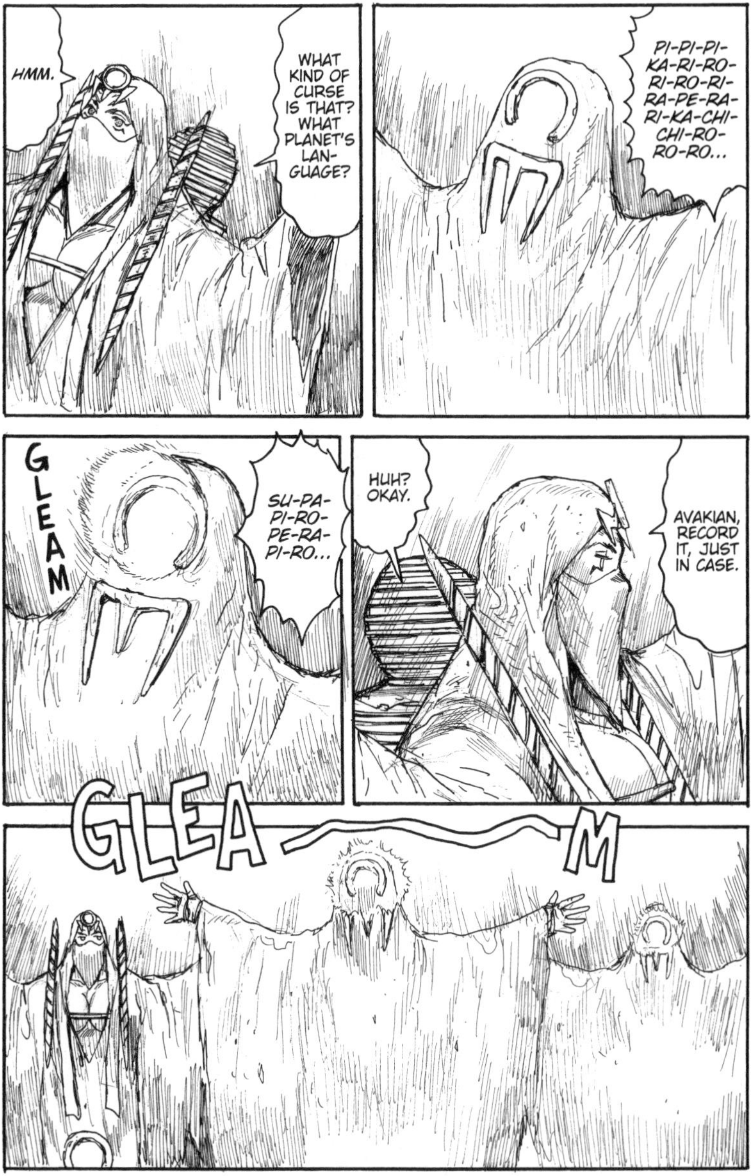
PI-PI-PI-KA-RI-RO-RI-RO-RI-RA-PE-RA-RI-KA-CHI-CHI-RO-RO-RO-RO...
WHAT KIND OF CURSE IS THAT? WHAT PLANET'S LAN-GUAGE?
HMM.
AVAKIAN, RECORD IT, JUST IN CASE.
HUH? OKAY.
SU-PA-PI-RO-PE-RA-PI-RO...
GLEAM
GLEA—M

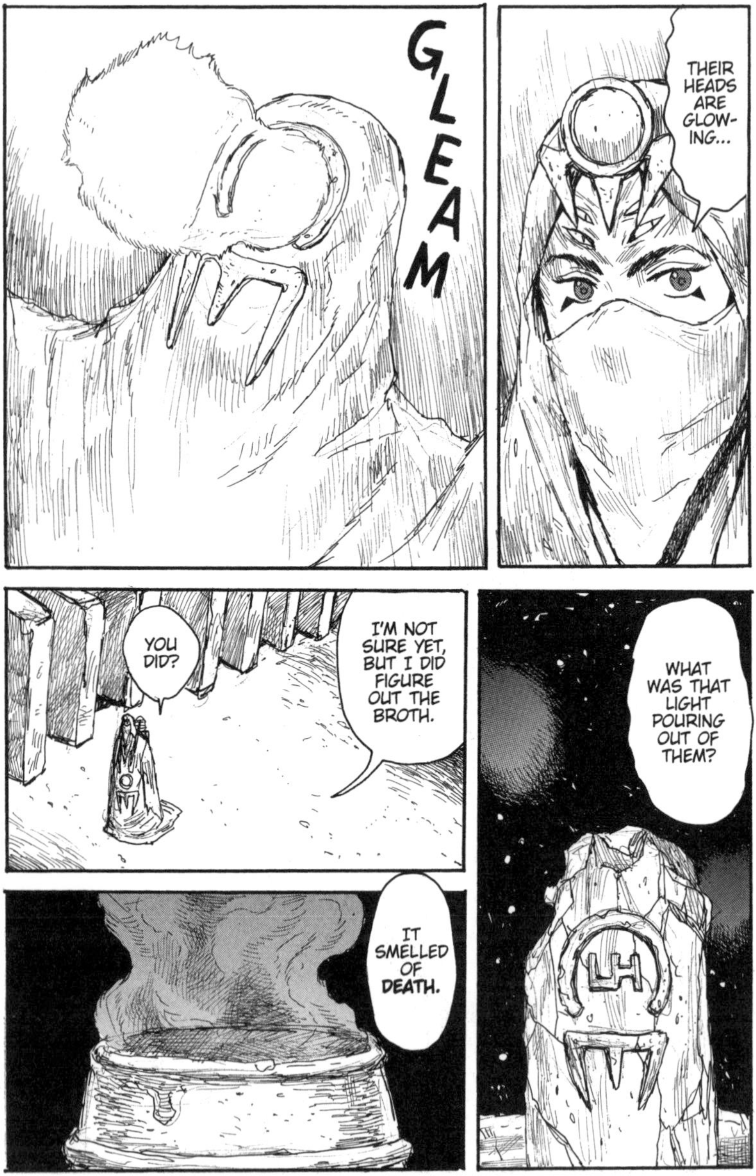
THEIR HEADS ARE GLOWING-ING...
GLEAM
WHAT WAS THAT LIGHT POURING OUT OF THEM?
I'M NOT SURE YET, BUT I DID FIGURE OUT THE BROTH.
YOU DID?
IT SMELLED OF **DEATH.**

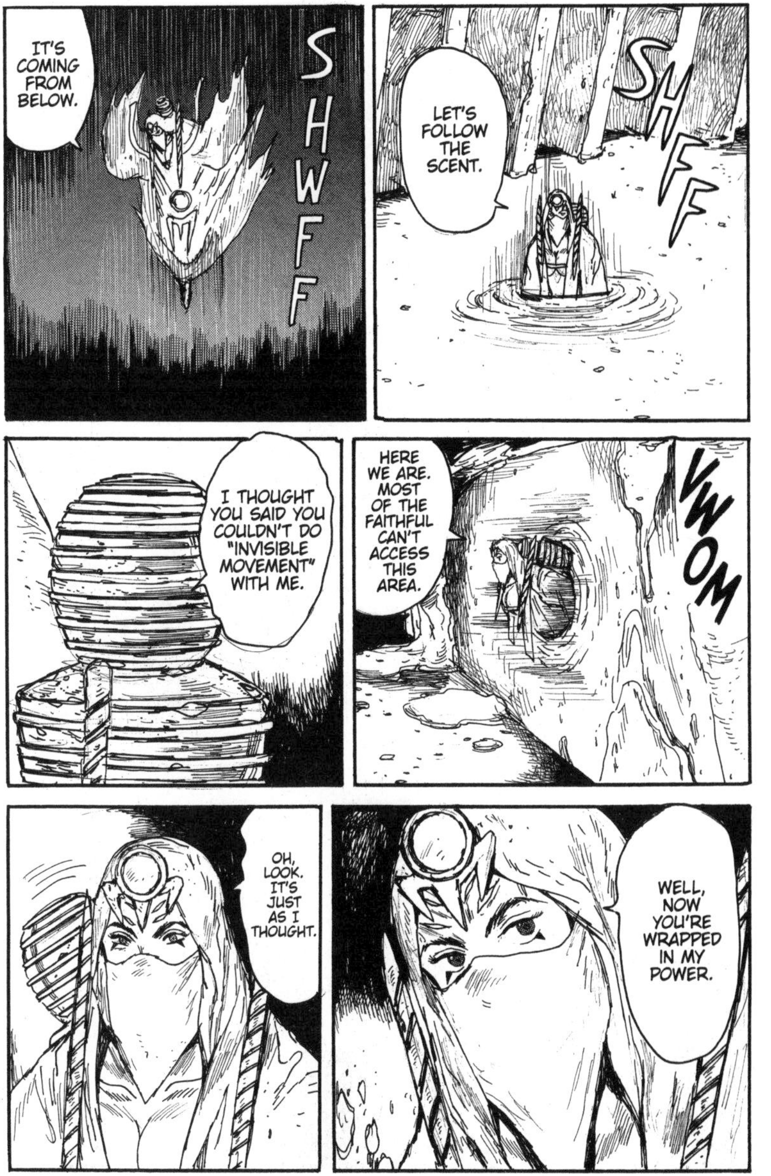
IT'S COMING FROM BELOW.
SHWFF
LET'S FOLLOW THE SCENT.
SHFF
I THOUGHT YOU SAID YOU COULDN'T DO "INVISIBLE MOVEMENT" WITH ME.
HERE WE ARE. MOST OF THE FAITHFUL CAN'T ACCESS THIS AREA.
VWOM
OH, LOOK. IT'S JUST AS I THOUGHT.
WELL, NOW YOU'RE WRAPPED IN MY POWER.

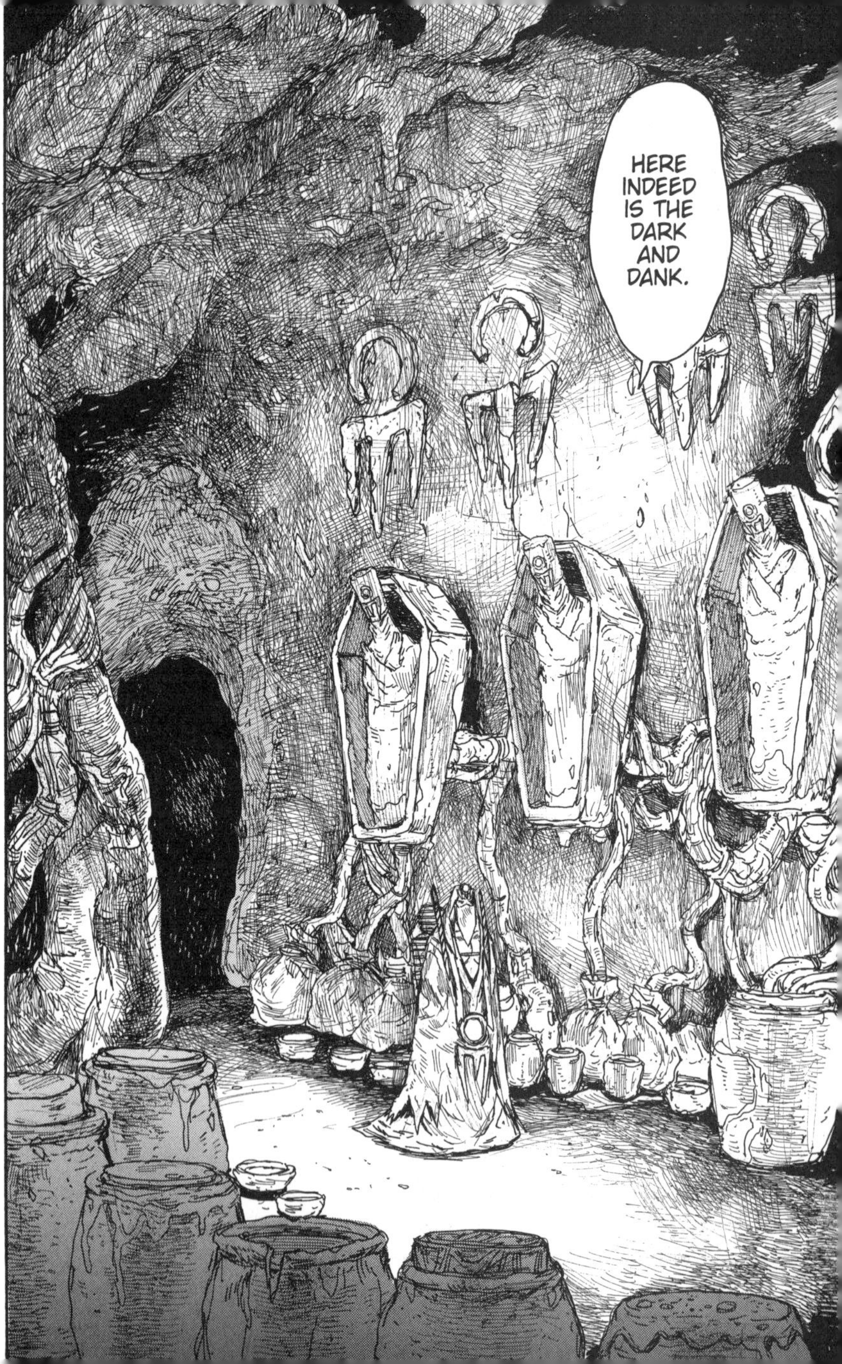
HERE INDEED IS THE DARK AND DANK.

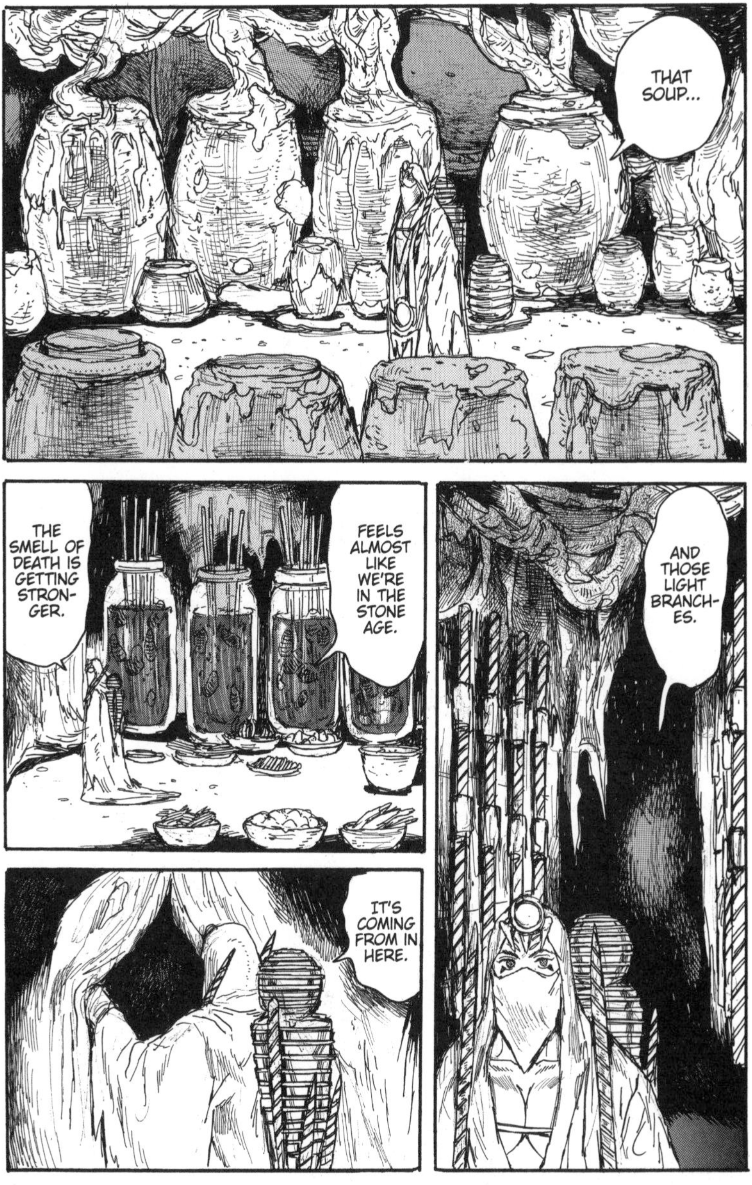
THAT SOUP...
AND THOSE LIGHT BRANCHES.
FEELS ALMOST LIKE WE'RE IN THE STONE AGE.
THE SMELL OF DEATH IS GETTING STRONGER.
IT'S COMING FROM IN HERE.

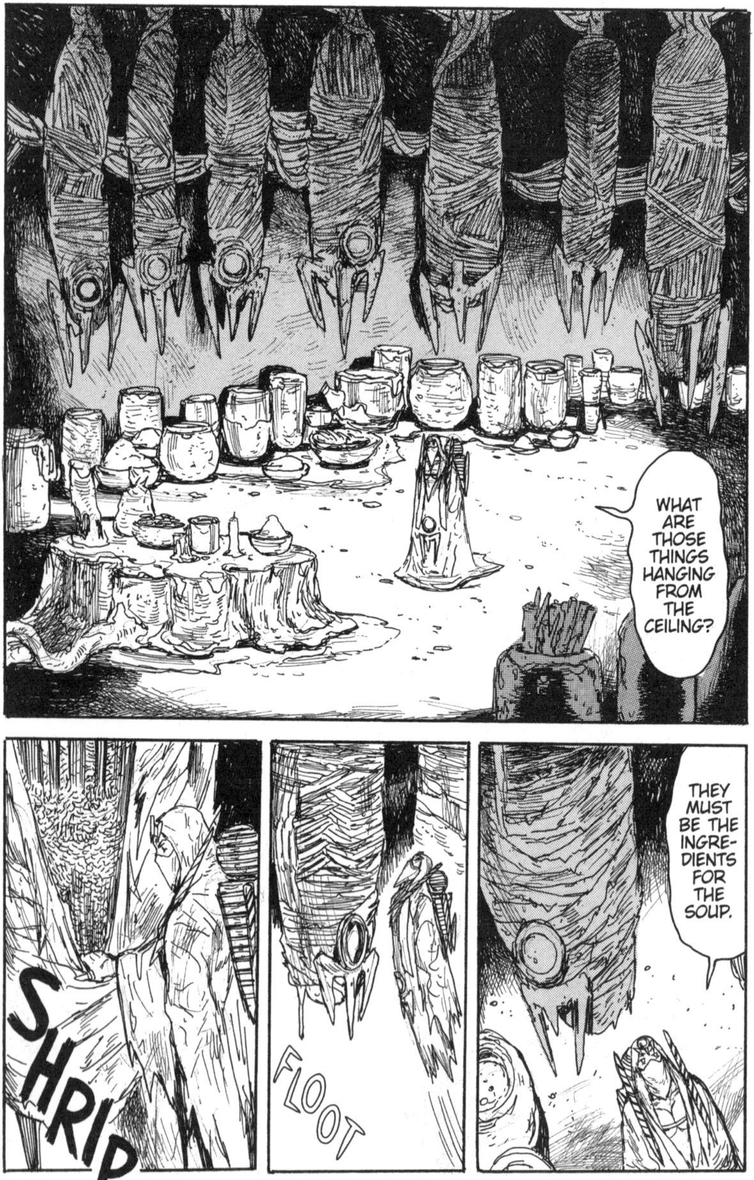
WHAT ARE THOSE THINGS HANGING FROM THE CEILING?
THEY MUST BE THE INGRE-DIENTS FOR THE SOUP.
FLOOT
SHRIP

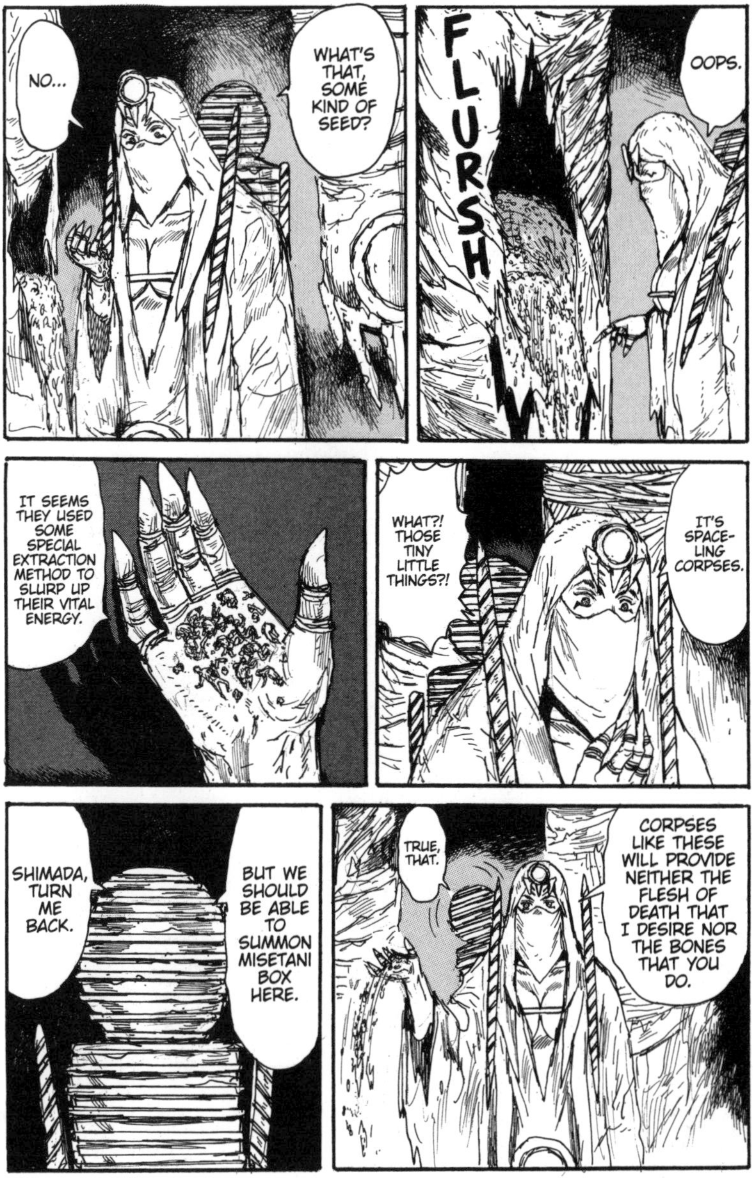
OOPS.
FLURSH
WHAT'S THAT, SOME KIND OF SEED?
NO...
IT'S SPACE-LING CORPSES.
WHAT?! THOSE TINY LITTLE THINGS?!
IT SEEMS THEY USED SOME SPECIAL EXTRACTION METHOD TO SLURP UP THEIR VITAL ENERGY.
CORPSES LIKE THESE WILL PROVIDE NEITHER THE FLESH OF DEATH THAT I DESIRE NOR THE BONES THAT YOU DO.
TRUE, THAT.
BUT WE SHOULD BE ABLE TO SUMMON MISETANI BOX HERE.
SHIMADA, TURN ME BACK.

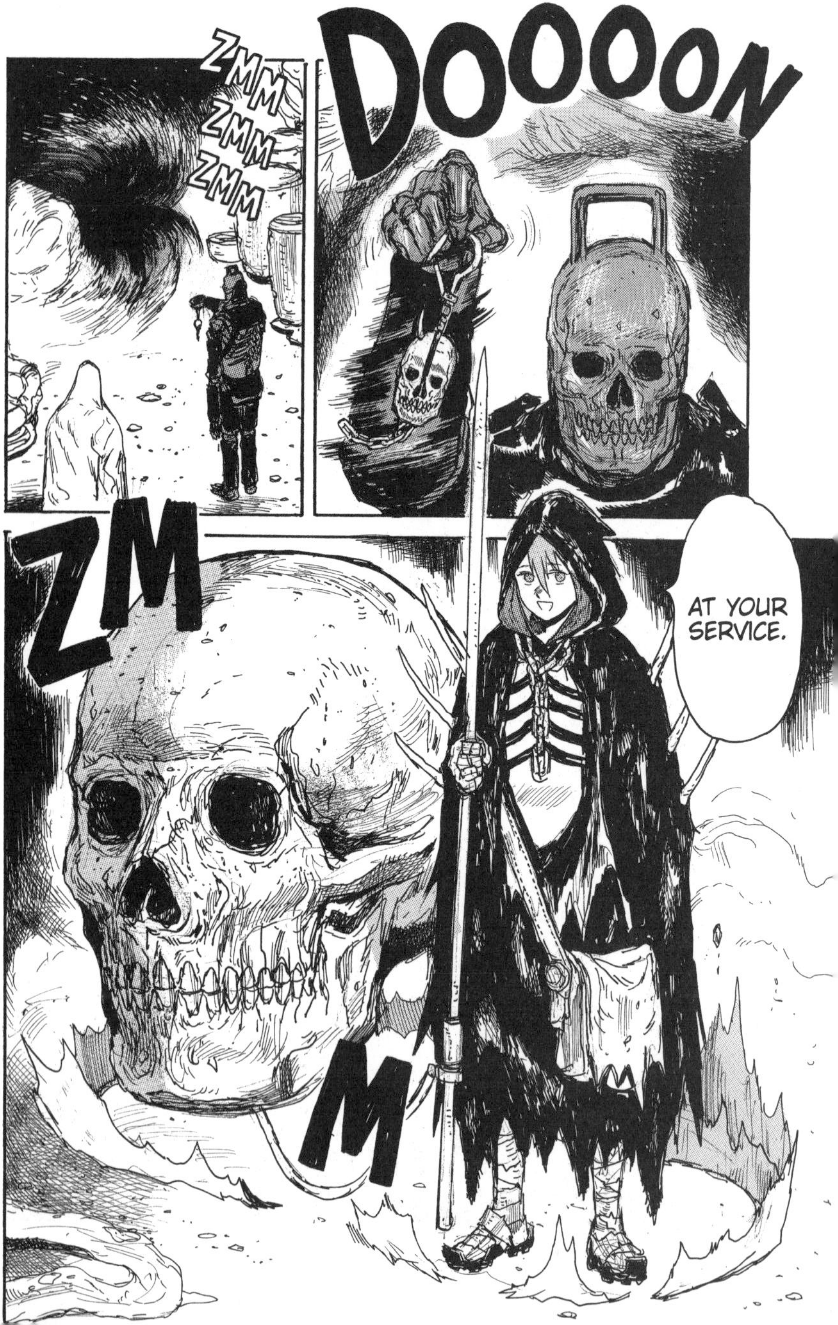
DOOOON
ZMM ZMM ZMM
AT YOUR SERVICE.
ZM
M

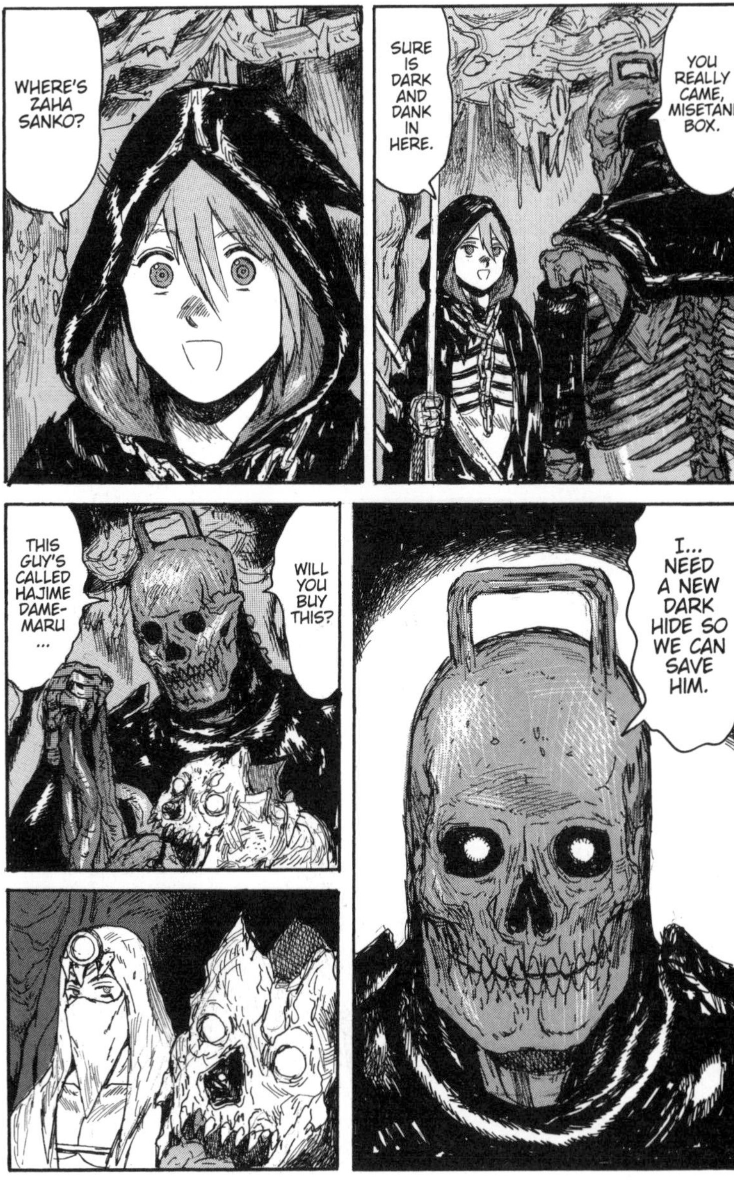
YOU REALLY CAME, MISETANI BOX.
SURE IS DARK AND DANK IN HERE.
WHERE'S ZAHA SANKO?
I... NEED A NEW DARK HIDE SO WE CAN SAVE HIM.
WILL YOU BUY THIS?
THIS GUY'S CALLED HAJIME DAME-MARU ...

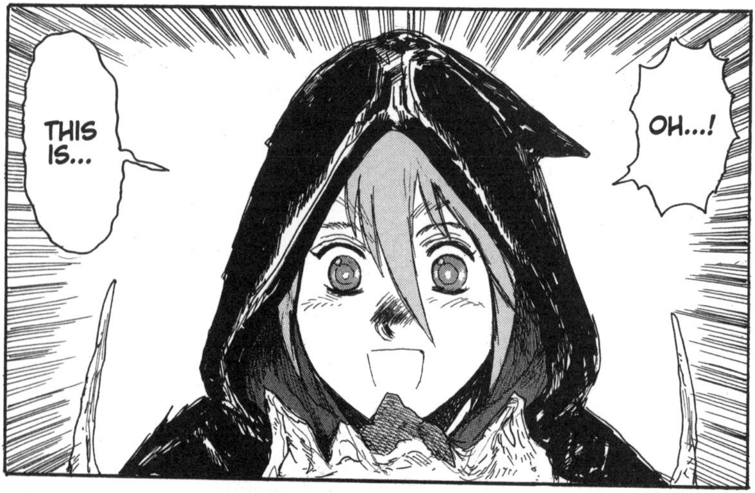
OH...!
THIS IS...

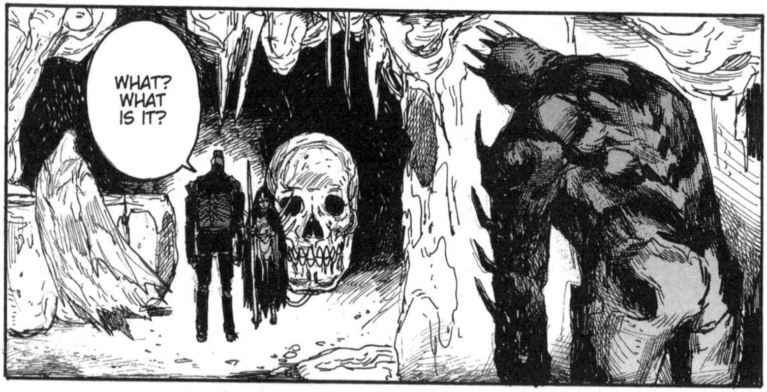
WHAT? WHAT IS IT?

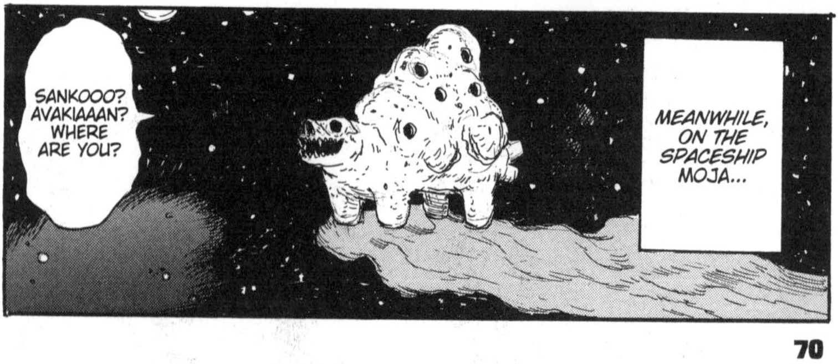
MEANWHILE, ON THE SPACESHIP MOJA...
SANKOOO? AVAKIAAAN? WHERE ARE YOU?

Bone 15: How Much for That Damemaru

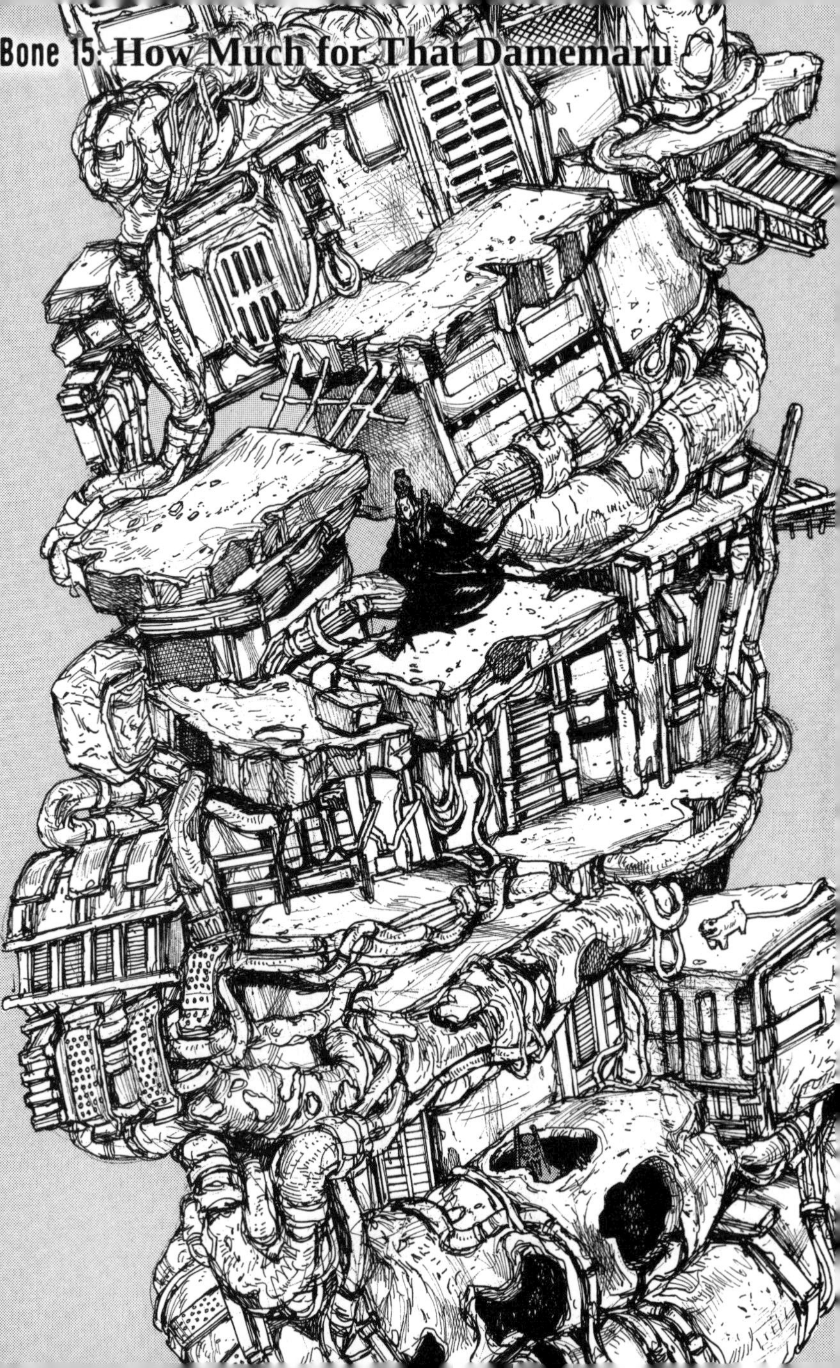

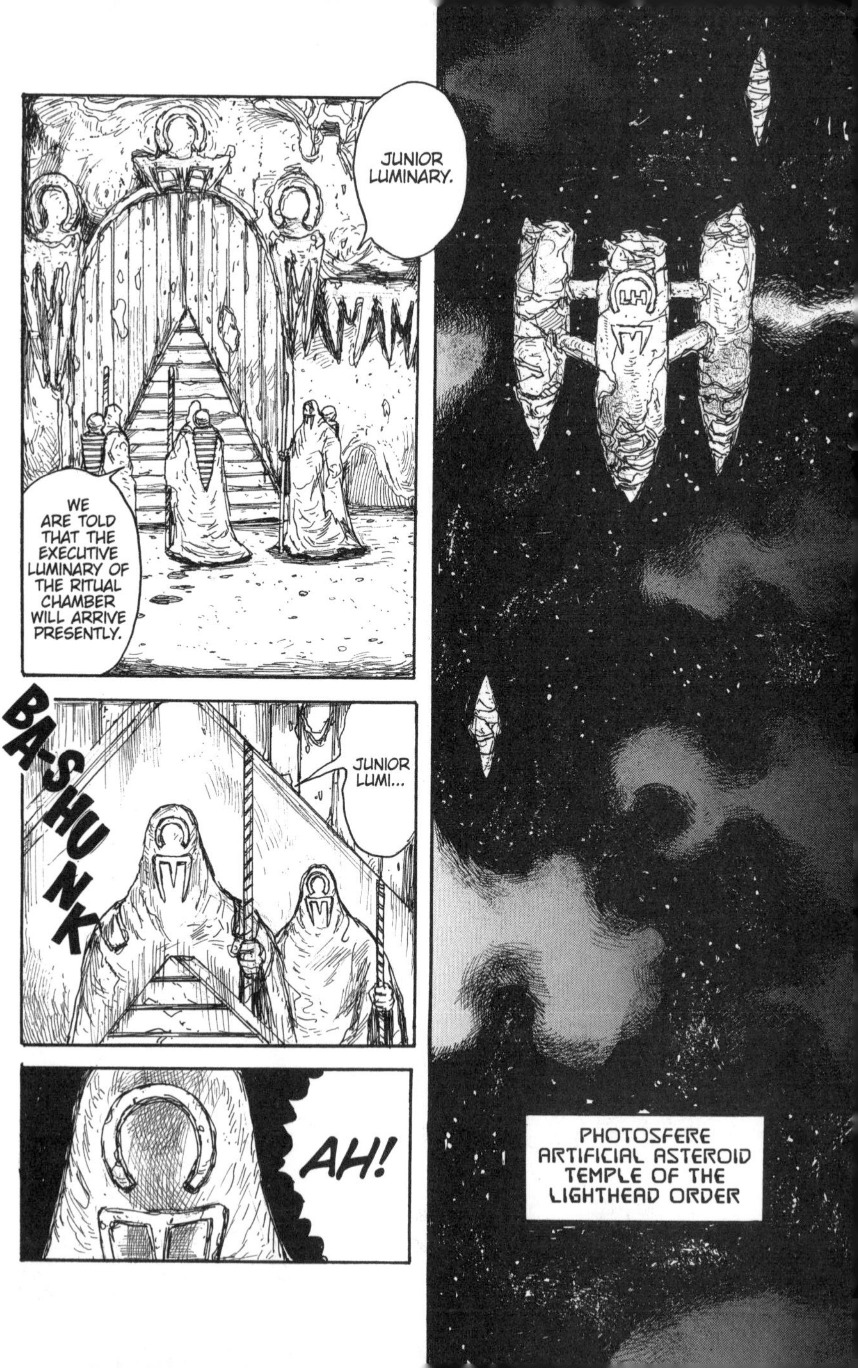

PHOTOSFERE ARTIFICIAL ASTEROID TEMPLE OF THE LIGHTHEAD ORDER
JUNIOR LUMINARY.
WE ARE TOLD THAT THE EXECUTIVE LUMINARY OF THE RITUAL CHAMBER WILL ARRIVE PRESENTLY.
JUNIOR LUMI...
BA-SHUNK
AH!

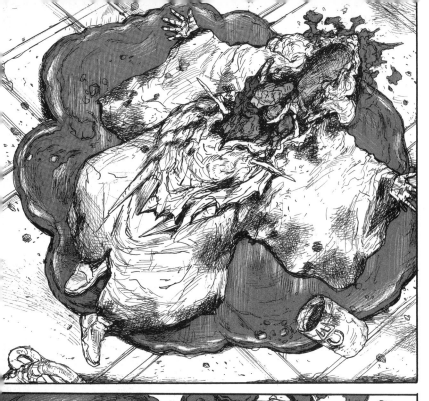

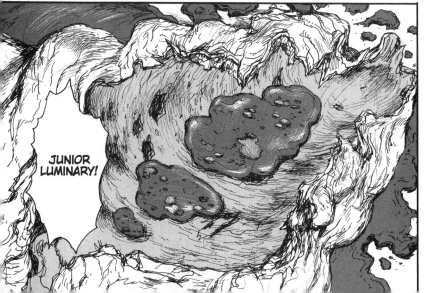

JUNIOR
LUMINARY!

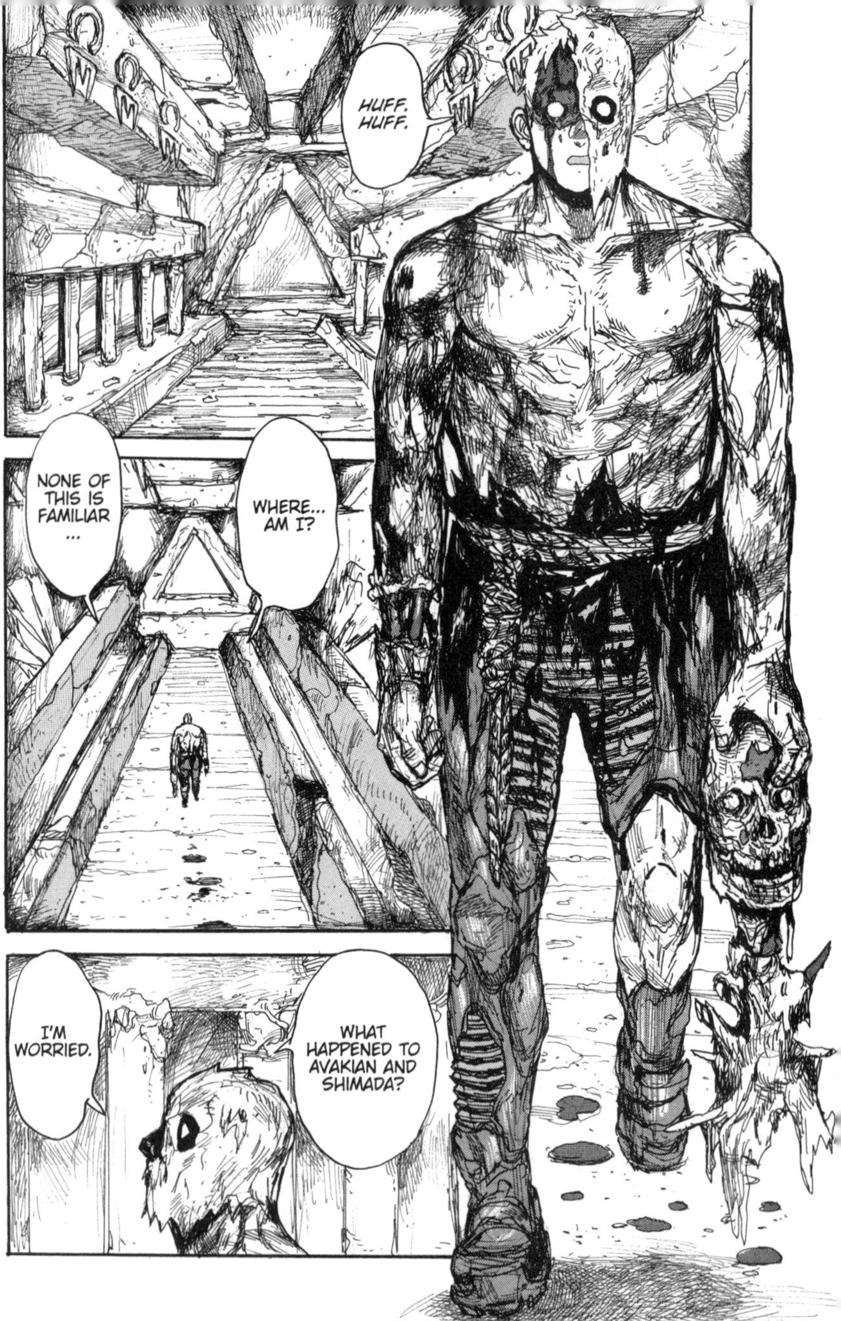
HUFF. HUFF.
WHERE... AM I?
NONE OF THIS IS FAMILIAR ...
WHAT HAPPENED TO AVAKIAN AND SHIMADA?
I'M WORRIED.

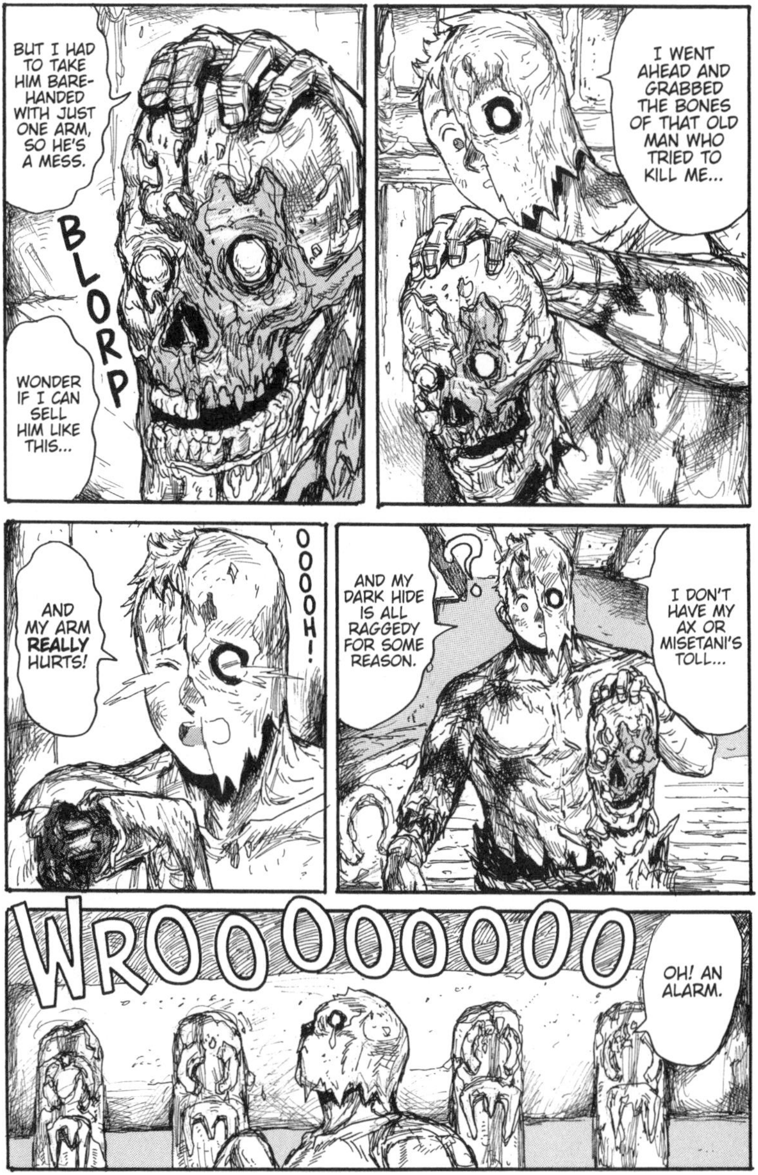
I WENT AHEAD AND GRABBED THE BONES OF THAT OLD MAN WHO TRIED TO KILL ME...
BUT I HAD TO TAKE HIM BARE-HANDED WITH JUST ONE ARM, SO HE'S A MESS.
BLORP
WONDER IF I CAN SELL HIM LIKE THIS...
I DON'T HAVE MY AX OR MISETANI'S TOLL...
AND MY DARK HIDE IS ALL RAGGEDY FOR SOME REASON.
OOOOOH!
AND MY ARM **REALLY** HURTS!
OH! AN ALARM.
WROOOOOOOOO

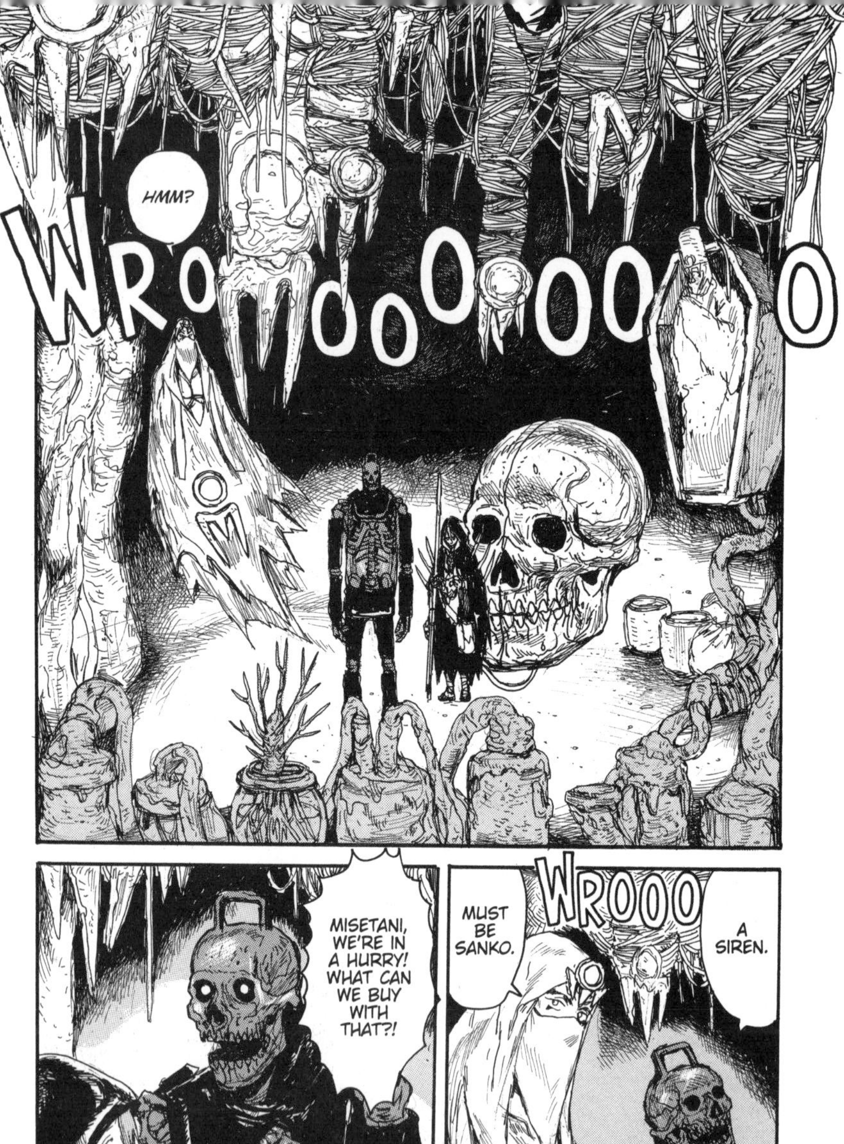
WROOOOOOO
HMM?
WROOO
A SIREN.
MUST BE SANKO.
MISETANI, WE'RE IN A HURRY! WHAT CAN WE BUY WITH THAT?!

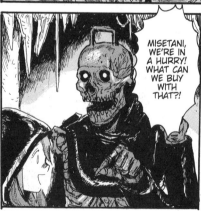

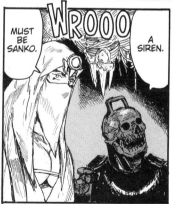

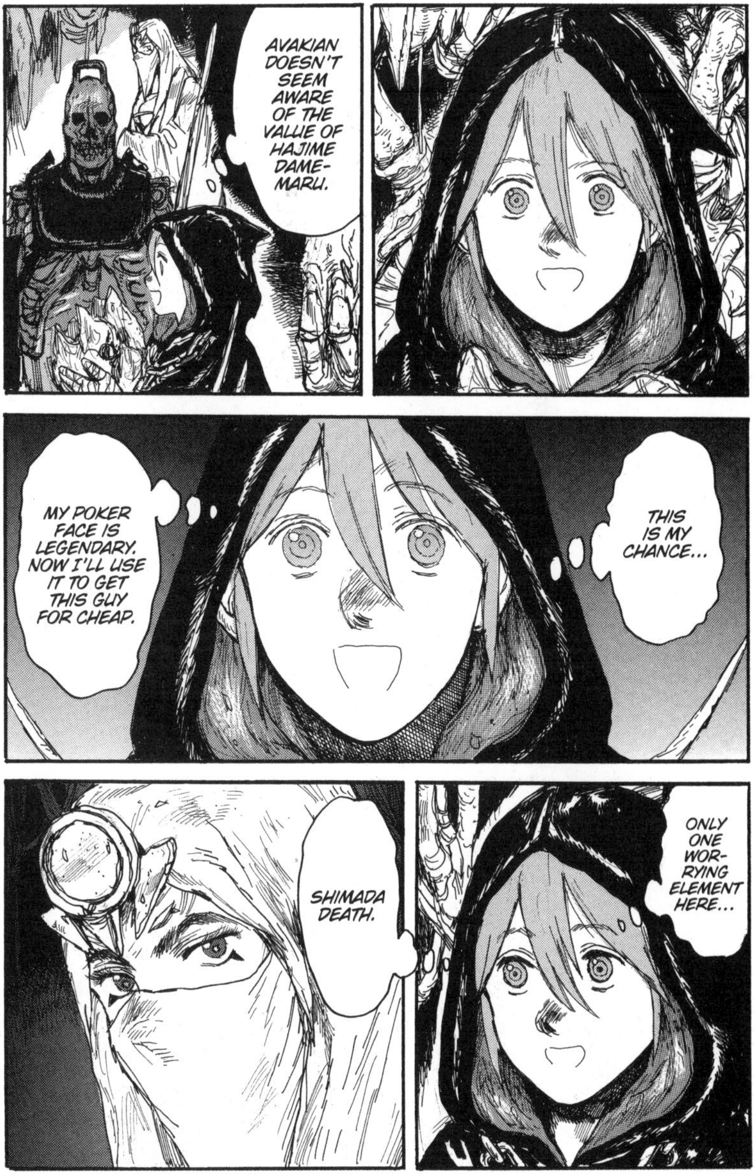
AVAKIAN DOESN'T SEEM AWARE OF THE VALUE OF HAJIME DAME-MARU.
THIS IS MY CHANCE...
MY POKER FACE IS LEGENDARY. NOW I'LL USE IT TO GET THIS GUY FOR CHEAP.
ONLY ONE WOR-RYING ELEMENT HERE...
SHIMADA DEATH.

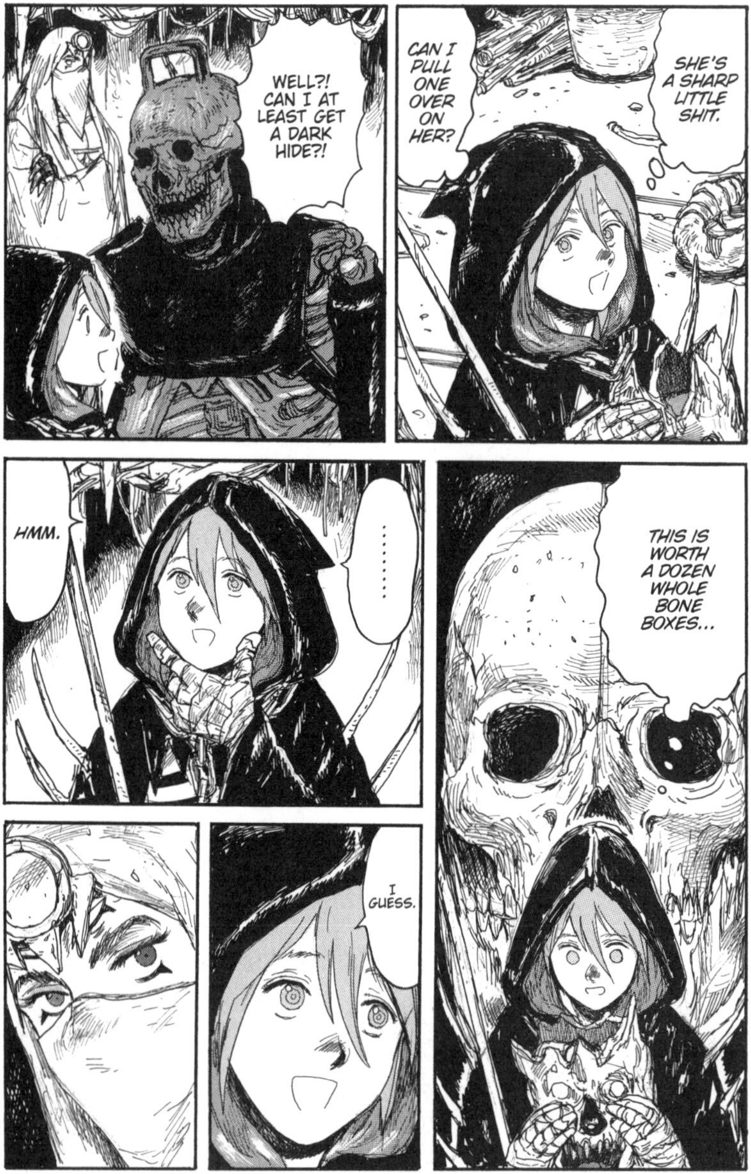
SHE'S A SHARP LITTLE SHIT.
CAN I PULL ONE OVER ON HER?
WELL?! CAN I AT LEAST GET A DARK HIDE?!
THIS IS WORTH A DOZEN WHOLE BONE BOXES...
......
HMM.
I GUESS.

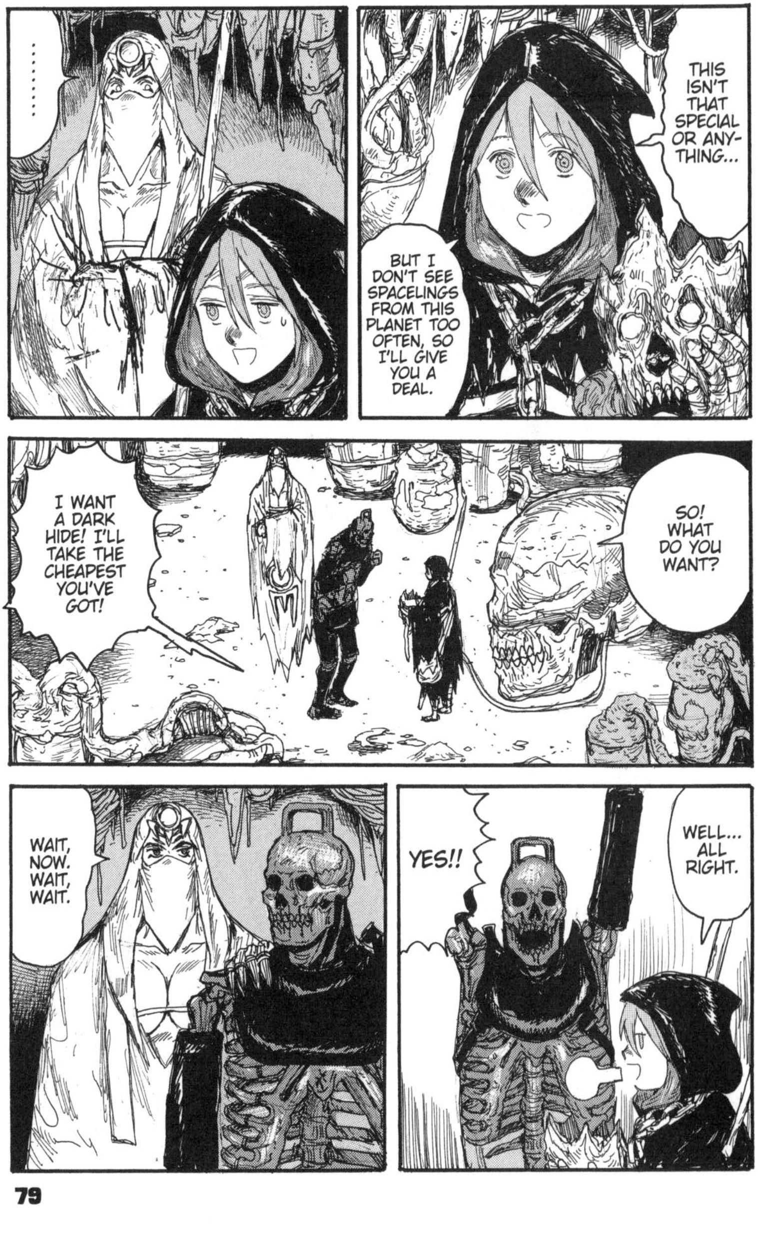
THIS ISN'T THAT SPECIAL OR ANY-THING...
BUT I DON'T SEE SPACELINGS FROM THIS PLANET TOO OFTEN, SO I'LL GIVE YOU A DEAL.
......
SO! WHAT DO YOU WANT?
I WANT A DARK HIDE! I'LL TAKE THE CHEAPEST YOU'VE GOT!
WELL... ALL RIGHT.
YES!!
WAIT, NOW. WAIT, WAIT.

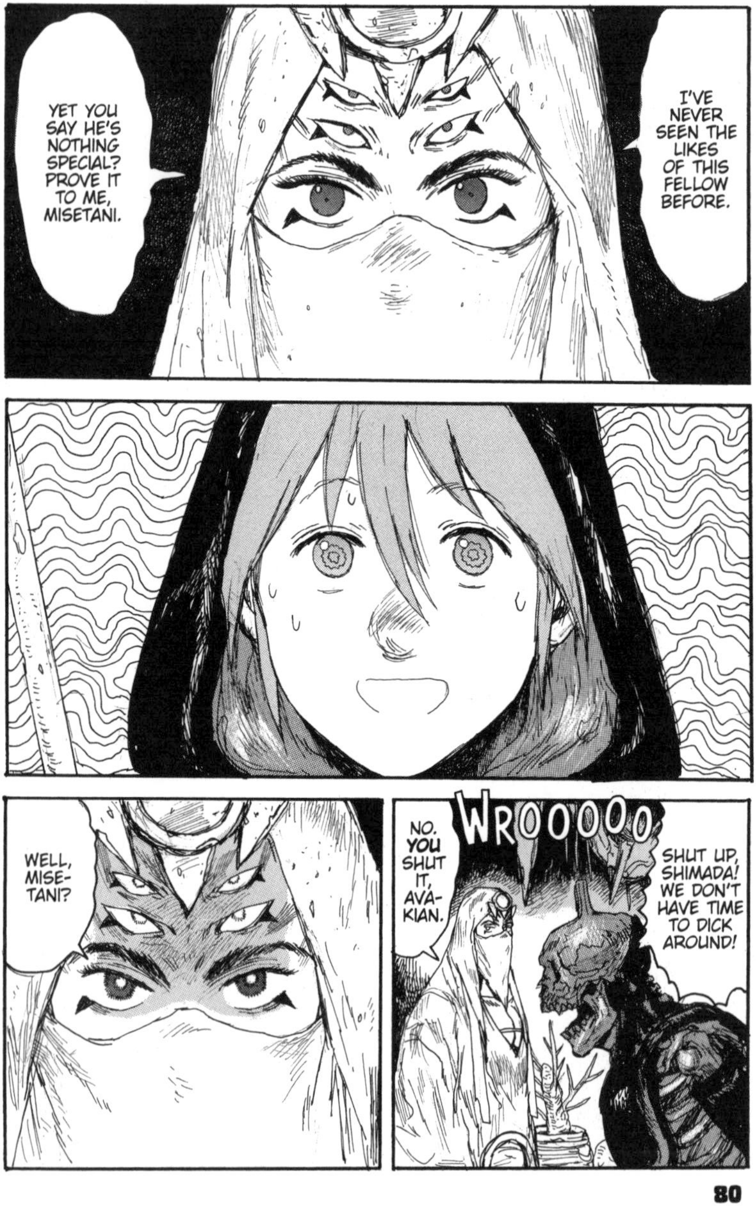
I'VE NEVER SEEN THE LIKES OF THIS FELLOW BEFORE.
YET YOU SAY HE'S NOTHING SPECIAL? PROVE IT TO ME, MISETANI.
WROOOOO
SHUT UP, SHIMADA! WE DON'T HAVE TIME TO DICK AROUND!
NO. **YOU** SHUT IT, AVAKIAN.
WELL, MISETANI?

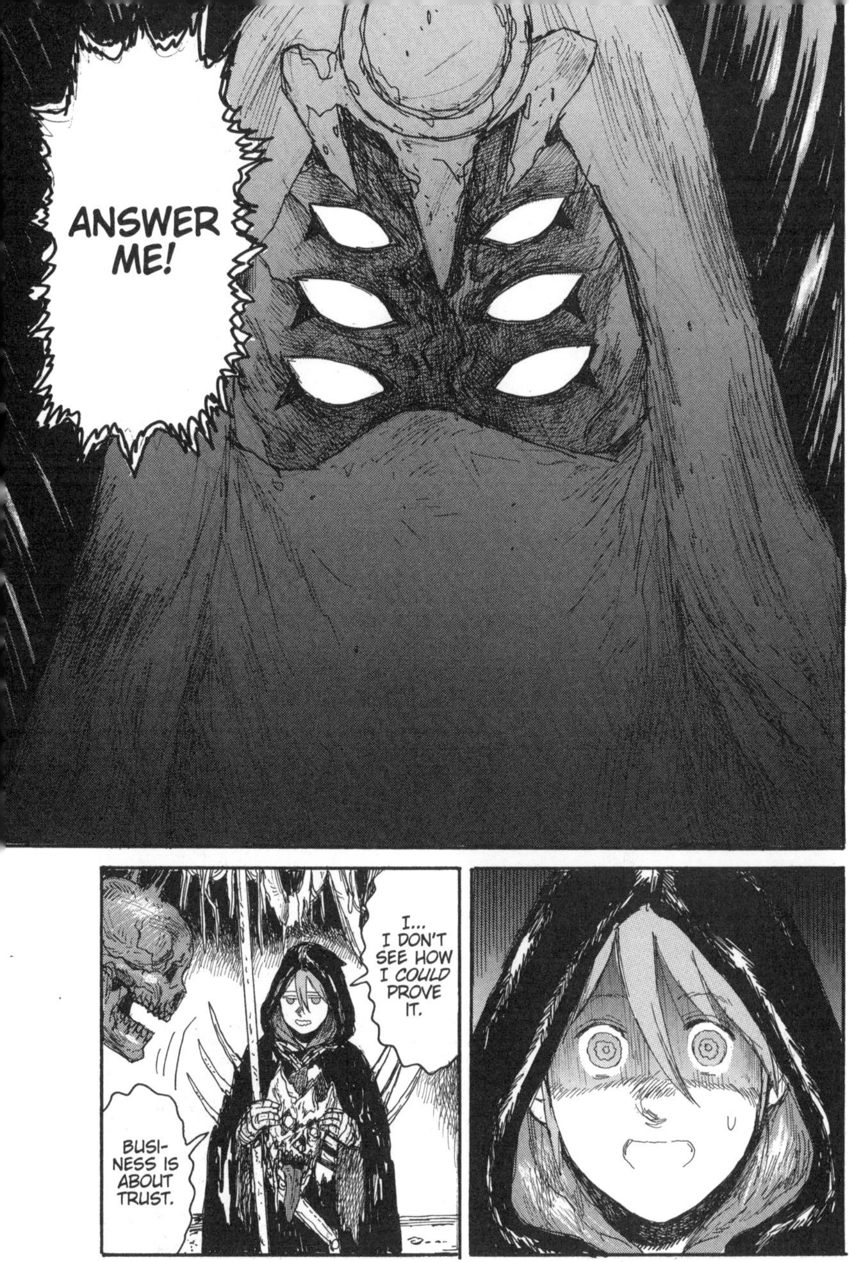
ANSWER ME!
I... I DON'T SEE HOW I COULD PROVE IT.
BUSI- NESS IS ABOUT TRUST.

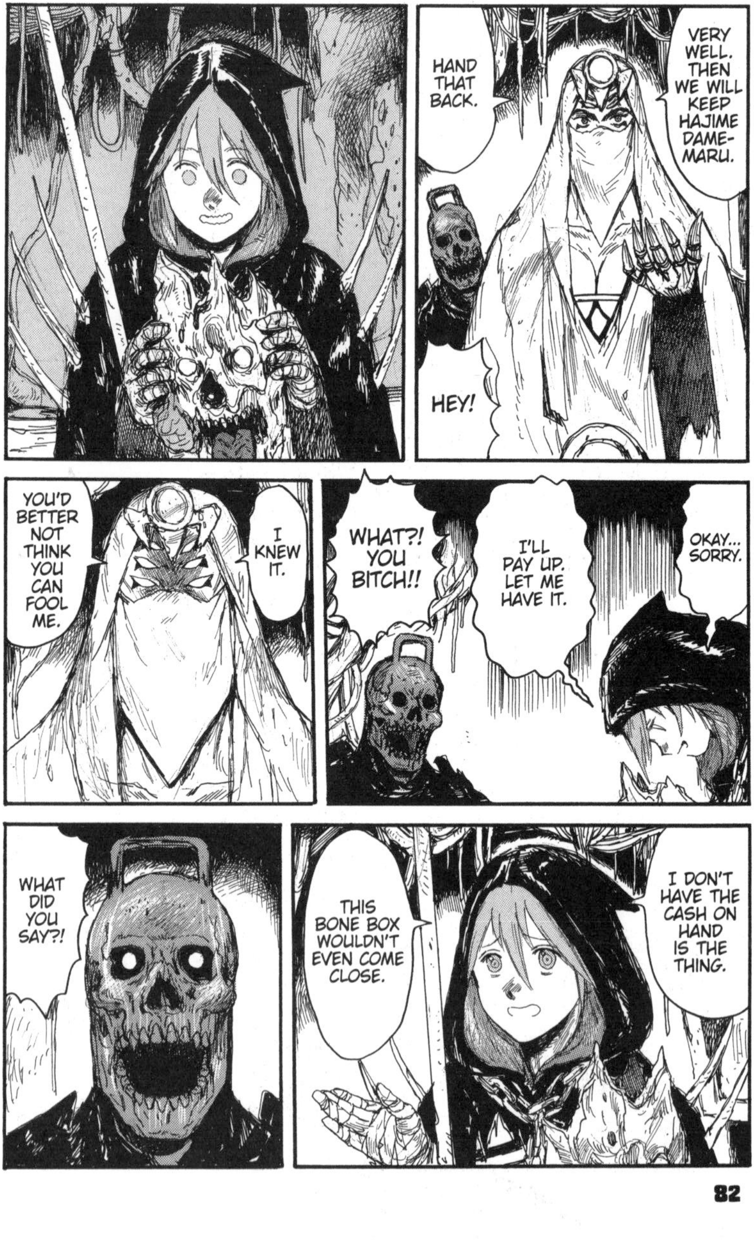
VERY WELL. THEN WE WILL KEEP HAJIME DAME-MARU.
HAND THAT BACK.
HEY!
OKAY... SORRY.
I'LL PAY UP. LET ME HAVE IT.
WHAT?! YOU BITCH!!
I KNEW IT.
YOU'D BETTER NOT THINK YOU CAN FOOL ME.
I DON'T HAVE THE CASH ON HAND IS THE THING.
THIS BONE BOX WOULDN'T EVEN COME CLOSE.
WHAT DID YOU SAY?!

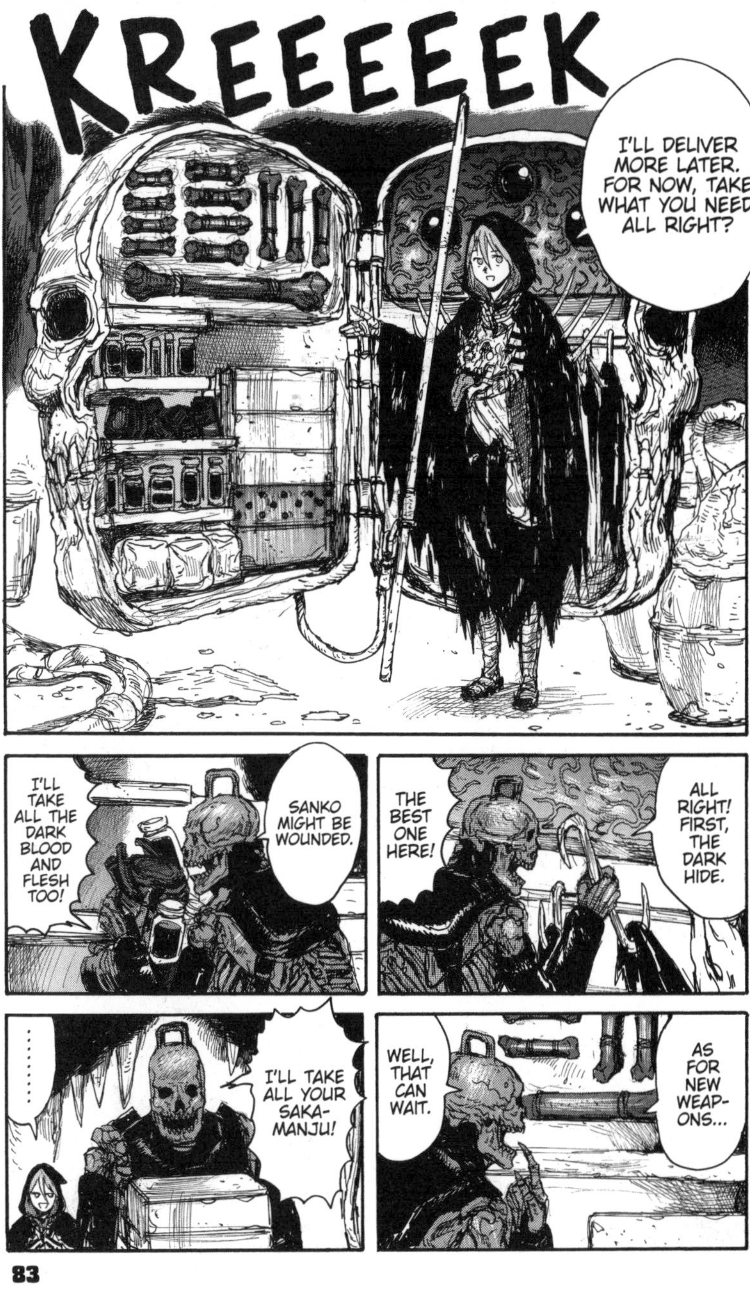
KREEEEEEK
I'LL DELIVER MORE LATER. FOR NOW, TAKE WHAT YOU NEED, ALL RIGHT?
ALL RIGHT! FIRST, THE DARK HIDE.
THE BEST ONE HERE!
SANKO MIGHT BE WOUNDED.
I'LL TAKE ALL THE DARK BLOOD AND FLESH TOO!
AS FOR NEW WEAP-ONS...
WELL, THAT CAN WAIT.
I'LL TAKE ALL YOUR SAKA-MANJU!
......

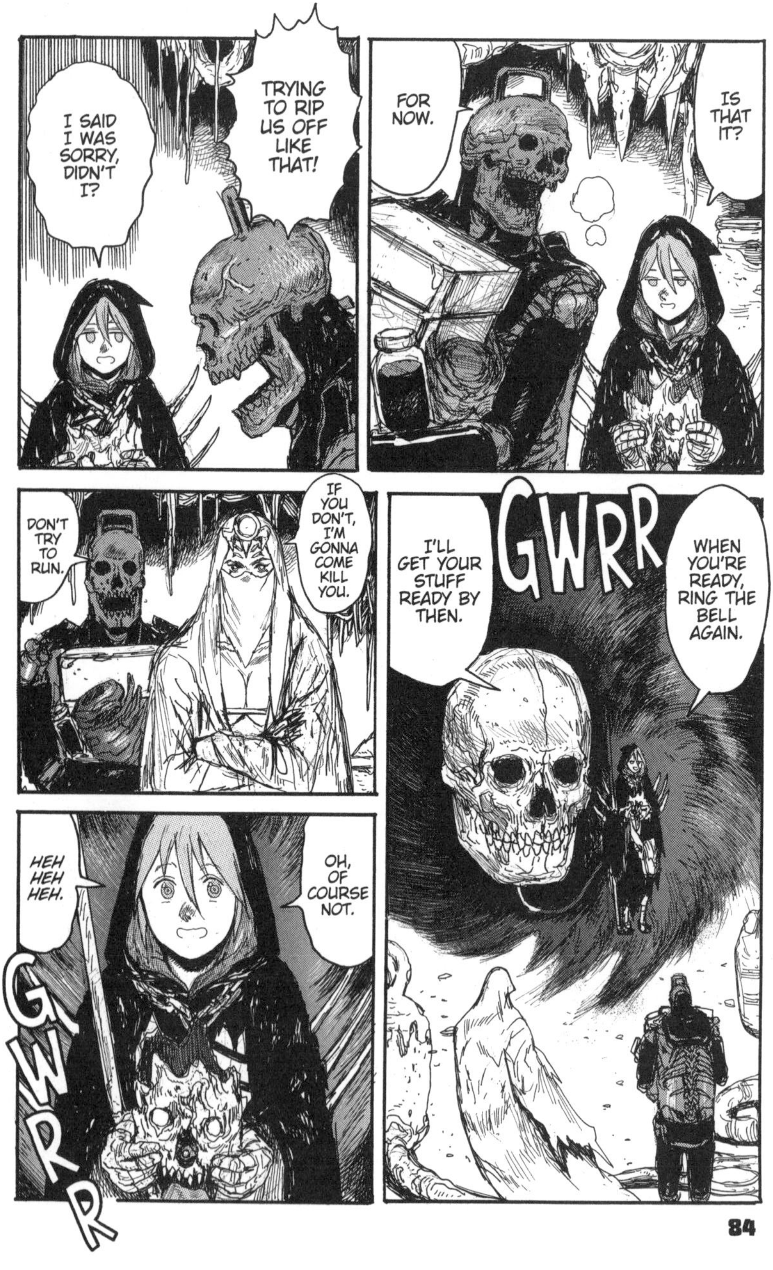
IS THAT IT?
FOR NOW.
TRYING TO RIP US OFF LIKE THAT!
I SAID I WAS SORRY, DIDN'T I?
WHEN YOU'RE READY, RING THE BELL AGAIN.
GWRR
I'LL GET YOUR STUFF READY BY THEN.
IF YOU DON'T, I'M GONNA COME KILL YOU.
DON'T TRY TO RUN.
OH, OF COURSE NOT.
HEH HEH HEH.
GWRR

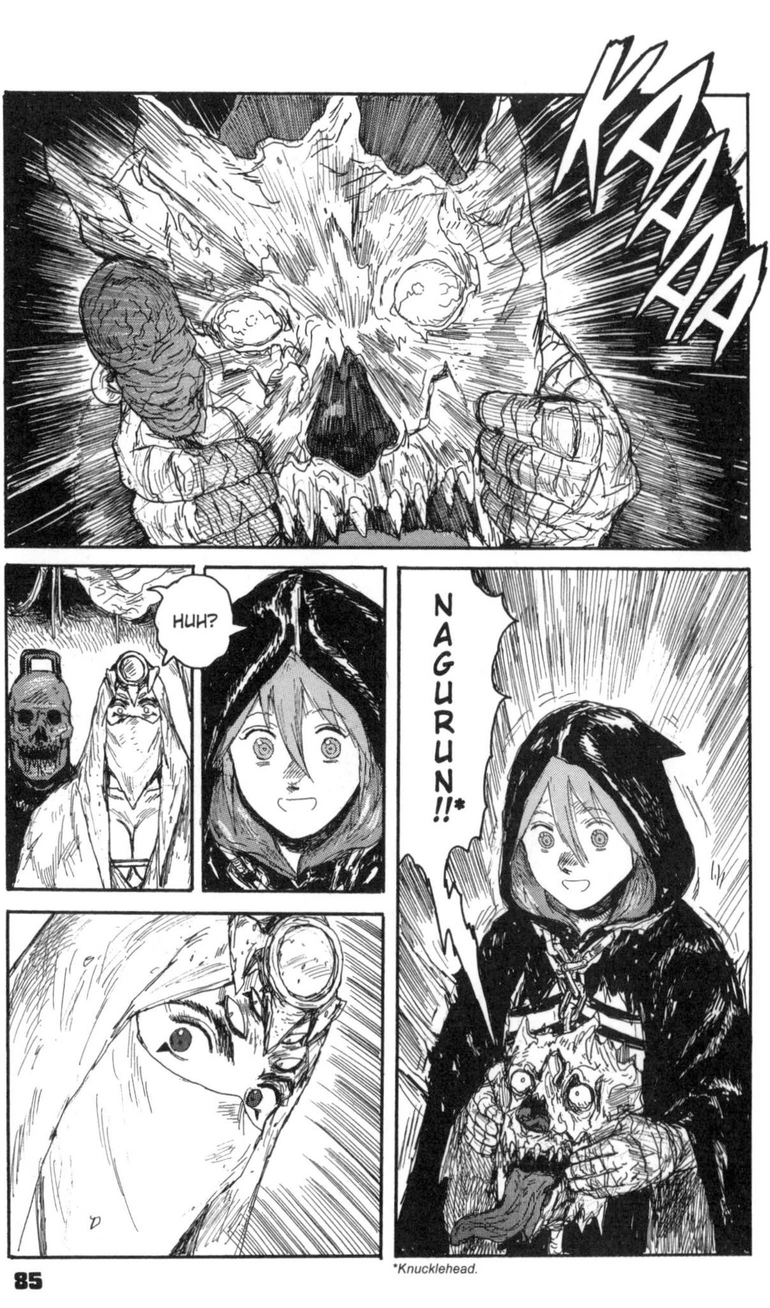
KAAAA
NAGURUN!!*
HUH?

*Knucklehead.

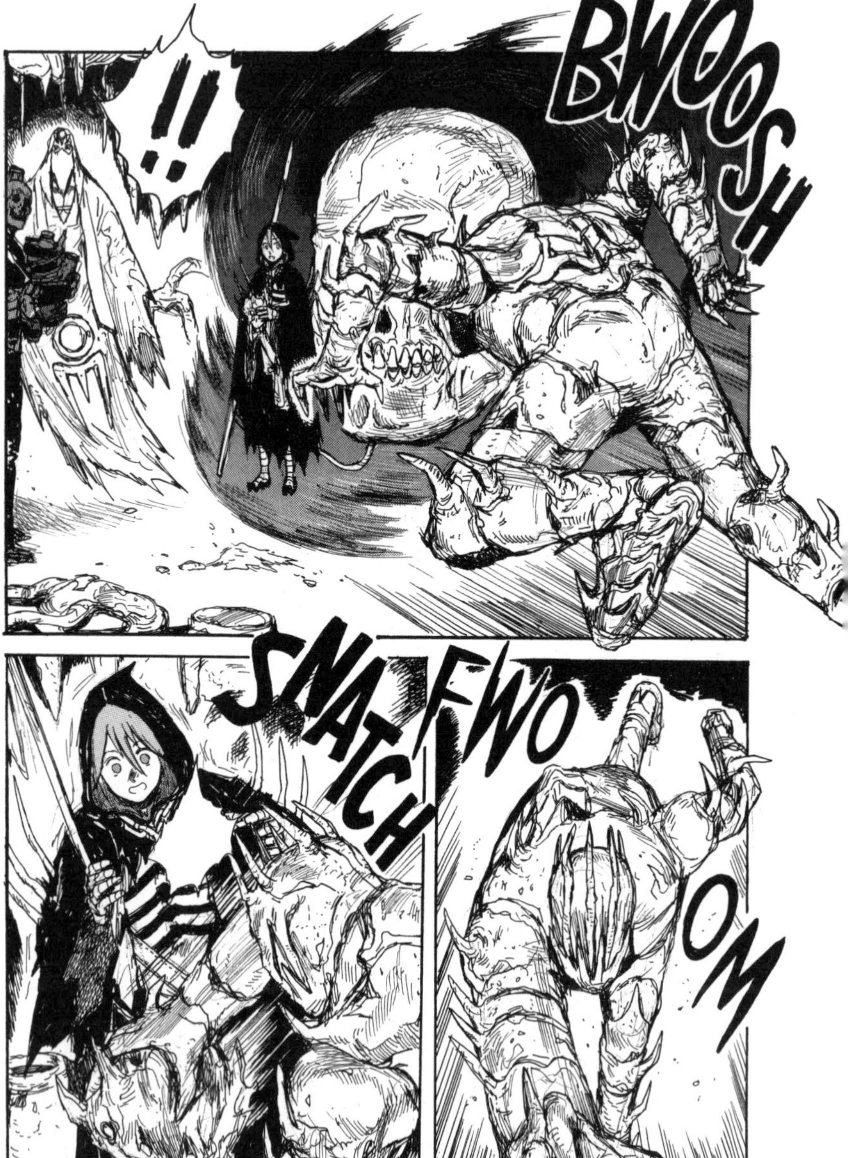
BWOOSH
!!
FWOOM
SNATCH

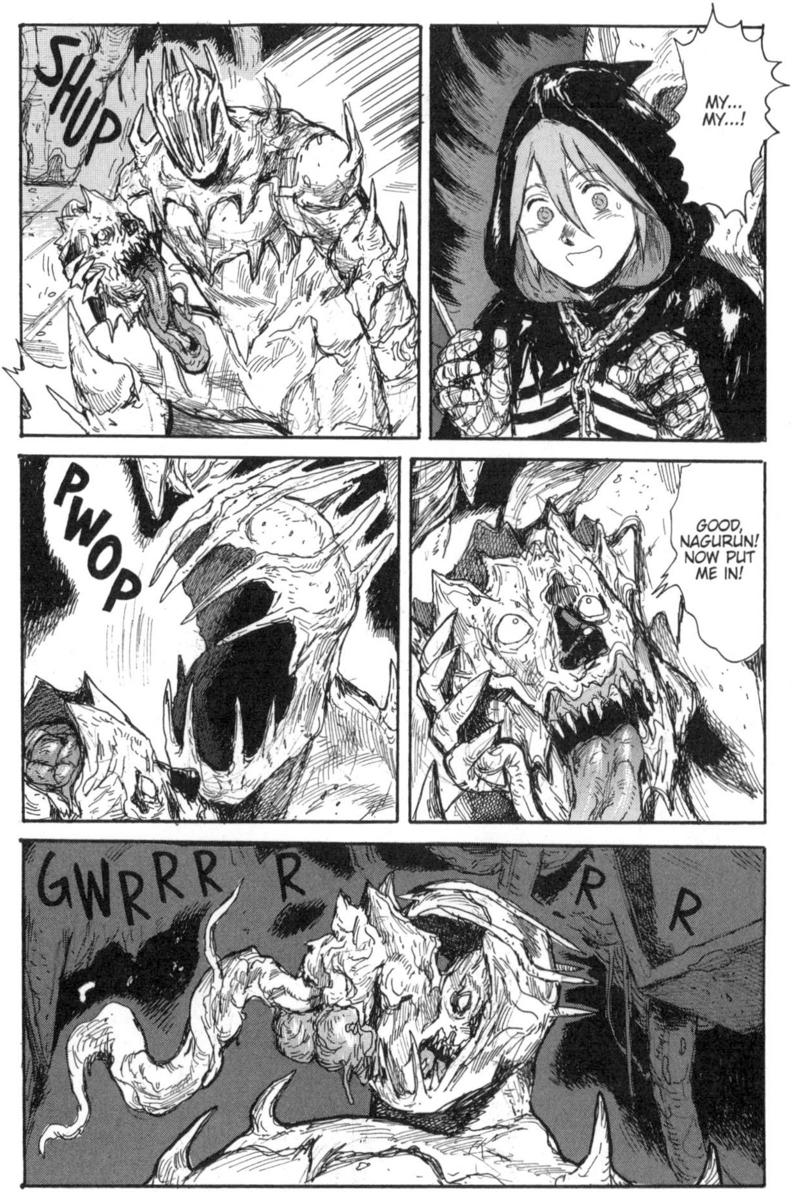
MY... MY...!
SHUP
GOOD, NAGURUN! NOW PUT ME IN!
PWOP
GWRRR R R R

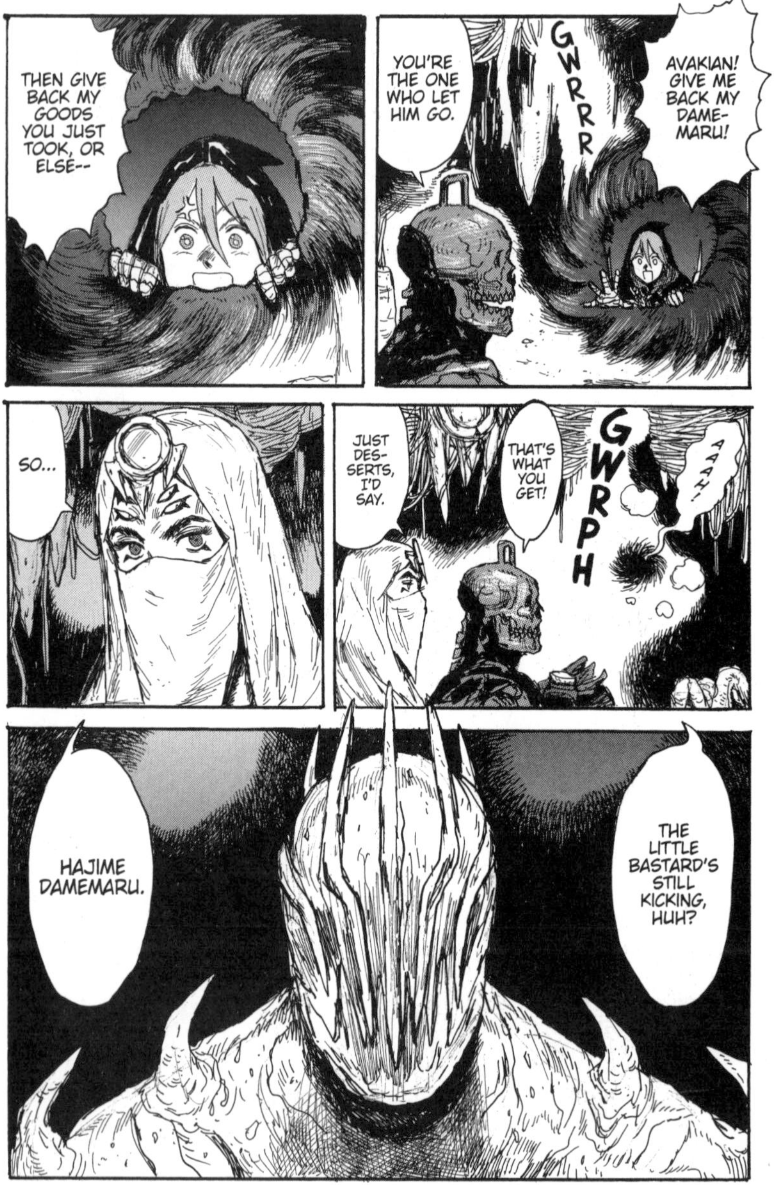
AVAKIAN! GIVE ME BACK MY DAMEMARU!
GWRRR
YOU'RE THE ONE WHO LET HIM GO.
THEN GIVE BACK MY GOODS YOU JUST TOOK, OR ELSE--
AAAH!
GWRPH
THAT'S WHAT YOU GET!
JUST DESSERTS, I'D SAY.
SO...
THE LITTLE BASTARD'S STILL KICKING, HUH?
HAJIME DAMEMARU.

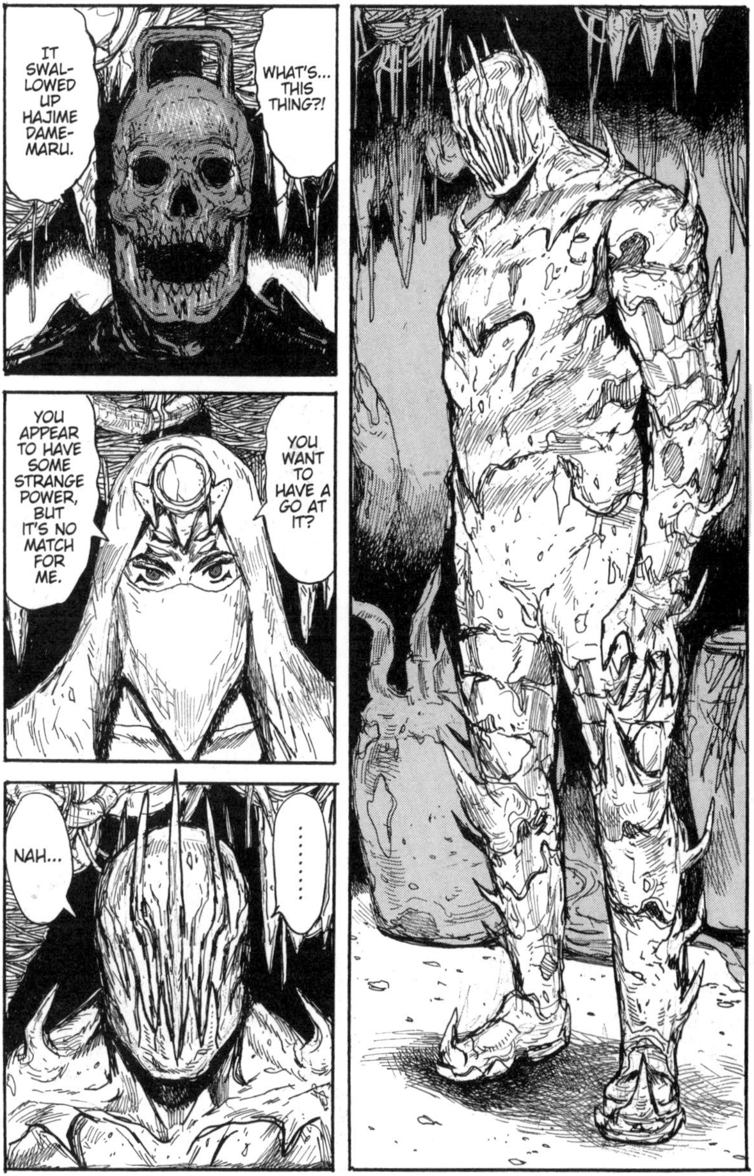
WHAT'S... THIS THING?!
IT SWAL-LOWED UP HAJIME DAME-MARU.
YOU WANT TO HAVE A GO AT IT?
YOU APPEAR TO HAVE SOME STRANGE POWER, BUT IT'S NO MATCH FOR ME.
....
NAH...

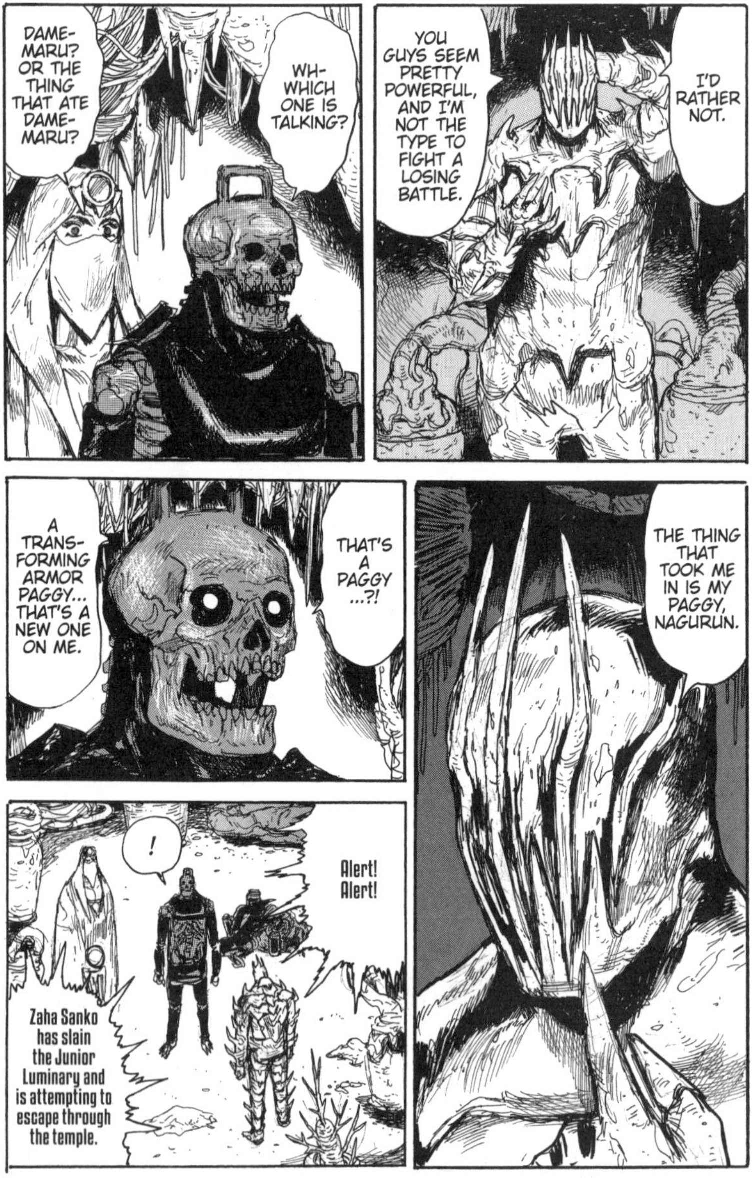
I'D RATHER NOT.
YOU GUYS SEEM PRETTY POWERFUL, AND I'M NOT THE TYPE TO FIGHT A LOSING BATTLE.
WH-WHICH ONE IS TALKING?
DAME-MARU? OR THE THING THAT ATE DAME-MARU?
THE THING THAT TOOK ME IN IS MY PAGGY, NAGURUN.
THAT'S A PAGGY...?!
A TRANS-FORMING ARMOR PAGGY... THAT'S A NEW ONE ON ME.
Alert! Alert!
!
Zaha Sanko has slain the Junior Luminary and is attempting to escape through the temple.

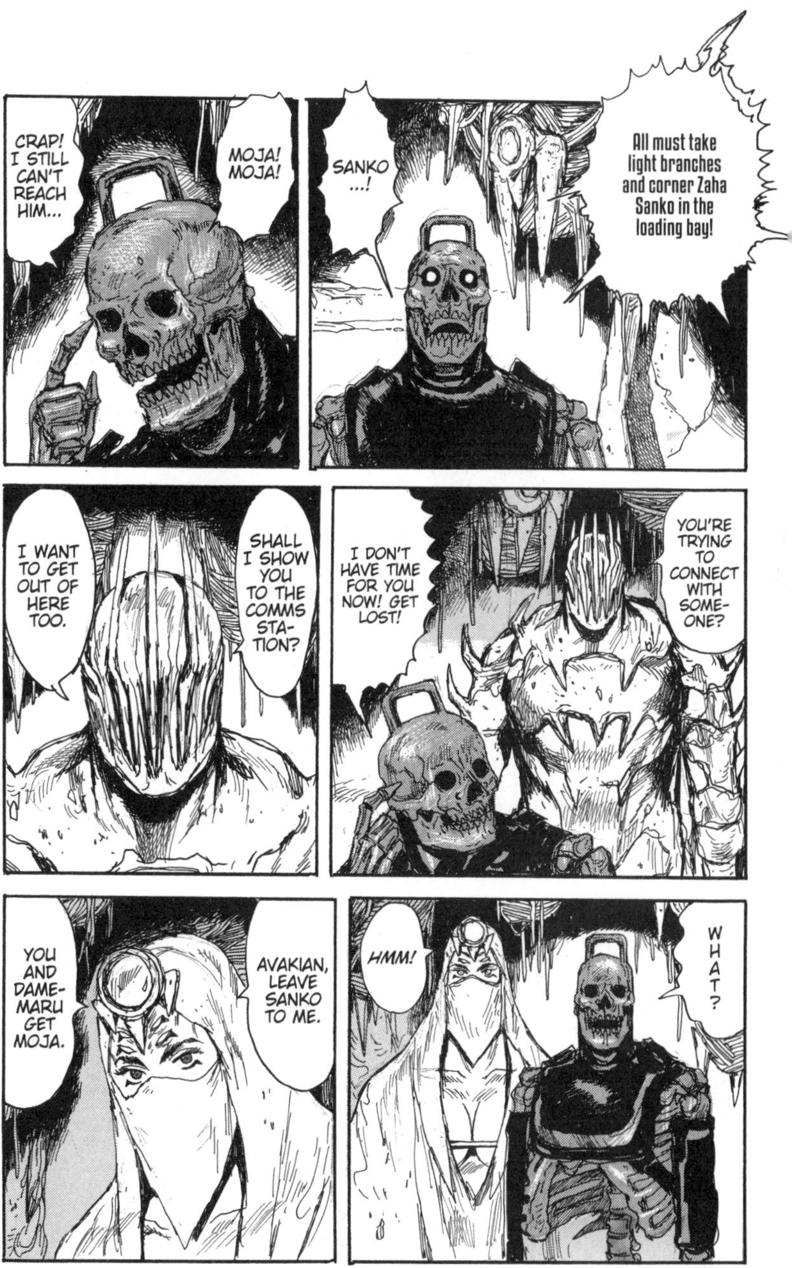
All must take light branches and corner Zaha Sanko in the loading bay!
SANKO ...!
MOJA! MOJA!
CRAP! I STILL CAN'T REACH HIM...
YOU'RE TRYING TO CONNECT WITH SOME-ONE?
I DON'T HAVE TIME FOR YOU NOW! GET LOST!
SHALL I SHOW YOU TO THE COMMS STATION?
I WANT TO GET OUT OF HERE TOO.
WHAT?
HMM!
AVAKIAN, LEAVE SANKO TO ME.
YOU AND DAME-MARU GET MOJA.

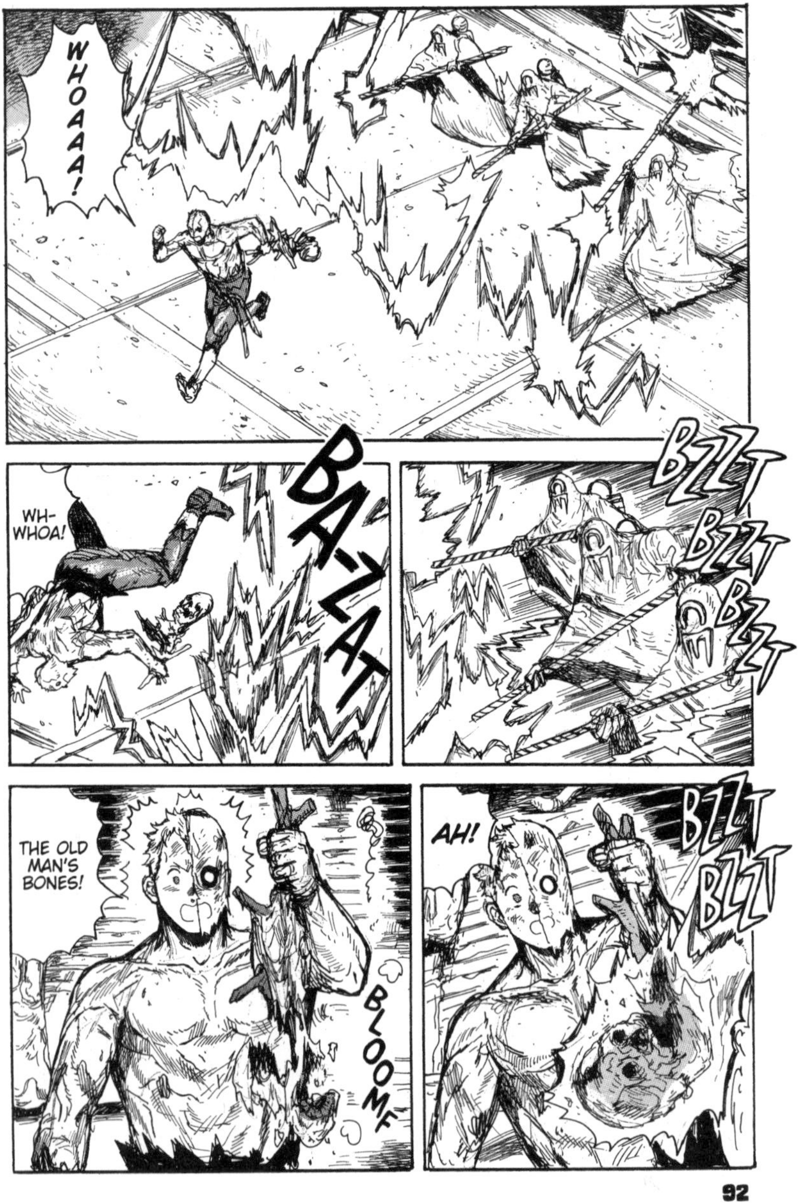
WHOAAAA!
BZZT
BZZT
BZZT
BZZT
WH-WHOA!
BA-ZAT
AH!
BZZT
BZZT
THE OLD MAN'S BONES!
BLOOMF

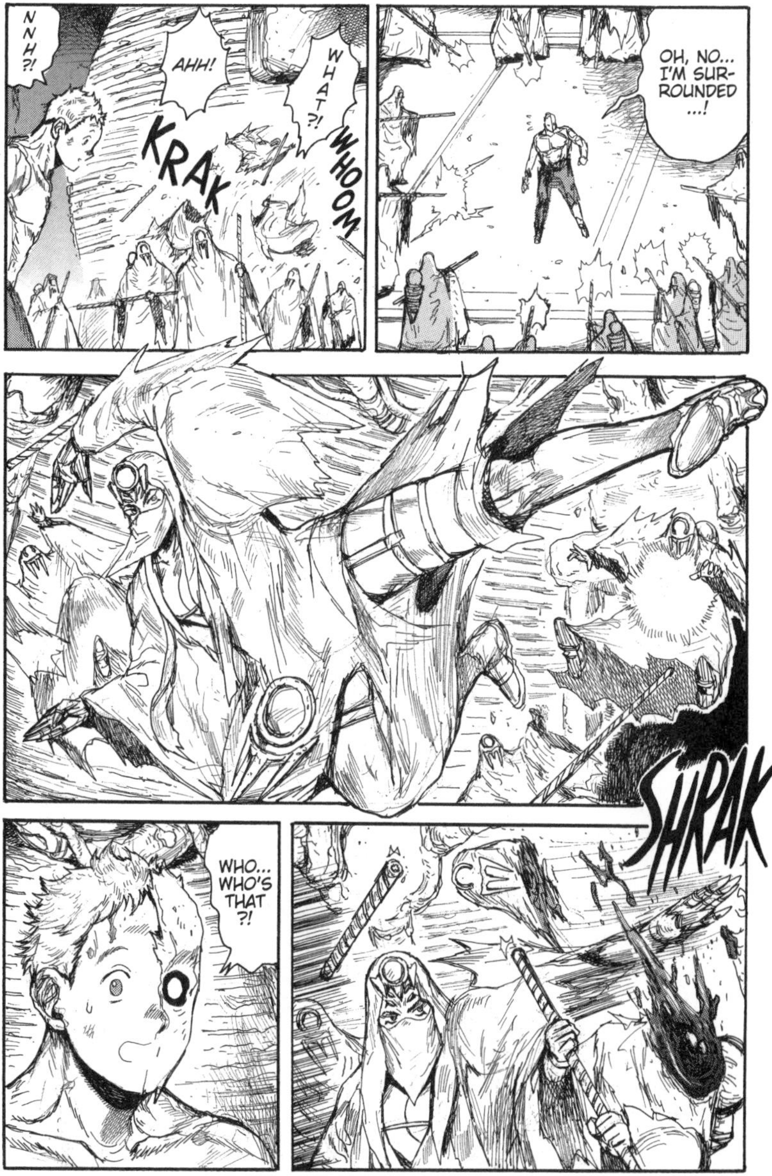
OH, NO... I'M SURROUNDED ...!
WHAT?!
AHH!
NNH?!
WHOOM
KRAK
SHRAK
WHO... WHO'S THAT?!

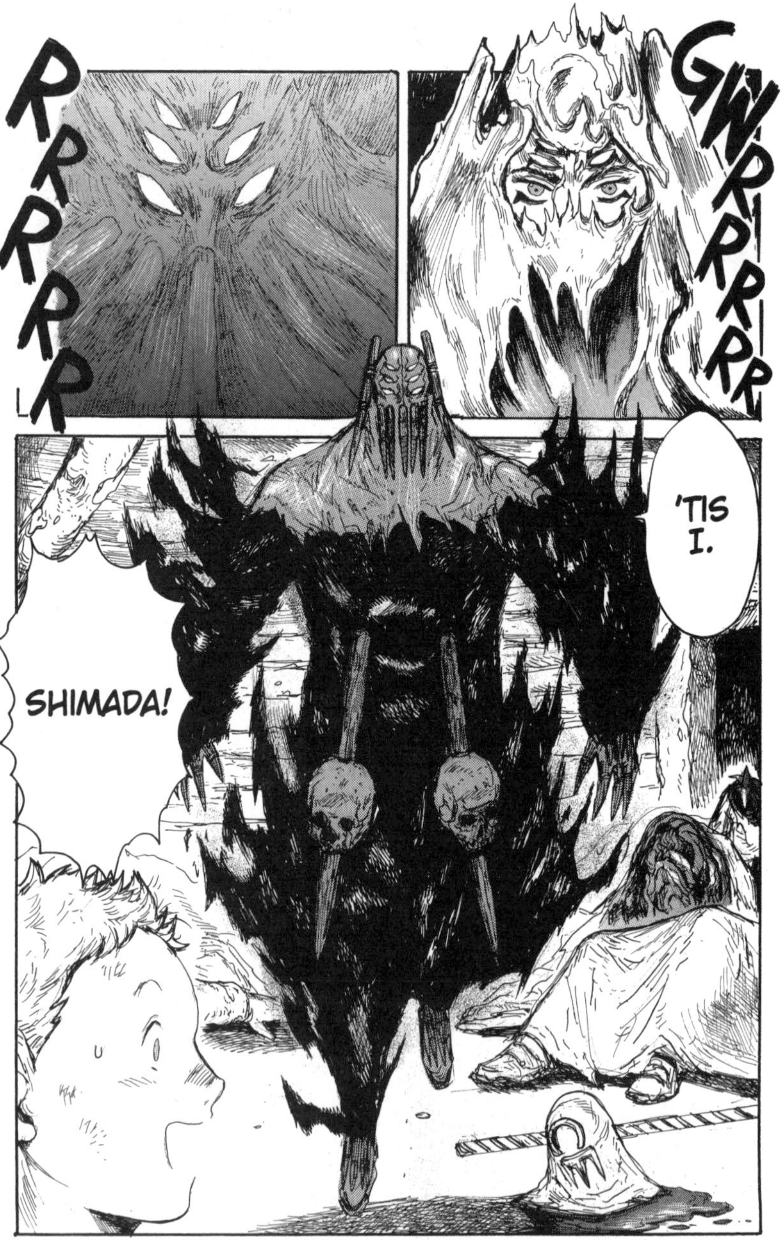
GWRRRRR
RRRRR
'TIS I.
SHIMADA!

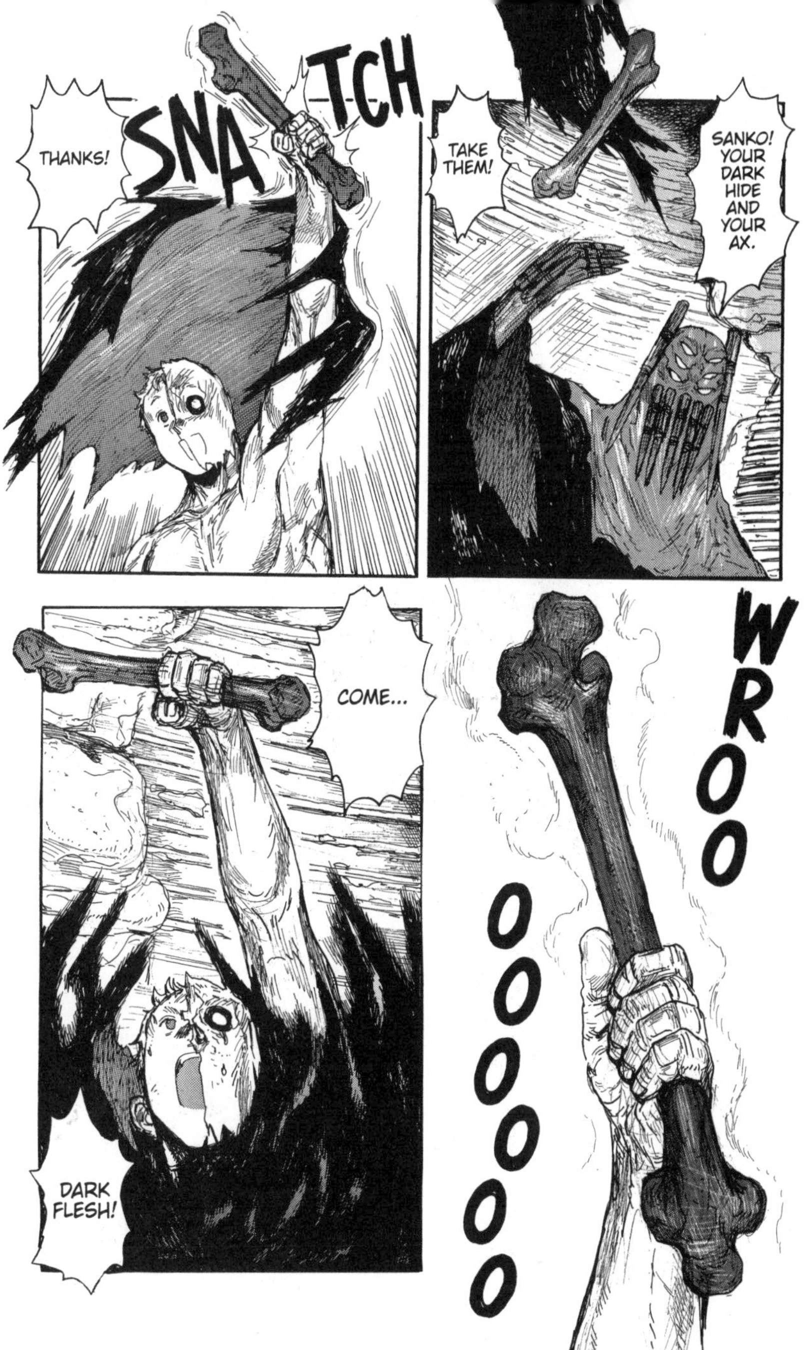
SANKO! YOUR DARK HIDE AND YOUR AX.
TAKE THEM!
SNATCH
THANKS!
WROOOOOOOOOO
COME...
DARK FLESH!

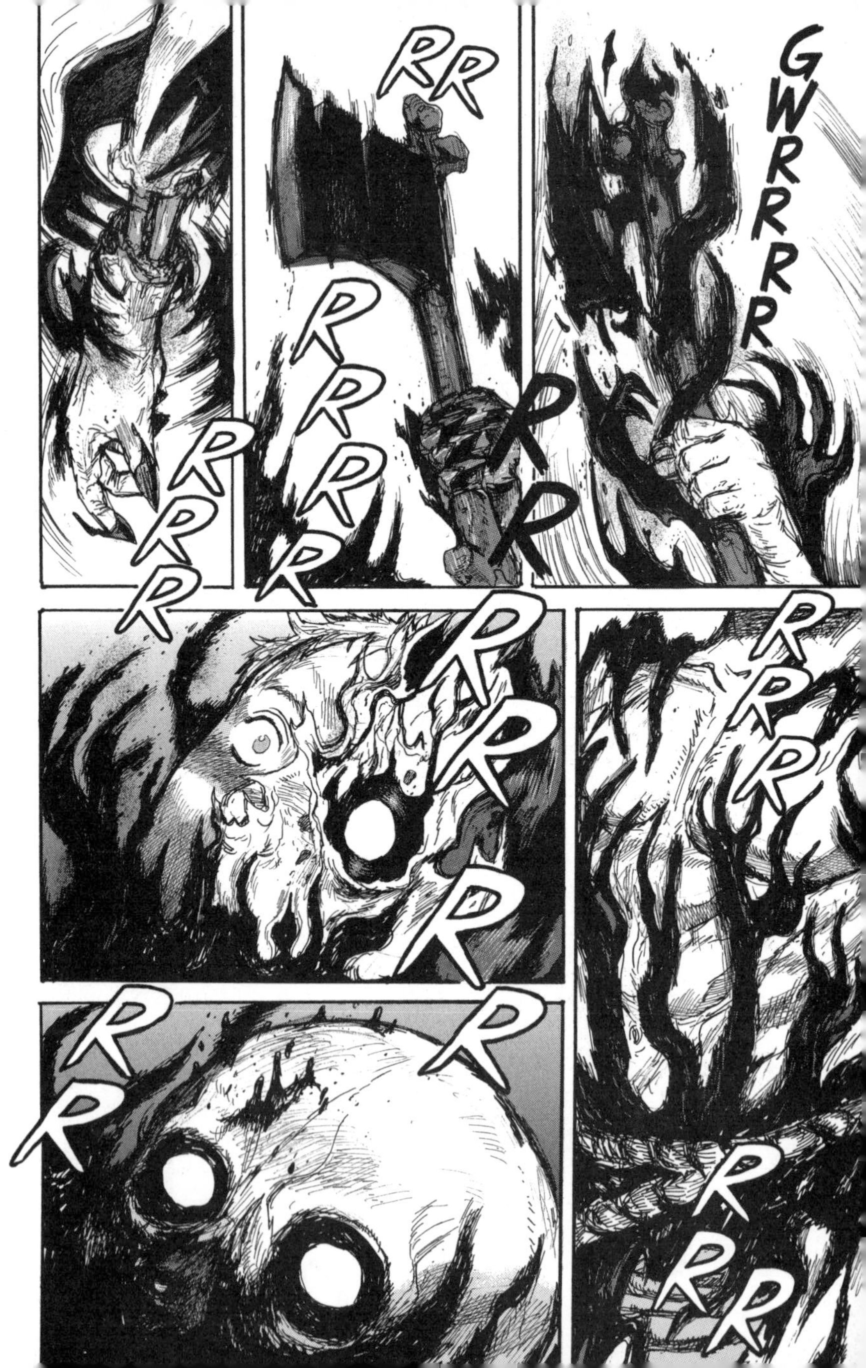

GWRRRRR
RR
RRRR
RR
RRRR
RRRR
RRRRR
RRRR
RR

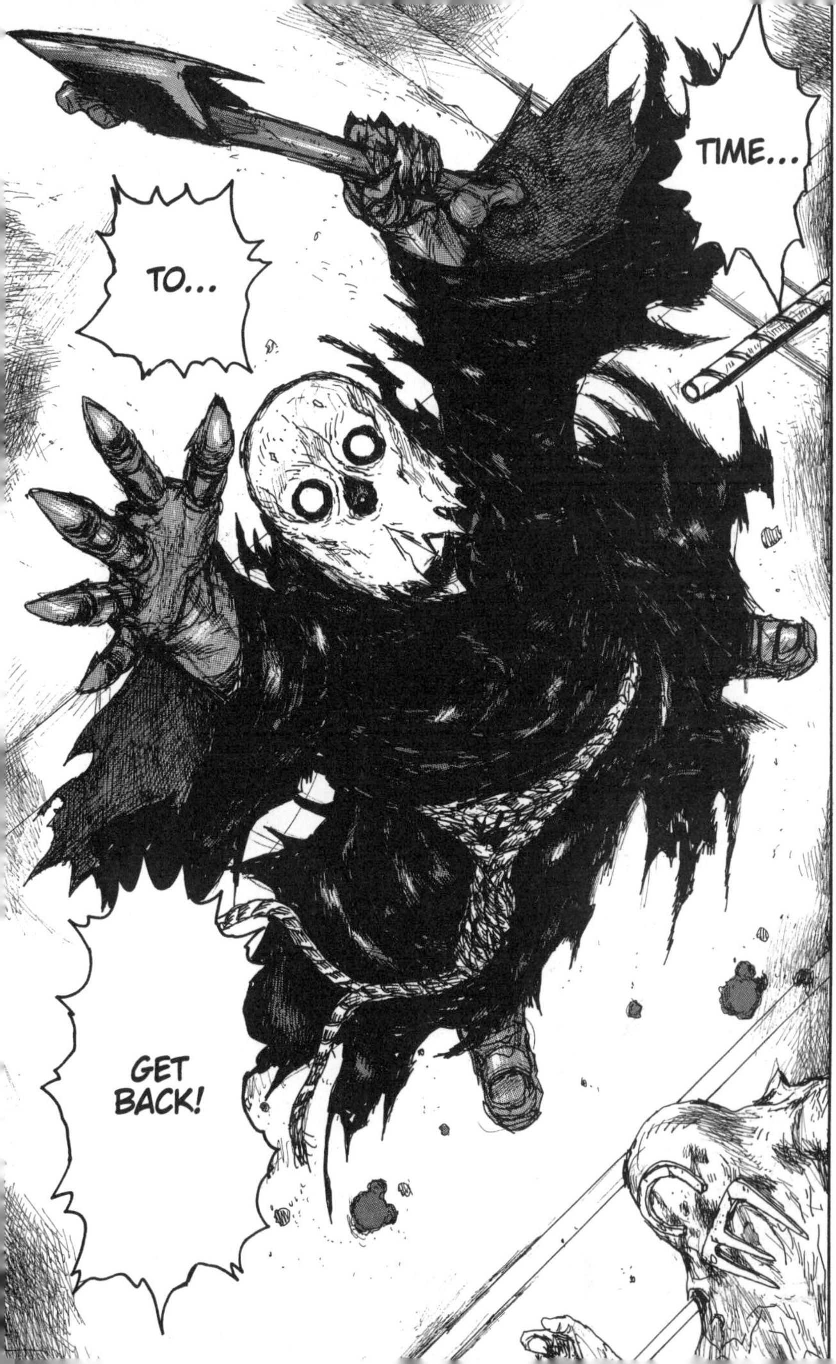
TIME...
TO...
GET BACK!

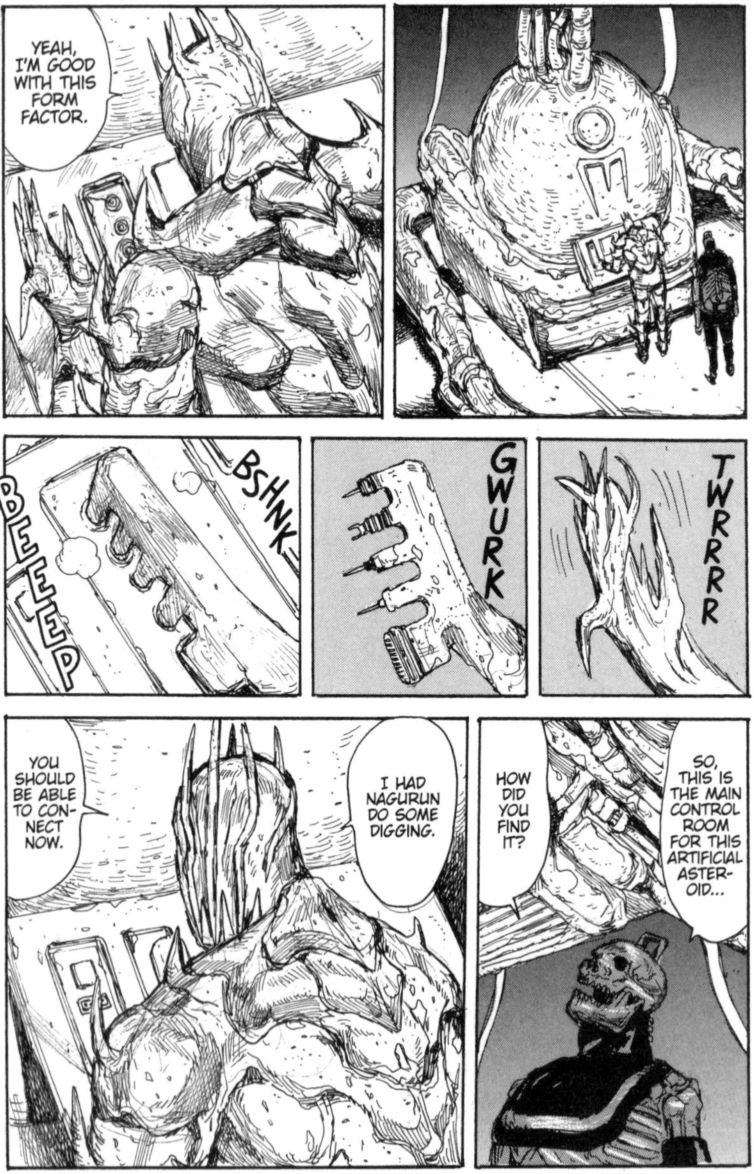
YEAH, I'M GOOD WITH THIS FORM FACTOR.
TWRRRR
GWURK
BSHNK
BEEEP
SO, THIS IS THE MAIN CONTROL ROOM FOR THIS ARTIFICIAL ASTEROID...
HOW DID YOU FIND IT?
I HAD NAGURUN DO SOME DIGGING.
YOU SHOULD BE ABLE TO CONNECT NOW.

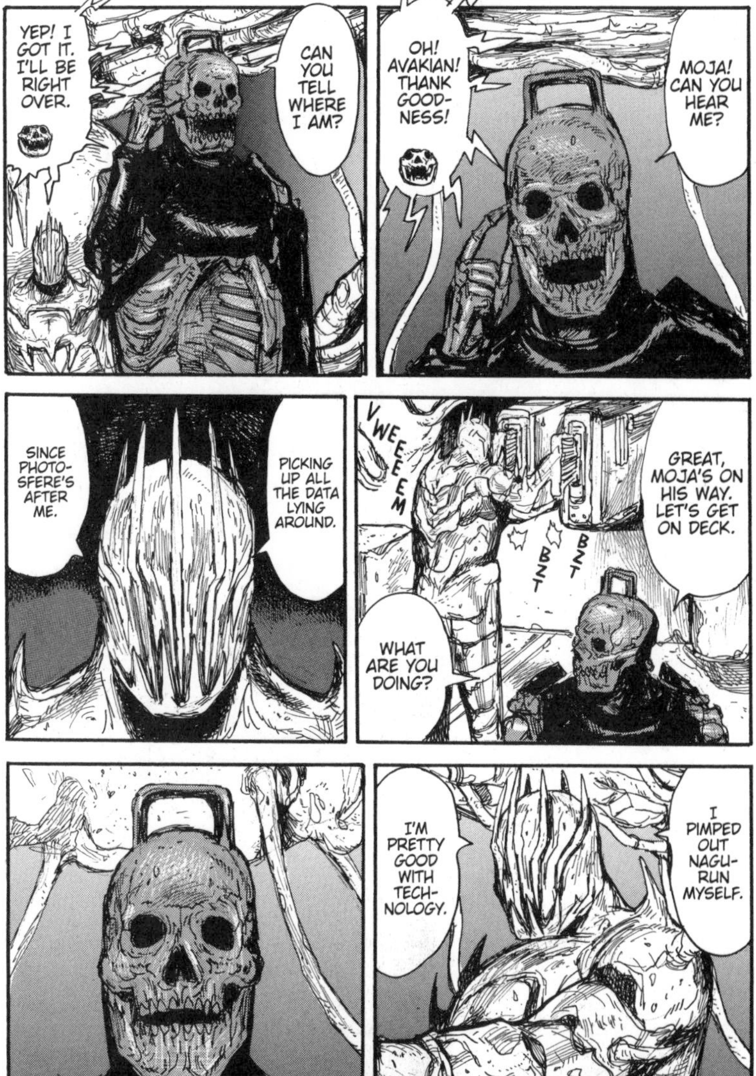
MOJA! CAN YOU HEAR ME?
OH! AVAKIAN! THANK GOOD-NESS!
CAN YOU TELL WHERE I AM?
YEP! I GOT IT. I'LL BE RIGHT OVER.
GREAT, MOJA'S ON HIS WAY. LET'S GET ON DECK.
VWEEEEEM
BZT BZT
WHAT ARE YOU DOING?
PICKING UP ALL THE DATA LYING AROUND.
SINCE PHOTO-SFERE'S AFTER ME.
I PIMPED OUT NAGU-RUN MYSELF.
I'M PRETTY GOOD WITH TECH-NOLOGY.

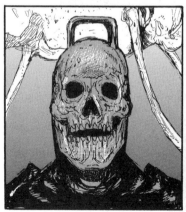

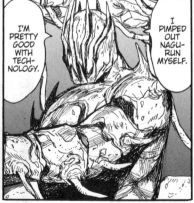

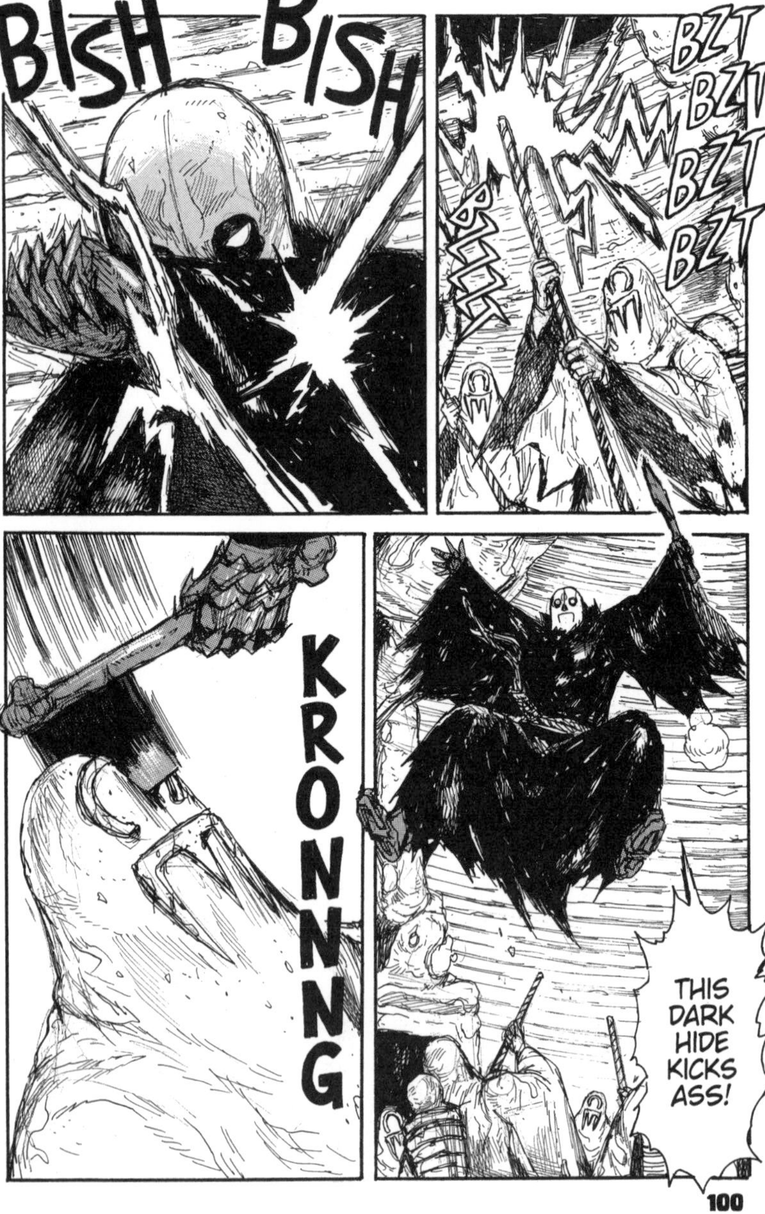
BZT
BZT
BZT
BZT
BISH
BISH
THIS DARK HIDE KICKS ASS!
KRONNNG

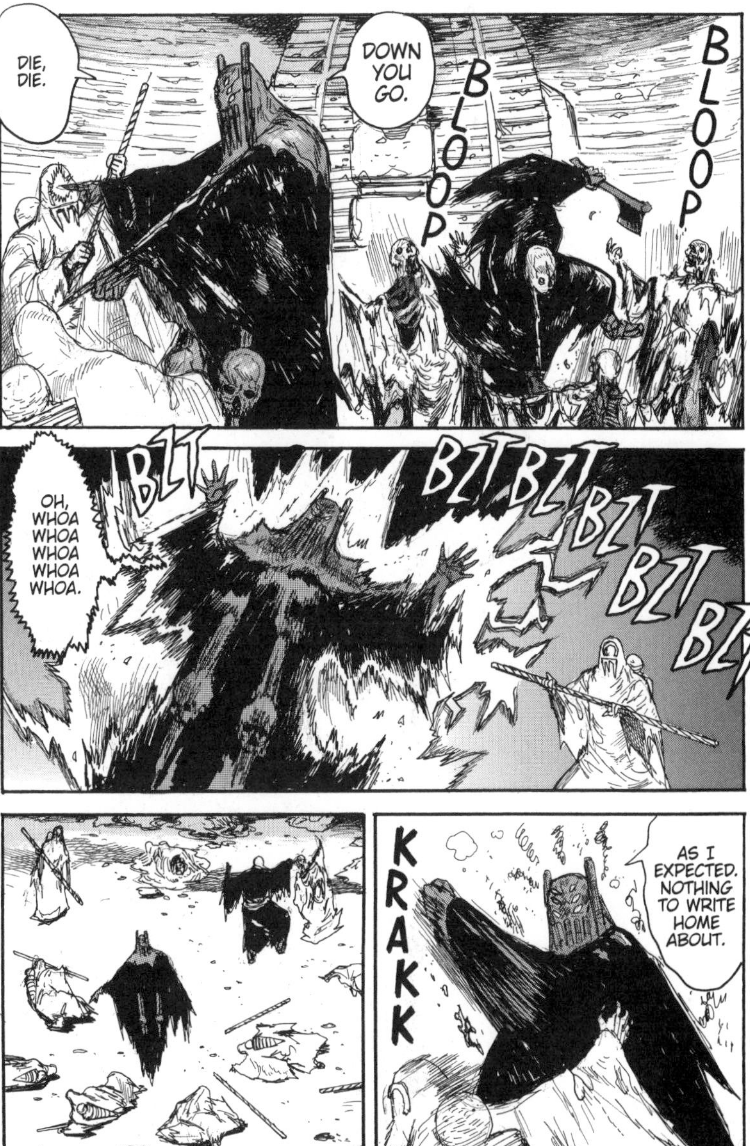
BLOOP
BLOOP
DOWN YOU GO.
DIE, DIE.
BZT BZT BZT BZT BZT
BZT
OH, WHOA WHOA WHOA WHOA WHOA.
AS I EXPECTED. NOTHING TO WRITE HOME ABOUT.
KRAKK

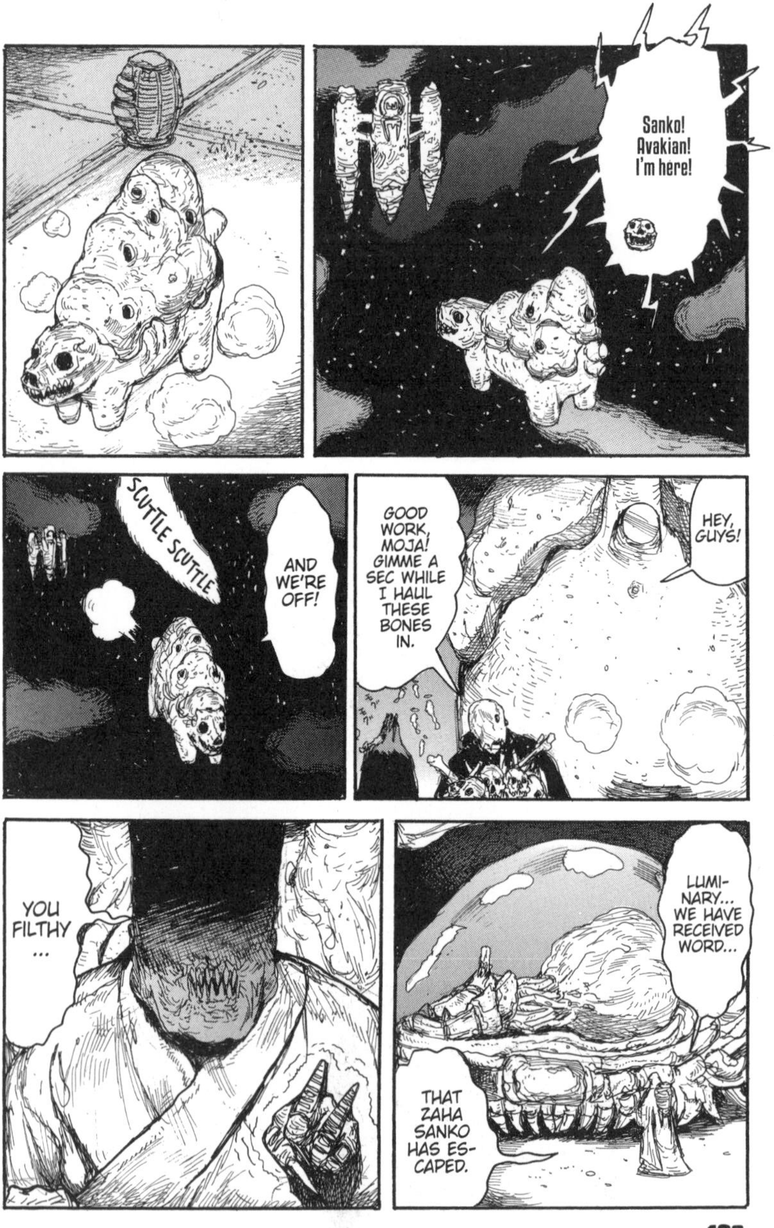
Sanko! Avakian! I'm here!
HEY, GUYS!
GOOD WORK, MOJA! GIMME A SEC WHILE I HAUL THESE BONES IN.
AND WE'RE OFF!
SCUTTLE SCUTTLE
LUMINARY... WE HAVE RECEIVED WORD...
THAT ZAHA SANKO HAS ES-CAPED.
YOU FILTHY ...

★ *Dai Dark* vol. 1 store special sheet, black-and-white version

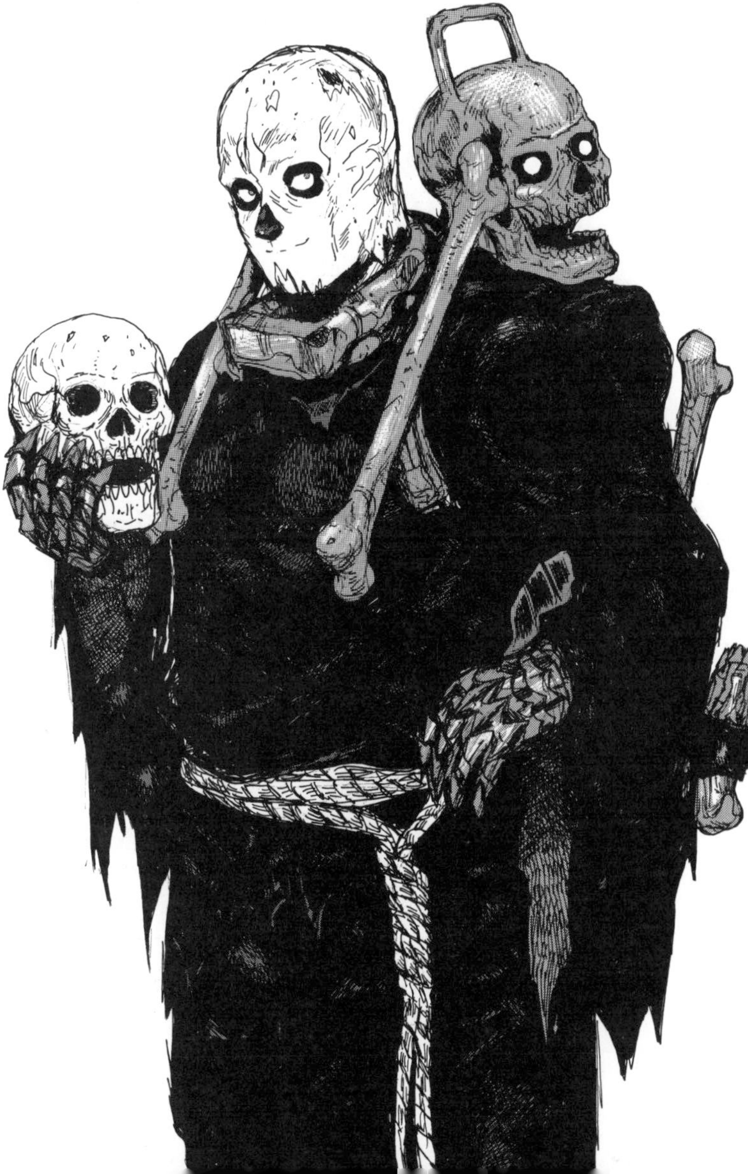

★ Design of Nagurun (front)

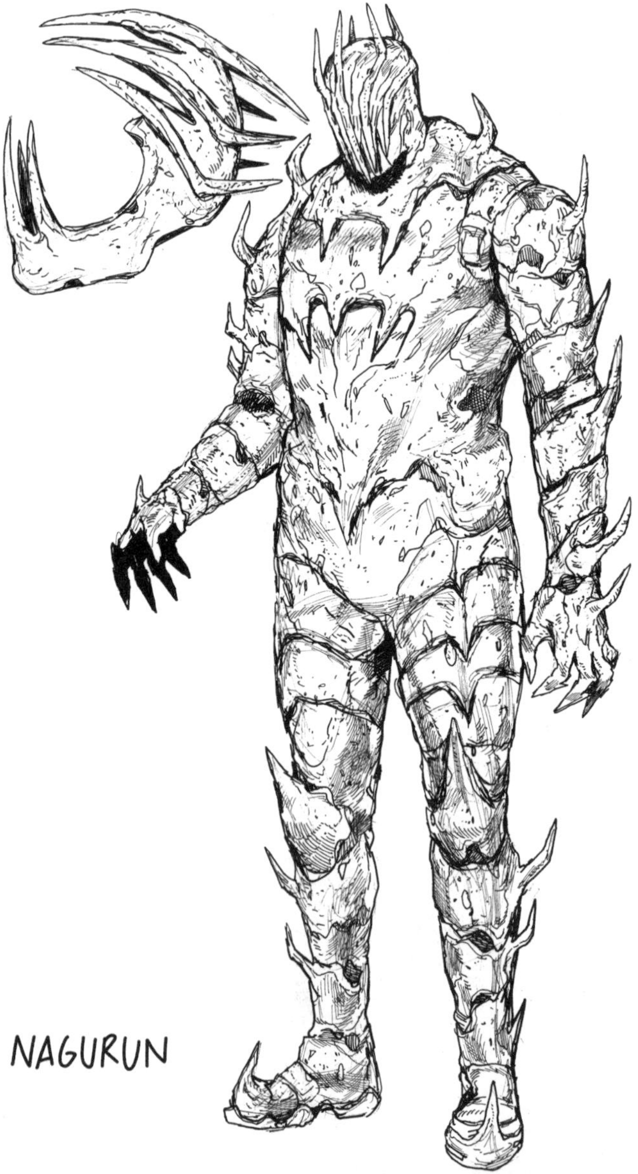
NAGURUN

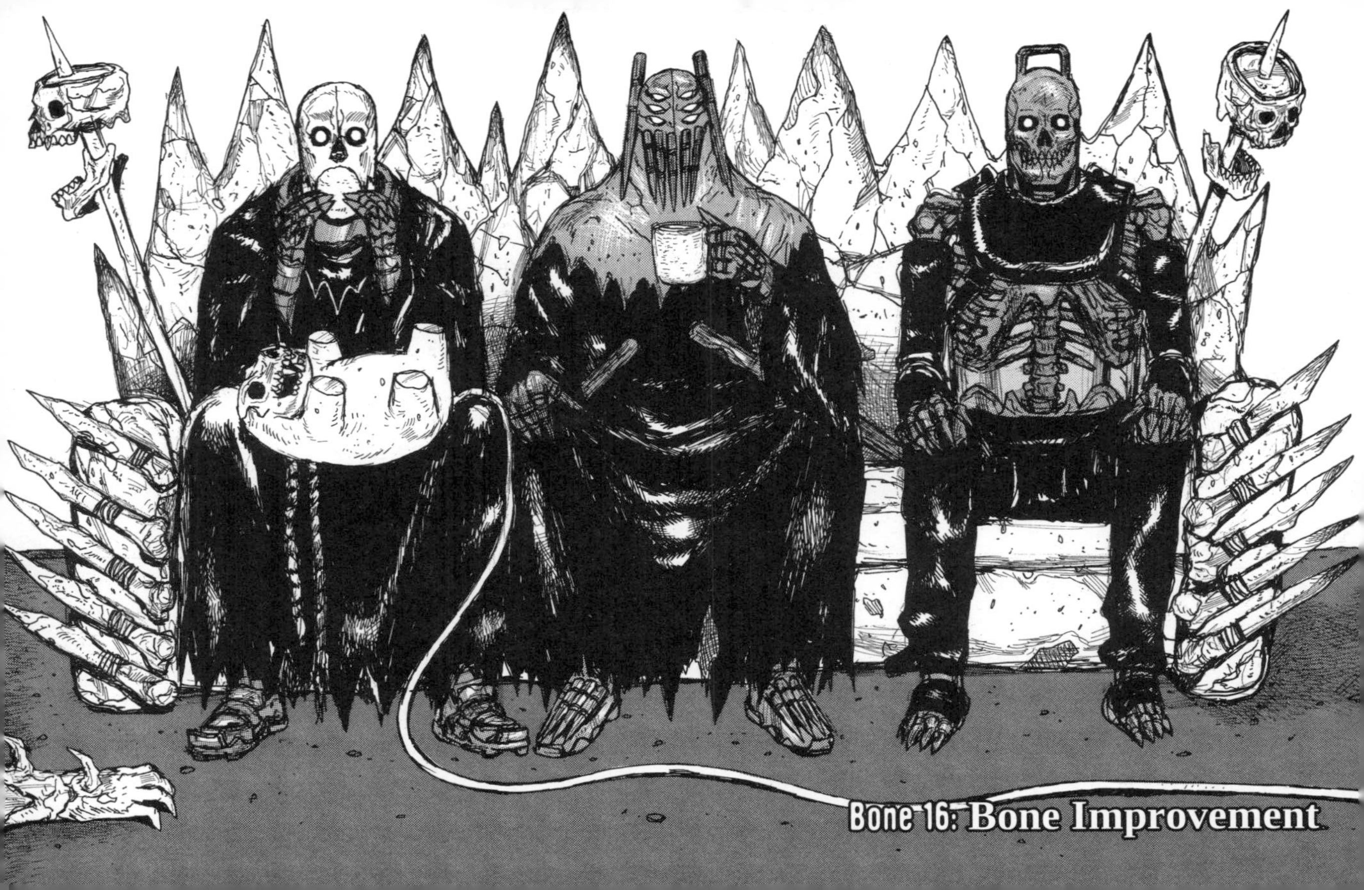
Bone 16: Bone Improvement

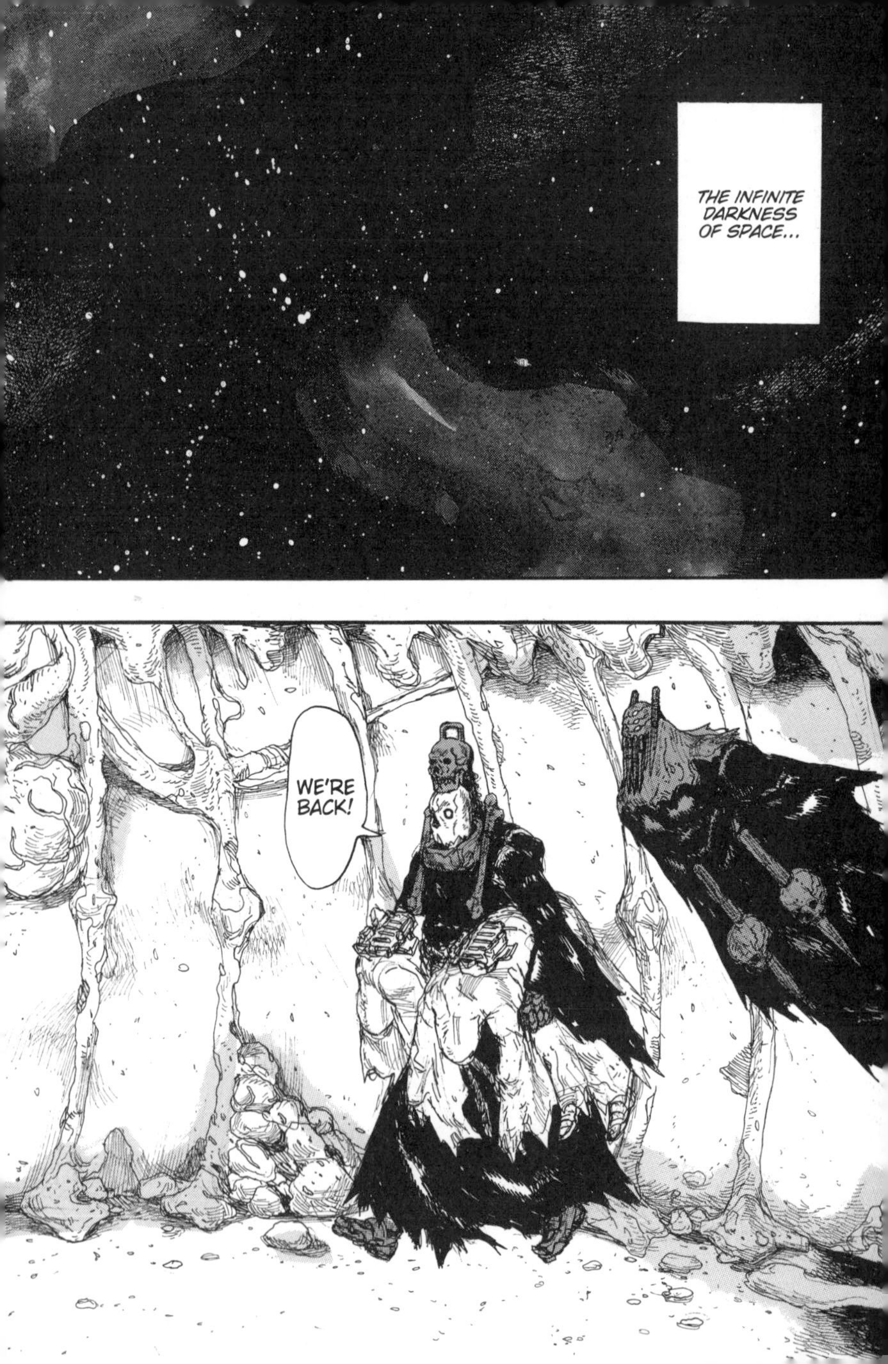
THE INFINITE DARKNESS OF SPACE...
WE'RE BACK!

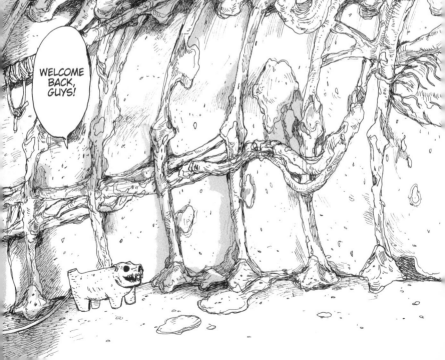

WELCOME BACK, GUYS!

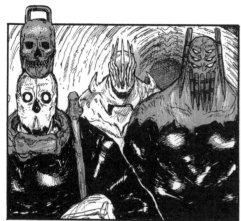

HUH?

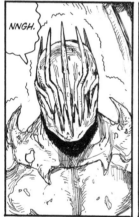

NNGH.

UH, THIS IS HAJIME DAME...

WHO'S THAT?!

UWAAAAH!

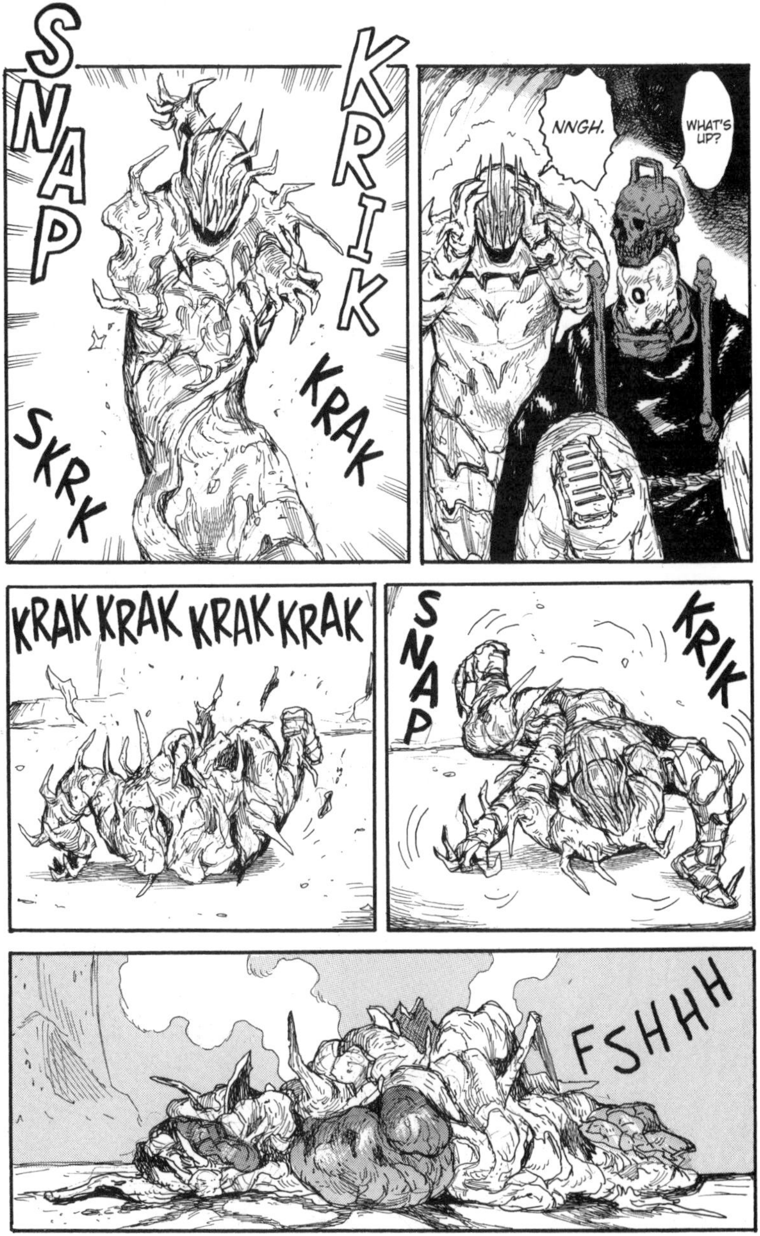
NNGH.
WHAT'S UP?
SNAP
KRIK
KRAK
SKRK
KRIK
SNAP
KRAK KRAK KRAK KRAK
FSHHH

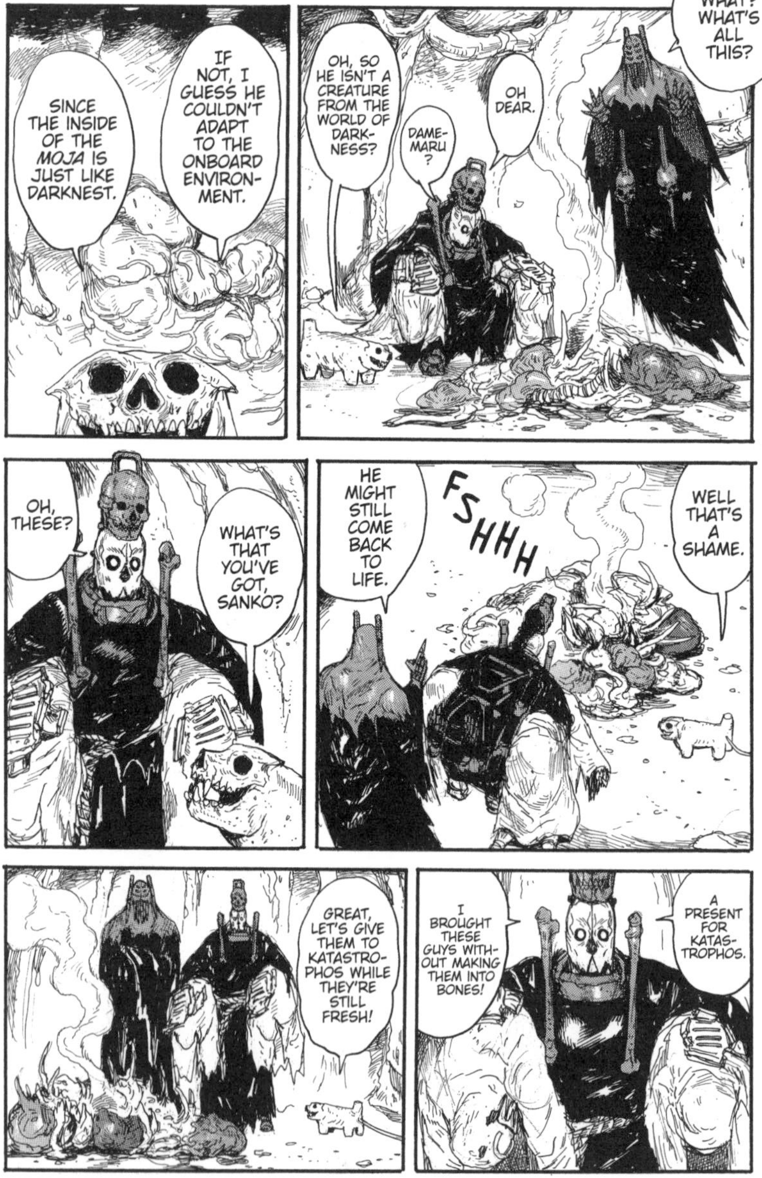
WHAT? WHAT'S ALL THIS?
OH DEAR.
DAME-MARU?
OH, SO HE ISN'T A CREATURE FROM THE WORLD OF DARKNESS?
IF NOT, I GUESS HE COULDN'T ADAPT TO THE ONBOARD ENVIRONMENT.
SINCE THE INSIDE OF THE *MOJA* IS JUST LIKE DARKNEST.
WELL THAT'S A SHAME.
FSHHHH
HE MIGHT STILL COME BACK TO LIFE.
WHAT'S THAT YOU'VE GOT, SANKO?
OH, THESE?
A PRESENT FOR KATASTROPHOS.
I BROUGHT THESE GUYS WITHOUT MAKING THEM INTO BONES!
GREAT, LET'S GIVE THEM TO KATASTROPHOS WHILE THEY'RE STILL FRESH!

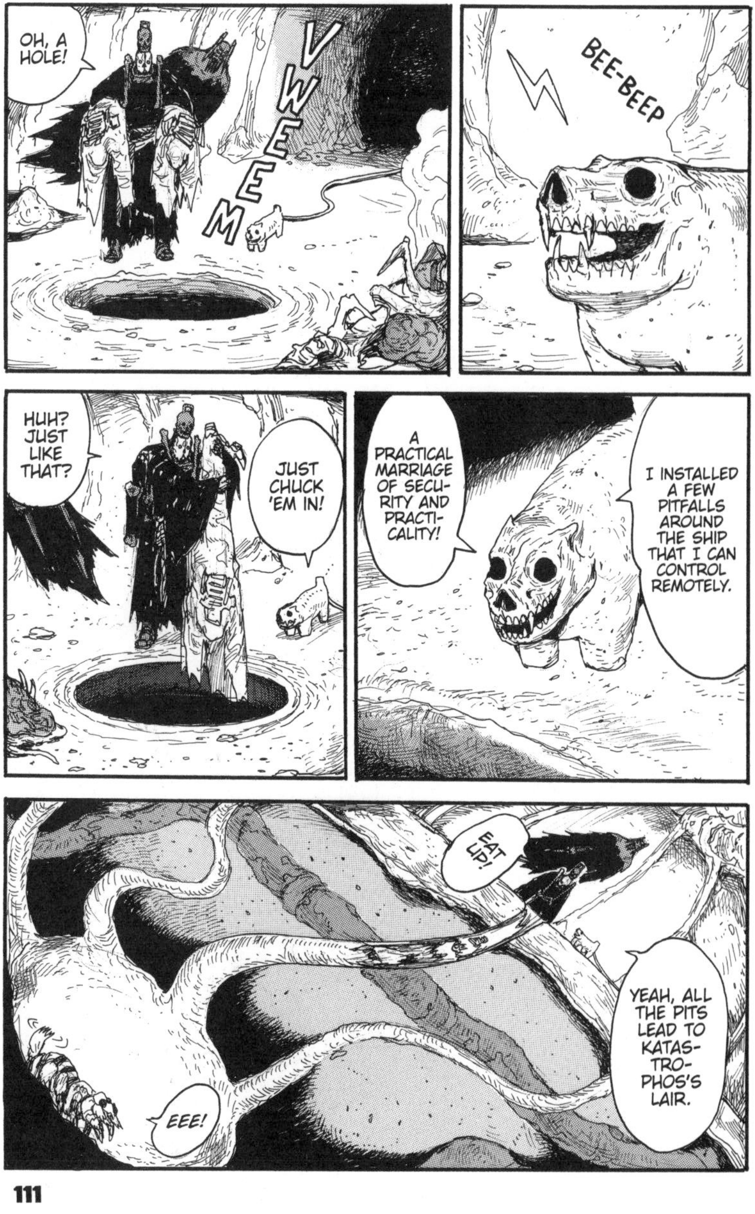
BEE-BEEP
OH, A HOLE!
VWEEM
I INSTALLED A FEW PITFALLS AROUND THE SHIP THAT I CAN CONTROL REMOTELY.
A PRACTICAL MARRIAGE OF SECURITY AND PRACTICALITY!
JUST CHUCK 'EM IN!
HUH? JUST LIKE THAT?
EAT UP!
YEAH, ALL THE PITS LEAD TO KATASTROPHOS'S LAIR.
EEE!

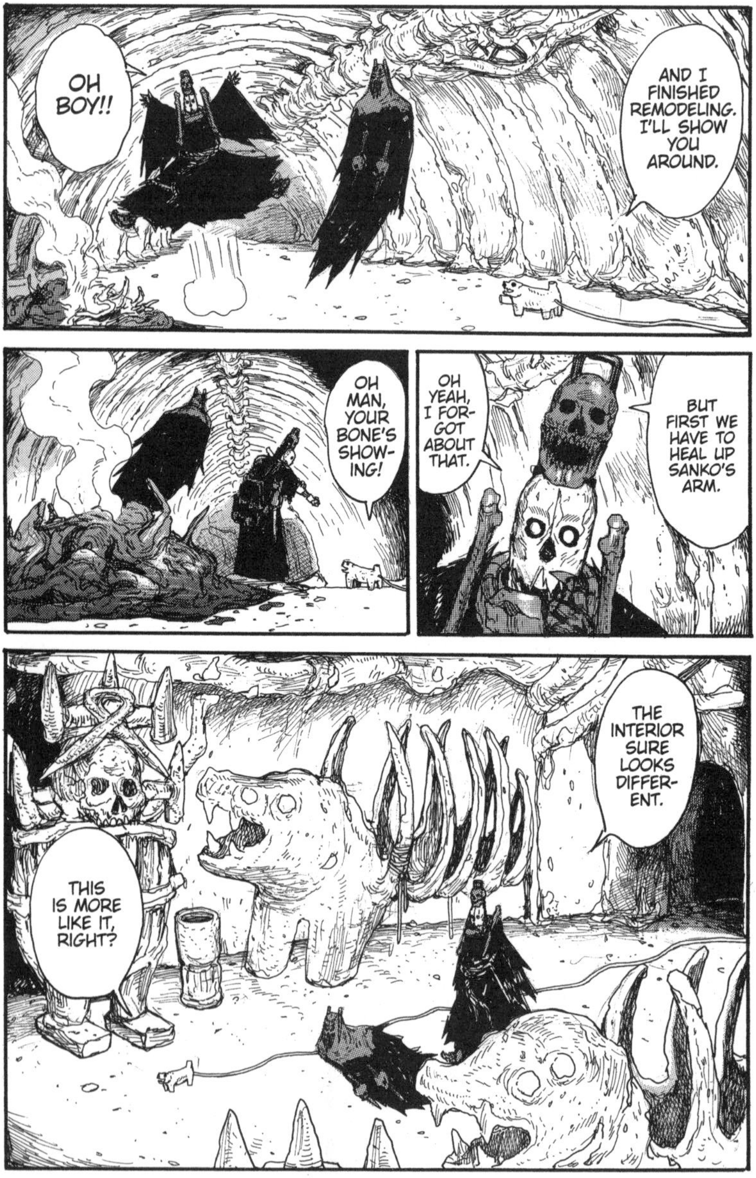
AND I FINISHED REMODELING. I'LL SHOW YOU AROUND.
OH BOY!!
BUT FIRST WE HAVE TO HEAL UP SANKO'S ARM.
OH YEAH, I FORGOT ABOUT THAT.
OH MAN, YOUR BONE'S SHOWING!
THE INTERIOR SURE LOOKS DIFFERENT.
THIS IS MORE LIKE IT, RIGHT?

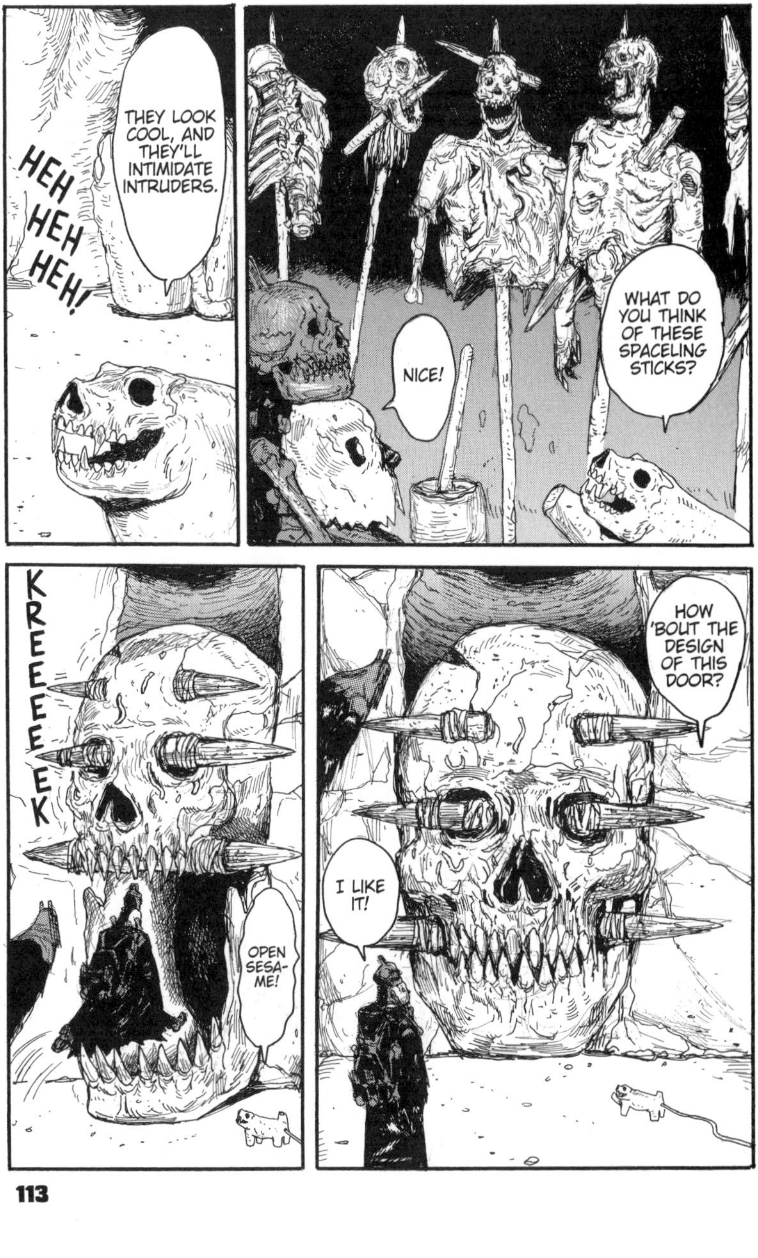
WHAT DO YOU THINK OF THESE SPACELING STICKS?
NICE!
THEY LOOK COOL, AND THEY'LL INTIMIDATE INTRUDERS.
HEH HEH HEH!
HOW 'BOUT THE DESIGN OF THIS DOOR?
I LIKE IT!
KREEEEEK
OPEN SESA-ME!

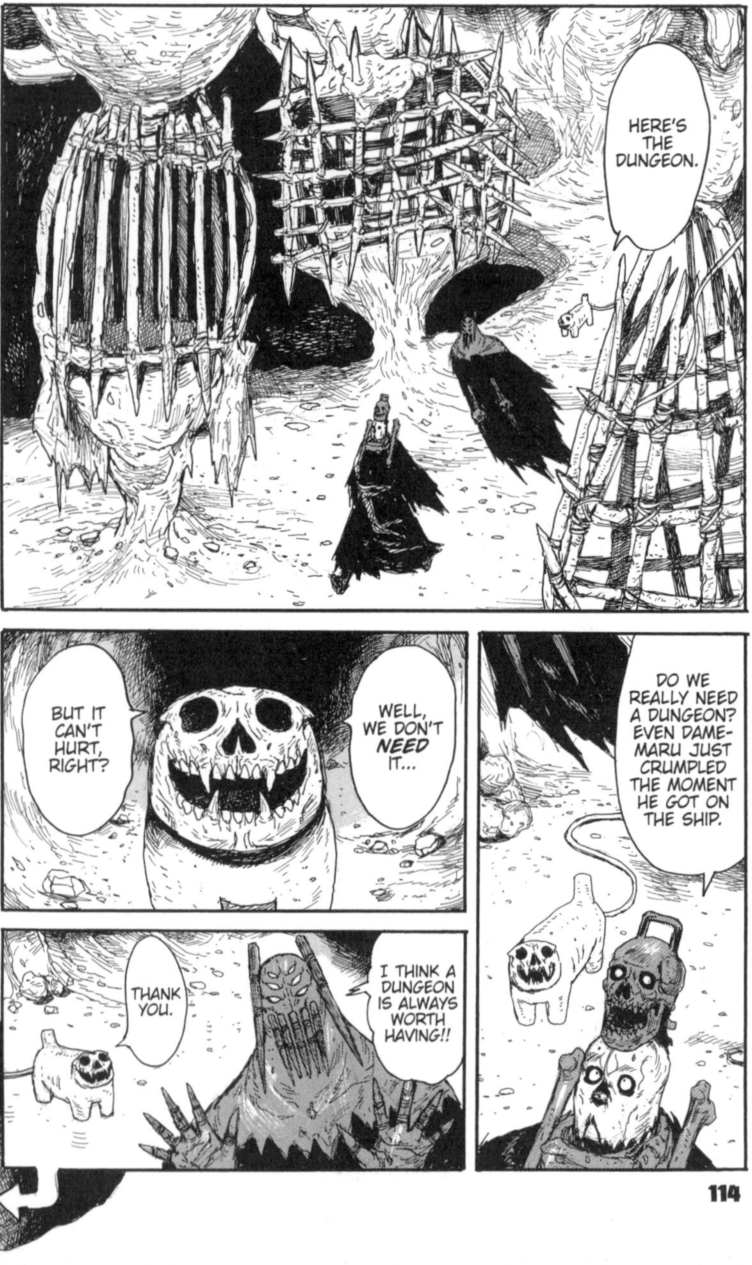
HERE'S THE DUNGEON.
DO WE REALLY NEED A DUNGEON? EVEN DAME-MARU JUST CRUMPLED THE MOMENT HE GOT ON THE SHIP.
WELL, WE DON'T **NEED** IT...
BUT IT CAN'T HURT, RIGHT?
I THINK A DUNGEON IS ALWAYS WORTH HAVING!!
THANK YOU.

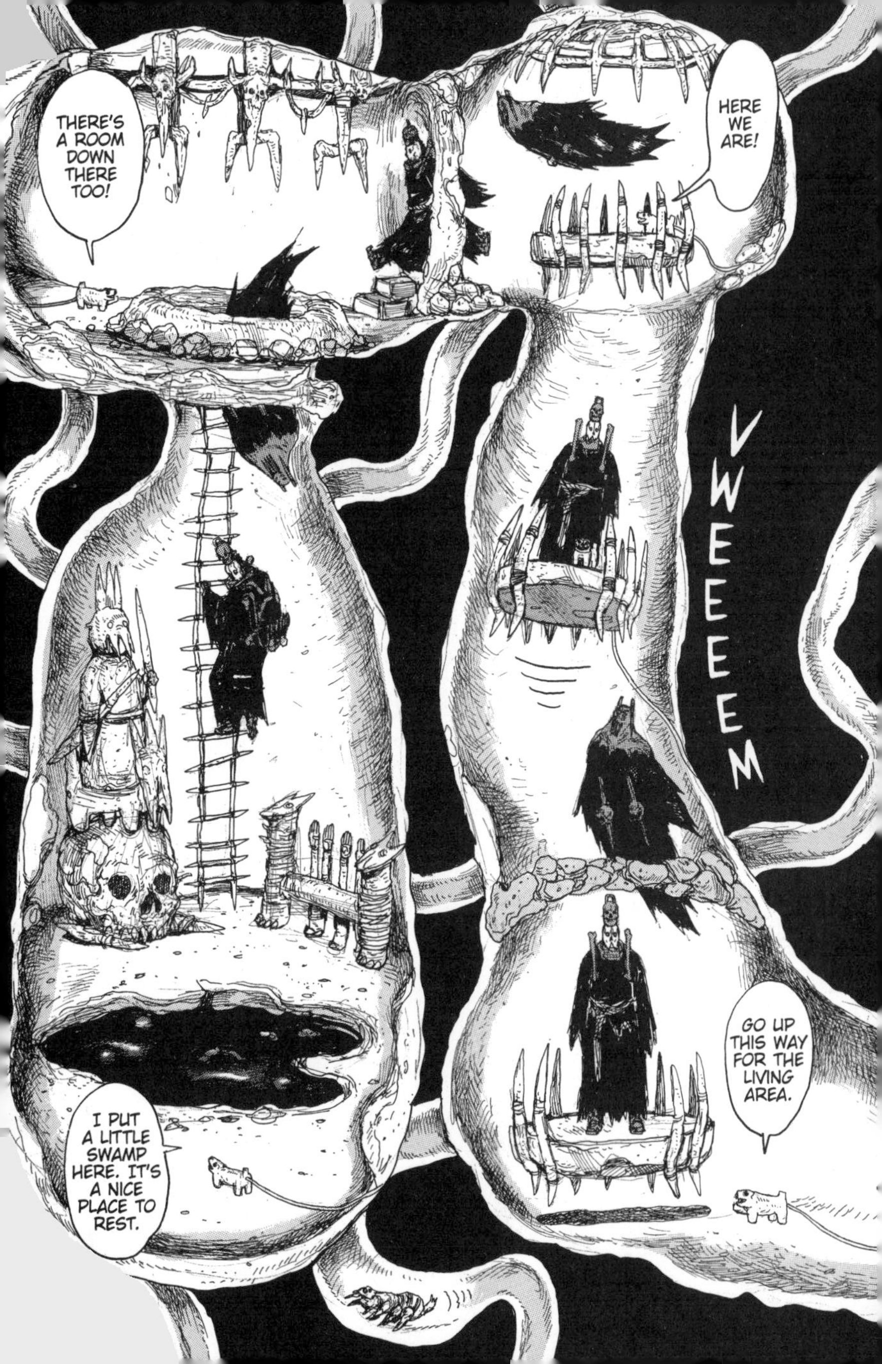
HERE WE ARE!
THERE'S A ROOM DOWN THERE TOO!
VWEEEEM
GO UP THIS WAY FOR THE LIVING AREA.
I PUT A LITTLE SWAMP HERE. IT'S A NICE PLACE TO REST.

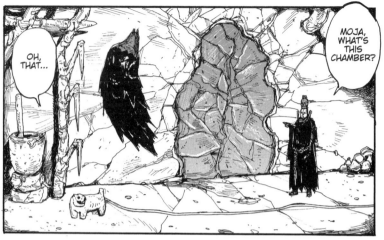

MOJA, WHAT'S THIS CHAMBER?
OH, THAT...
IT'S JUST HOW IT IS WHEN YOU USE A DARK CORE.
THERE ALWAYS END UP BEING A FEW "MYSTERY ROOMS."
MYSTERY ROOMS?!
YEAH. THERE'S NOTHING TO DO ABOUT IT, SO LEAVE IT ALONE.

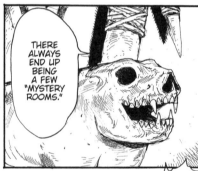

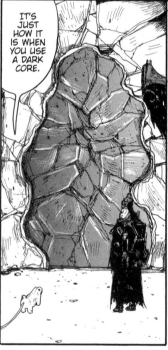

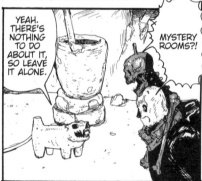

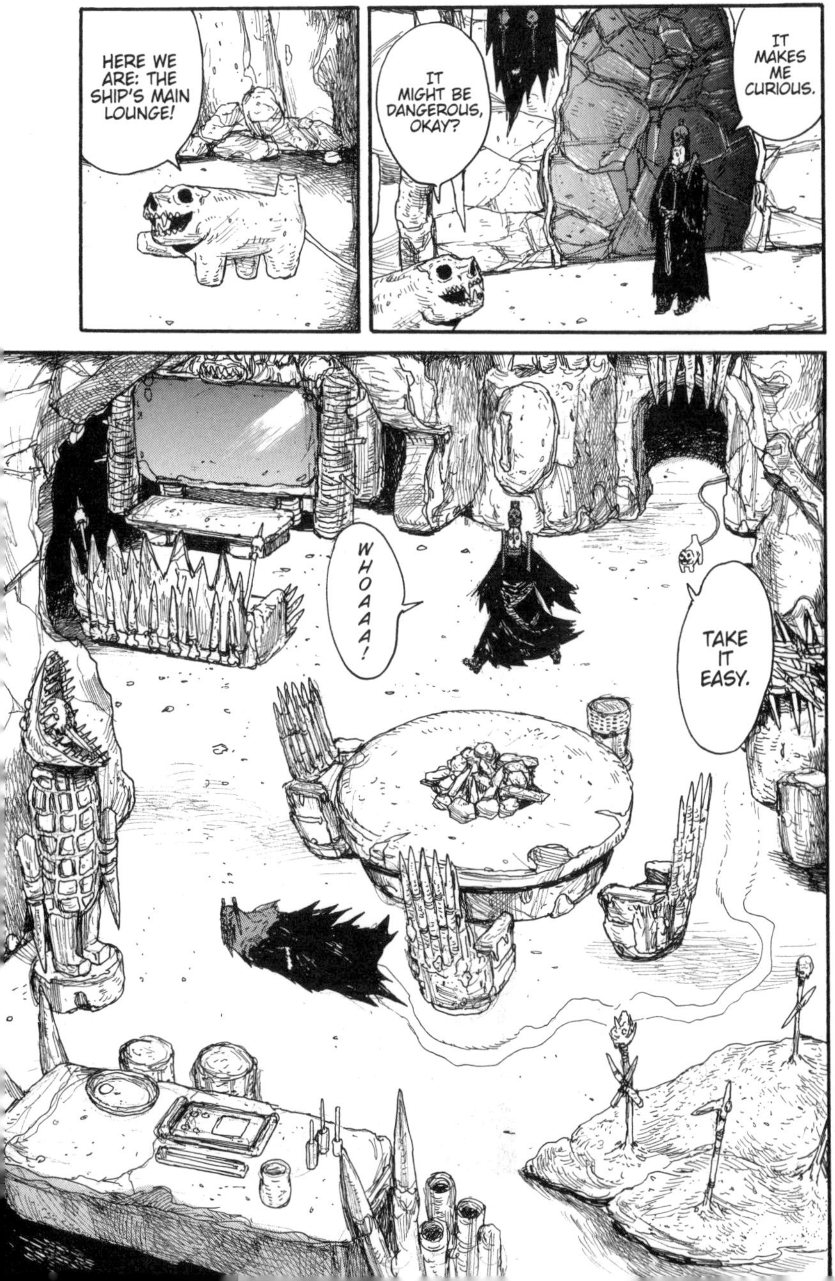
IT MAKES ME CURIOUS.
IT MIGHT BE DANGEROUS, OKAY?
HERE WE ARE: THE SHIP'S MAIN LOUNGE!
TAKE IT EASY.
WHOAAAA!

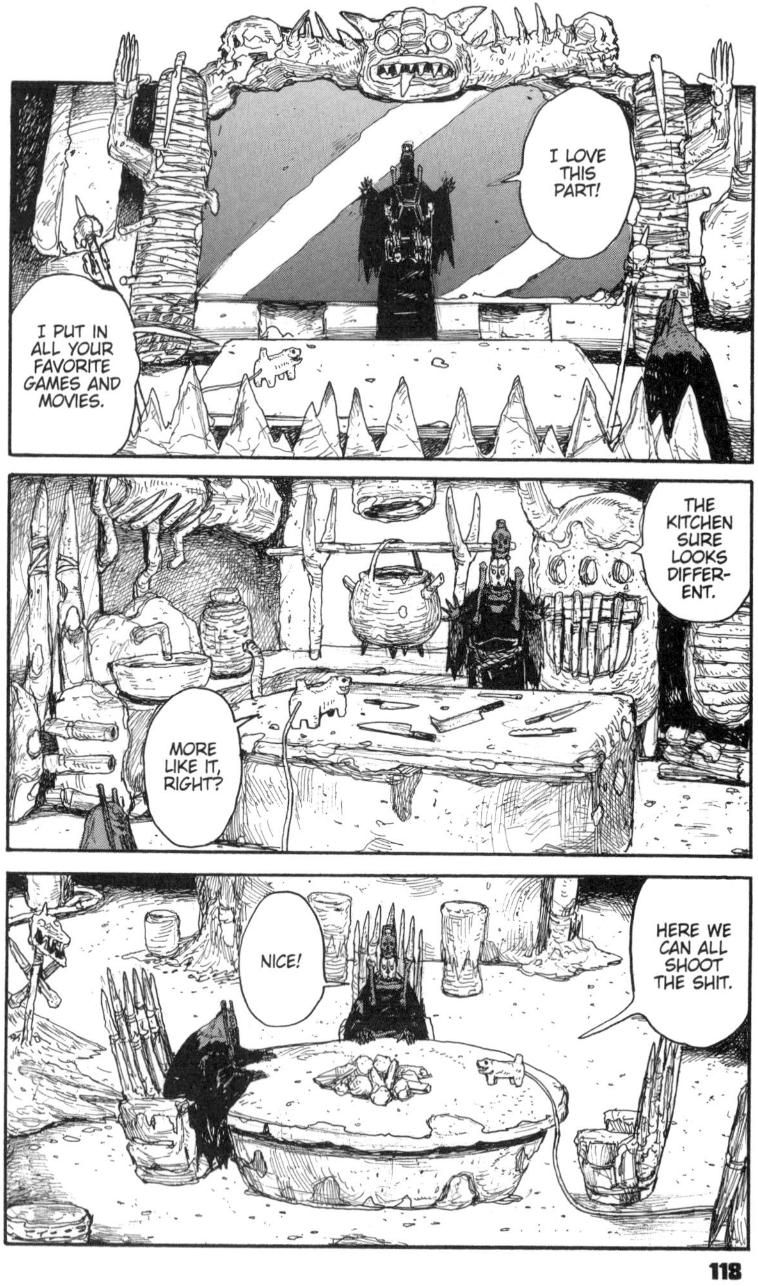
I LOVE THIS PART!
I PUT IN ALL YOUR FAVORITE GAMES AND MOVIES.
THE KITCHEN SURE LOOKS DIFFER-ENT.
MORE LIKE IT, RIGHT?
HERE WE CAN ALL SHOOT THE SHIT.
NICE!

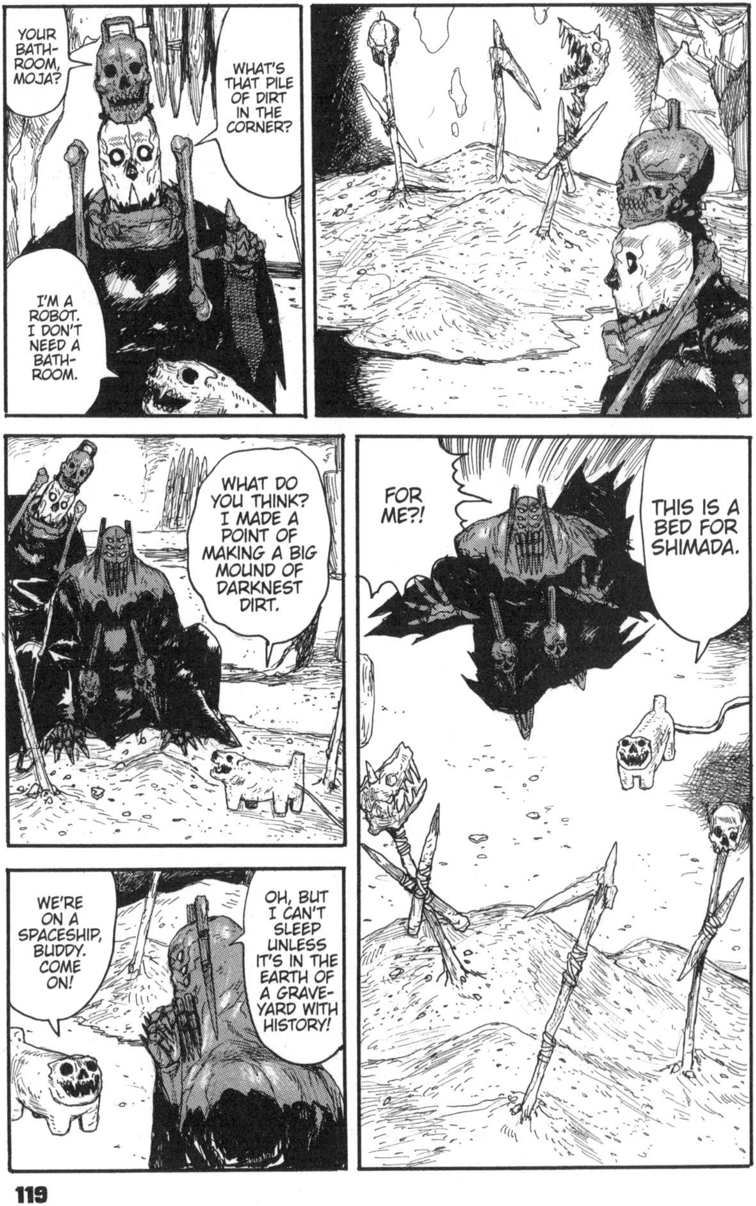
WHAT'S THAT PILE OF DIRT IN THE CORNER?
YOUR BATHROOM, MOJA?
I'M A ROBOT. I DON'T NEED A BATHROOM.
THIS IS A BED FOR SHIMADA.
FOR ME?!
WHAT DO YOU THINK? I MADE A POINT OF MAKING A BIG MOUND OF DARKNEST DIRT.
OH, BUT I CAN'T SLEEP UNLESS IT'S IN THE EARTH OF A GRAVEYARD WITH HISTORY!
WE'RE ON A SPACESHIP, BUDDY. COME ON!

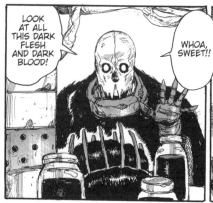

WHOA, SWEET!!
LOOK AT ALL THIS DARK FLESH AND DARK BLOOD!
THIS SHOULD BE ENOUGH TO HEAL YOUR ARM.
AND A WHOLE CASE OF SAKA-MANJU!
HOW'D YOU GET ALL THIS?
HAJIME DAMEMARU.

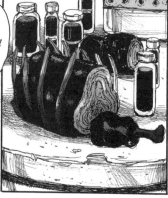

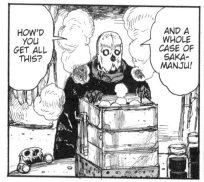

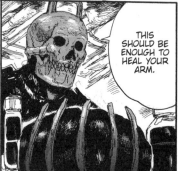

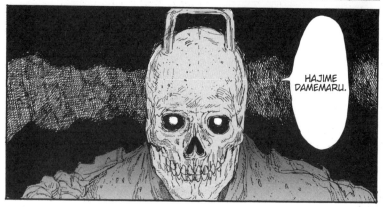

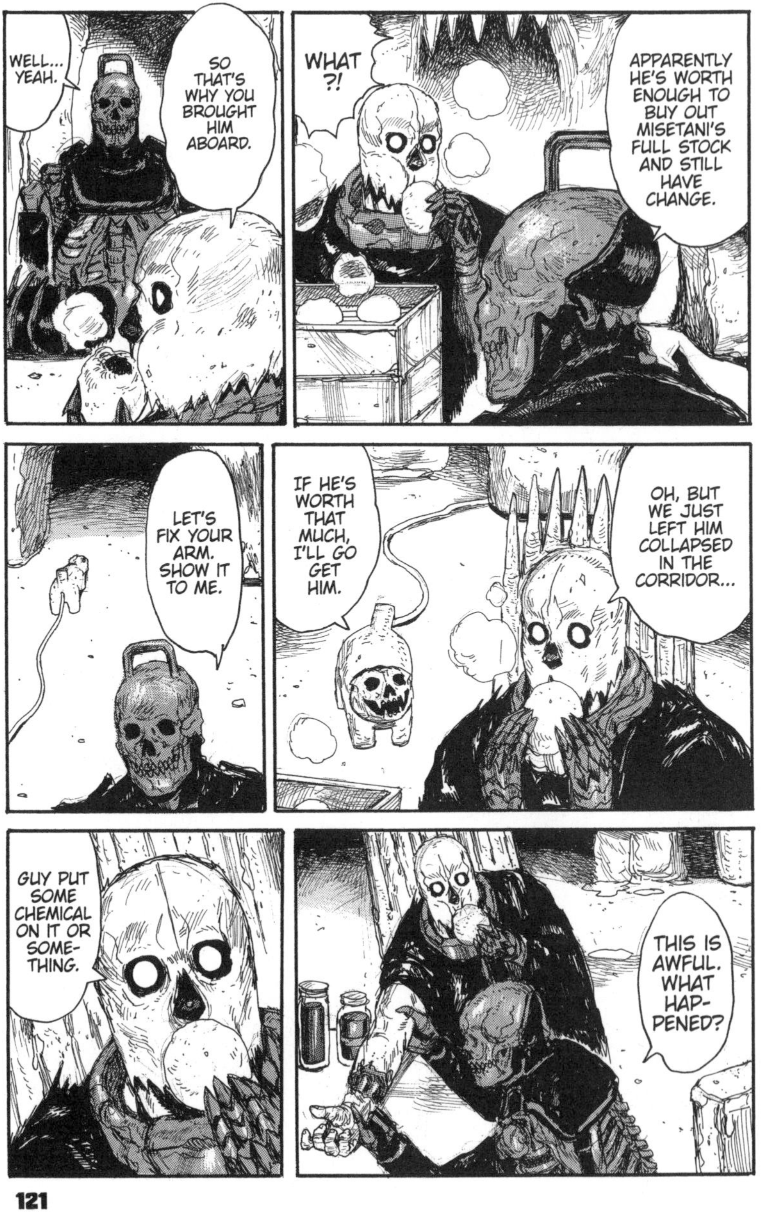
APPARENTLY HE'S WORTH ENOUGH TO BUY OUT MISETANI'S FULL STOCK AND STILL HAVE CHANGE.
WHAT ?!
SO THAT'S WHY YOU BROUGHT HIM ABOARD.
WELL... YEAH.
OH, BUT WE JUST LEFT HIM COLLAPSED IN THE CORRIDOR...
IF HE'S WORTH THAT MUCH, I'LL GO GET HIM.
LET'S FIX YOUR ARM. SHOW IT TO ME.
THIS IS AWFUL. WHAT HAP-PENED?
GUY PUT SOME CHEMICAL ON IT OR SOME-THING.

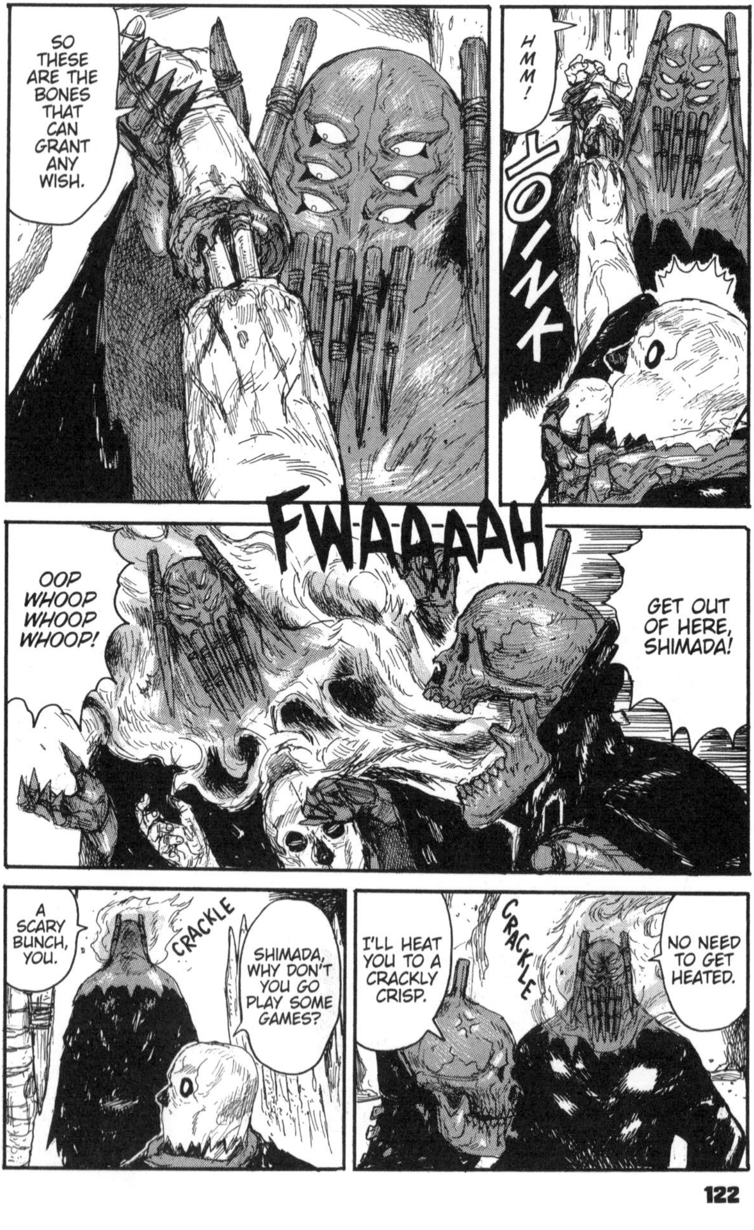
HMM!
YOINK
SO THESE ARE THE BONES THAT CAN GRANT ANY WISH.
FWAAAAH
GET OUT OF HERE, SHIMADA!
OOP WHOOP WHOOP WHOOP!
NO NEED TO GET HEATED.
CRACKLE
I'LL HEAT YOU TO A CRACKLY CRISP.
SHIMADA, WHY DON'T YOU GO PLAY SOME GAMES?
CRACKLE
A SCARY BUNCH, YOU.

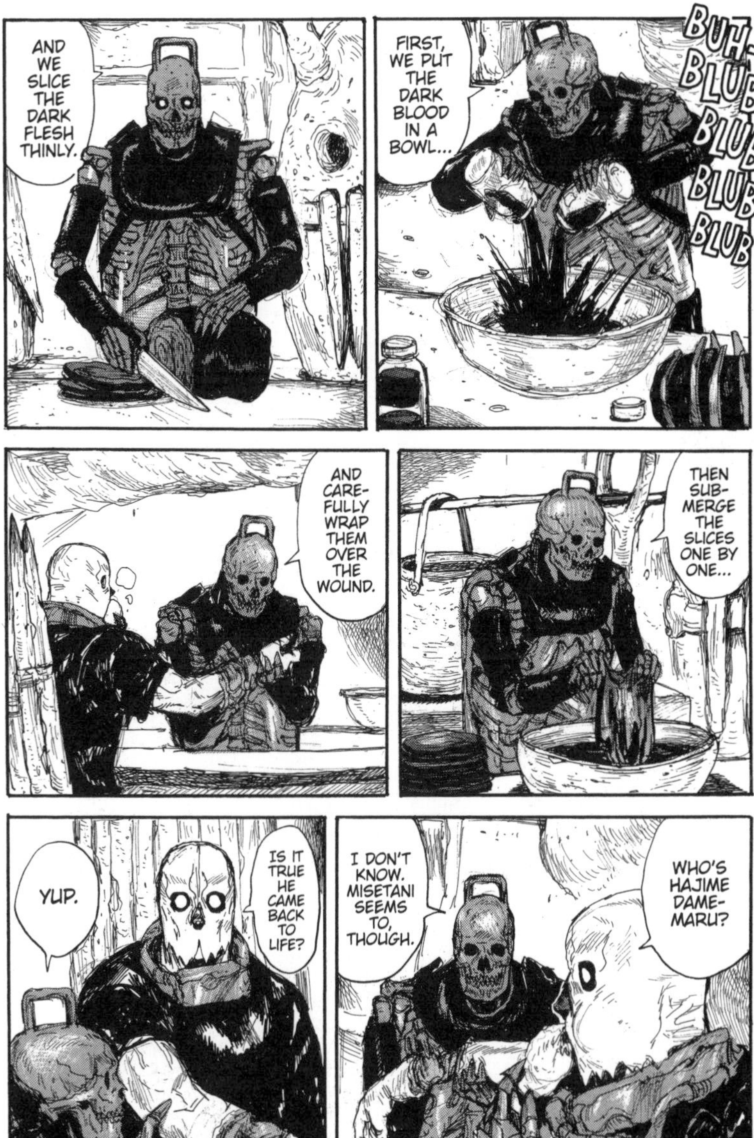
FIRST, WE PUT THE DARK BLOOD IN A BOWL...
BUH-BLUB BLUB BLUB BLUB
AND WE SLICE THE DARK FLESH THINLY.
THEN SUBMERGE THE SLICES ONE BY ONE...
AND CAREFULLY WRAP THEM OVER THE WOUND.
WHO'S HAJIME DAMEMARU?
I DON'T KNOW. MISETANI SEEMS TO, THOUGH.
IS IT TRUE HE CAME BACK TO LIFE?
YUP.

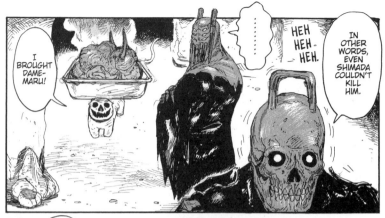

IN OTHER WORDS, EVEN SHIMADA COULDN'T KILL HIM.
HEH HEH HEH.
......
I BROUGHT DAME-MARU!
GOOD, THE DARK FLESH IS ADHERING.
SHAKE SHAKE SHAKE
LAST THING, WE TAKE A DARK BLOOD SPRAY ...
CAREFULLY COAT THE AREA...
PSHHHT

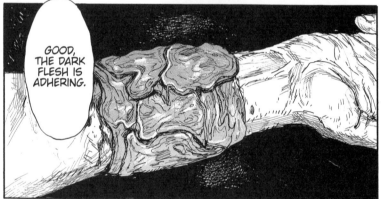

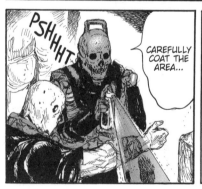

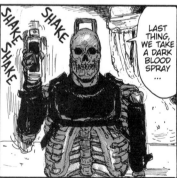

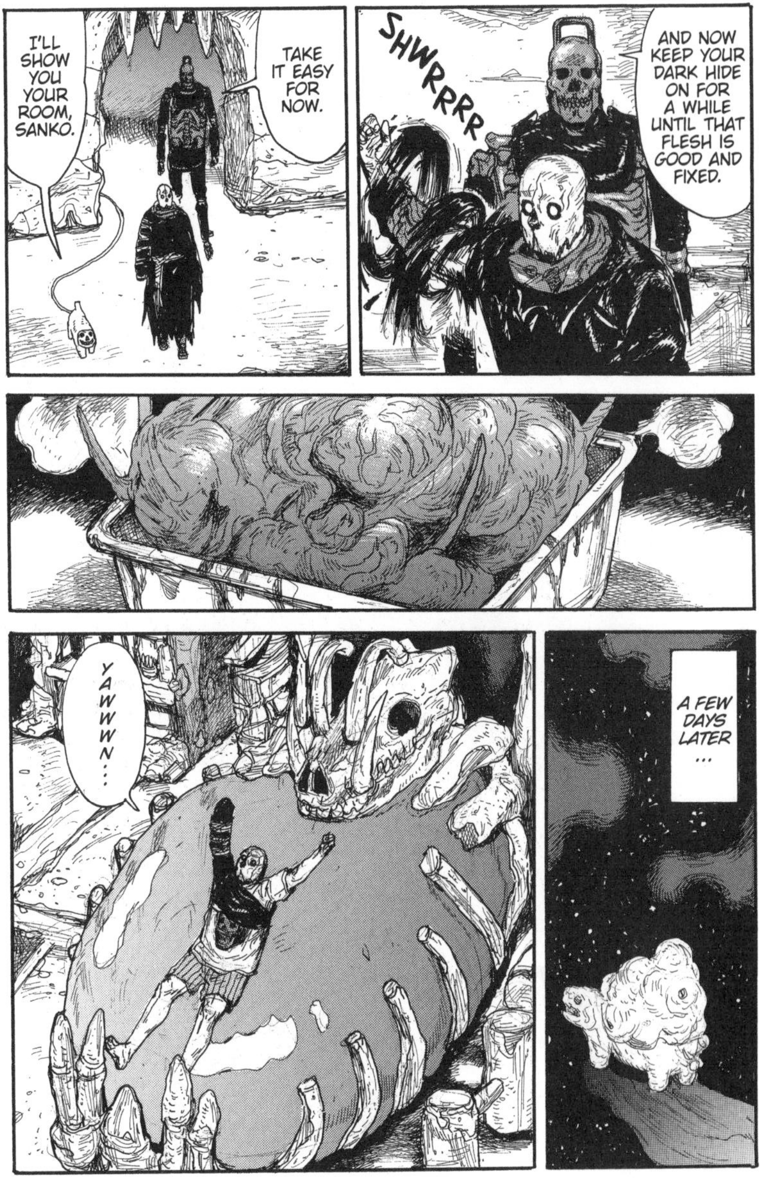
AND NOW KEEP YOUR DARK HIDE ON FOR A WHILE UNTIL THAT FLESH IS GOOD AND FIXED.
SHWRRRR
TAKE IT EASY FOR NOW.
I'LL SHOW YOU YOUR ROOM, SANKO.
A FEW DAYS LATER...
YAWWWN...

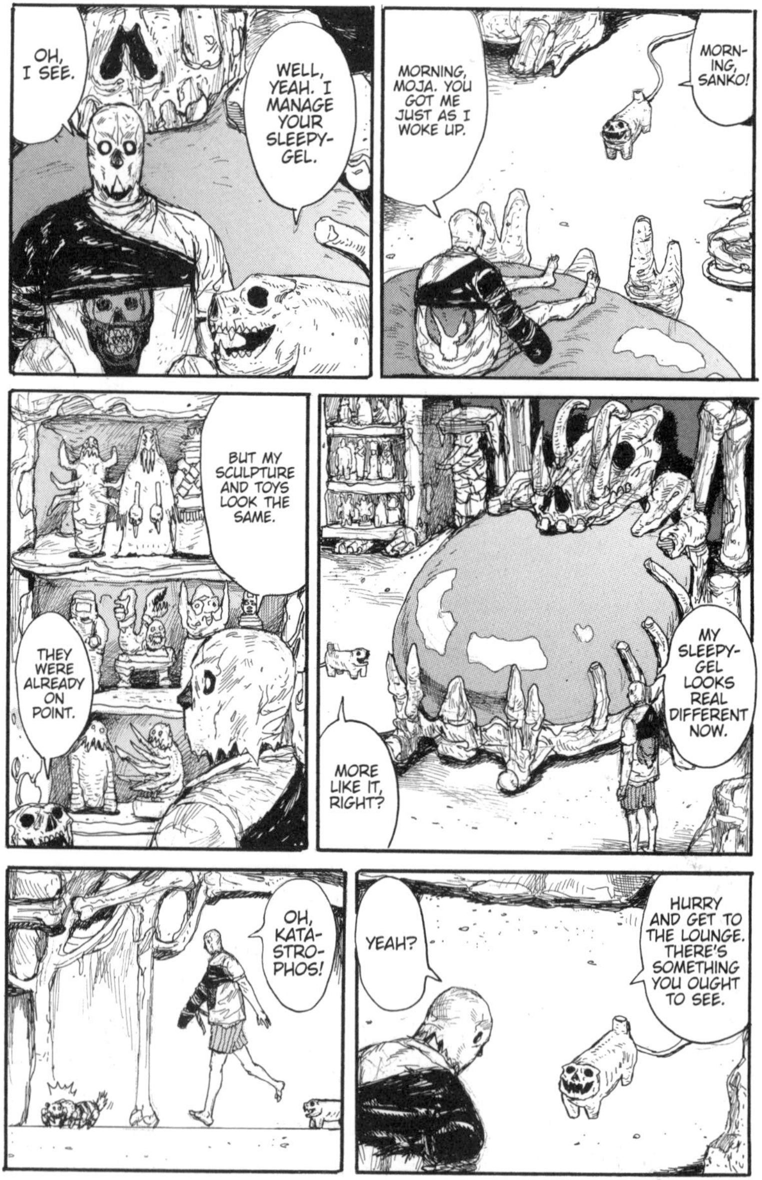
MORN-ING, SANKO!
MORNING, MOJA. YOU GOT ME JUST AS I WOKE UP.
WELL, YEAH. I MANAGE YOUR SLEEPY-GEL.
OH, I SEE.
MY SLEEPY-GEL LOOKS REAL DIFFERENT NOW.
MORE LIKE IT, RIGHT?
BUT MY SCULPTURE AND TOYS LOOK THE SAME.
THEY WERE ALREADY ON POINT.
HURRY AND GET TO THE LOUNGE. THERE'S SOMETHING YOU OUGHT TO SEE.
YEAH?
OH, KATA-STROPHOS!

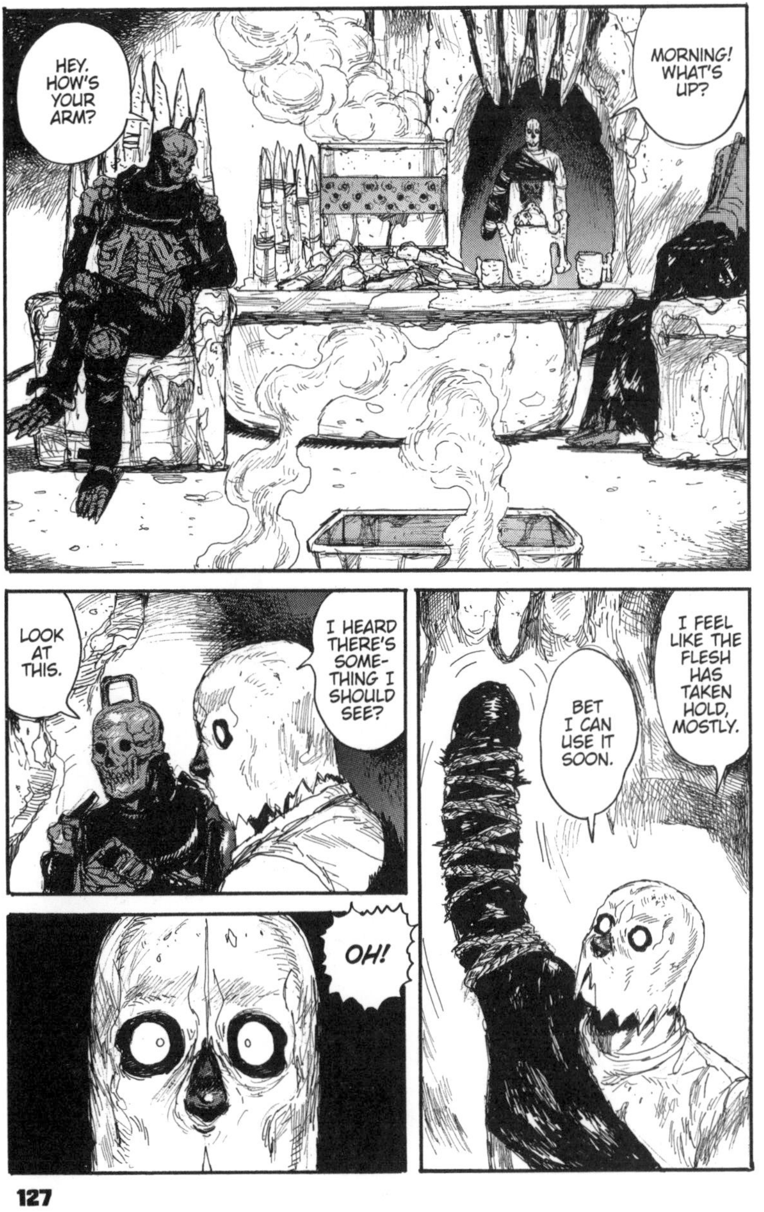
MORNING! WHAT'S UP?
HEY. HOW'S YOUR ARM?
I FEEL LIKE THE FLESH HAS TAKEN HOLD, MOSTLY.
BET I CAN USE IT SOON.
I HEARD THERE'S SOME-THING I SHOULD SEE?
LOOK AT THIS.
OH!

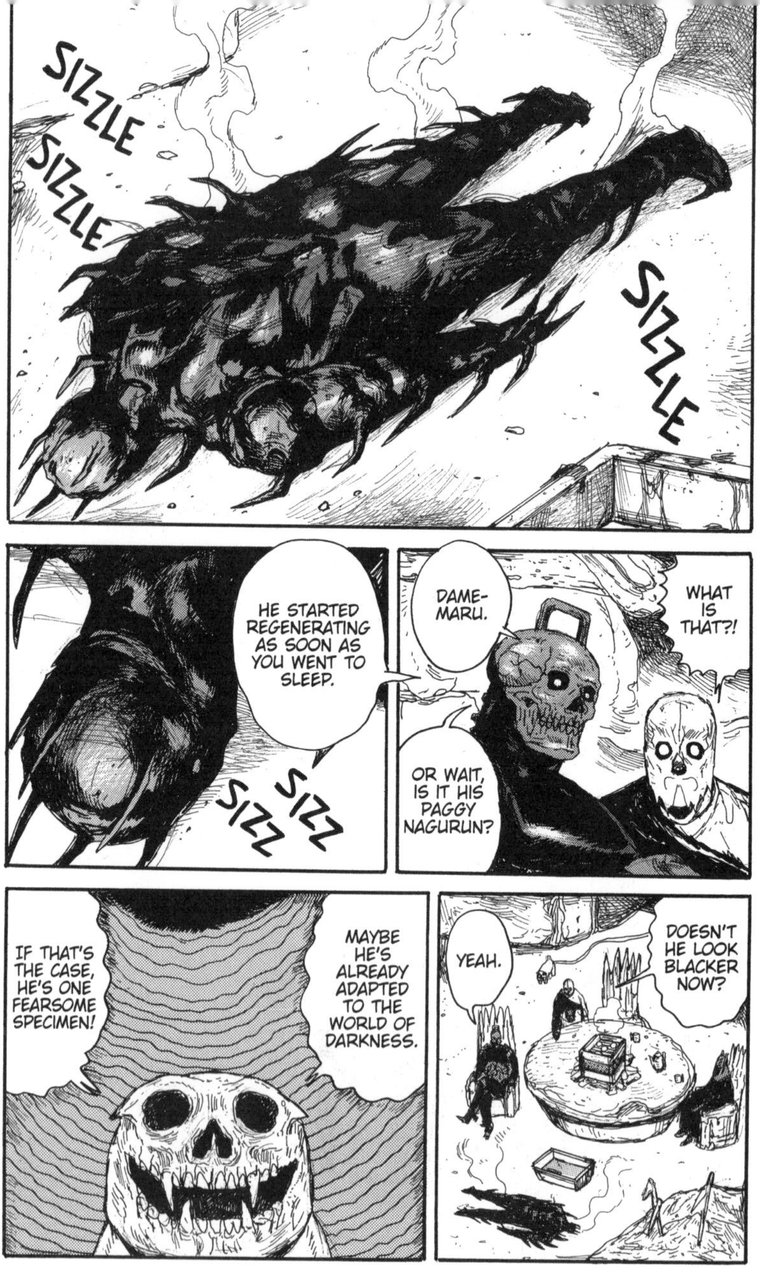
SIZZLE
SIZZLE
SIZZLE
SIZZLE
WHAT IS THAT?!
DAME-MARU.
OR WAIT, IS IT HIS PAGGY NAGURUN?
HE STARTED REGENERATING AS SOON AS YOU WENT TO SLEEP.
SIZZ
SIZZ
DOESN'T HE LOOK BLACKER NOW?
YEAH.
MAYBE HE'S ALREADY ADAPTED TO THE WORLD OF DARKNESS.
IF THAT'S THE CASE, HE'S ONE FEARSOME SPECIMEN!

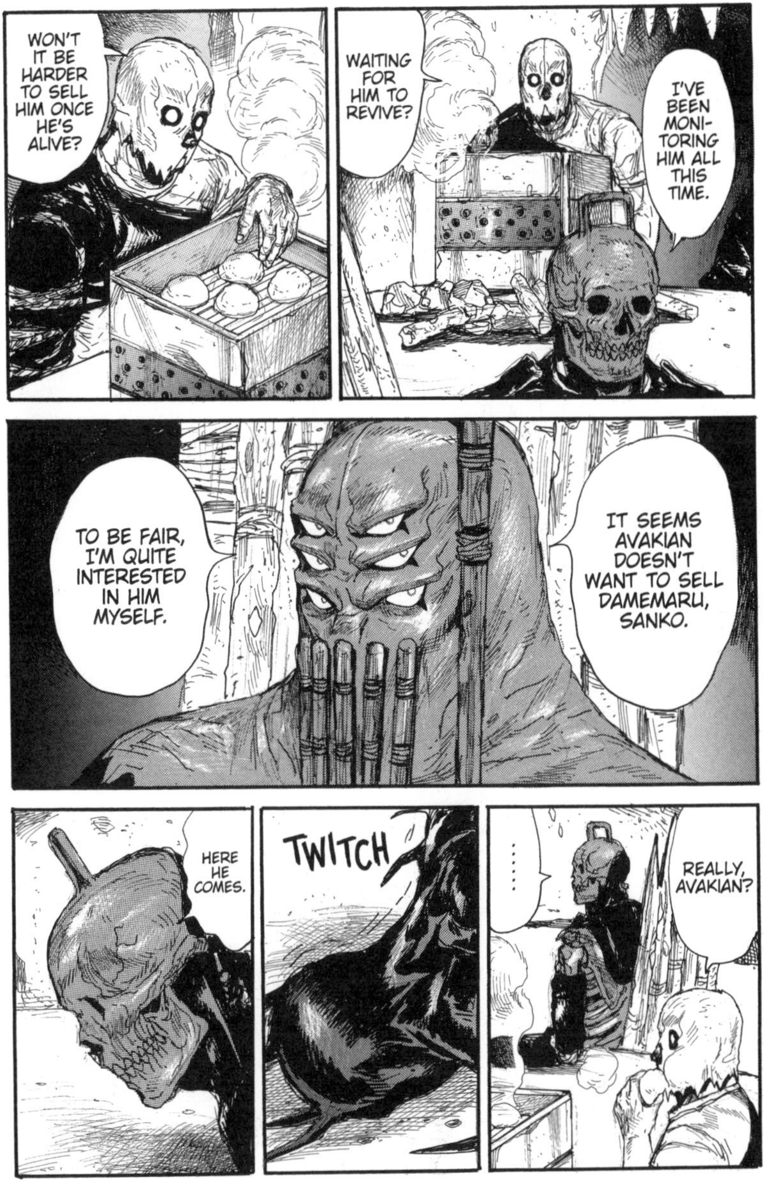

WAITING FOR HIM TO REVIVE?
I'VE BEEN MONITORING HIM ALL THIS TIME.
WON'T IT BE HARDER TO SELL HIM ONCE HE'S ALIVE?
IT SEEMS AVAKIAN DOESN'T WANT TO SELL DAMEMARU, SANKO.
TO BE FAIR, I'M QUITE INTERESTED IN HIM MYSELF.
REALLY, AVAKIAN?
......
TWITCH
HERE HE COMES.

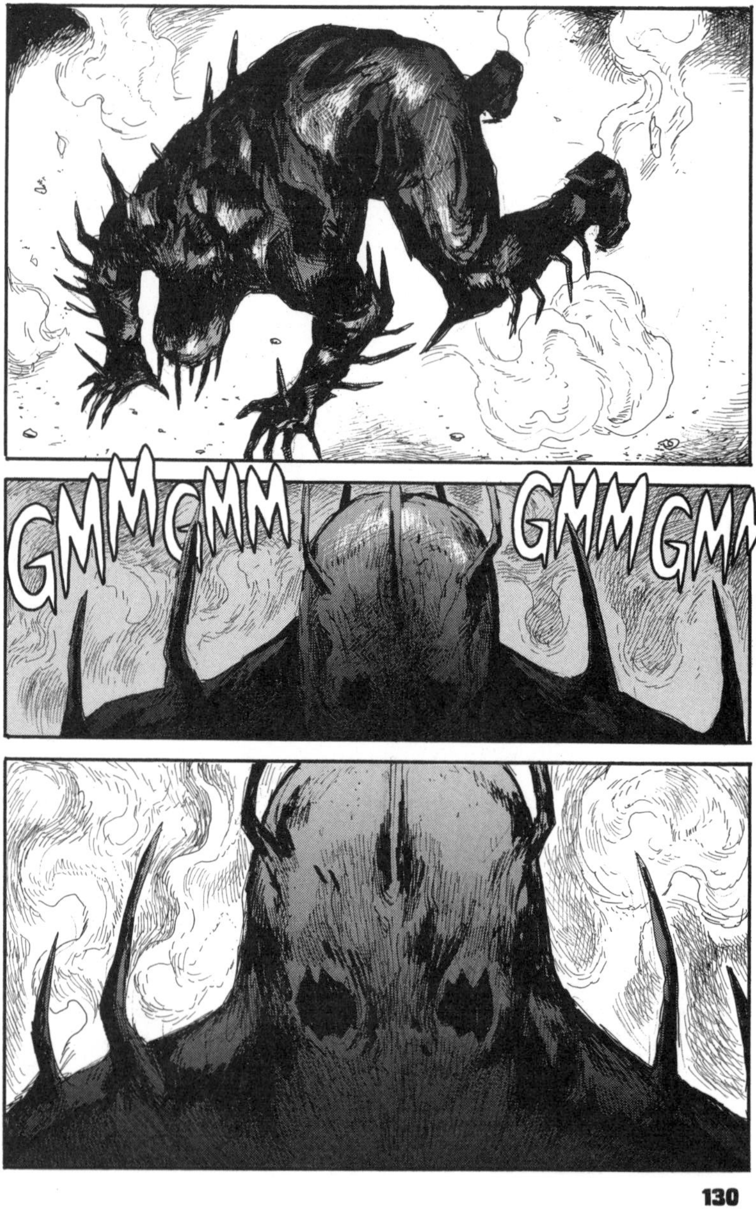
GMMGMM
GMMGMM

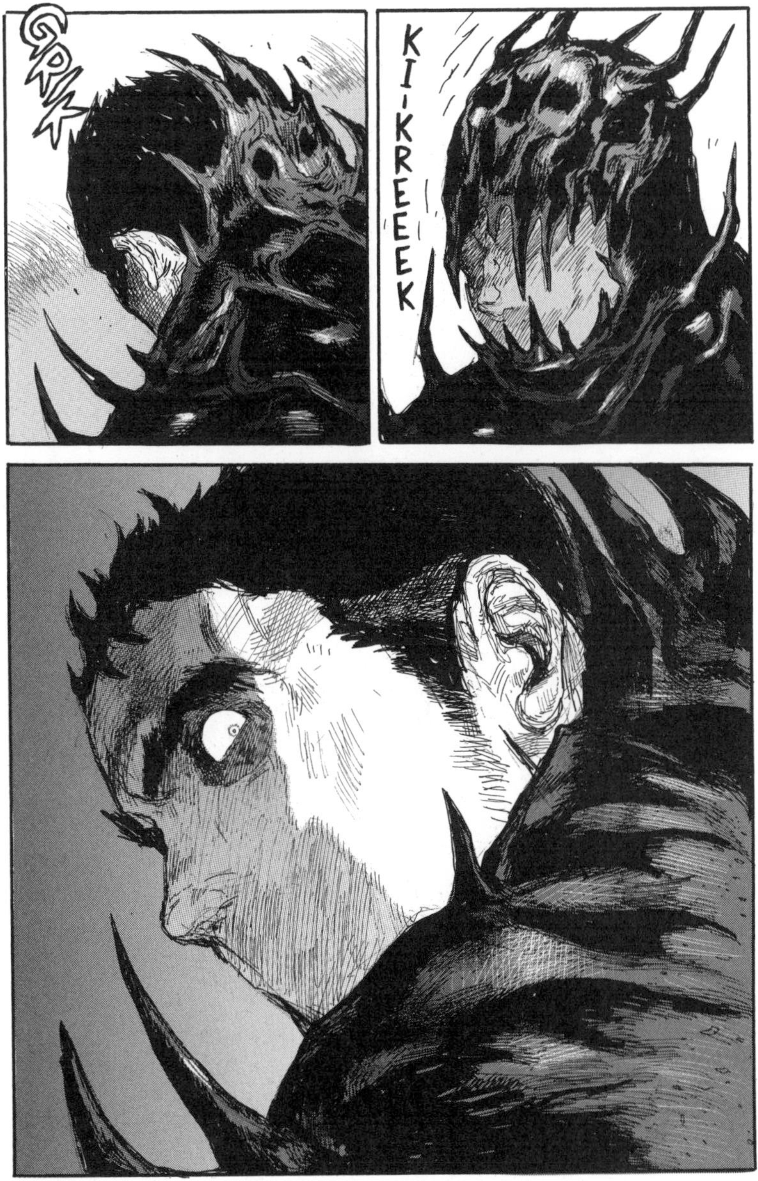
KI-KREEEK
GRIK

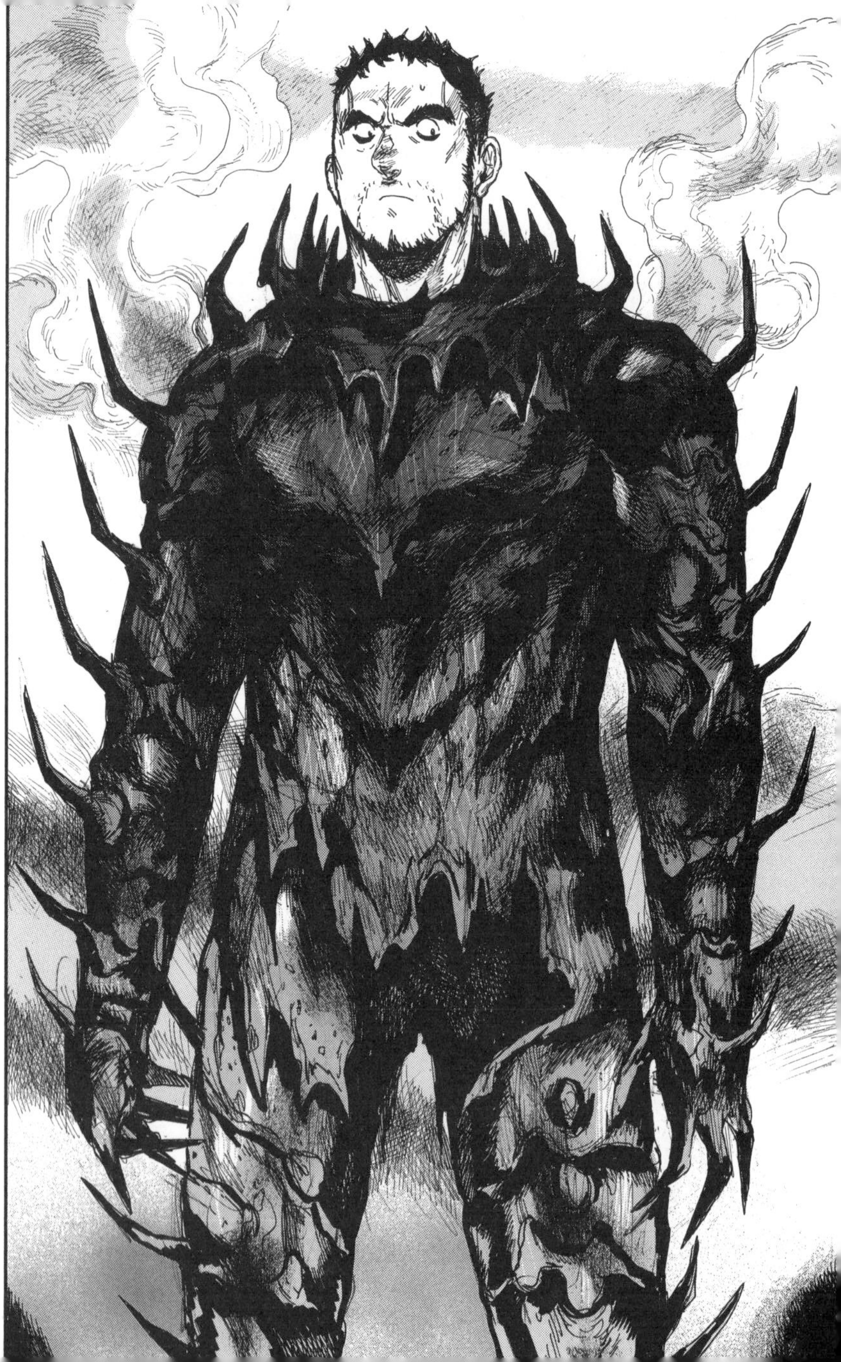

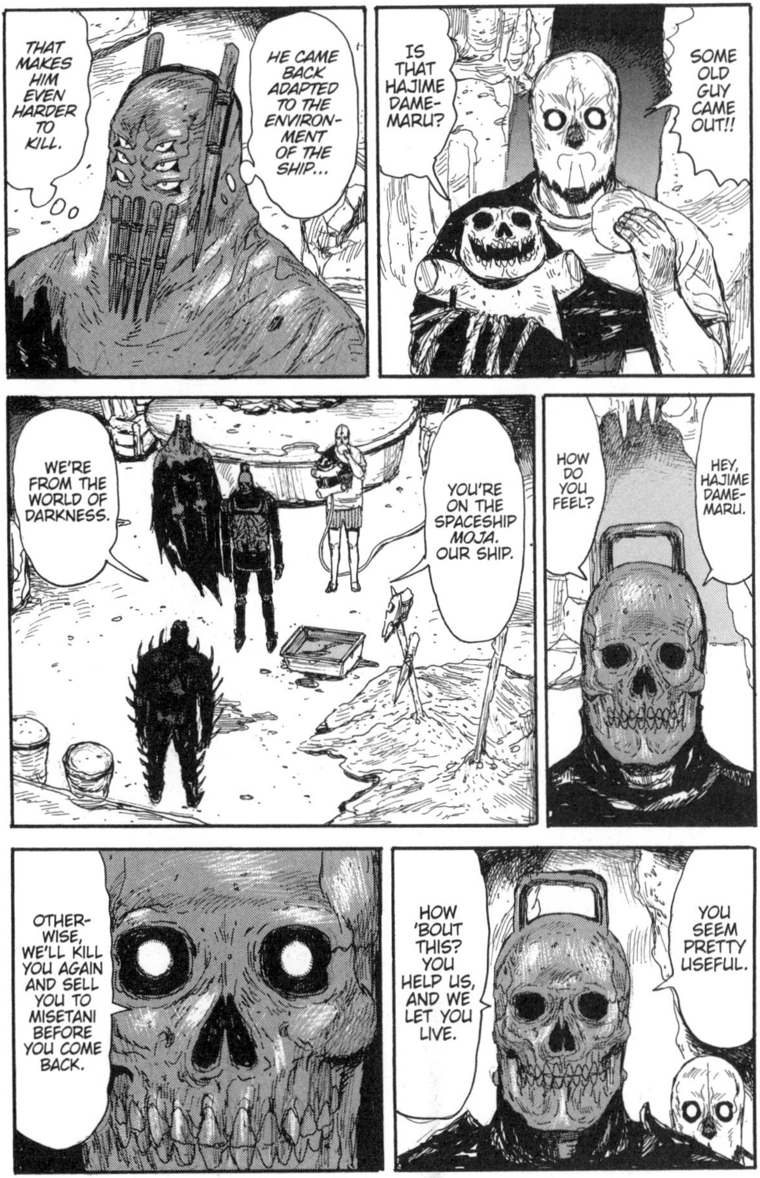
SOME OLD GUY CAME OUT!!
IS THAT HAJIME DAME-MARU?
HE CAME BACK ADAPTED TO THE ENVIRONMENT OF THE SHIP...
THAT MAKES HIM EVEN HARDER TO KILL.
HEY, HAJIME DAME-MARU.
HOW DO YOU FEEL?
YOU'RE ON THE SPACESHIP MOJA. OUR SHIP.
WE'RE FROM THE WORLD OF DARKNESS.
YOU SEEM PRETTY USEFUL.
HOW 'BOUT THIS? YOU HELP US, AND WE LET YOU LIVE.
OTHERWISE, WE'LL KILL YOU AGAIN AND SELL YOU TO MISETANI BEFORE YOU COME BACK.

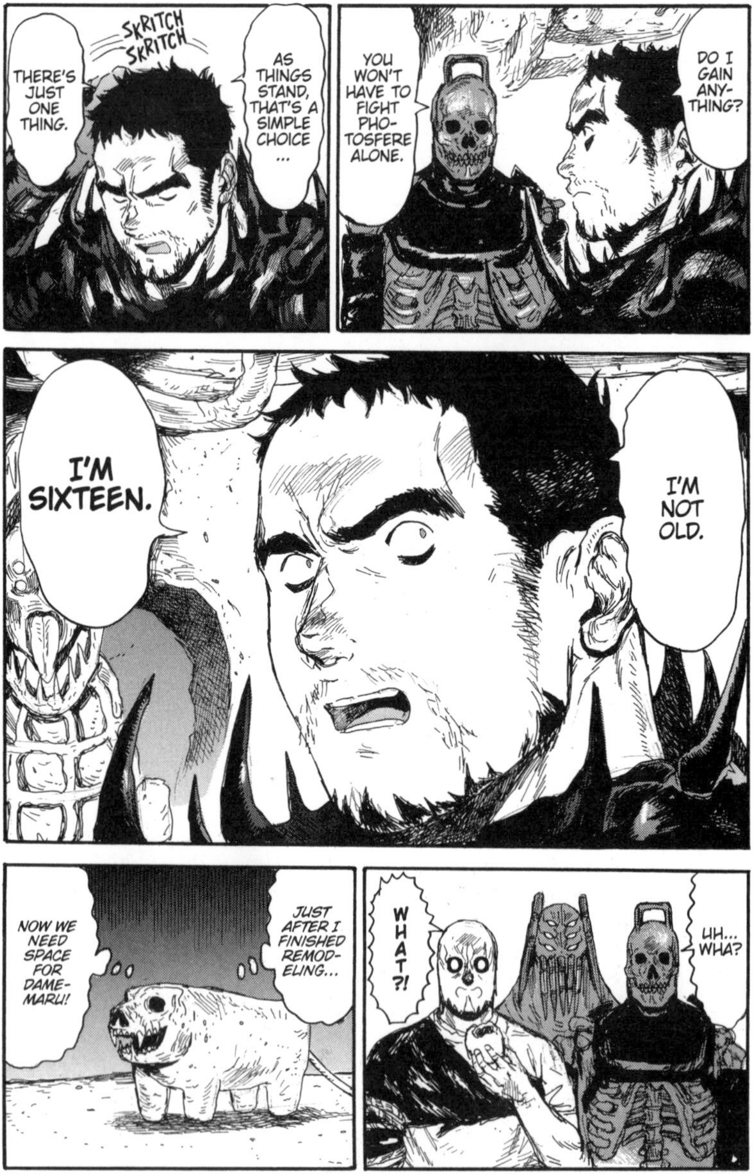
DO I GAIN ANY-THING?
YOU WON'T HAVE TO FIGHT PHO-TOSFERE ALONE.
AS THINGS STAND, THAT'S A SIMPLE CHOICE ...
SKRITCH SKRITCH
THERE'S JUST ONE THING.
I'M NOT OLD.
I'M SIXTEEN.
UH... WHA?
WHAT?!
JUST AFTER I FINISHED REMOD-ELING...
NOW WE NEED SPACE FOR DAME-MARU!

★ Design of Nagurun (rear)

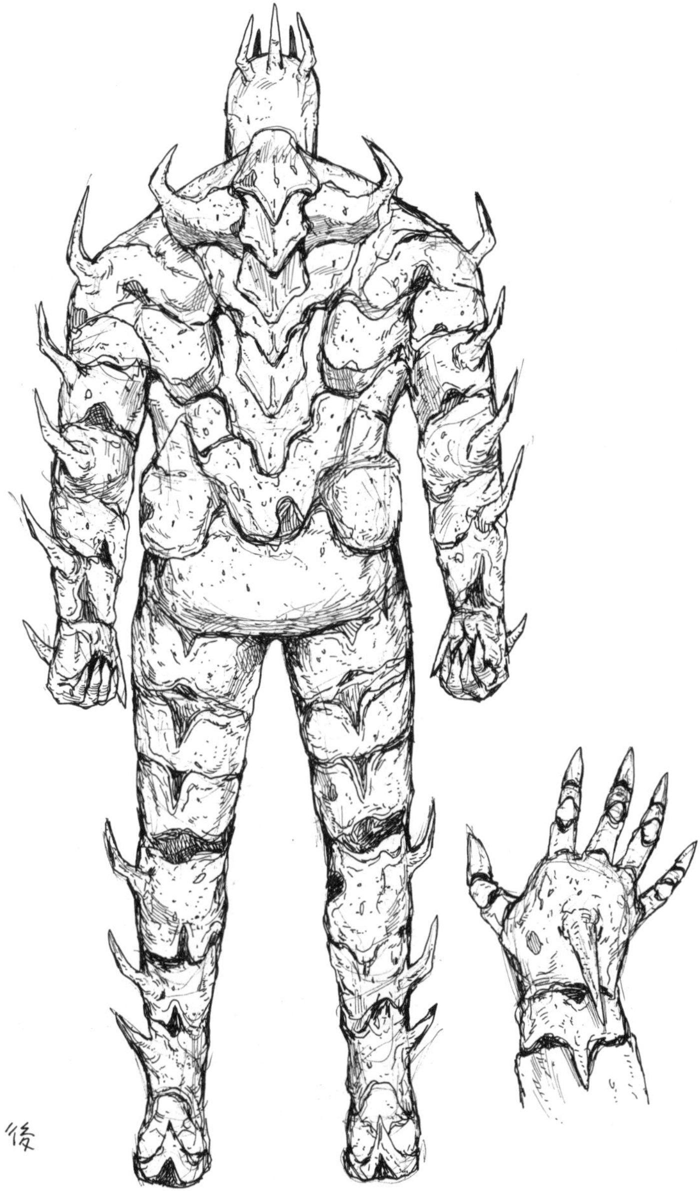
後

★ Hajime Damemaru, armored

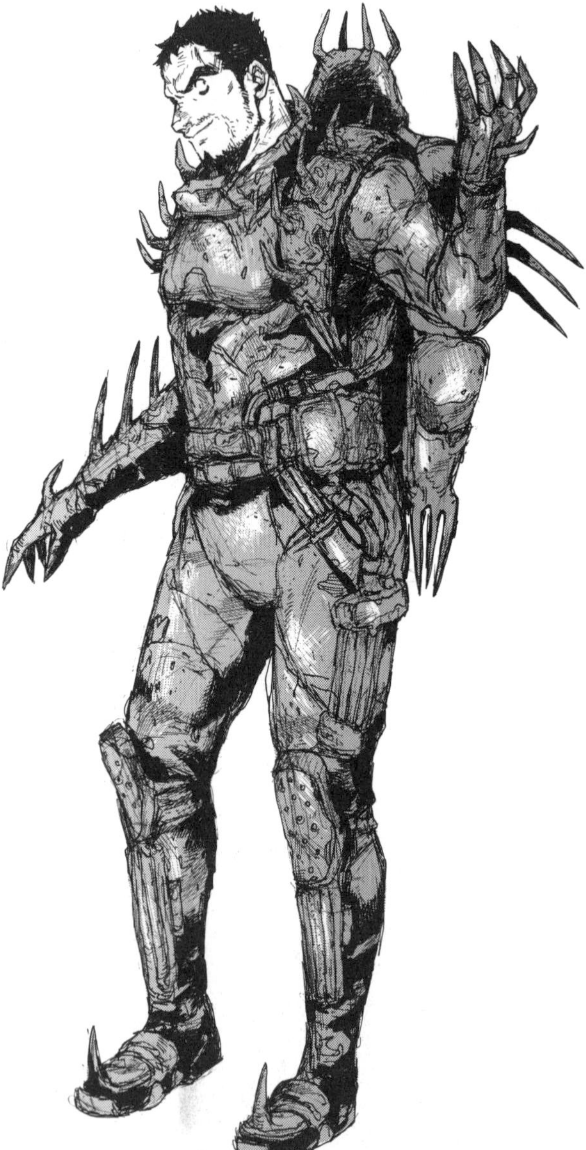

DAI DARK

DAI DARK

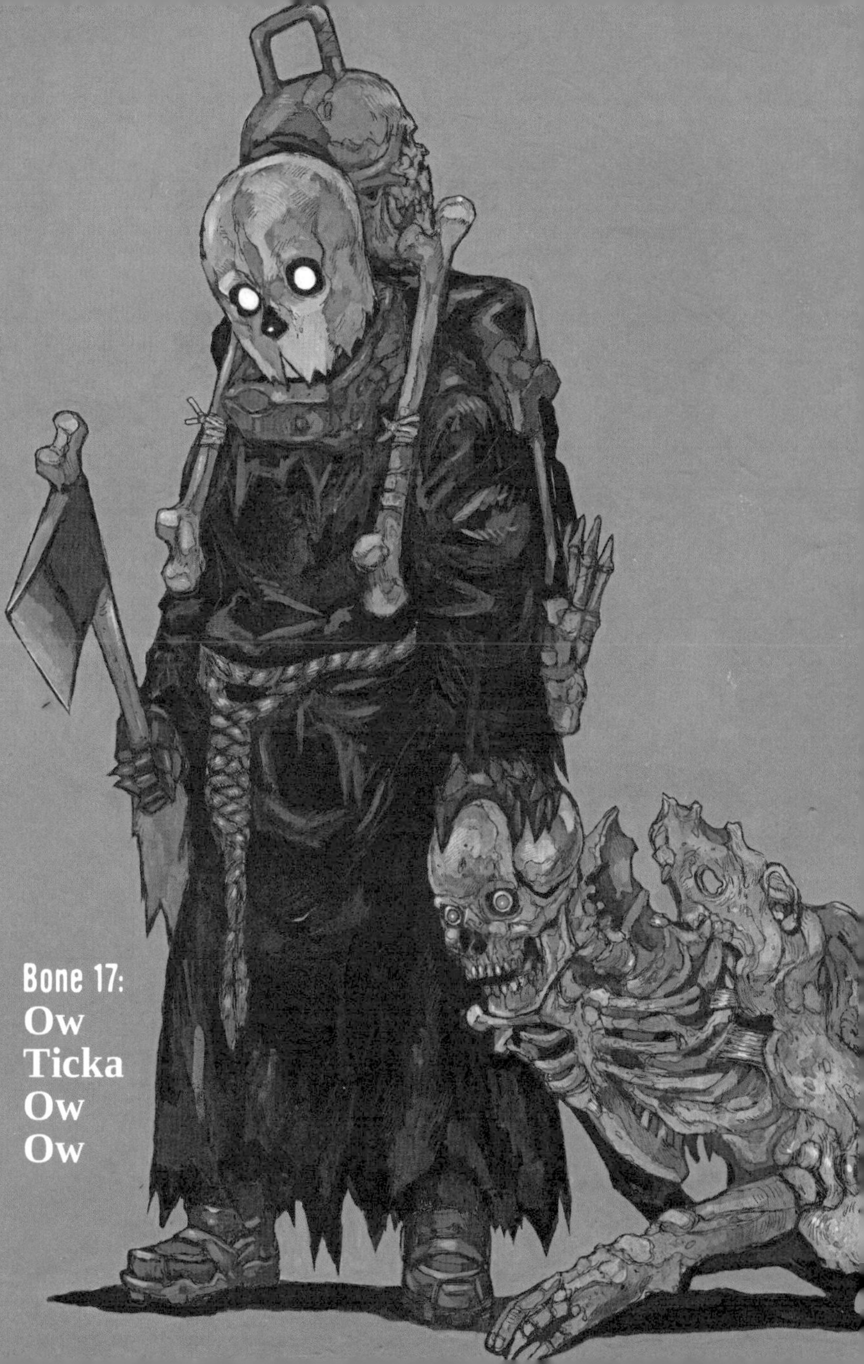

Bone 17: Ow Ticka Ow Ow

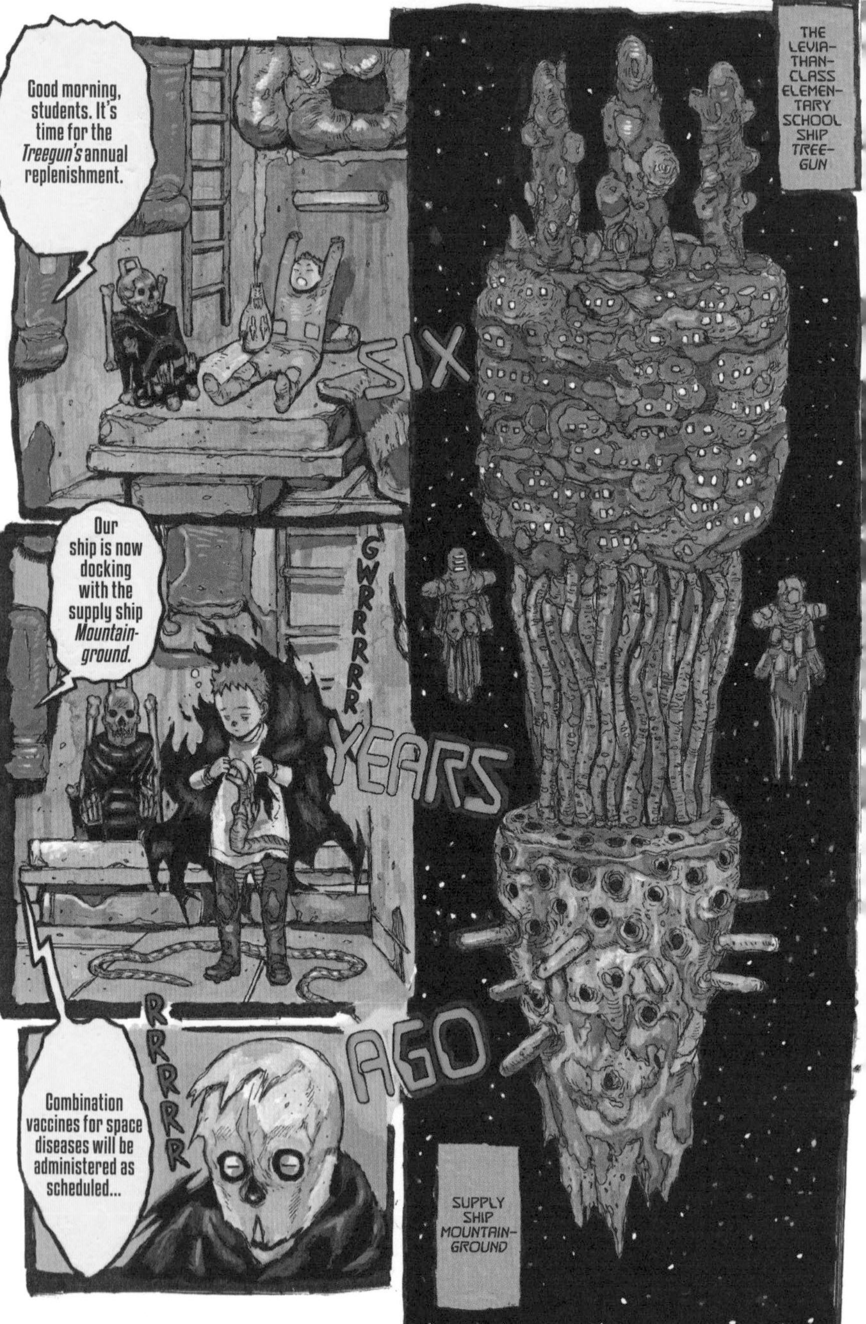
THE LEVIA-THAN-CLASS ELEMEN-TARY SCHOOL SHIP TREE-GUN
SUPPLY SHIP MOUNTAIN-GROUND
SIX YEARS AGO
Good morning, students. It's time for the *Treegun's* annual replenishment.
Our ship is now docking with the supply ship *Mountain-ground*.
GWRRRRRR
RRRRR
Combination vaccines for space diseases will be administered as scheduled...

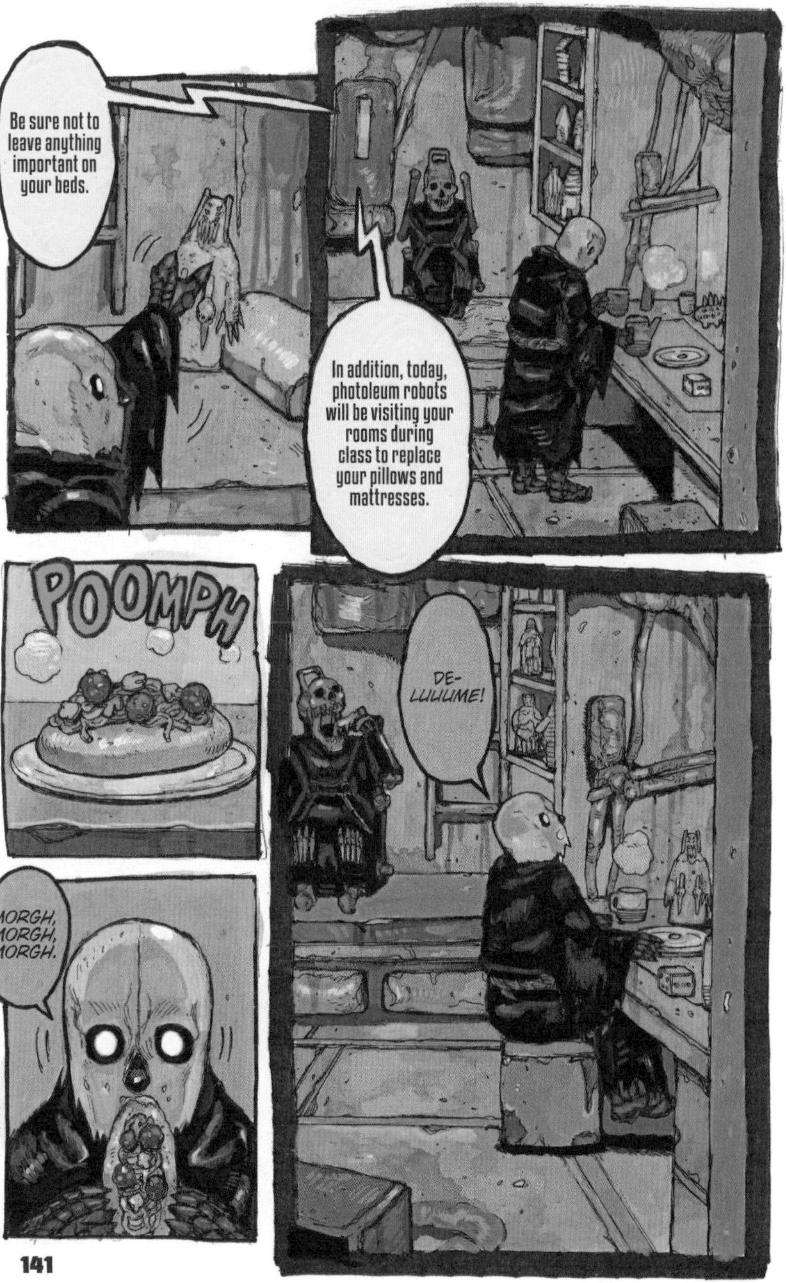

Be sure not to leave anything important on your beds.
In addition, today, photoleum robots will be visiting your rooms during class to replace your pillows and mattresses.
DE-LUUUME!
POOMPH
MORGH, MORGH, MORGH.

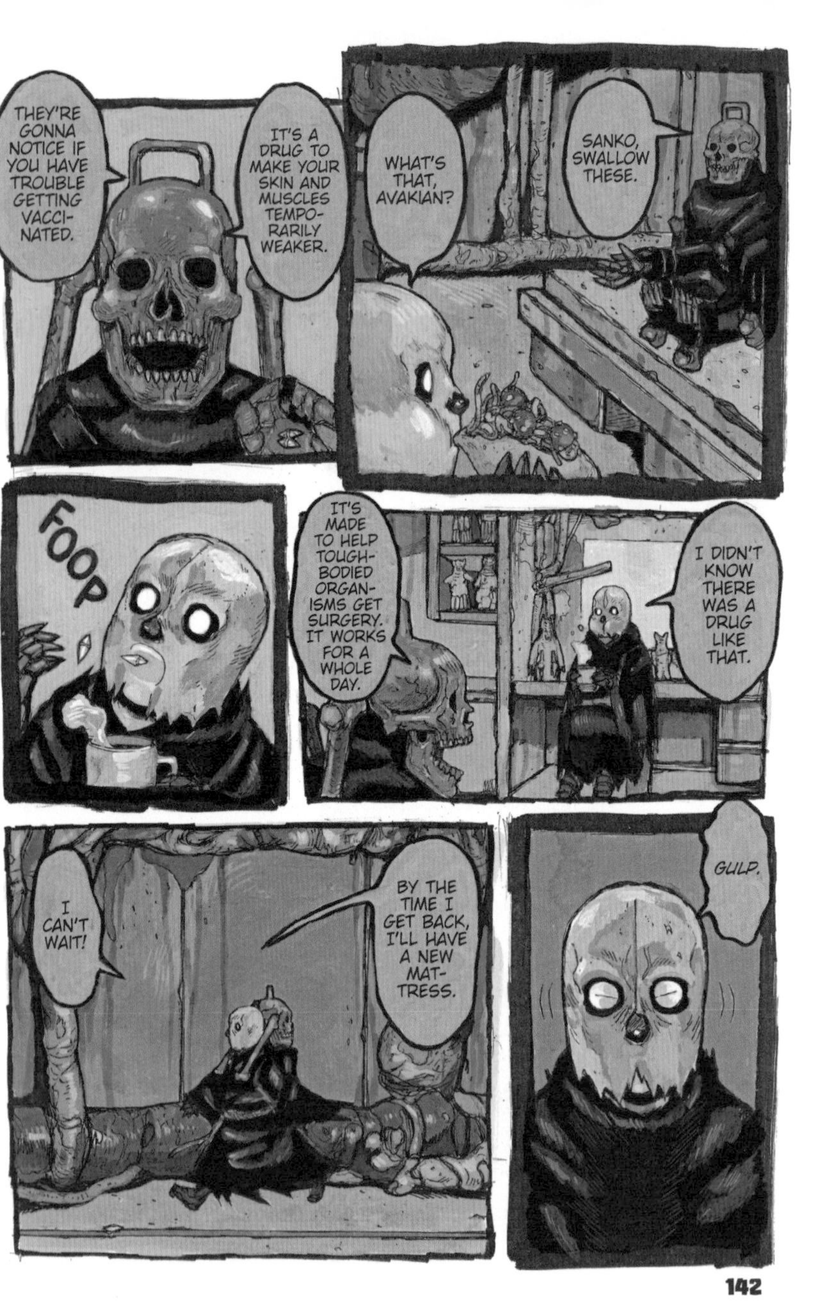
SANKO, SWALLOW THESE.
WHAT'S THAT, AVAKIAN?
IT'S A DRUG TO MAKE YOUR SKIN AND MUSCLES TEMPO-RARILY WEAKER.
THEY'RE GONNA NOTICE IF YOU HAVE TROUBLE GETTING VACCI-NATED.
I DIDN'T KNOW THERE WAS A DRUG LIKE THAT.
IT'S MADE TO HELP TOUGH-BODIED ORGAN-ISMS GET SURGERY. IT WORKS FOR A WHOLE DAY.
FOOP
GULP.
BY THE TIME I GET BACK, I'LL HAVE A NEW MAT-TRESS.
I CAN'T WAIT!

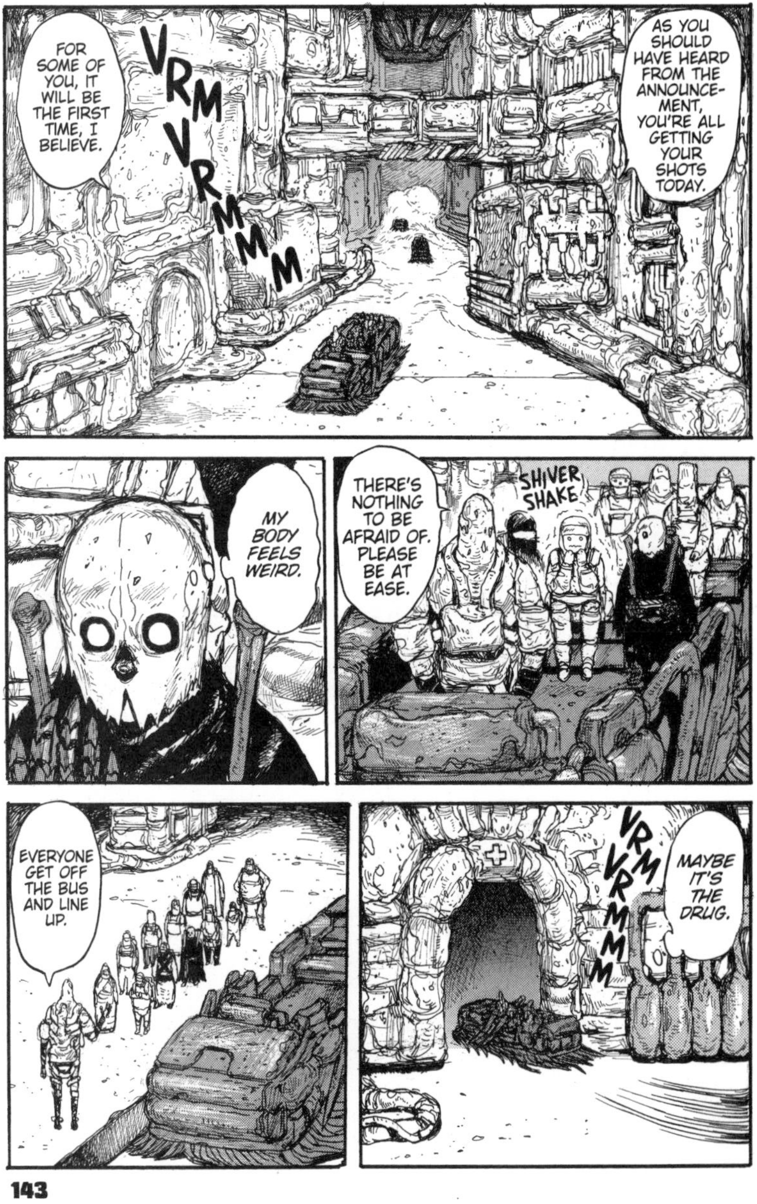
AS YOU SHOULD HAVE HEARD FROM THE ANNOUNCEMENT, YOU'RE ALL GETTING YOUR SHOTS TODAY.
VRM VRM VRMMMM
FOR SOME OF YOU, IT WILL BE THE FIRST TIME, I BELIEVE.
SHIVER SHAKE
THERE'S NOTHING TO BE AFRAID OF. PLEASE BE AT EASE.
MY BODY FEELS WEIRD.
VRM VRMMMM
MAYBE IT'S THE DRUG.
EVERYONE GET OFF THE BUS AND LINE UP.

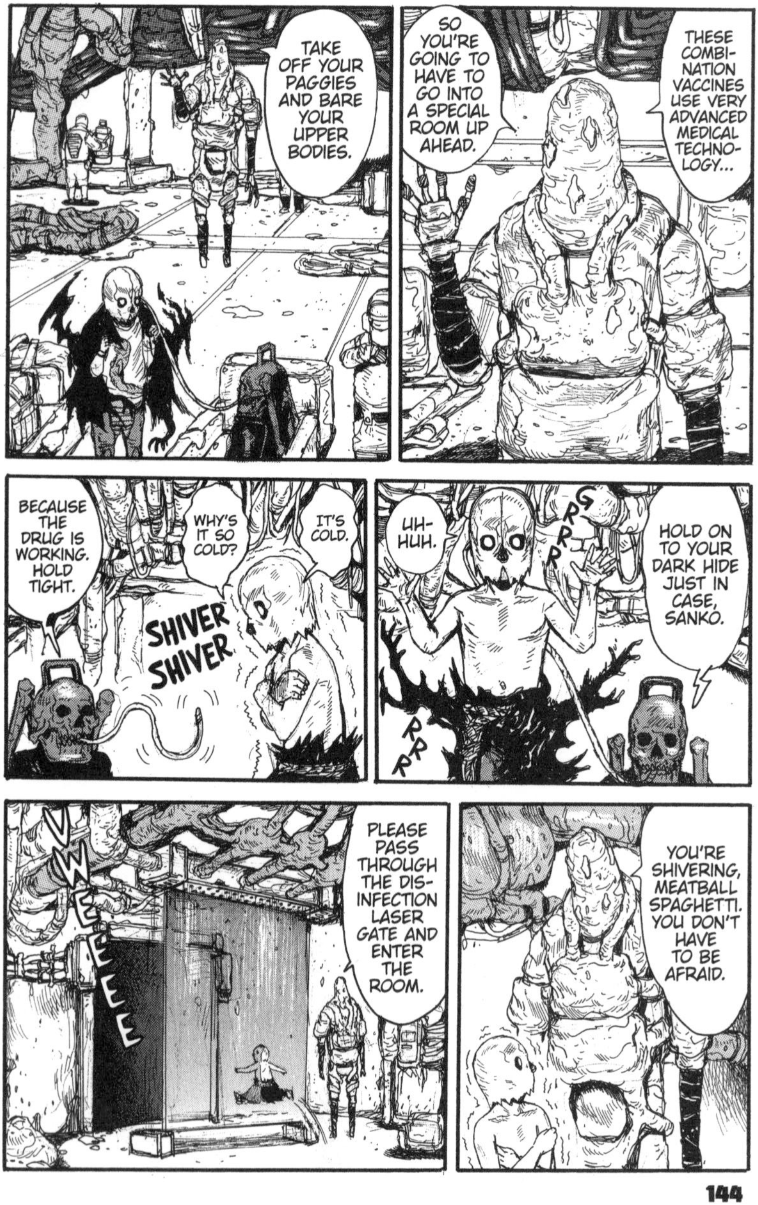
THESE COMBINATION VACCINES USE VERY ADVANCED MEDICAL TECHNOLOGY...
SO YOU'RE GOING TO HAVE TO GO INTO A SPECIAL ROOM UP AHEAD.
TAKE OFF YOUR PAGGIES AND BARE YOUR UPPER BODIES.
GRRR
HOLD ON TO YOUR DARK HIDE JUST IN CASE, SANKO.
UH-HUH.
RRR
IT'S COLD.
WHY'S IT SO COLD?
BECAUSE THE DRUG IS WORKING. HOLD TIGHT.
SHIVER SHIVER
YOU'RE SHIVERING, MEATBALL SPAGHETTI. YOU DON'T HAVE TO BE AFRAID.
PLEASE PASS THROUGH THE DISINFECTION LASER GATE AND ENTER THE ROOM.
VWEEEE

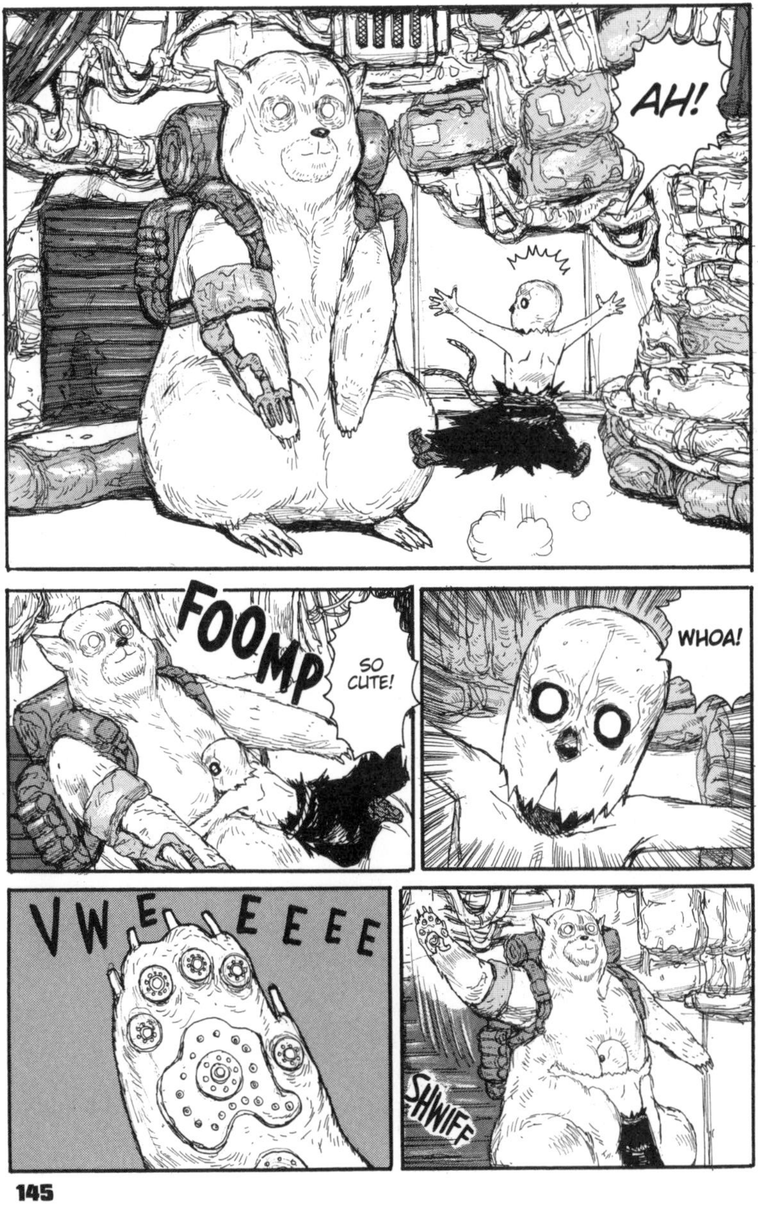
AH!
WHOA!
FOOMP
SO CUTE!
SHWIFF
VWEEEEE

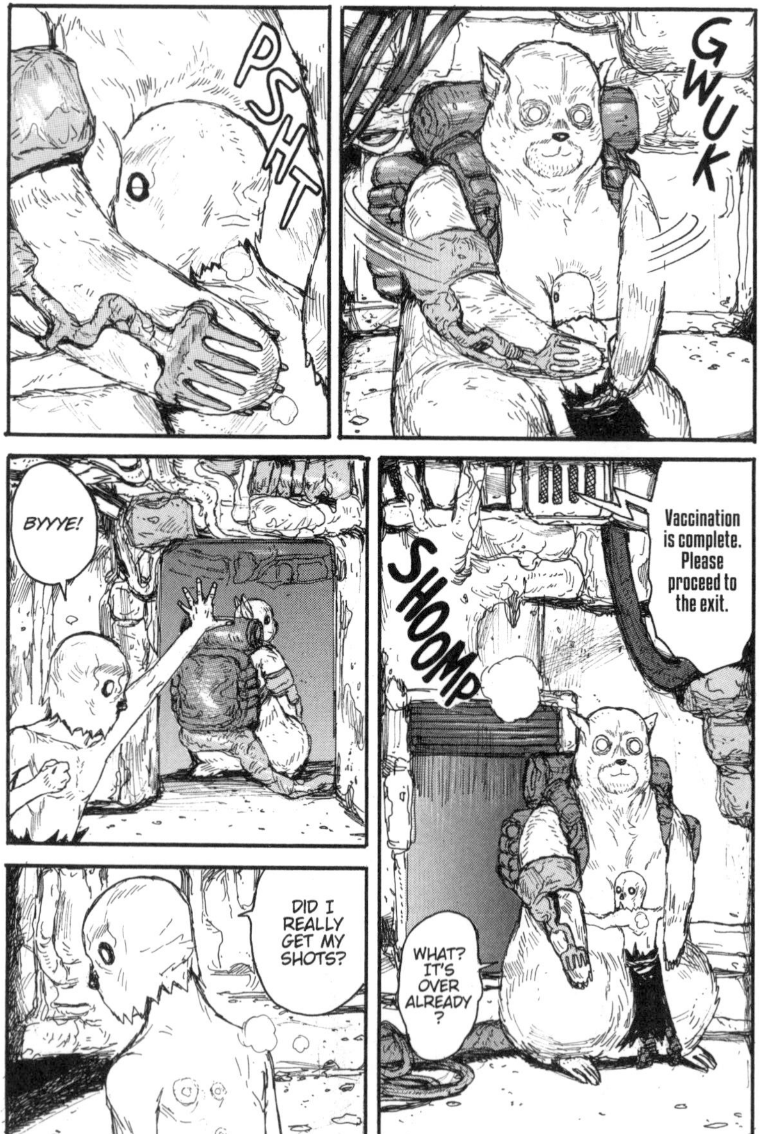
GWUK
PSHT
Vaccination is complete. Please proceed to the exit.
SHOOMP
WHAT? IT'S OVER ALREADY?
BYYYE!
DID I REALLY GET MY SHOTS?

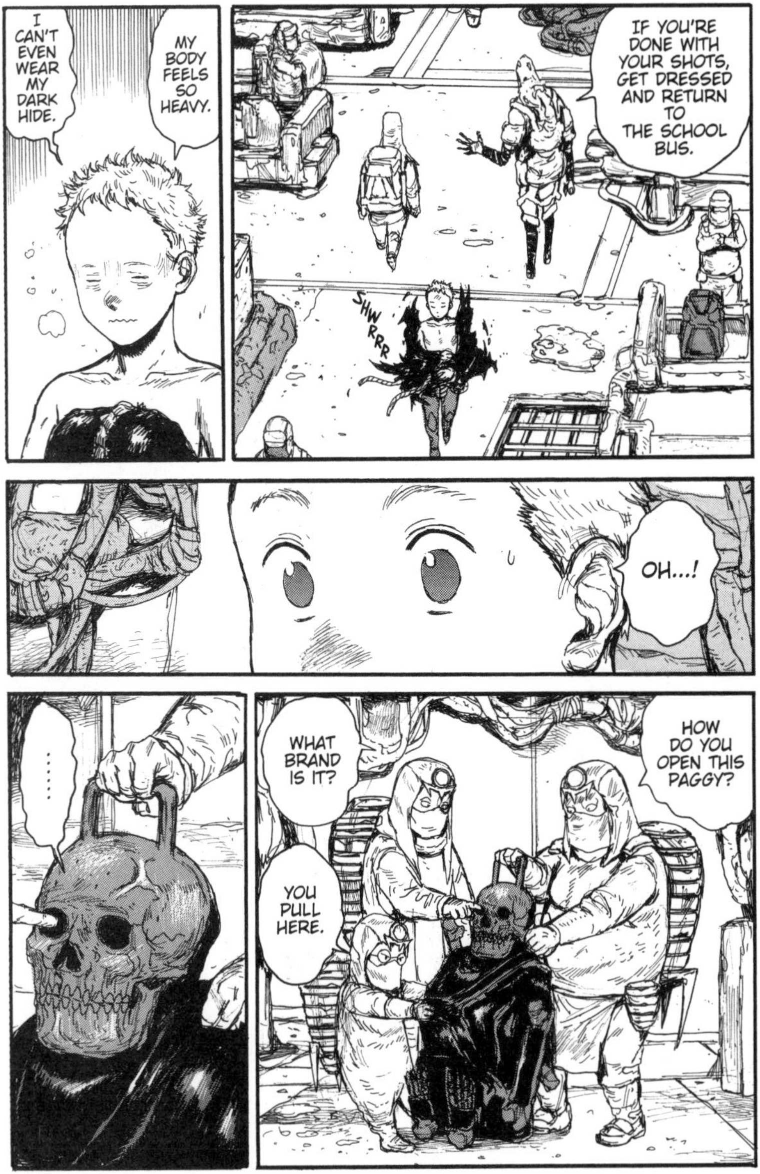
IF YOU'RE DONE WITH YOUR SHOTS, GET DRESSED AND RETURN TO THE SCHOOL BUS.
SHWRRR
MY BODY FEELS SO HEAVY.
I CAN'T EVEN WEAR MY DARK HIDE.
OH...!
HOW DO YOU OPEN THIS PAGGY?
WHAT BRAND IS IT?
YOU PULL HERE.
......

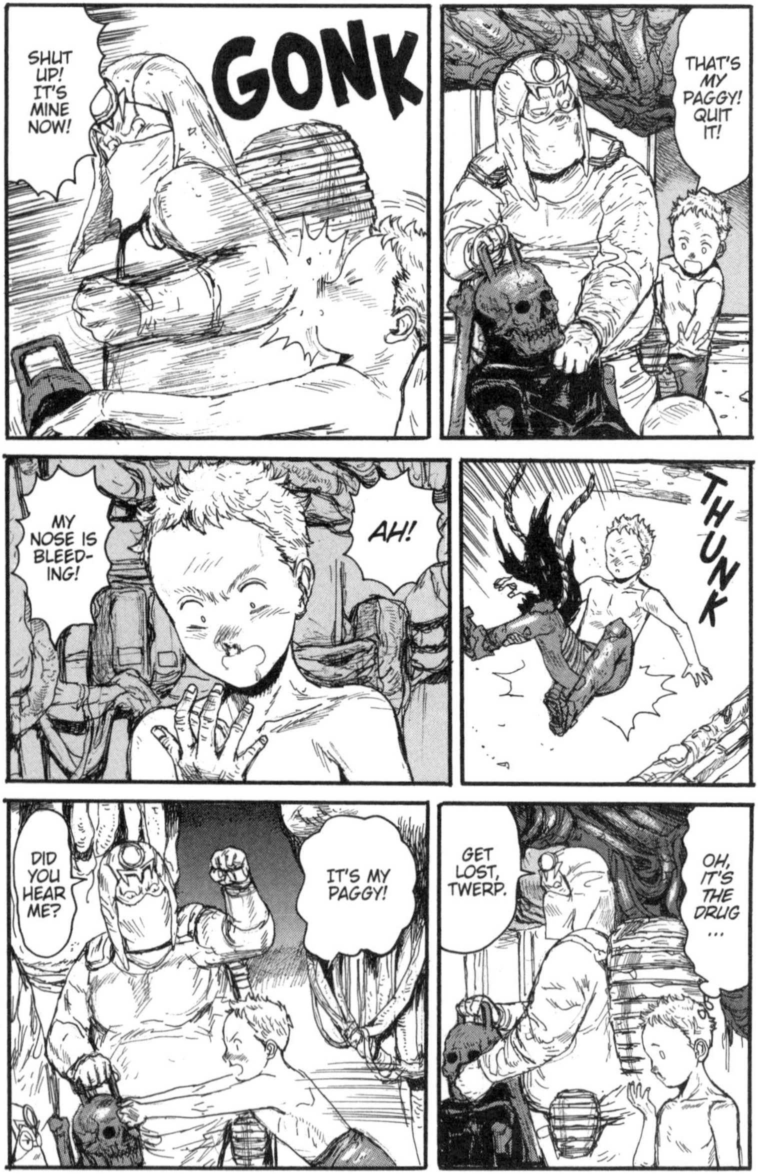
THAT'S MY PAGGY! QUIT IT!
GONK
SHUT UP! IT'S MINE NOW!
THUNK
AH!
MY NOSE IS BLEEDING!
OH, IT'S THE DRUG ...
GET LOST, TWERP.
IT'S MY PAGGY!
DID YOU HEAR ME?

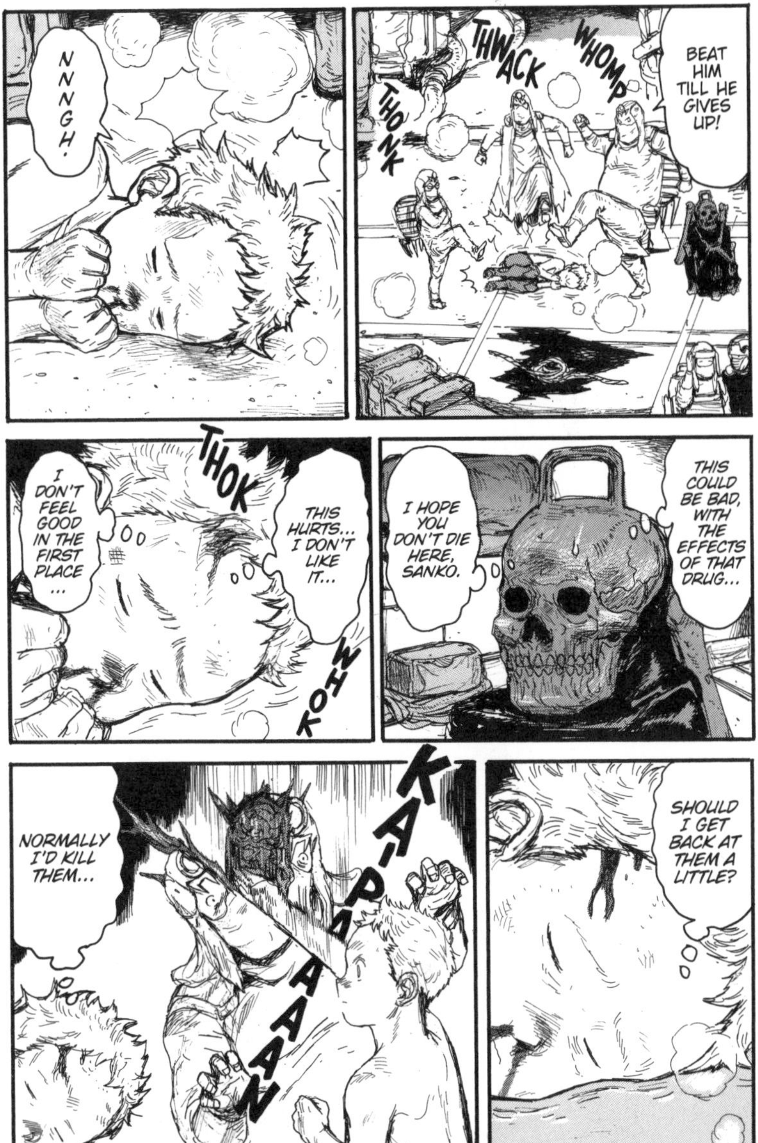
BEAT HIM TILL HE GIVES UP!
WHOMP
THWACK
THONK
NNNNGH!
THIS COULD BE BAD, WITH THE EFFECTS OF THAT DRUG...
I HOPE YOU DON'T DIE HERE, SANKO.
THOK
THIS HURTS... I DON'T LIKE IT...
I DON'T FEEL GOOD IN THE FIRST PLACE...
WHOK
SHOULD I GET BACK AT THEM A LITTLE?
KA-PAAAAAN
NORMALLY I'D KILL THEM...

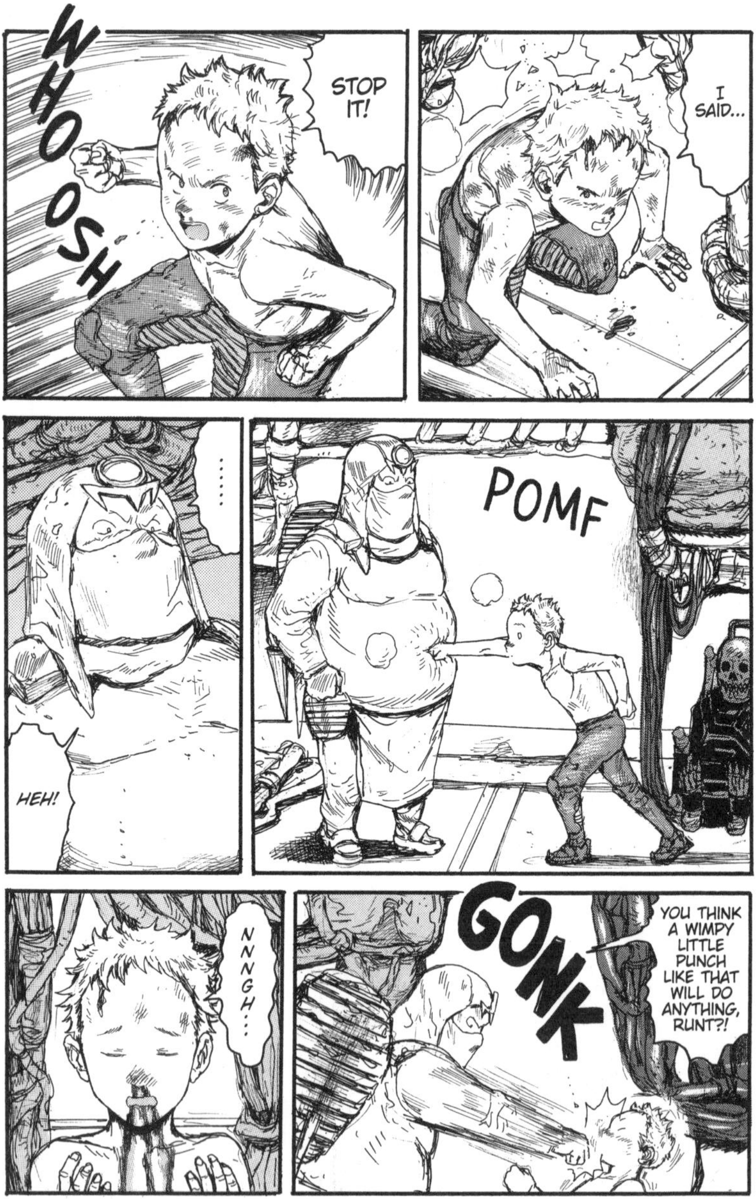
I SAID...
WHOOSH
STOP IT!
POMF
......
HEH!
GONK
YOU THINK A WIMPY LITTLE PUNCH LIKE THAT WILL DO ANYTHING, RUNT?!
NNNGH...

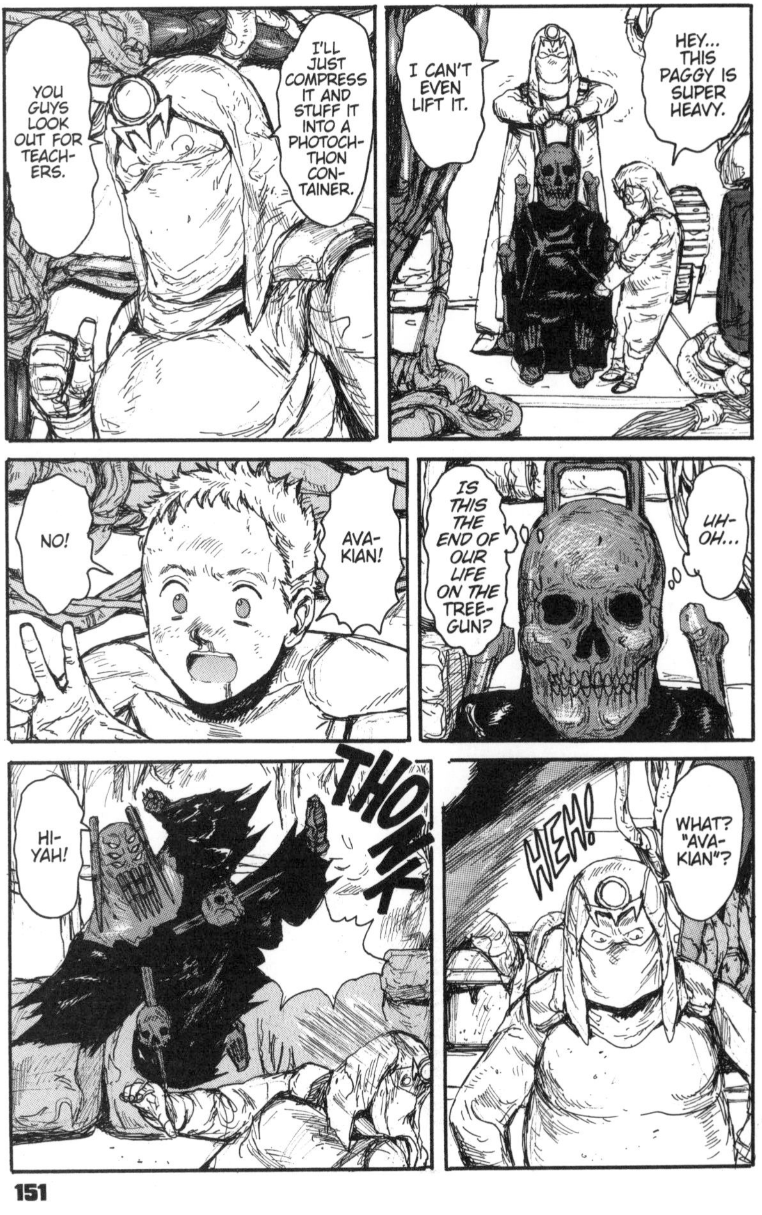
HEY... THIS PAGGY IS SUPER HEAVY.
I CAN'T EVEN LIFT IT.
I'LL JUST COMPRESS IT AND STUFF IT INTO A PHOTOCHTHON CONTAINER.
YOU GUYS LOOK OUT FOR TEACHERS.
UH-OH...
IS THIS THE END OF OUR LIFE ON THE TREE-GUN?
AVAKIAN!
NO!
WHAT? "AVAKIAN"?
HEH!
THONK
HI-YAH!

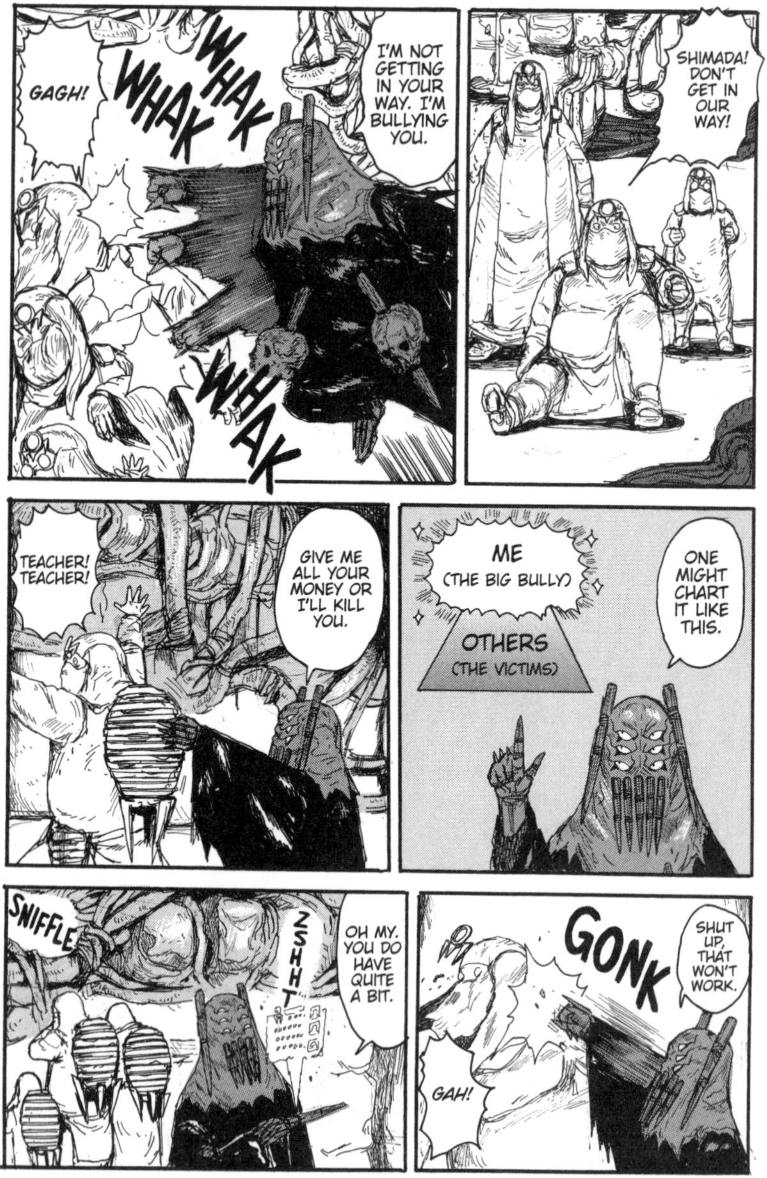
SHIMADA! DON'T GET IN OUR WAY!
I'M NOT GETTING IN YOUR WAY. I'M BULLYING YOU.
WHAK WHAK
GAGH!
WHAK
ONE MIGHT CHART IT LIKE THIS.
ME (THE BIG BULLY)
OTHERS (THE VICTIMS)
GIVE ME ALL YOUR MONEY OR I'LL KILL YOU.
TEACHER! TEACHER!
SHUT UP, THAT WON'T WORK.
GONK
GAH!
OH MY. YOU DO HAVE QUITE A BIT.
ZSHHT
SNIFFLE

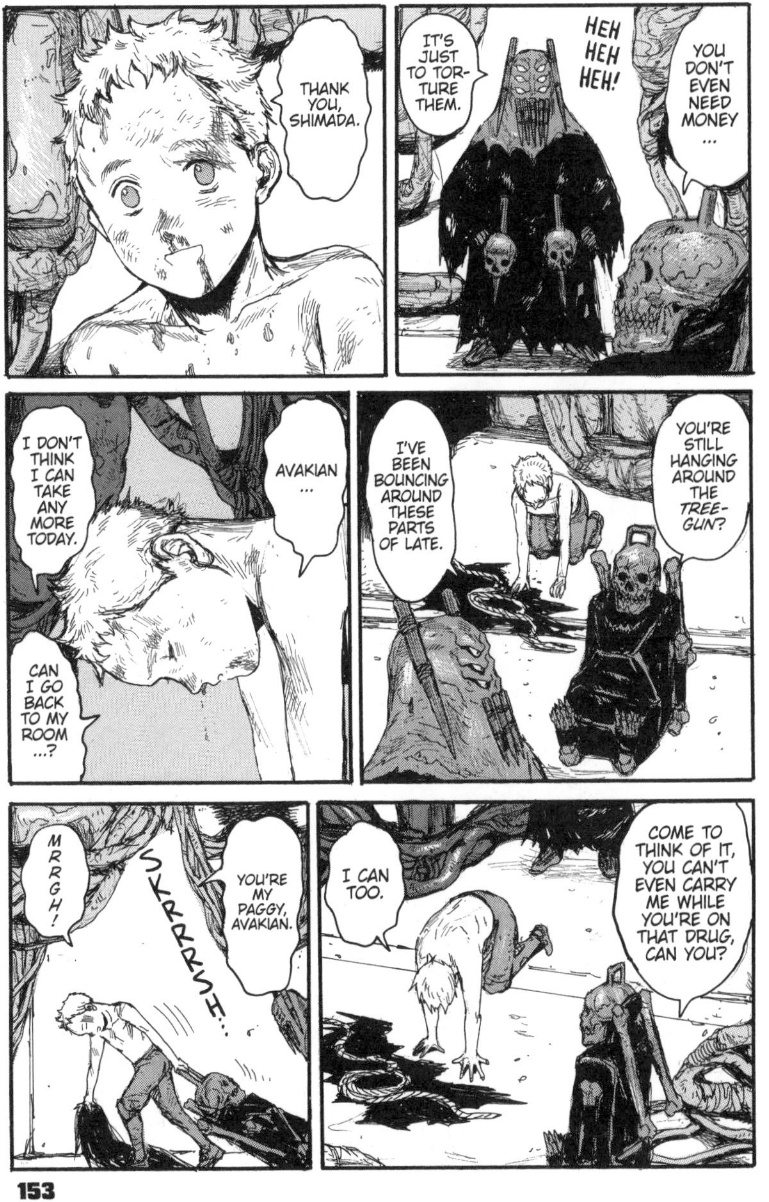
YOU DON'T EVEN NEED MONEY ...
HEH HEH HEH!
IT'S JUST TO TORTURE THEM.
THANK YOU, SHIMADA.
YOU'RE STILL HANGING AROUND THE *TREE-GUN*?
I'VE BEEN BOUNCING AROUND THESE PARTS OF LATE.
AVAKIAN ...
I DON'T THINK I CAN TAKE ANY MORE TODAY.
CAN I GO BACK TO MY ROOM ...?
COME TO THINK OF IT, YOU CAN'T EVEN CARRY ME WHILE YOU'RE ON THAT DRUG, CAN YOU?
I CAN TOO.
YOU'RE MY PAGGY, AVAKIAN.
SKRRRSH...
MRRGH!

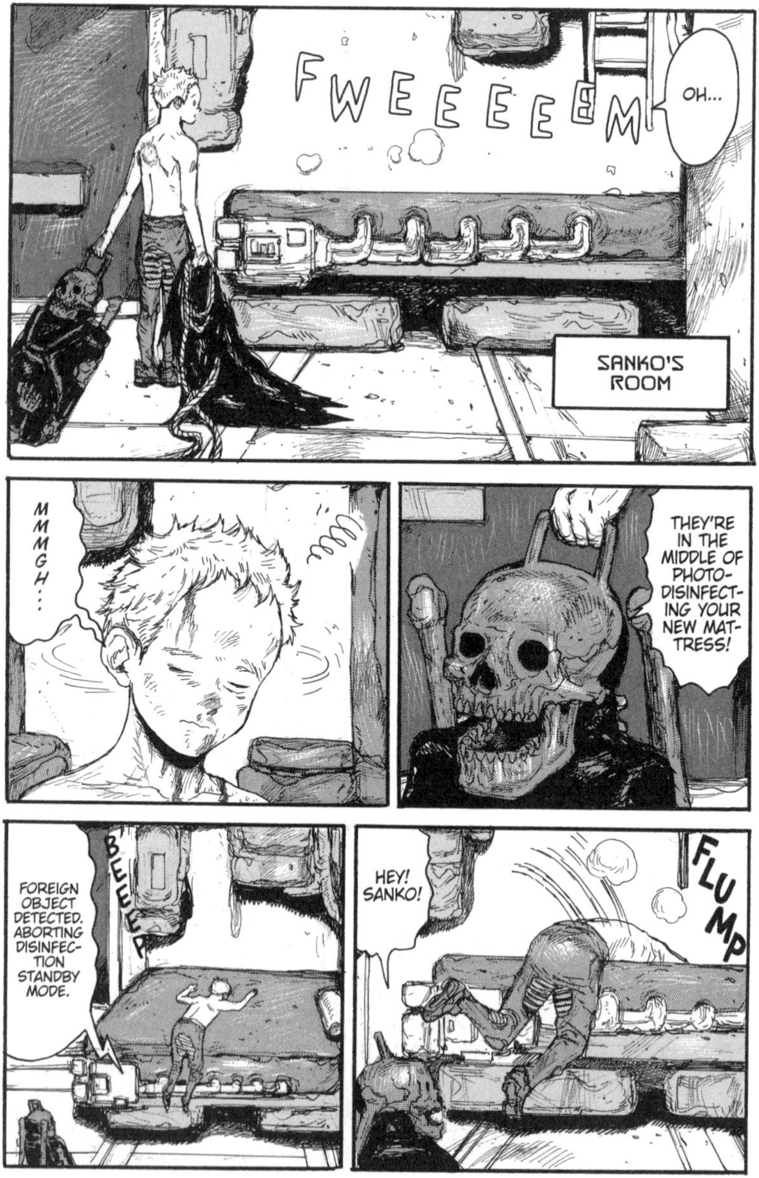

OH...
FWEEEEEM
SANKO'S ROOM
THEY'RE IN THE MIDDLE OF PHOTO-DISINFECTING YOUR NEW MATTRESS!
MMMGH...
FLUMP
HEY! SANKO!
BEEEEP
FOREIGN OBJECT DETECTED. ABORTING DISINFECTION STANDBY MODE.

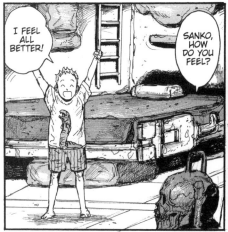

THE NEXT DAY...
SANKO, HOW DO YOU FEEL?
I FEEL ALL BETTER!
BEE-BEEEP
Resuming photodis-infection.
WHAT'S THAT FOR?
WELL, CARGO GOES THROUGH A LOT OF HANDS TO GET HERE, YOU KNOW?
YOU NEVER KNOW WHAT IT MIGHT HAVE.
HMM.
MM?
SANKO, YOU LOOK THINNER.
YOU THINK?

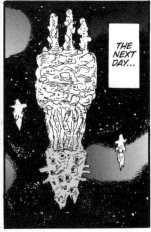

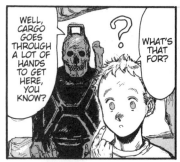

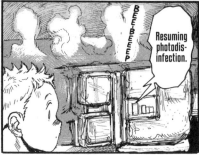

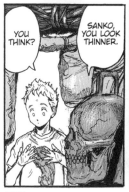

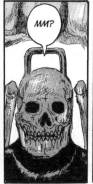

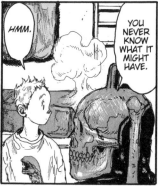

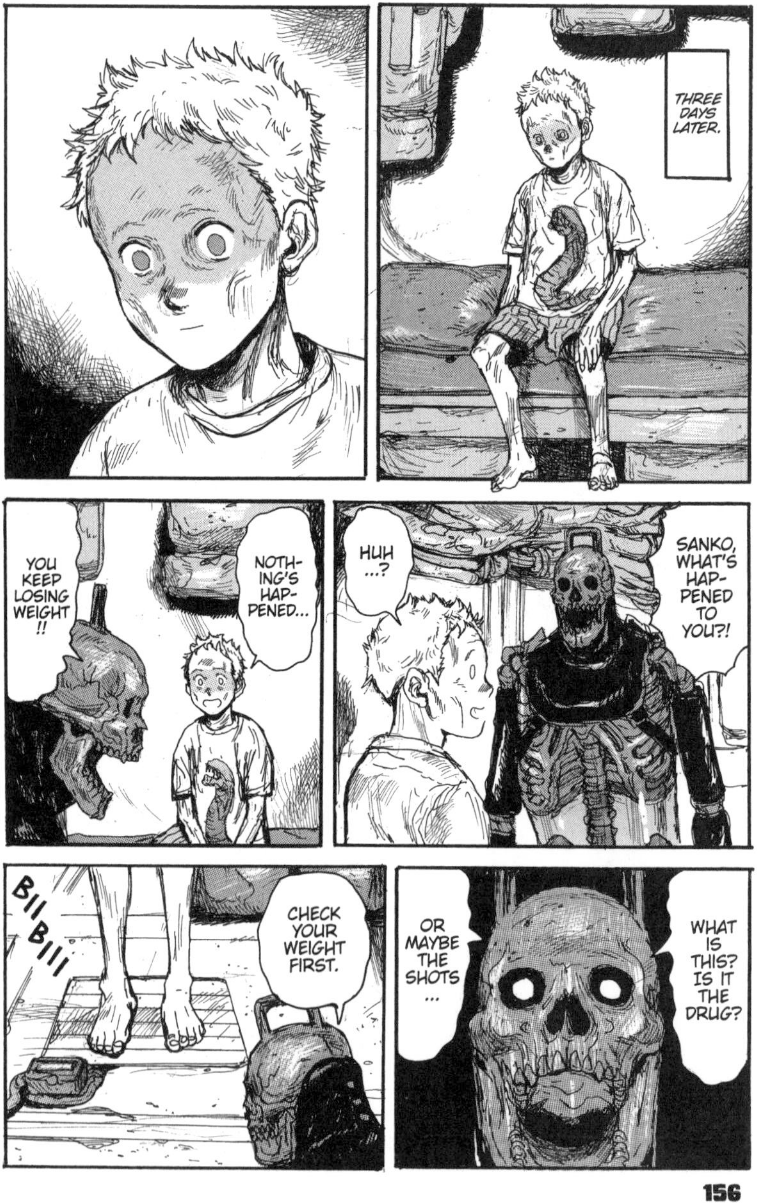
THREE DAYS LATER.
SANKO, WHAT'S HAP-PENED TO YOU?!
HUH ...?
NOTH-ING'S HAP-PENED...
YOU KEEP LOSING WEIGHT !!
WHAT IS THIS? IS IT THE DRUG?
OR MAYBE THE SHOTS ...
CHECK YOUR WEIGHT FIRST.
BIIBIII

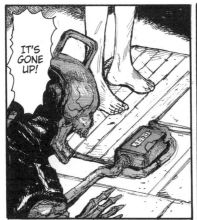

IT'S GONE UP!

WHAT?!

H-HOW COULD THIS BE?!

SANKO!

FLOP

NNNNGH...

MNGH, MNGH.

157

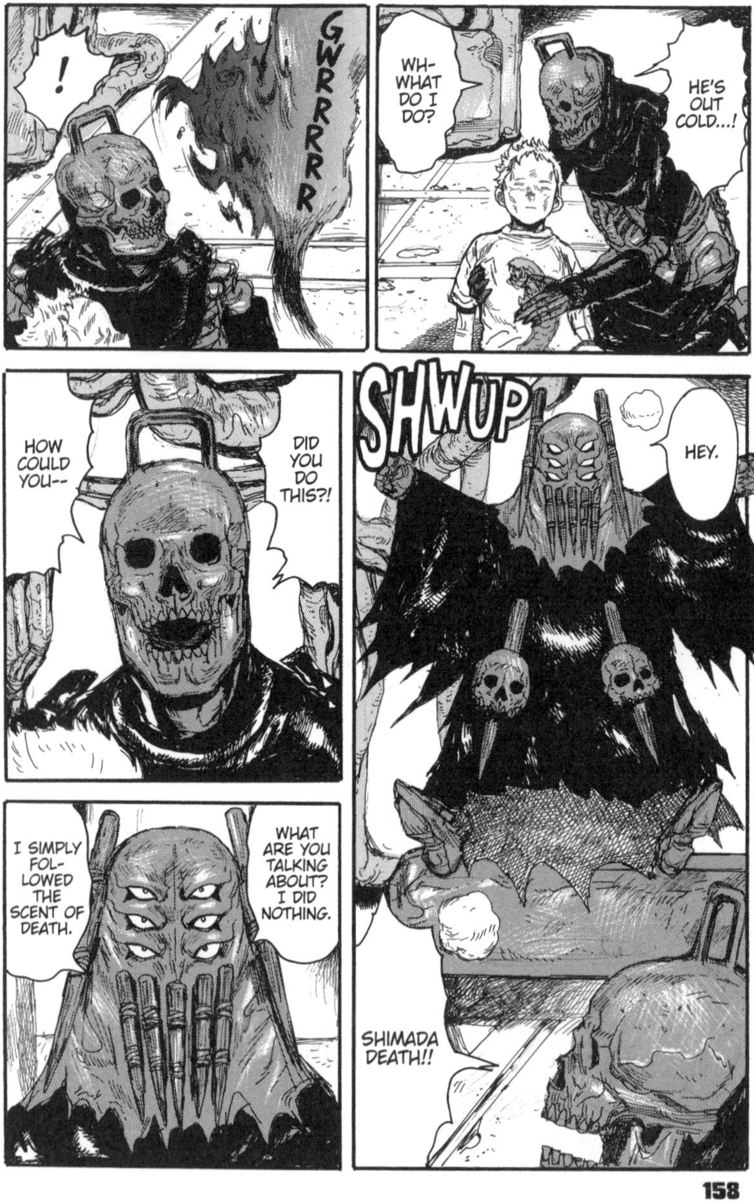
HE'S OUT COLD...!
WH- WHAT DO I DO?
GWRRRRR
!
SHWUP
HEY.
SHIMADA DEATH!!
DID YOU DO THIS?!
HOW COULD YOU--
WHAT ARE YOU TALKING ABOUT? I DID NOTHING.
I SIMPLY FOL-LOWED THE SCENT OF DEATH.

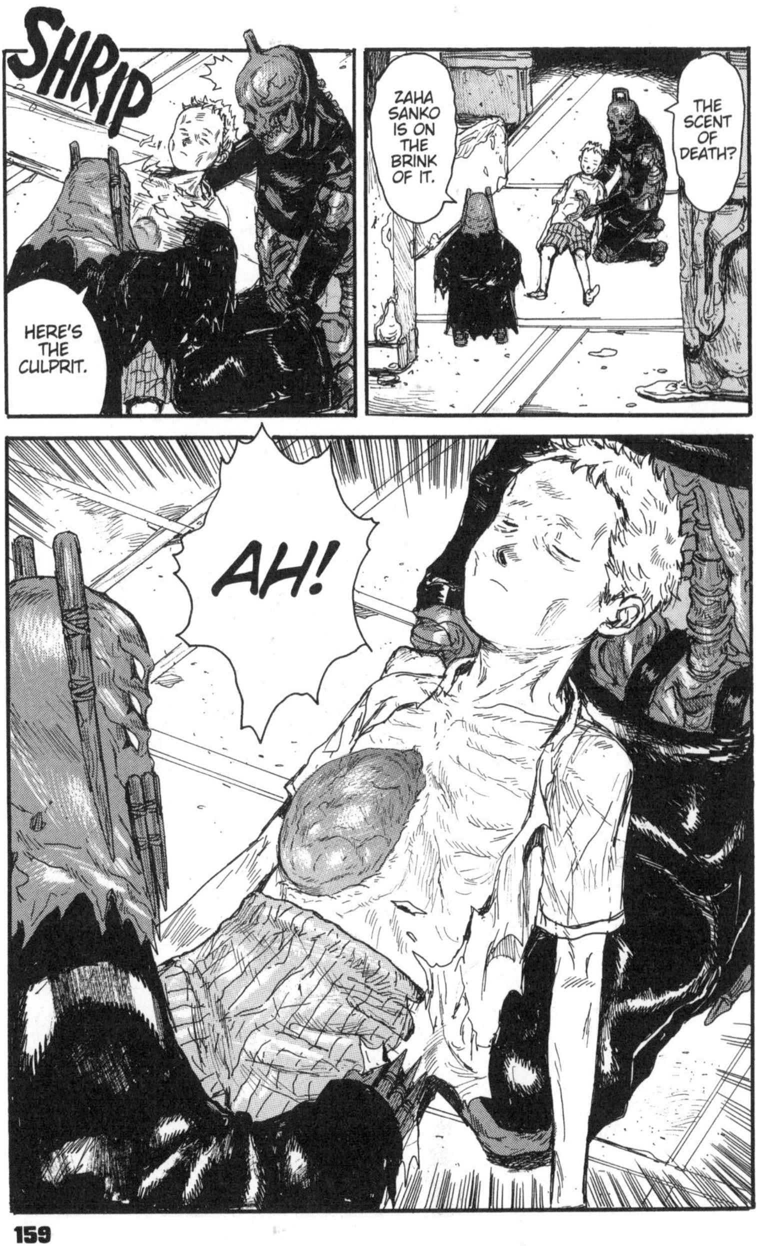
THE SCENT OF DEATH?
ZAHA SANKO IS ON THE BRINK OF IT.
SHRIP
HERE'S THE CULPRIT.
AH!

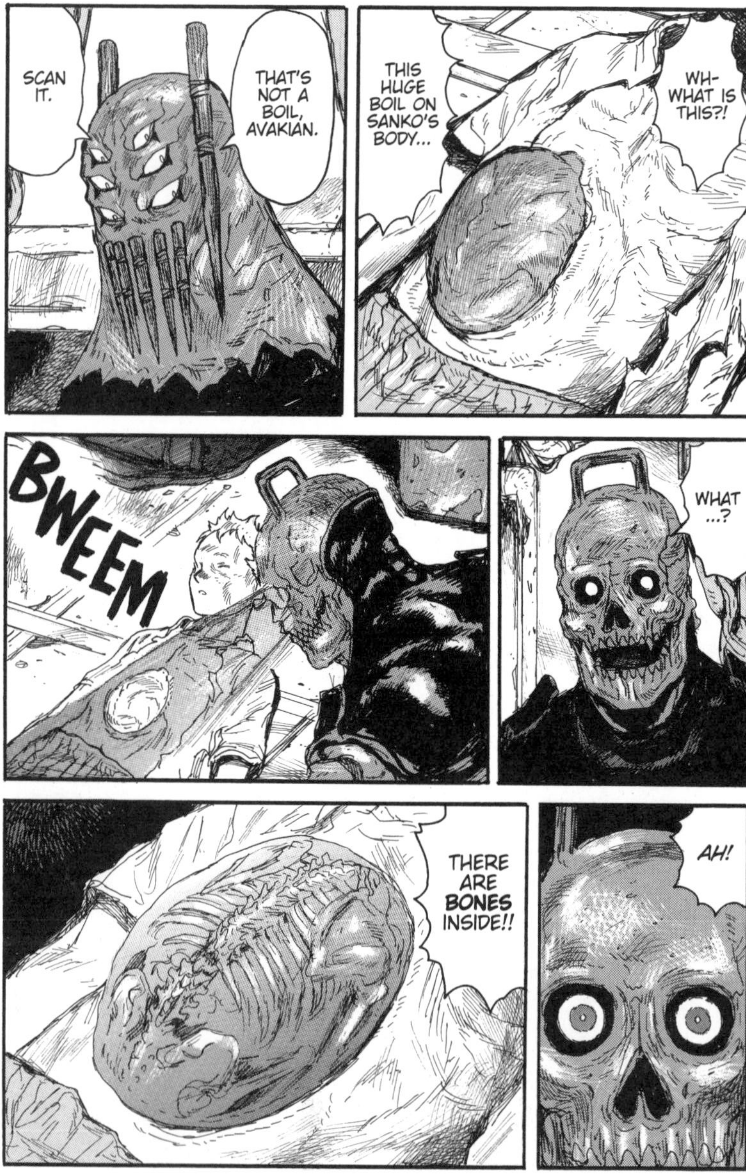
WH- WHAT IS THIS?!
THIS HUGE BOIL ON SANKO'S BODY...
THAT'S NOT A BOIL, AVAKIAN.
SCAN IT.
WHAT ...?
BWEEM
AH!
THERE ARE **BONES** INSIDE!!

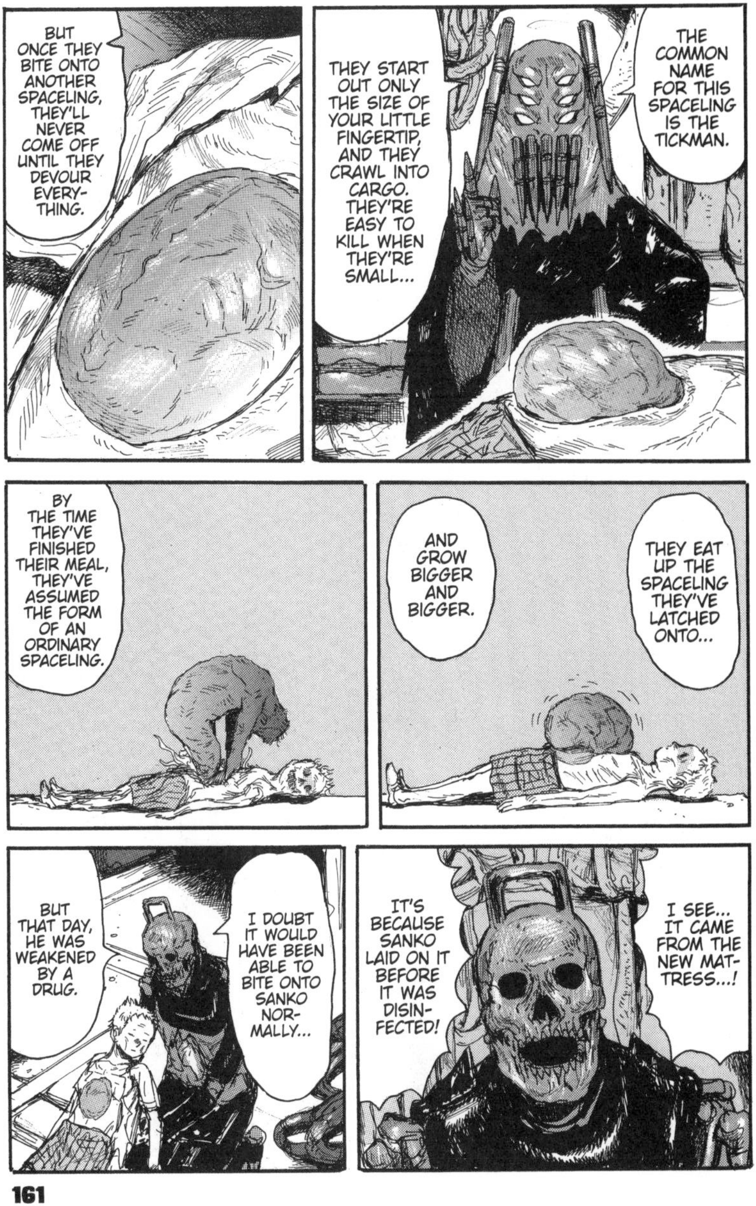
THE COMMON NAME FOR THIS SPACELING IS THE TICKMAN.
THEY START OUT ONLY THE SIZE OF YOUR LITTLE FINGERTIP, AND THEY CRAWL INTO CARGO. THEY'RE EASY TO KILL WHEN THEY'RE SMALL...
BUT ONCE THEY BITE ONTO ANOTHER SPACELING, THEY'LL NEVER COME OFF UNTIL THEY DEVOUR EVERY-THING.
THEY EAT UP THE SPACELING THEY'VE LATCHED ONTO...
AND GROW BIGGER AND BIGGER.
BY THE TIME THEY'VE FINISHED THEIR MEAL, THEY'VE ASSUMED THE FORM OF AN ORDINARY SPACELING.
I SEE... IT CAME FROM THE NEW MAT-TRESS...!
IT'S BECAUSE SANKO LAID ON IT BEFORE IT WAS DISIN-FECTED!
I DOUBT IT WOULD HAVE BEEN ABLE TO BITE ONTO SANKO NOR-MALLY...
BUT THAT DAY, HE WAS WEAKENED BY A DRUG.

PWA

SHOOMP

I'LL REDUCE THE BASTARD TO BONES WITH THIS DARK AX.

YOU'D BETTER NOT. THE TICKMAN IS ALREADY TIGHTLY WOUND INTO SANKO'S BODY.

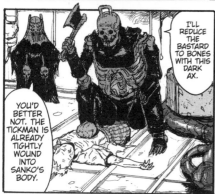

GWRRRRR

COME...

BUH-BLOOP

USE THAT AX AND YOU MIGHT REDUCE **SANKO** TO BONES.

DARK FLESH!

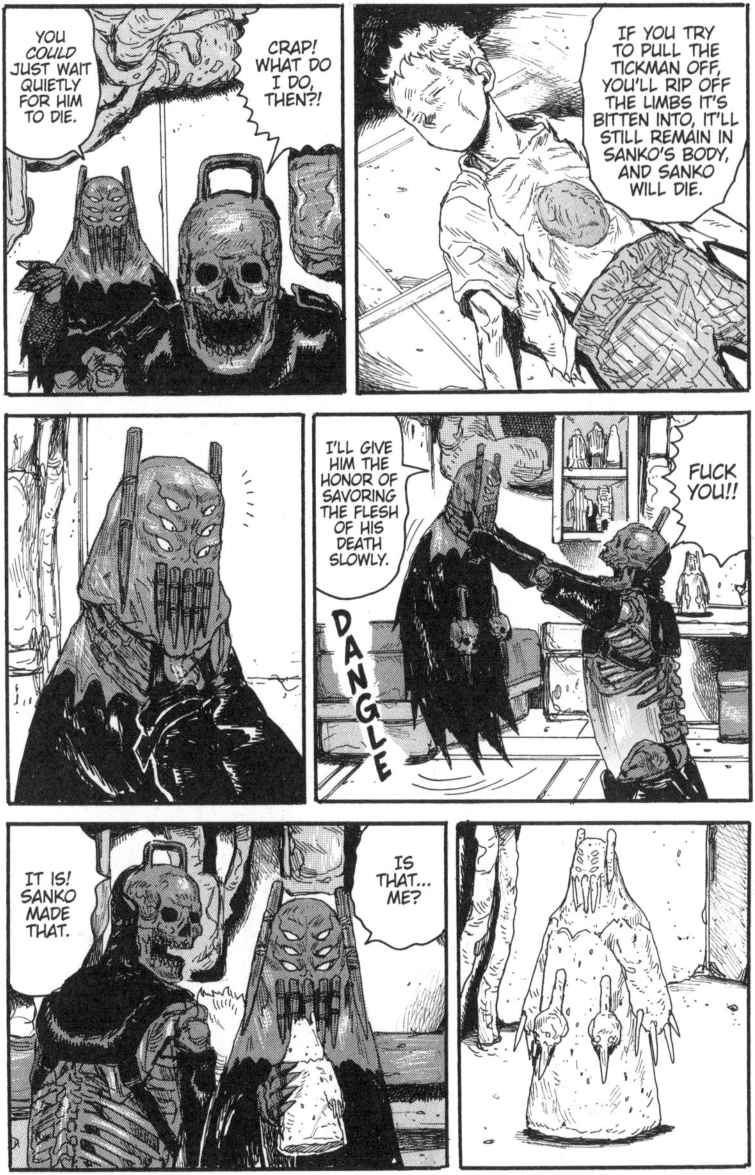

IF YOU TRY TO PULL THE TICKMAN OFF, YOU'LL RIP OFF THE LIMBS IT'S BITTEN INTO, IT'LL STILL REMAIN IN SANKO'S BODY, AND SANKO WILL DIE.
CRAP! WHAT DO I DO, THEN?!
YOU COULD JUST WAIT QUIETLY FOR HIM TO DIE.
I'LL GIVE HIM THE HONOR OF SAVORING THE FLESH OF HIS DEATH SLOWLY.
FUCK YOU!!
DANGLE
IS THAT... ME?
IT IS! SANKO MADE THAT.

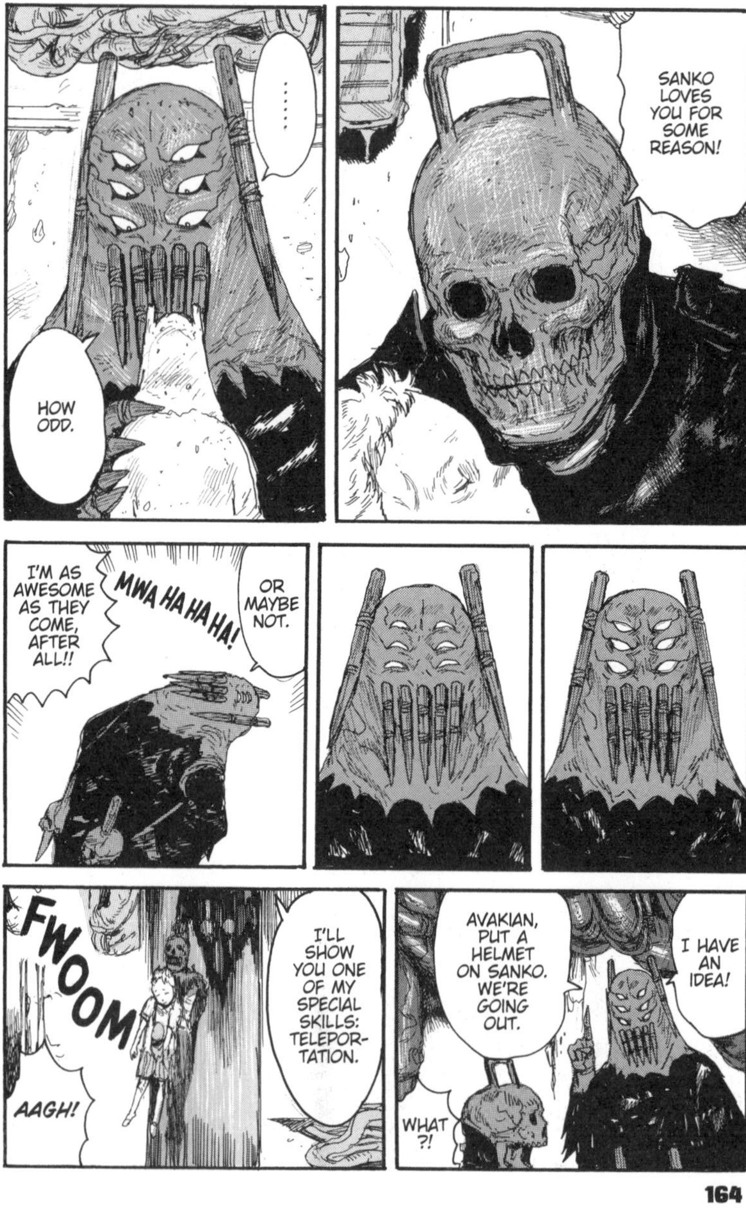
SANKO LOVES YOU FOR SOME REASON!
......
HOW ODD.
OR MAYBE NOT.
MWA HA HA HA HA!
I'M AS AWESOME AS THEY COME, AFTER ALL!!
I HAVE AN IDEA!
AVAKIAN, PUT A HELMET ON SANKO. WE'RE GOING OUT.
WHAT?!
I'LL SHOW YOU ONE OF MY SPECIAL SKILLS: TELEPOR-TATION.
FWOOM
AAGH!

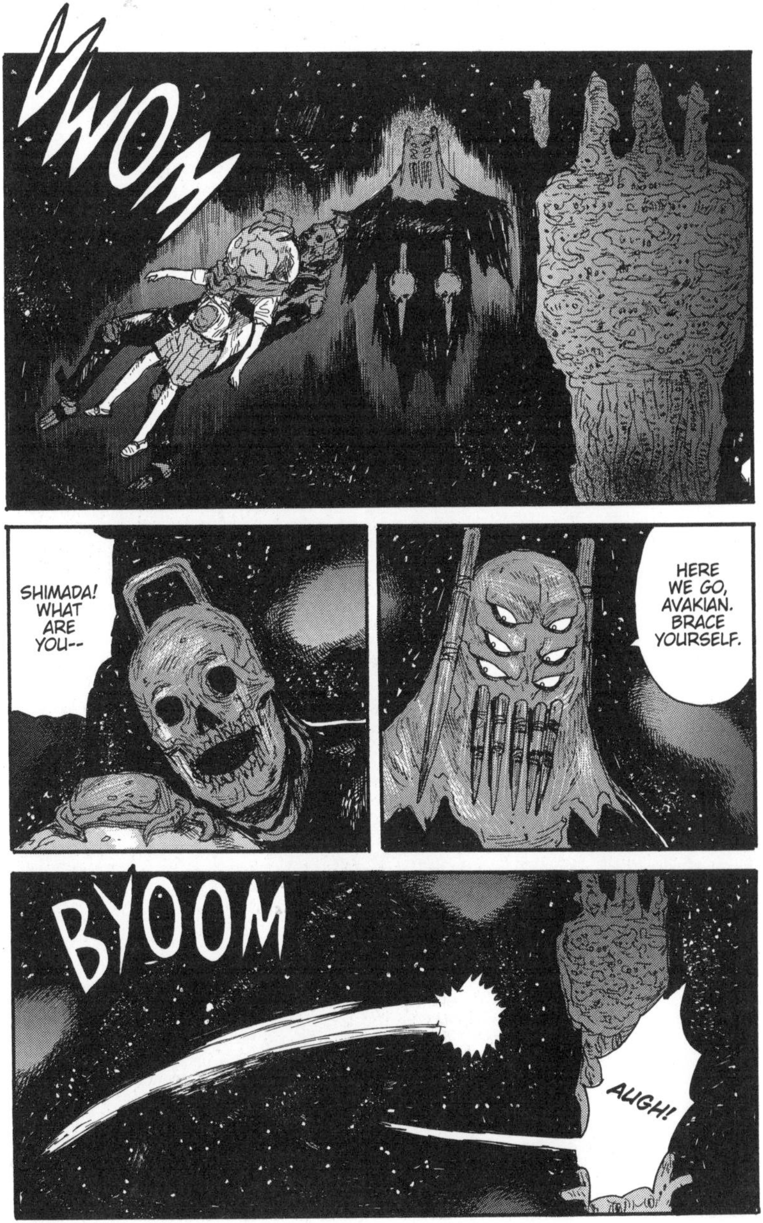
VWOM
HERE WE GO, AVAKIAN. BRACE YOURSELF.
SHIMADA! WHAT ARE YOU--
BYOOM
AUGH!

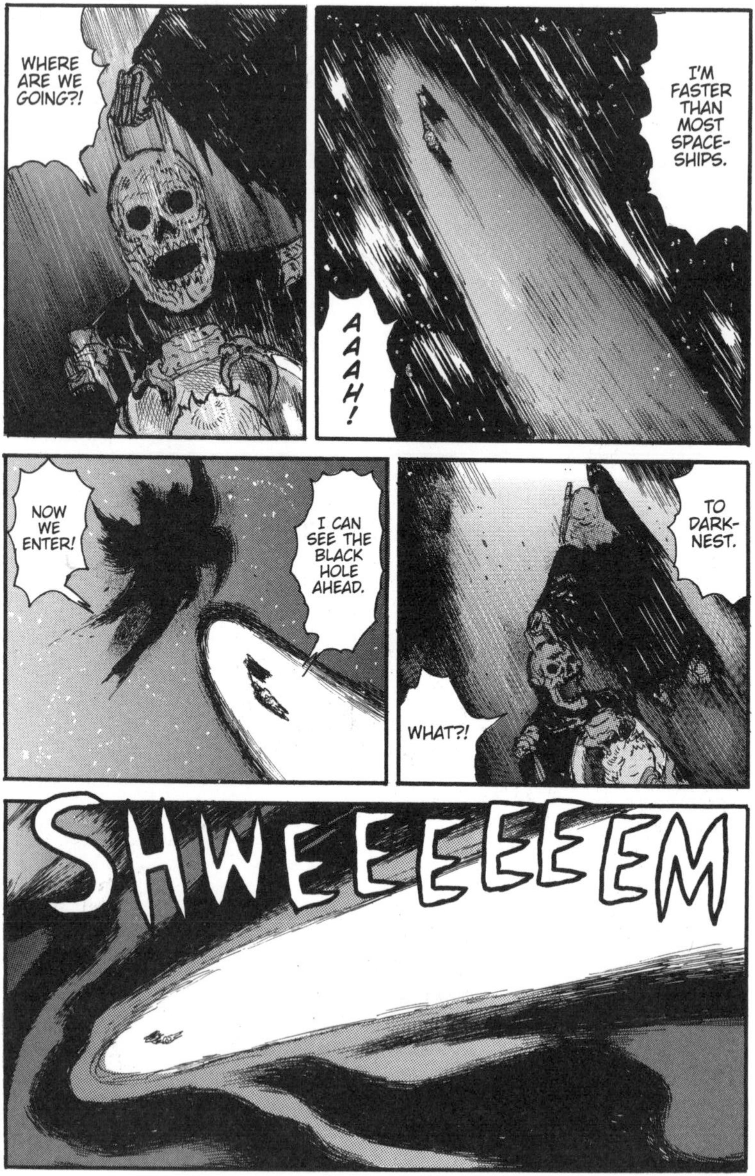
I'M FASTER THAN MOST SPACE-SHIPS.
AAAH!
WHERE ARE WE GOING?!
TO DARK-NEST.
WHAT?!
I CAN SEE THE BLACK HOLE AHEAD.
NOW WE ENTER!
SHWEEEEEEM

BRIIIP

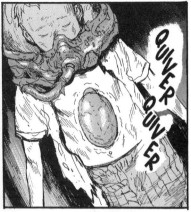

QUIVER QUIVER

ONLY CREATURES OF THE WORLD OF DARKNESS CAN WITHSTAND THIS ENVIRONMENT.

THE TICKMAN...!

GYAAAAH

GWORRRD

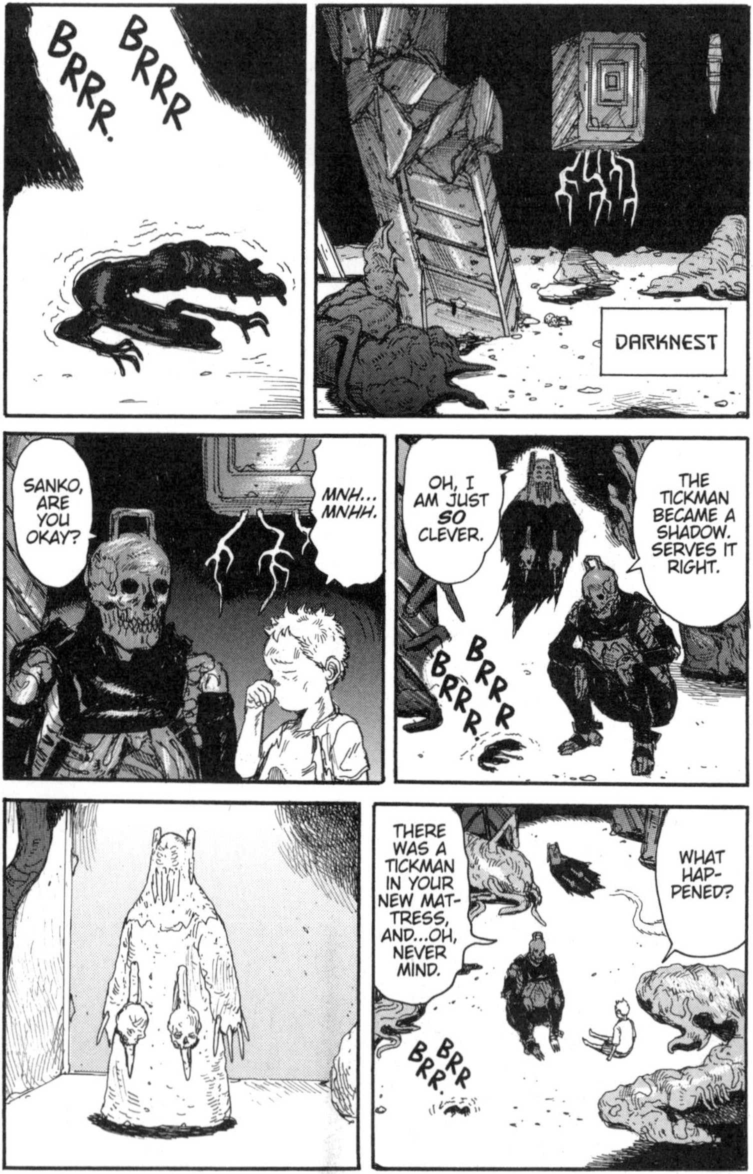
DARKNEST
BRRRR
BRRRR.
THE TICKMAN BECAME A SHADOW. SERVES IT RIGHT.
OH, I AM JUST SO CLEVER.
BRRRR
BRRRR.
MNH... MNHH.
SANKO, ARE YOU OKAY?
WHAT HAP-PENED?
THERE WAS A TICKMAN IN YOUR NEW MAT-TRESS, AND...OH, NEVER MIND.
BRR
BRR.

DAI DARK

DAI DARK

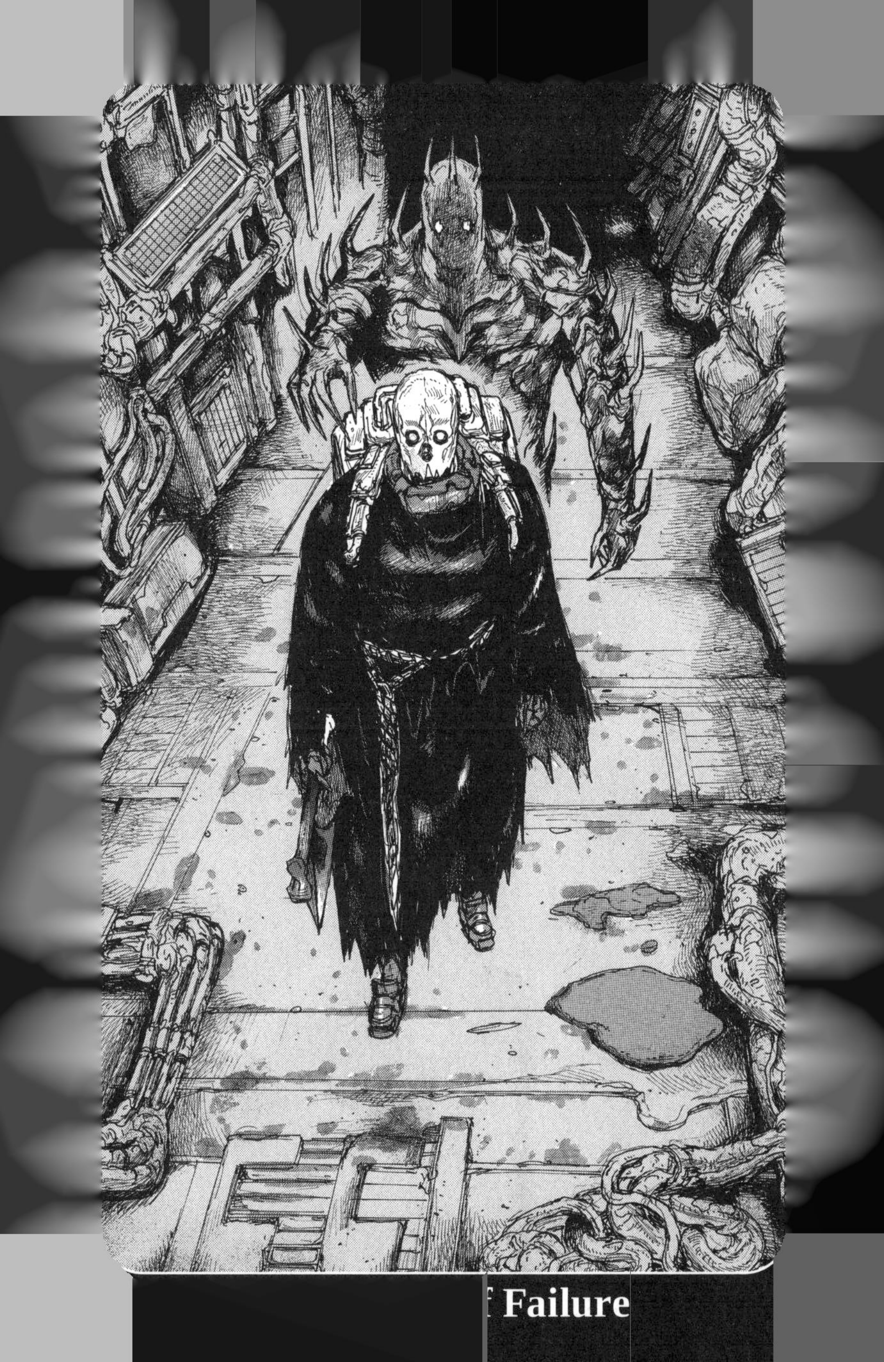

f Failure

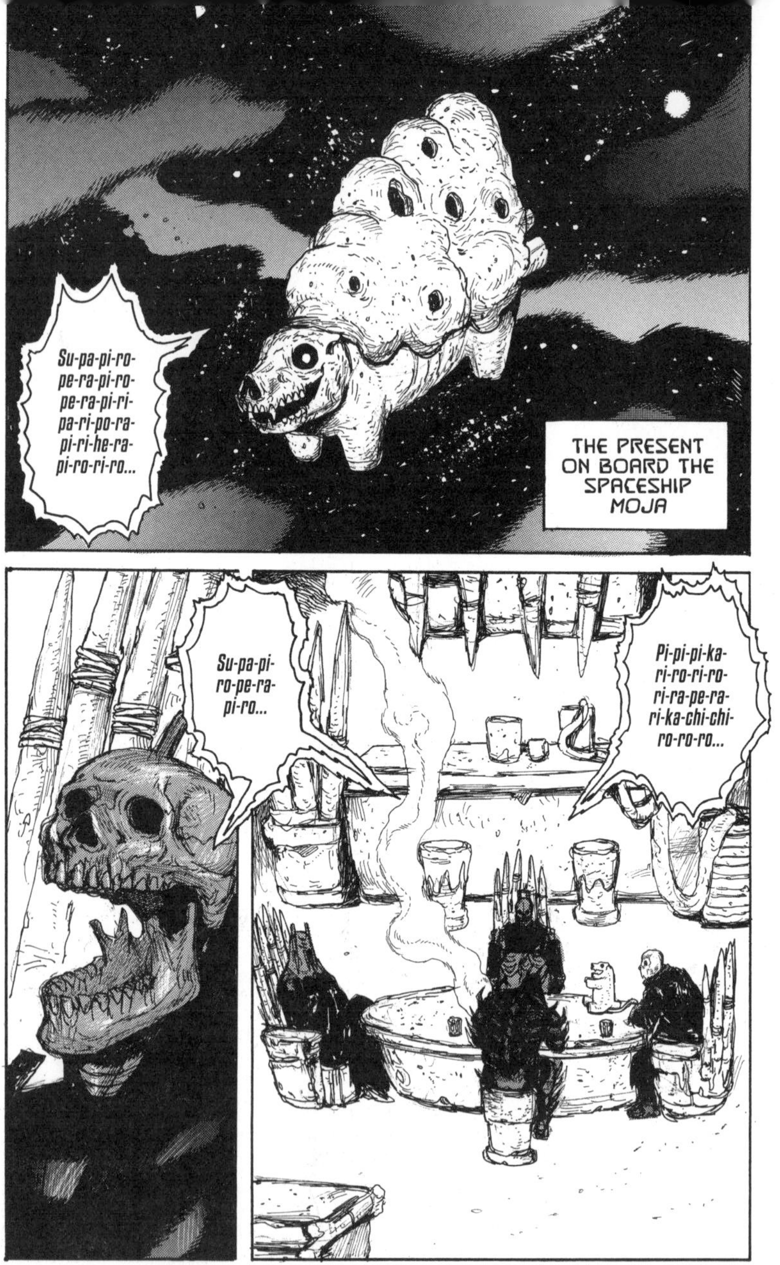
THE PRESENT ON BOARD THE SPACESHIP MOJA
Su-pa-pi-ro-pe-ra-pi-ro-pe-ra-pi-ri-pa-ri-po-ra-pi-ri-he-ra-pi-ro-ri-ro...
Pi-pi-pi-ka-ri-ro-ri-ro-ri-ra-pe-ra-ri-ka-chi-chi-ro-ro-ro...
Su-pa-pi-ro-pe-ra-pi-ro...

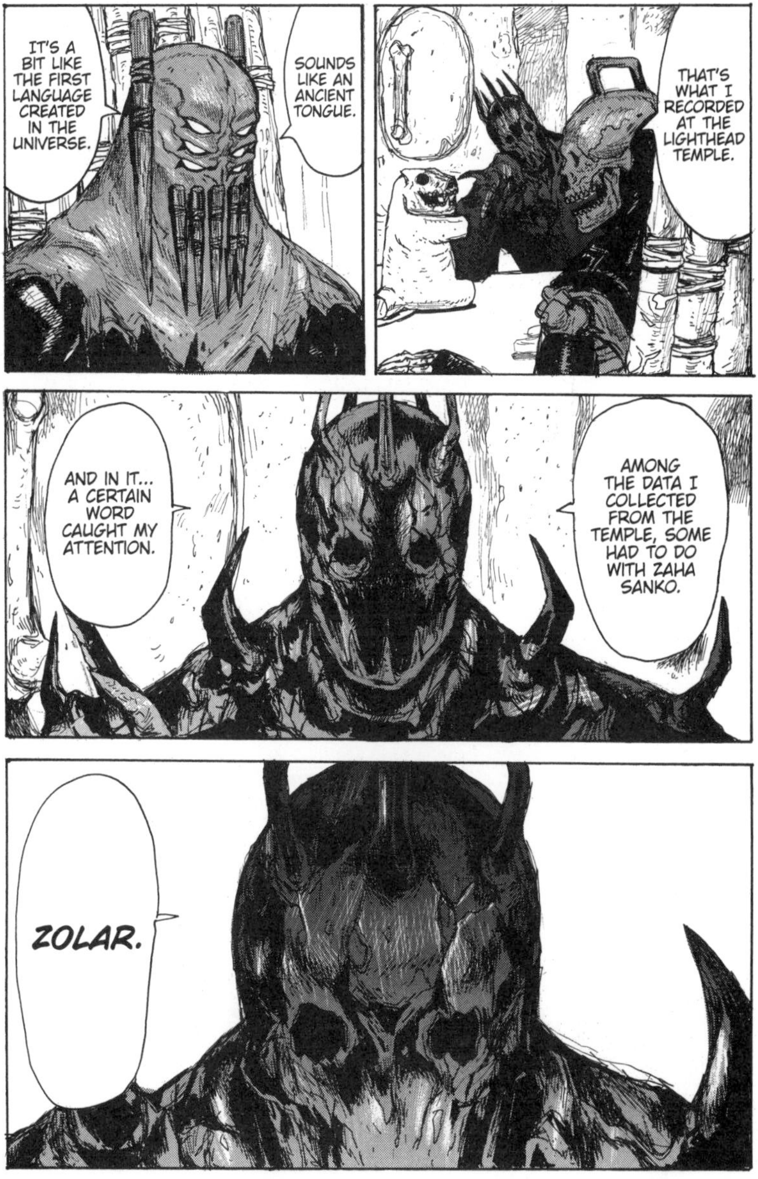
THAT'S WHAT I RECORDED AT THE LIGHTHEAD TEMPLE.
SOUNDS LIKE AN ANCIENT TONGUE.
IT'S A BIT LIKE THE FIRST LANGUAGE CREATED IN THE UNIVERSE.
AMONG THE DATA I COLLECTED FROM THE TEMPLE, SOME HAD TO DO WITH ZAHA SANKO.
AND IN IT... A CERTAIN WORD CAUGHT MY ATTENTION.
ZOLAR.

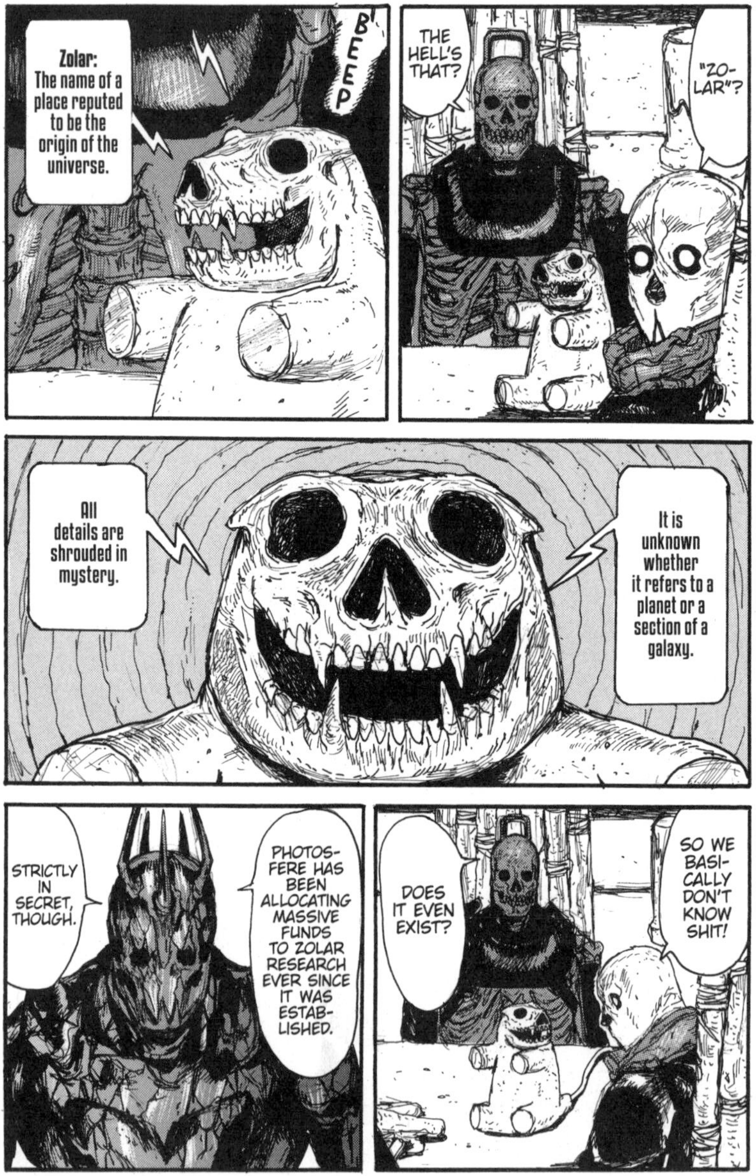
"ZO-LAR"?
THE HELL'S THAT?
BEEP
Zolar: The name of a place reputed to be the origin of the universe.
It is unknown whether it refers to a planet or a section of a galaxy.
All details are shrouded in mystery.
SO WE BASI-CALLY DON'T KNOW SHIT!
DOES IT EVEN EXIST?
PHOTOS-FERE HAS BEEN ALLOCATING MASSIVE FUNDS TO ZOLAR RESEARCH EVER SINCE IT WAS ESTAB-LISHED.
STRICTLY IN SECRET, THOUGH.

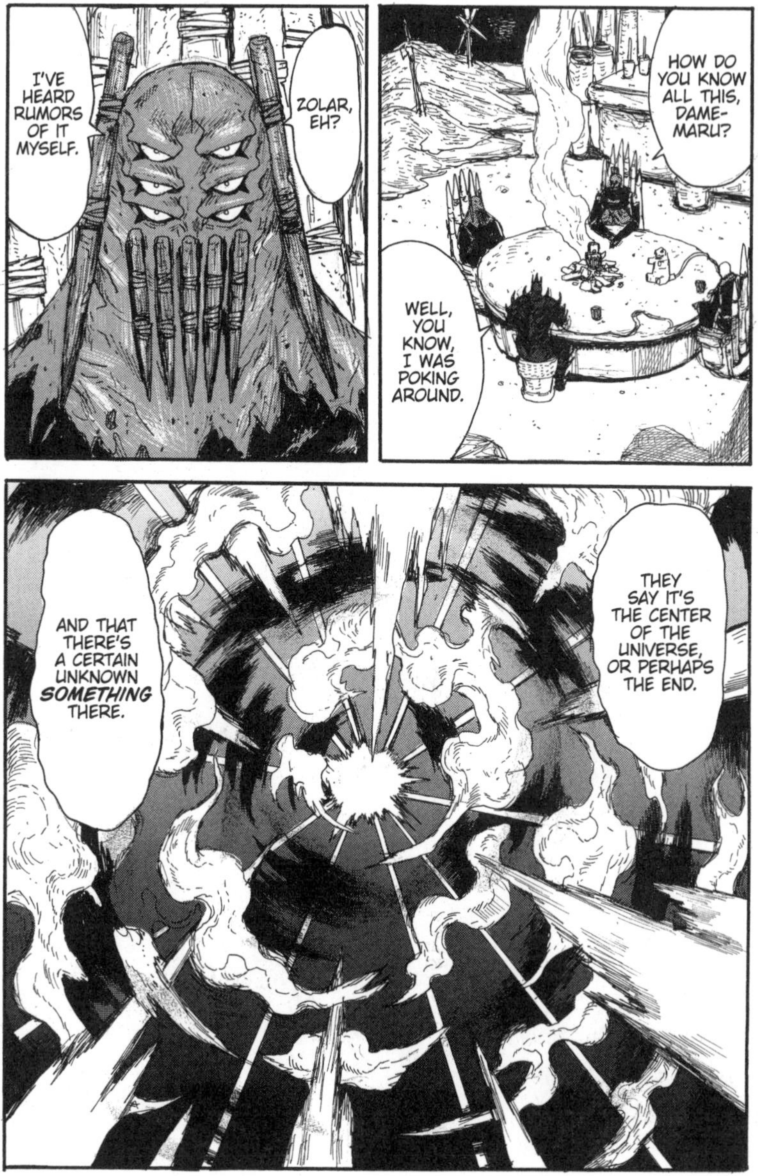
HOW DO YOU KNOW ALL THIS, DAME-MARU?
WELL, YOU KNOW, I WAS POKING AROUND.
ZOLAR, EH?
I'VE HEARD RUMORS OF IT MYSELF.
THEY SAY IT'S THE CENTER OF THE UNIVERSE, OR PERHAPS THE END.
AND THAT THERE'S A CERTAIN UNKNOWN *SOMETHING* THERE.

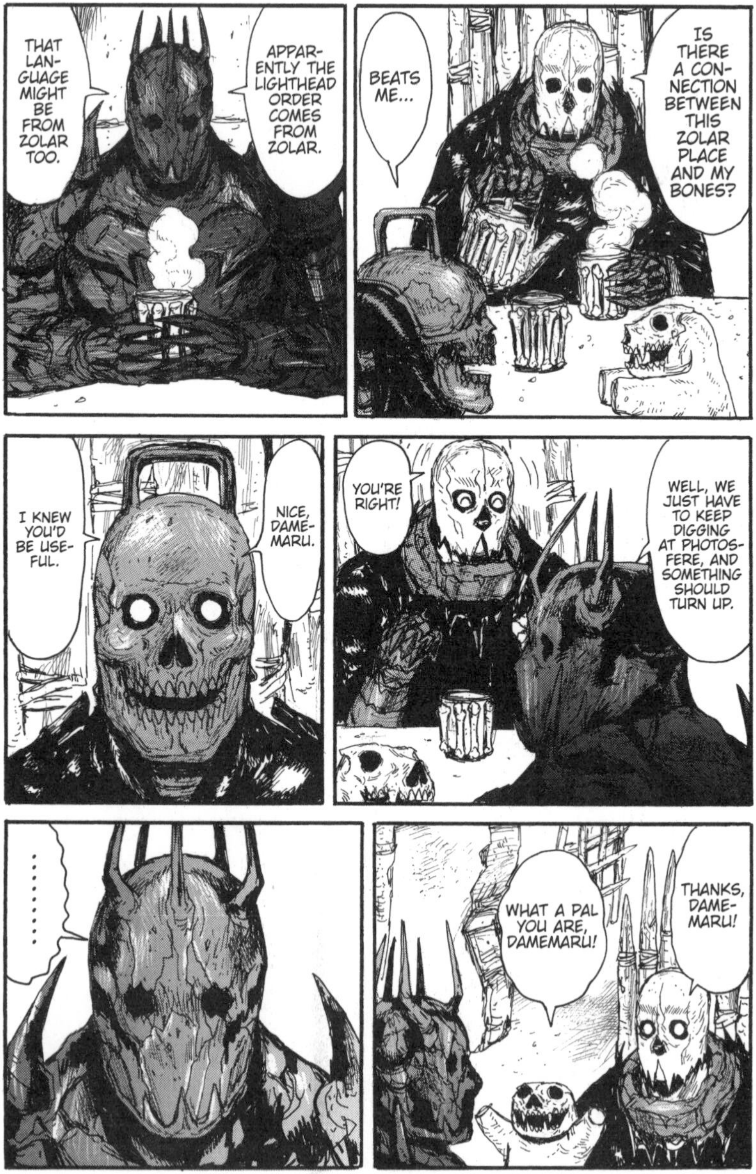
IS THERE A CONNECTION BETWEEN THIS ZOLAR PLACE AND MY BONES?
BEATS ME...
APPARENTLY THE LIGHTHEAD ORDER COMES FROM ZOLAR.
THAT LANGUAGE MIGHT BE FROM ZOLAR TOO.
WELL, WE JUST HAVE TO KEEP DIGGING AT PHOTOSFERE, AND SOMETHING SHOULD TURN UP.
YOU'RE RIGHT!
NICE, DAMEMARU.
I KNEW YOU'D BE USEFUL.
THANKS, DAMEMARU!
WHAT A PAL YOU ARE, DAMEMARU!
....

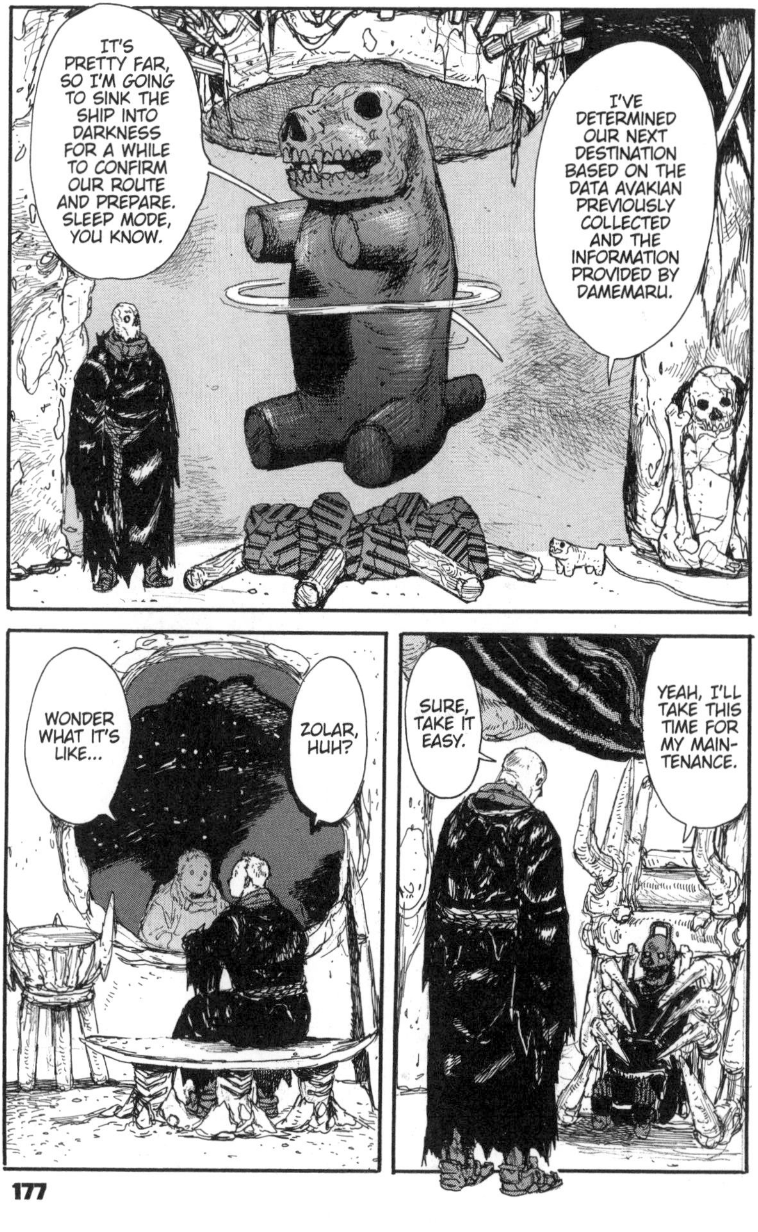
I'VE DETERMINED OUR NEXT DESTINATION BASED ON THE DATA AVAKIAN PREVIOUSLY COLLECTED AND THE INFORMATION PROVIDED BY DAMEMARU.
IT'S PRETTY FAR, SO I'M GOING TO SINK THE SHIP INTO DARKNESS FOR A WHILE TO CONFIRM OUR ROUTE AND PREPARE. SLEEP MODE, YOU KNOW.
YEAH, I'LL TAKE THIS TIME FOR MY MAIN-TENANCE.
SURE, TAKE IT EASY.
ZOLAR, HUH?
WONDER WHAT IT'S LIKE...

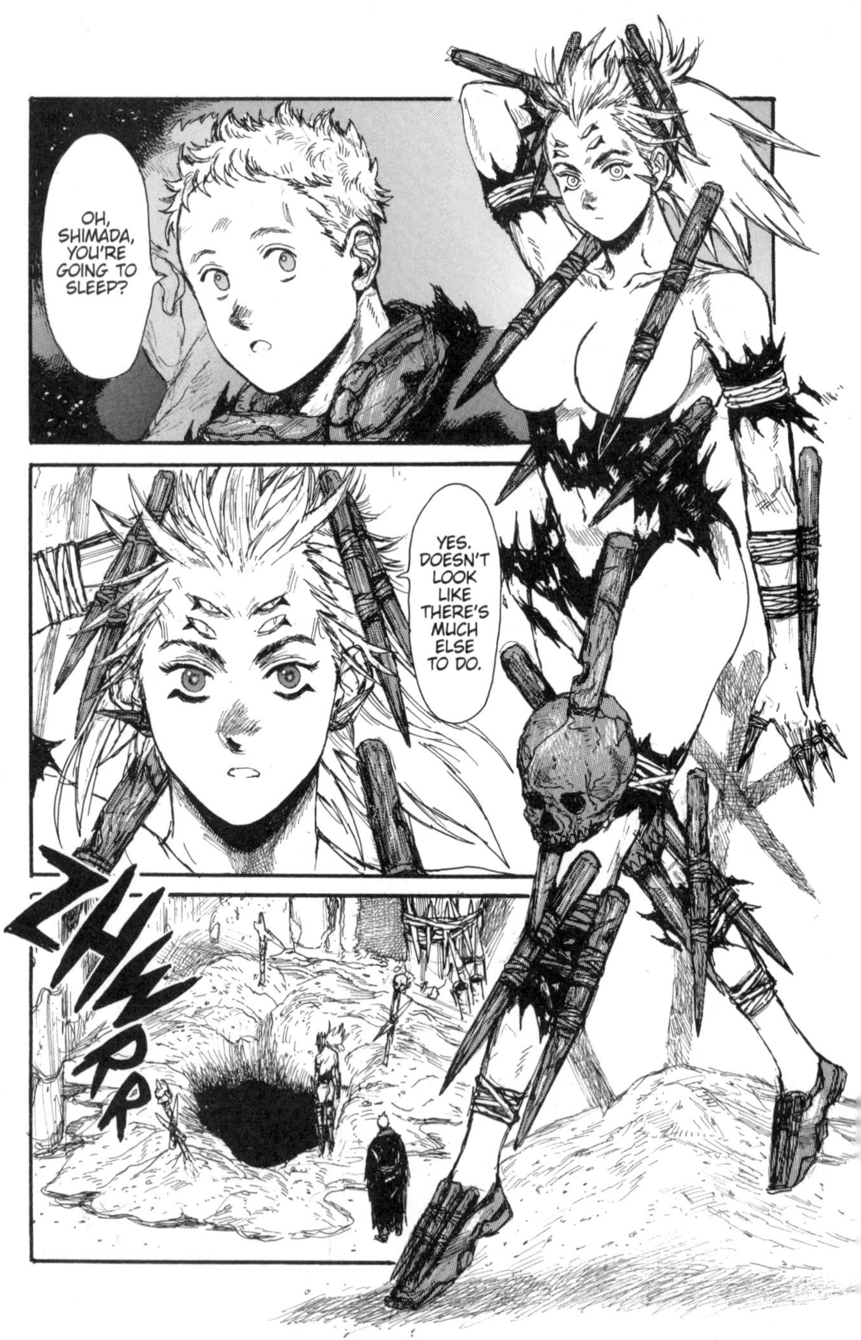
OH, SHIMADA, YOU'RE GOING TO SLEEP?
YES. DOESN'T LOOK LIKE THERE'S MUCH ELSE TO DO.
ZHWRR

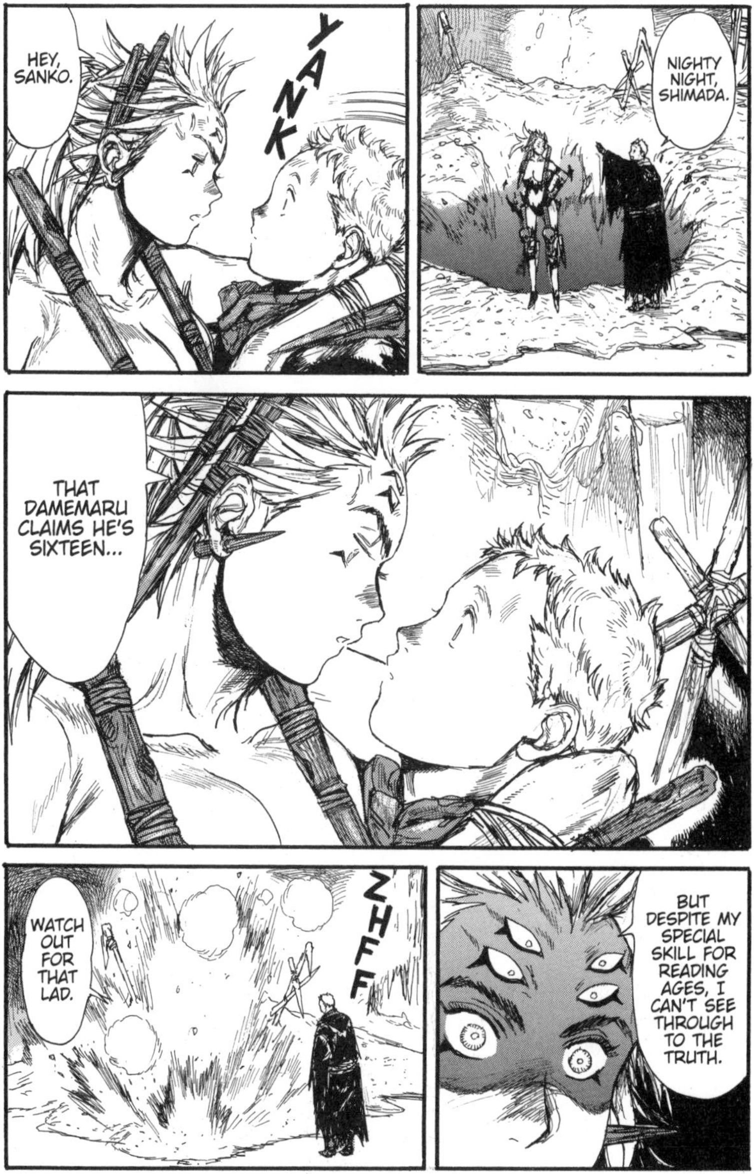
NIGHTY NIGHT, SHIMADA.
YANK
HEY, SANKO.
THAT DAMEMARU CLAIMS HE'S SIXTEEN...
BUT DESPITE MY SPECIAL SKILL FOR READING AGES, I CAN'T SEE THROUGH TO THE TRUTH.
ZHFF
WATCH OUT FOR THAT LAD.

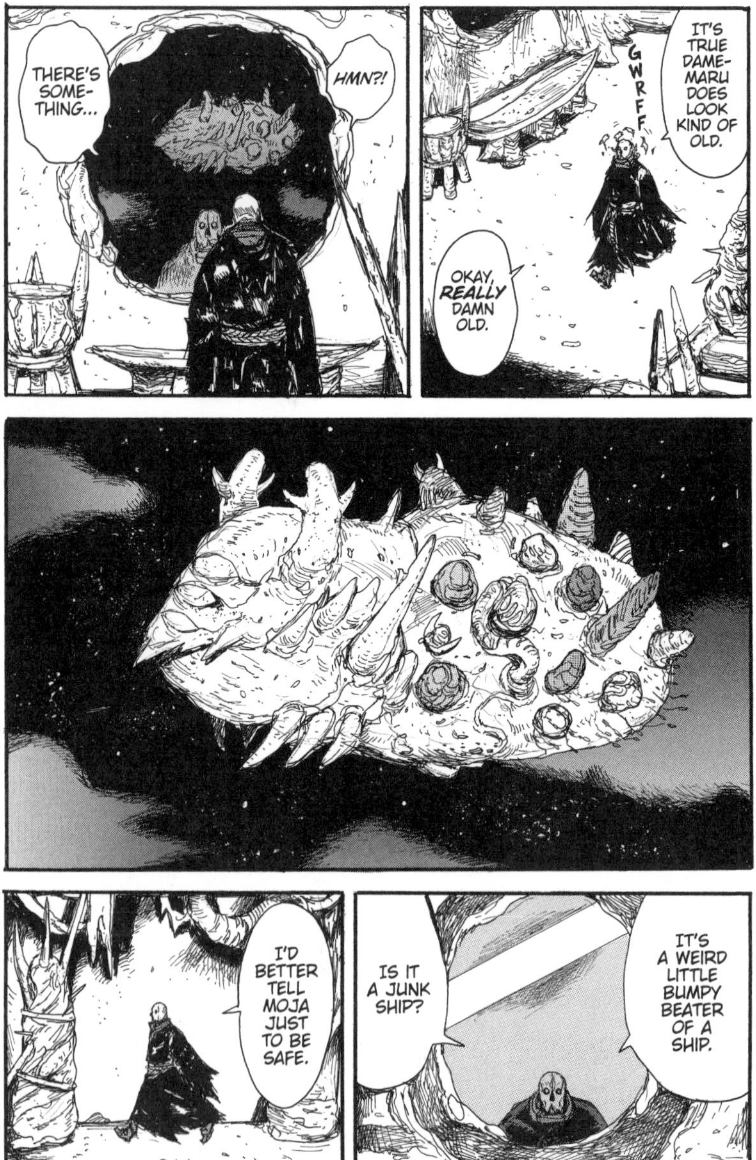
IT'S TRUE DAME-MARU DOES LOOK KIND OF OLD.
GWRFF
OKAY, *REALLY* DAMN OLD.
HMN?!
THERE'S SOME-THING...
IT'S A WEIRD LITTLE BUMPY BEATER OF A SHIP.
IS IT A JUNK SHIP?
I'D BETTER TELL MOJA JUST TO BE SAFE.

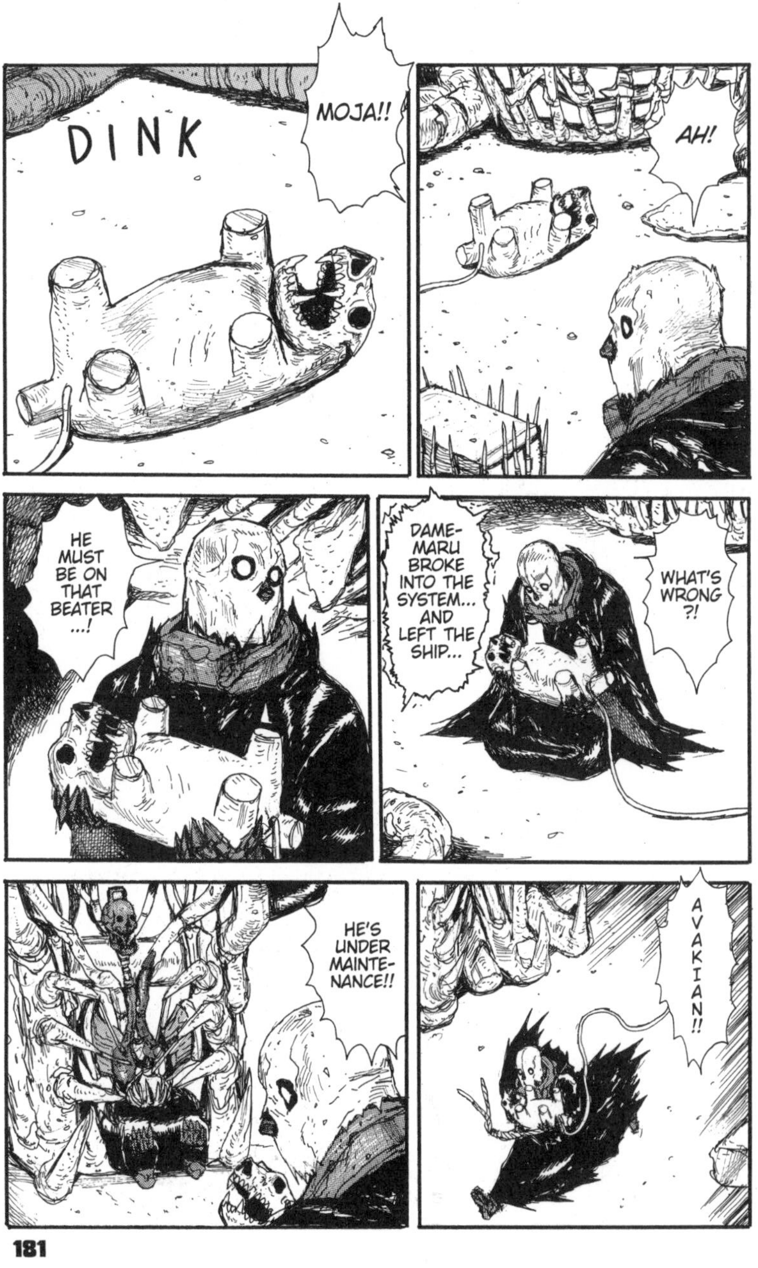
AH!
MOJA!!
DINK
WHAT'S WRONG ?!
DAME-MARU BROKE INTO THE SYSTEM... AND LEFT THE SHIP...
HE MUST BE ON THAT BEATER ...!
AVAKIAN!!
HE'S UNDER MAINTENANCE!!

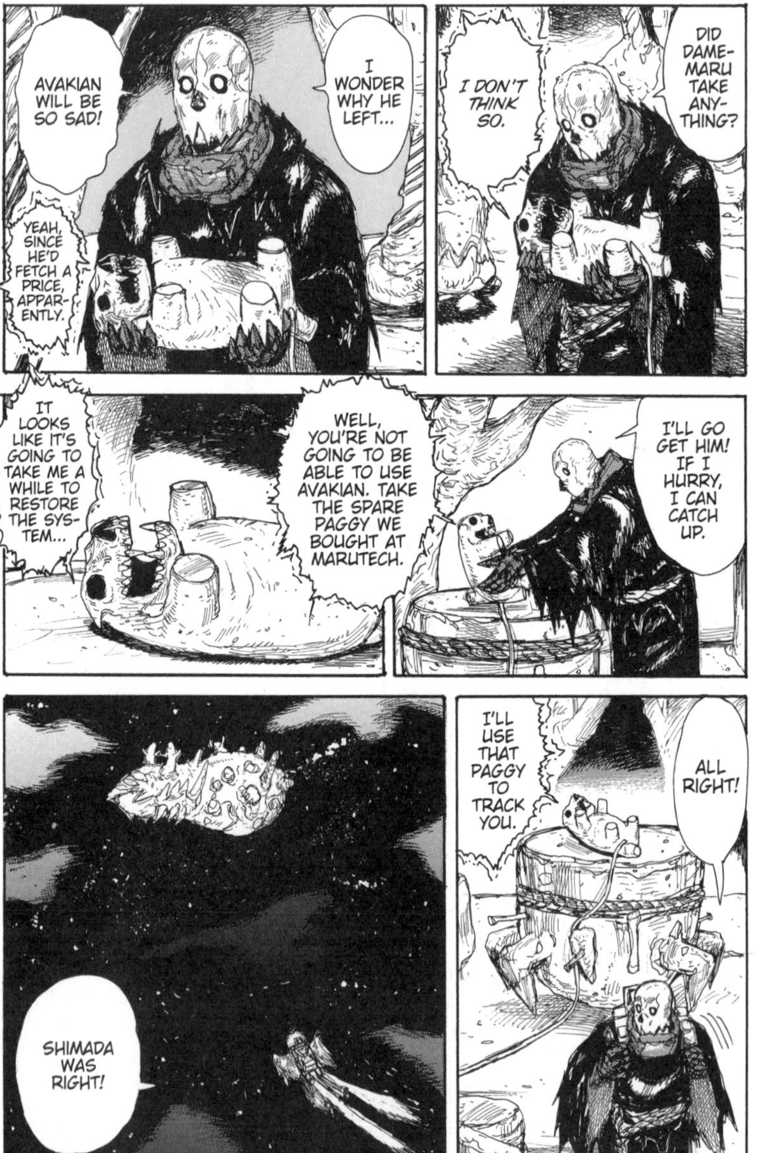
DID DAME-MARU TAKE ANY-THING?
I DON'T THINK SO.
I WONDER WHY HE LEFT...
AVAKIAN WILL BE SO SAD!
YEAH, SINCE HE'D FETCH A PRICE, APPARENTLY.
I'LL GO GET HIM! IF I HURRY, I CAN CATCH UP.
WELL, YOU'RE NOT GOING TO BE ABLE TO USE AVAKIAN. TAKE THE SPARE PAGGY WE BOUGHT AT MARUTECH.
IT LOOKS LIKE IT'S GOING TO TAKE ME A WHILE TO RESTORE THE SYS-TEM...
ALL RIGHT!
I'LL USE THAT PAGGY TO TRACK YOU.
SHIMADA WAS RIGHT!

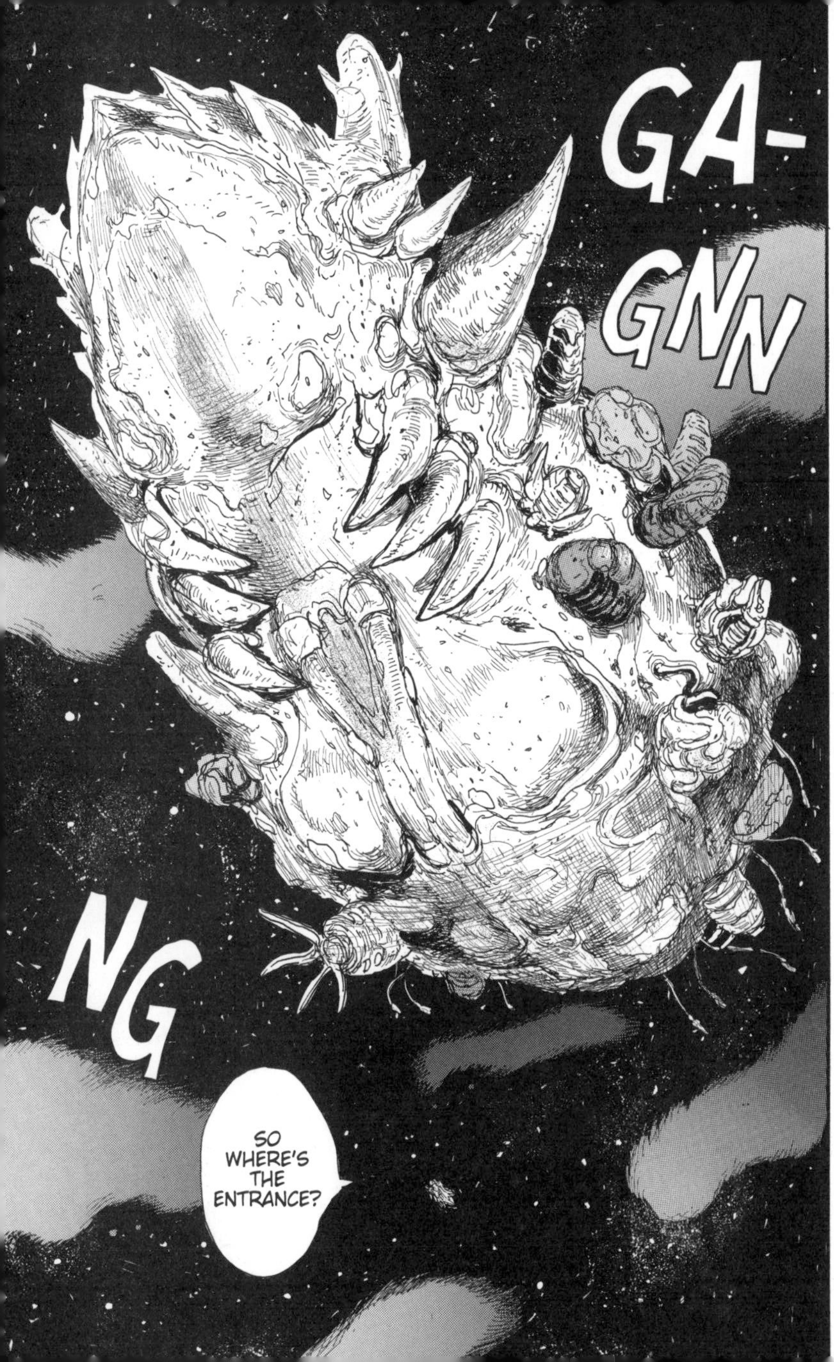
GA-
GNN
NG
SO WHERE'S THE ENTRANCE?

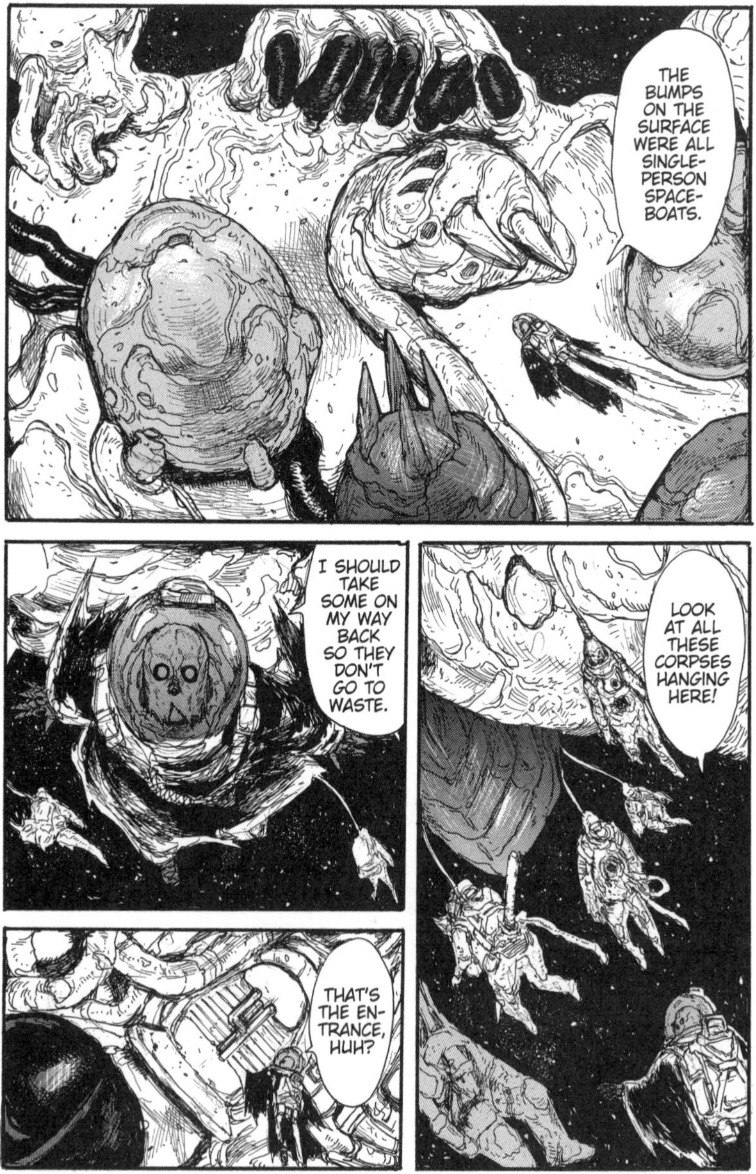
THE BUMPS ON THE SURFACE WERE ALL SINGLE-PERSON SPACE-BOATS.
LOOK AT ALL THESE CORPSES HANGING HERE!
I SHOULD TAKE SOME ON MY WAY BACK SO THEY DON'T GO TO WASTE.
THAT'S THE EN-TRANCE, HUH?

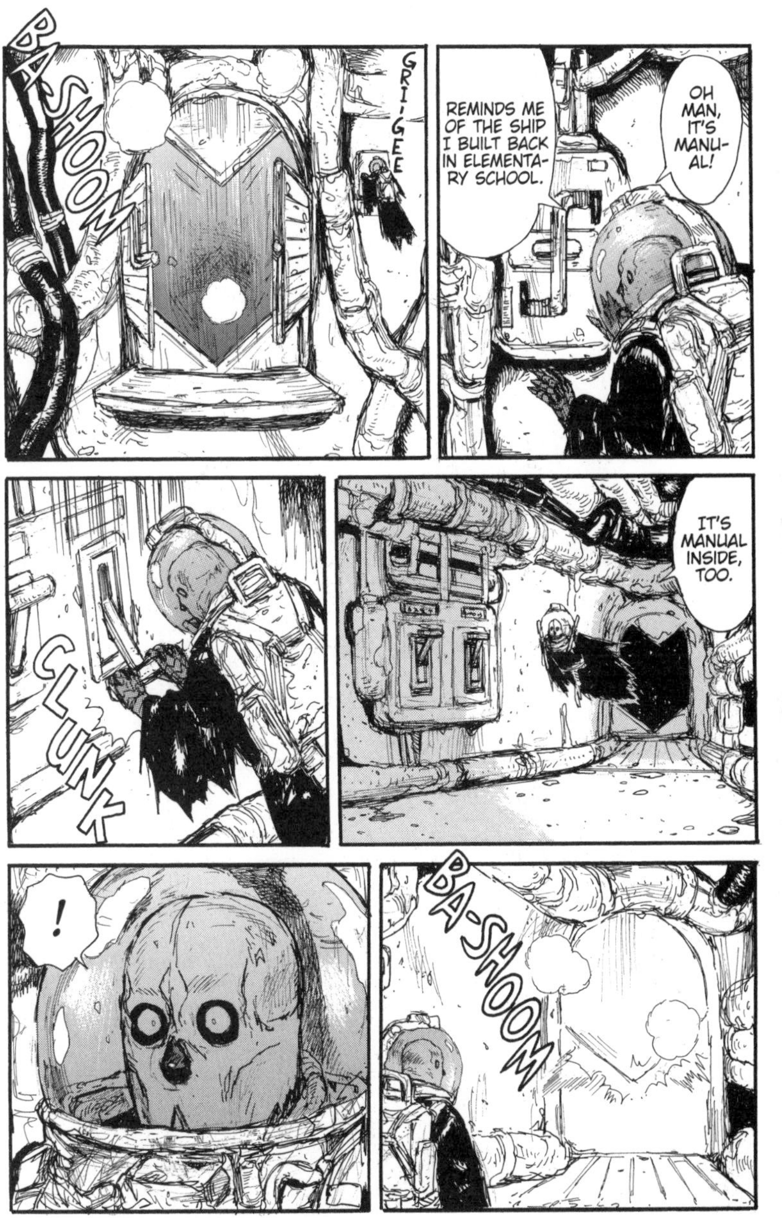
OH MAN, IT'S MANUAL!
REMINDS ME OF THE SHIP I BUILT BACK IN ELEMENTARY SCHOOL.
GRI-GEE
BA-SHOOM
IT'S MANUAL INSIDE, TOO.
CLUNK
BA-SHOOM
!

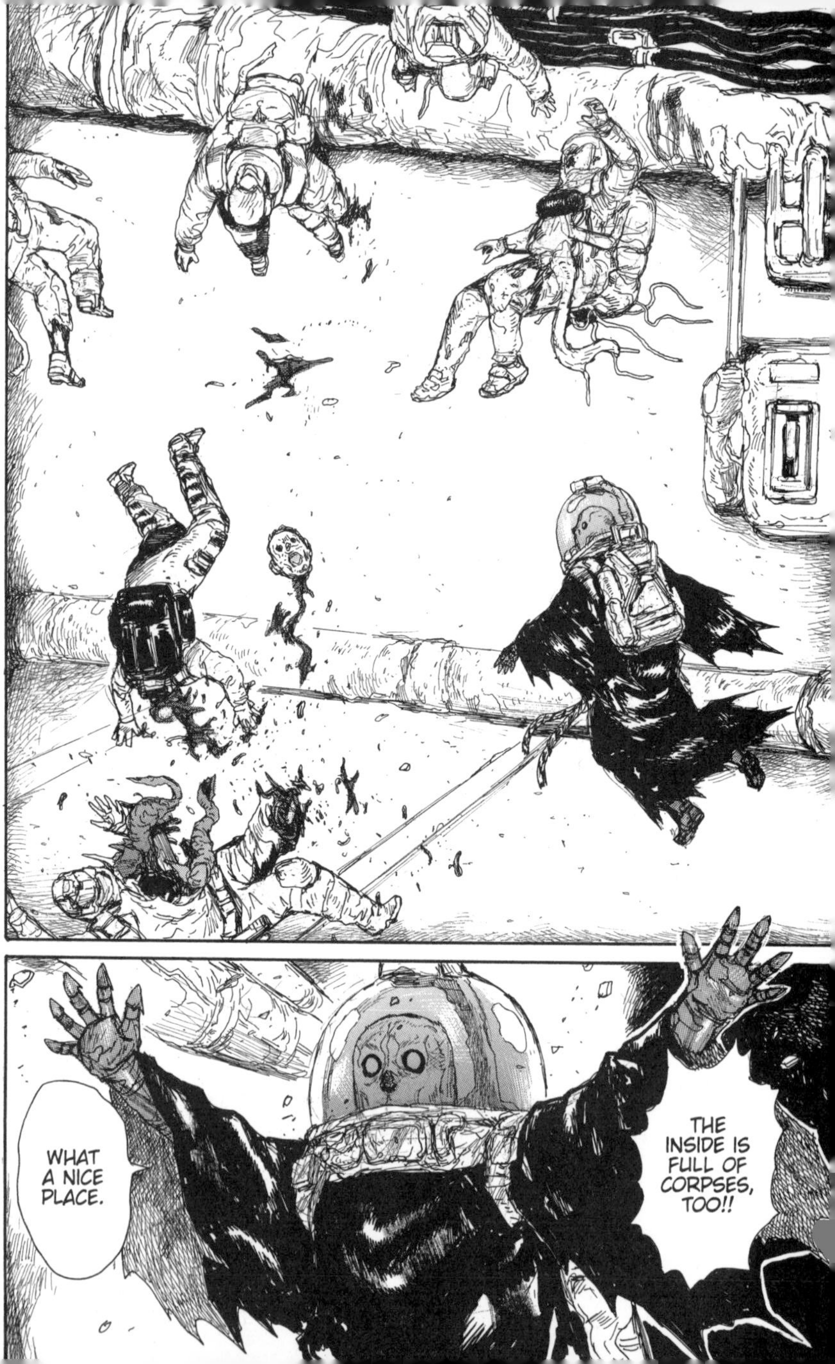
THE INSIDE IS FULL OF CORPSES, TOO!!
WHAT A NICE PLACE.

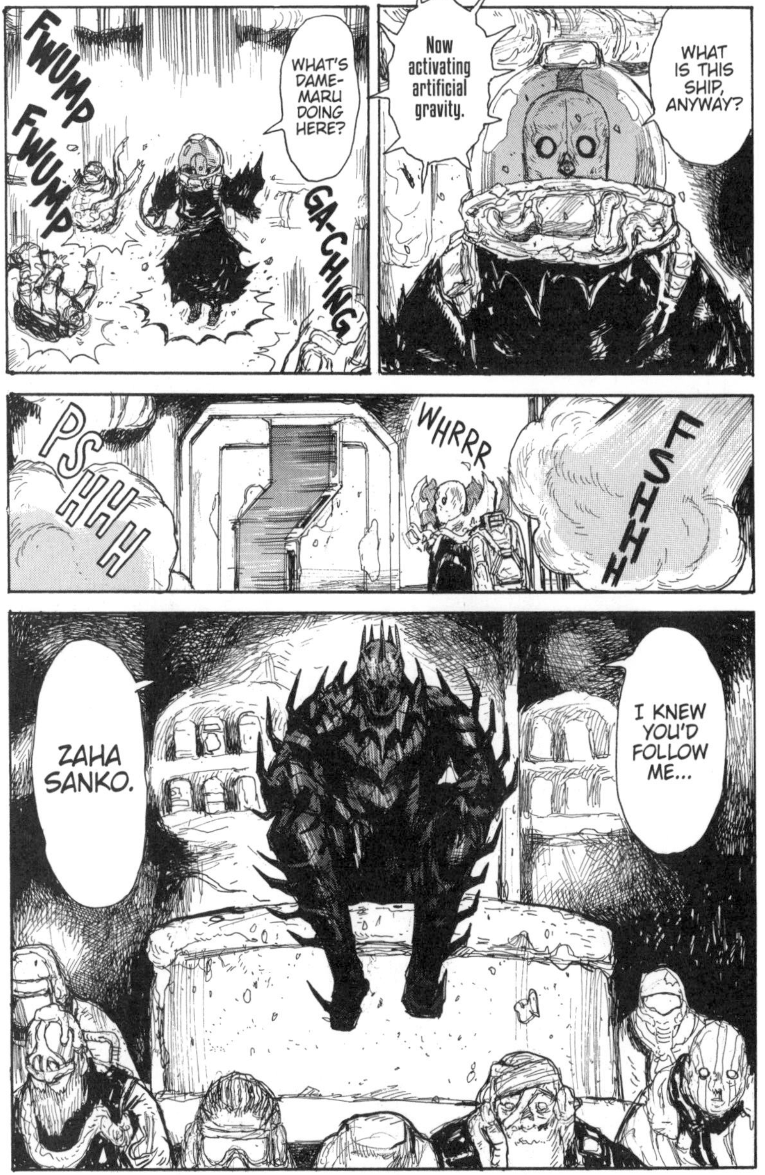
WHAT IS THIS SHIP, ANYWAY?
Now activating artificial gravity.
WHAT'S DAME-MARU DOING HERE?
FWUMP FWUMP
GA-CHING
FSHHHH
WHRRR
PSHHHH
I KNEW YOU'D FOLLOW ME...
ZAHA SANKO.

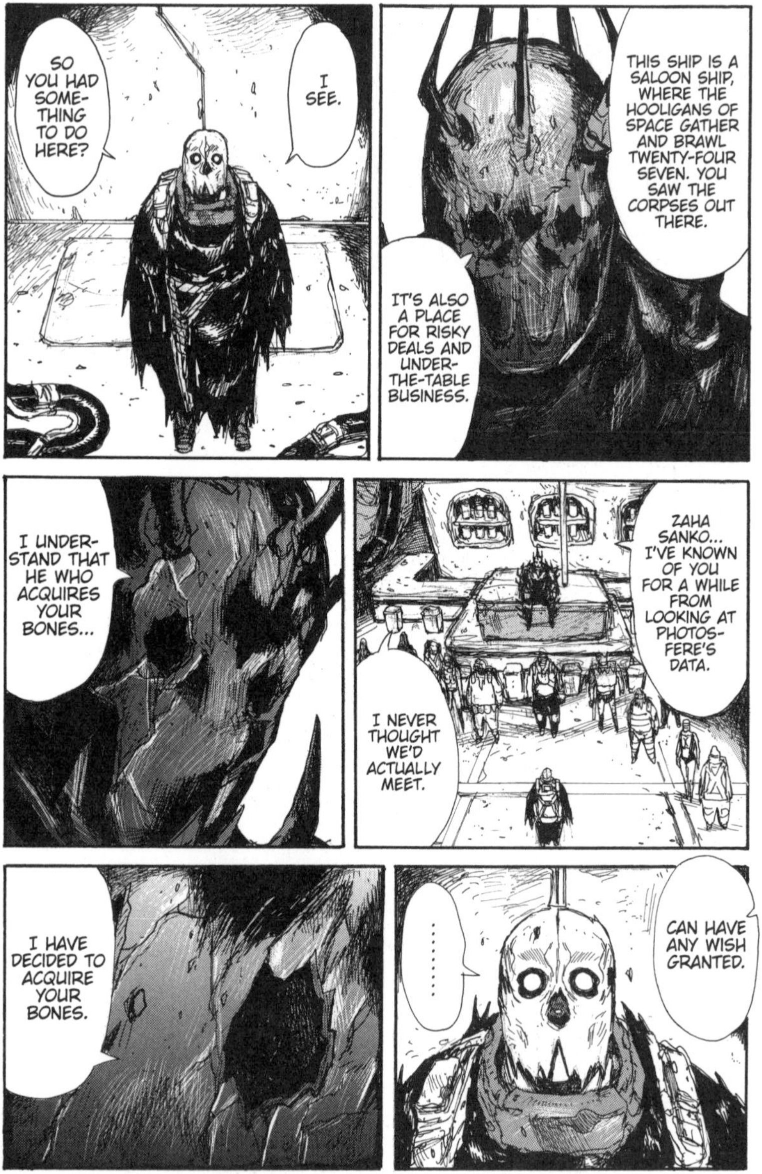
THIS SHIP IS A SALOON SHIP, WHERE THE HOOLIGANS OF SPACE GATHER AND BRAWL TWENTY-FOUR SEVEN. YOU SAW THE CORPSES OUT THERE.
IT'S ALSO A PLACE FOR RISKY DEALS AND UNDER-THE-TABLE BUSINESS.
I SEE.
SO YOU HAD SOME-THING TO DO HERE?
ZAHA SANKO... I'VE KNOWN OF YOU FOR A WHILE FROM LOOKING AT PHOTOS-FERE'S DATA.
I NEVER THOUGHT WE'D ACTUALLY MEET.
I UNDER-STAND THAT HE WHO ACQUIRES YOUR BONES...
CAN HAVE ANY WISH GRANTED.
....
I HAVE DECIDED TO ACQUIRE YOUR BONES.

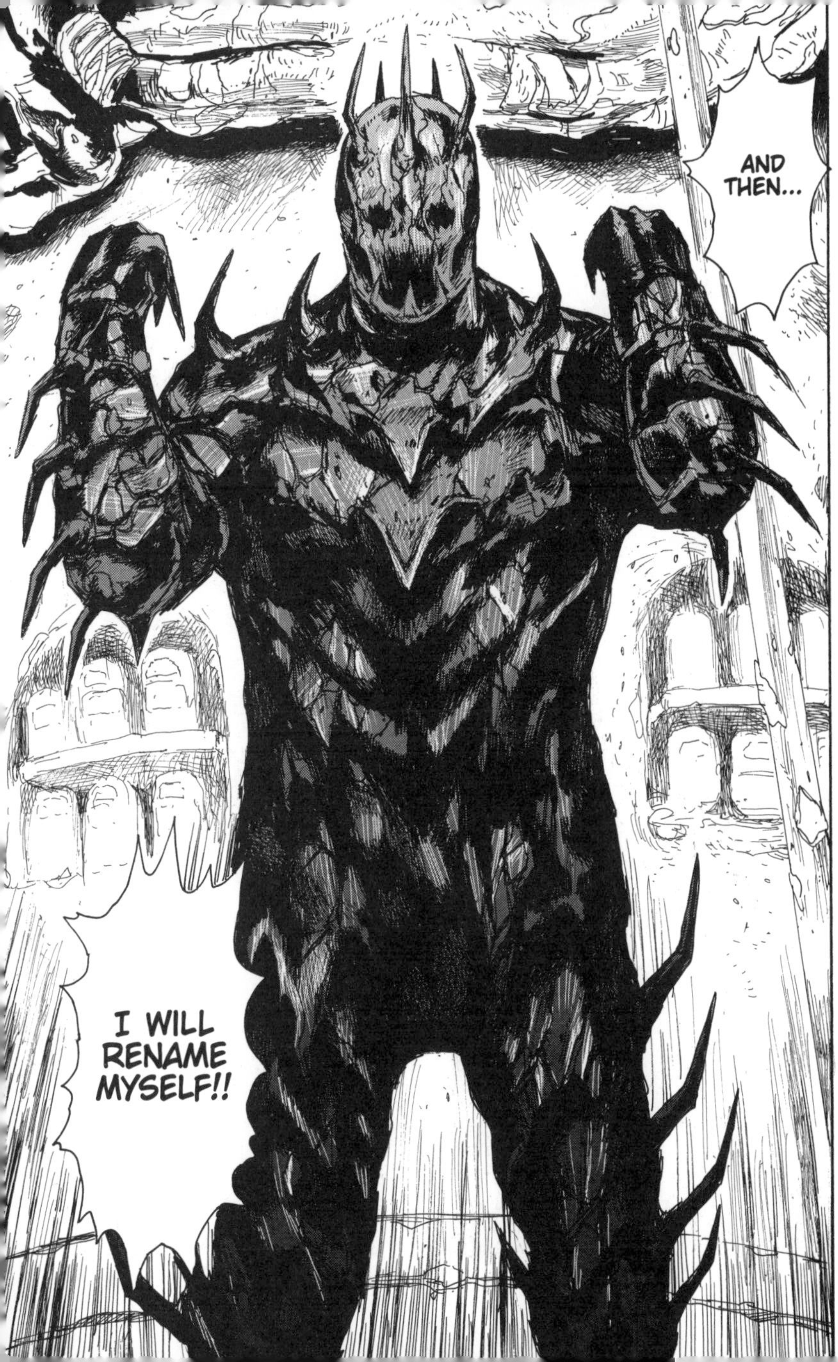
AND THEN...
I WILL RENAME MYSELF!!

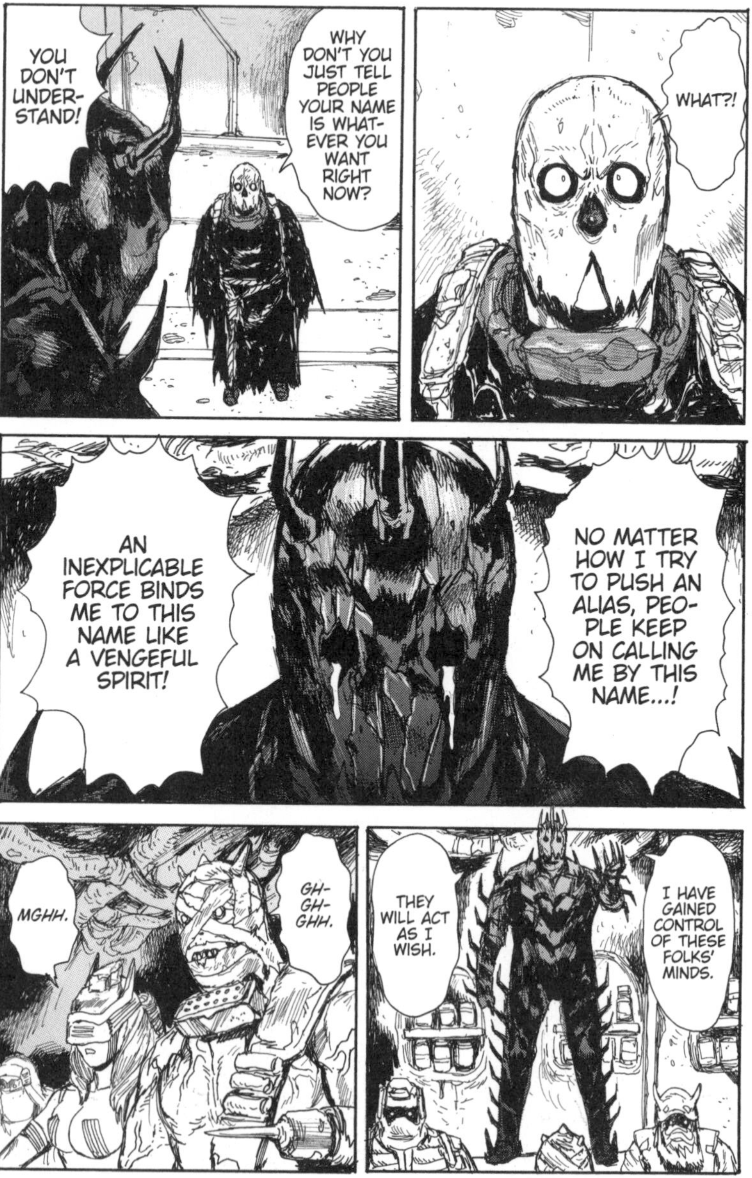
WHAT?!
WHY DON'T YOU JUST TELL PEOPLE YOUR NAME IS WHATEVER YOU WANT RIGHT NOW?
YOU DON'T UNDERSTAND!
NO MATTER HOW I TRY TO PUSH AN ALIAS, PEOPLE KEEP ON CALLING ME BY THIS NAME...!
AN INEXPLICABLE FORCE BINDS ME TO THIS NAME LIKE A VENGEFUL SPIRIT!
I HAVE GAINED CONTROL OF THESE FOLKS' MINDS.
THEY WILL ACT AS I WISH.
GH-GH-GHH.
MGHH.

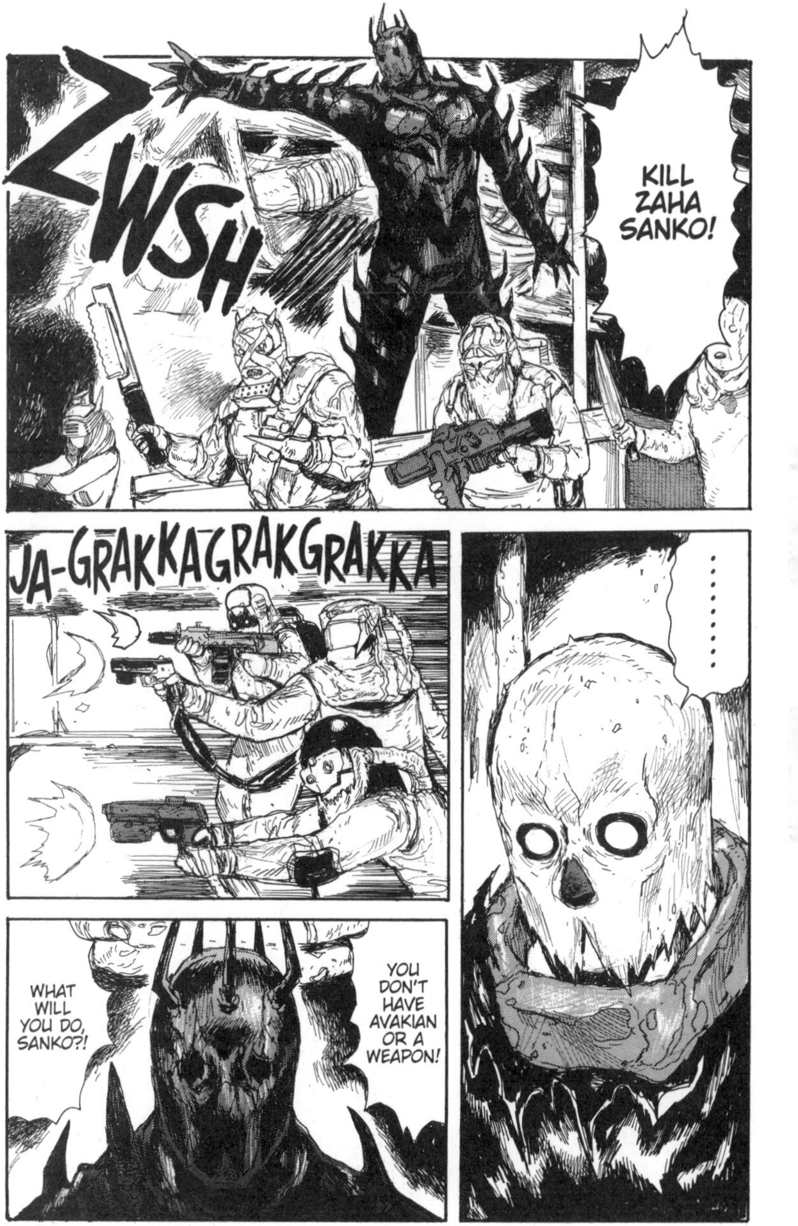
KILL ZAHA SANKO!
ZWSH
......
JA-GRAKKAGRAKGRAKKA
YOU DON'T HAVE AVAKIAN OR A WEAPON!
WHAT WILL YOU DO, SANKO?!

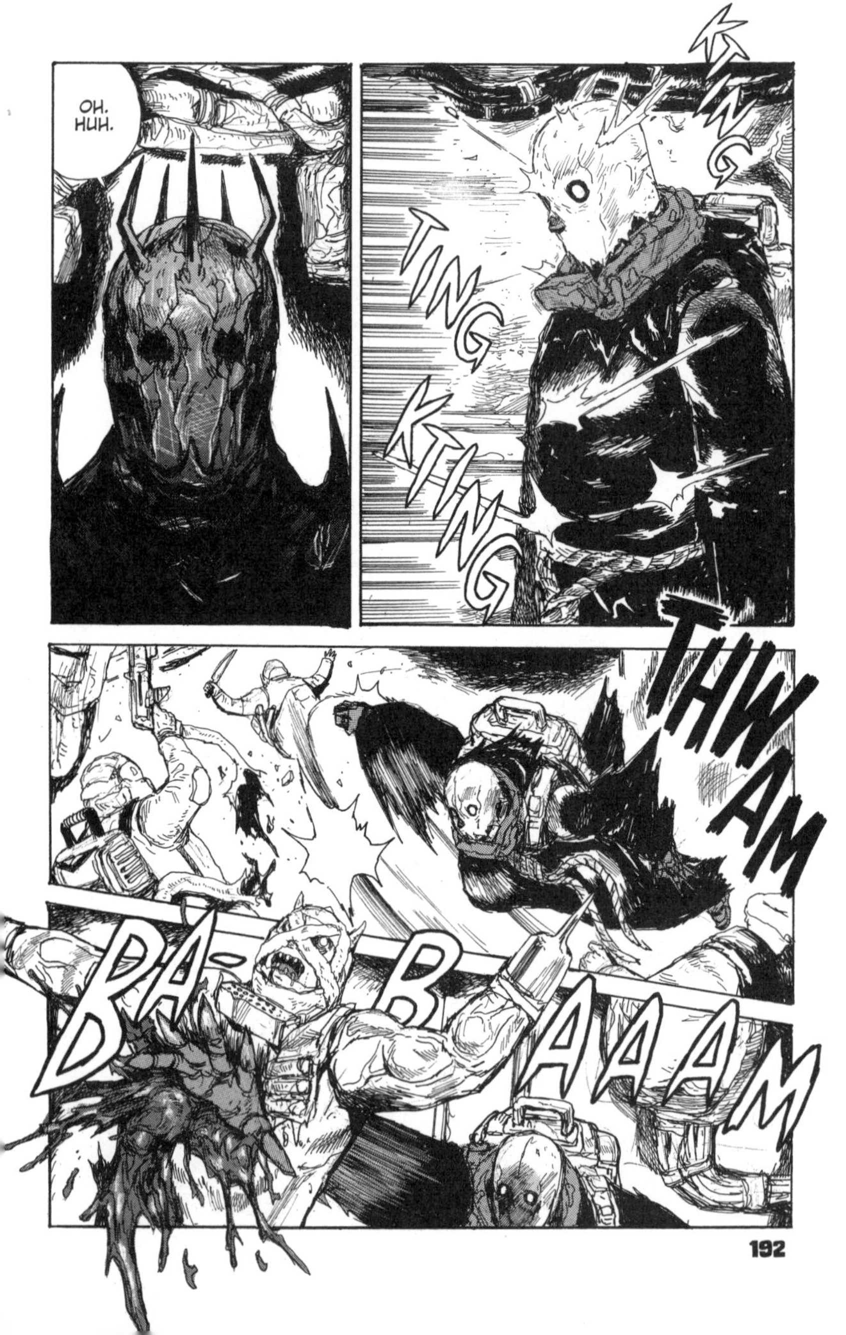

KTING
TING
KTING
OH. HUH.
THWAM
BA-BAAAAM

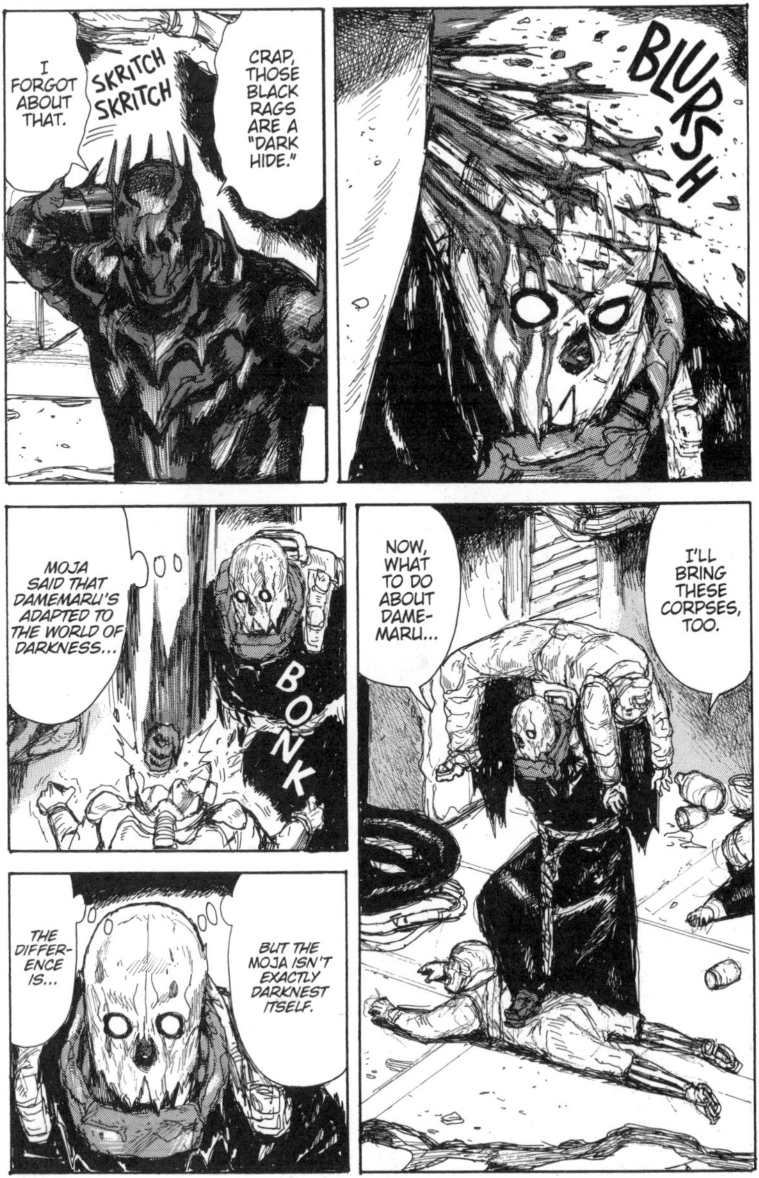
BLURSH
CRAP, THOSE BLACK RAGS ARE A "DARK HIDE."
SKRITCH SKRITCH
I FORGOT ABOUT THAT.
I'LL BRING THESE CORPSES, TOO.
NOW, WHAT TO DO ABOUT DAME-MARU...
MOJA SAID THAT DAMEMARU'S ADAPTED TO THE WORLD OF DARKNESS...
BONK
BUT THE MOJA ISN'T EXACTLY DARKNEST ITSELF.
THE DIFFER-ENCE IS...

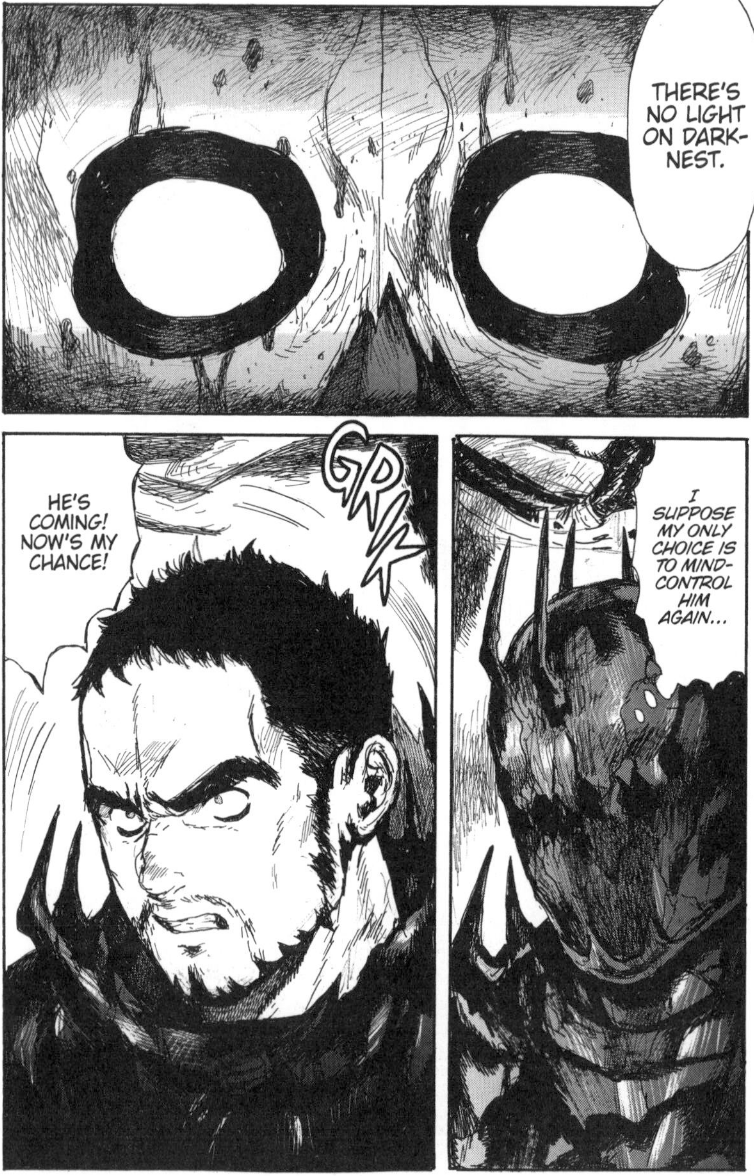
THERE'S NO LIGHT ON DARK-NEST.
I SUPPOSE MY ONLY CHOICE IS TO MIND-CONTROL HIM AGAIN...
GRIK
HE'S COMING! NOW'S MY CHANCE!

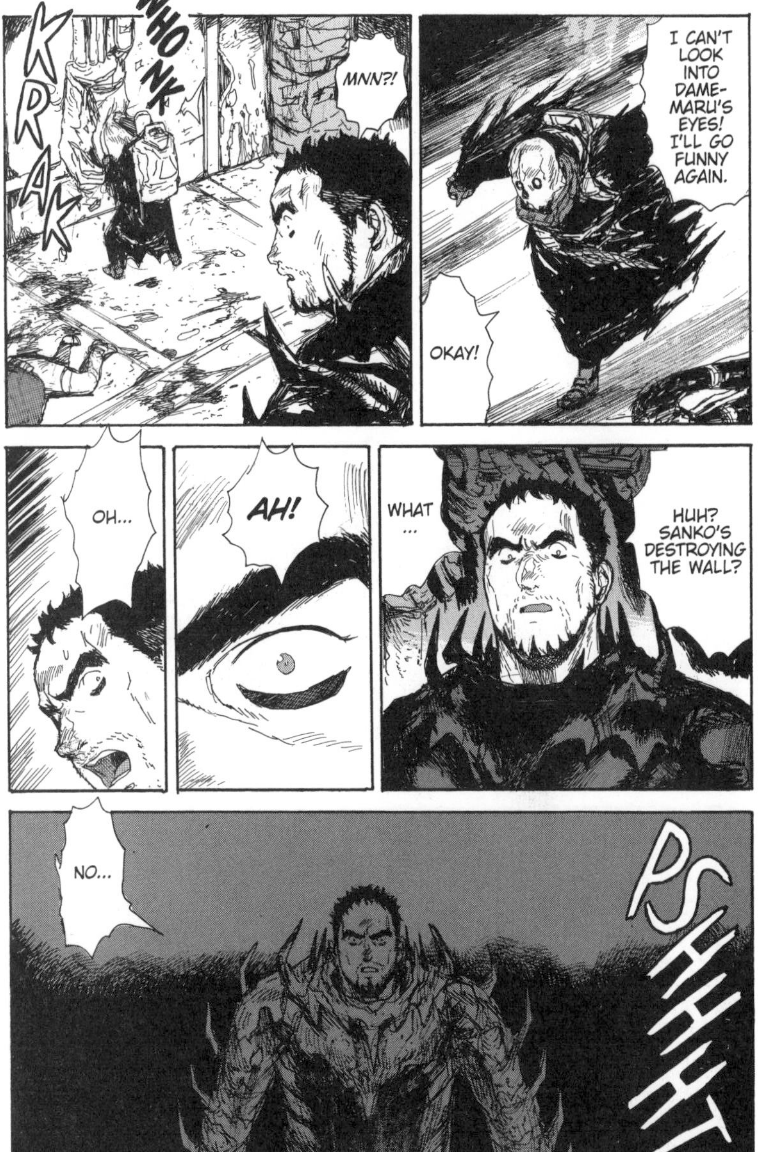
I CAN'T LOOK INTO DAME-MARU'S EYES! I'LL GO FUNNY AGAIN.
OKAY!
MNN?!
WHONK
KRAK
HUH? SANKO'S DESTROYING THE WALL?
WHAT ...
AH!
OH...
PSHHHT
NO...

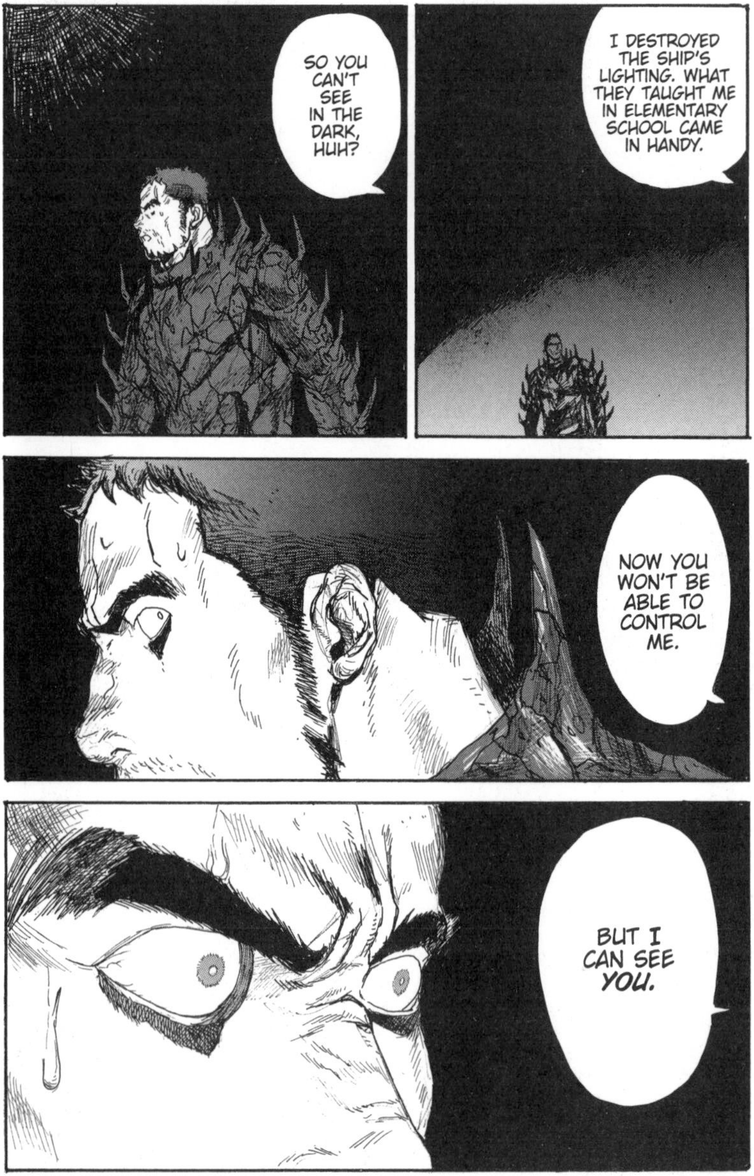
I DESTROYED THE SHIP'S LIGHTING. WHAT THEY TAUGHT ME IN ELEMENTARY SCHOOL CAME IN HANDY.
SO YOU CAN'T SEE IN THE DARK, HUH?
NOW YOU WON'T BE ABLE TO CONTROL ME.
BUT I CAN SEE *YOU.*

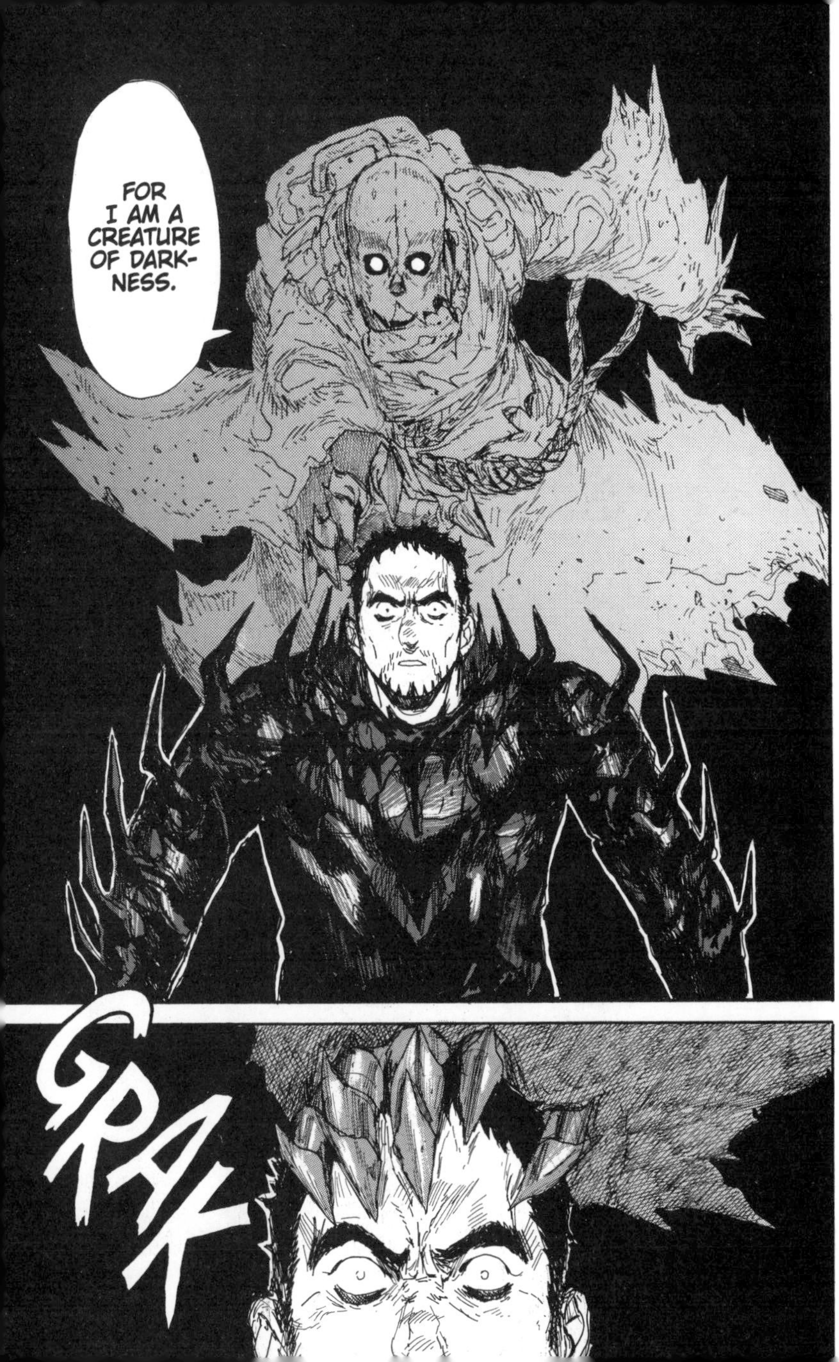
FOR I AM A CREATURE OF DARK-NESS.
GRAK

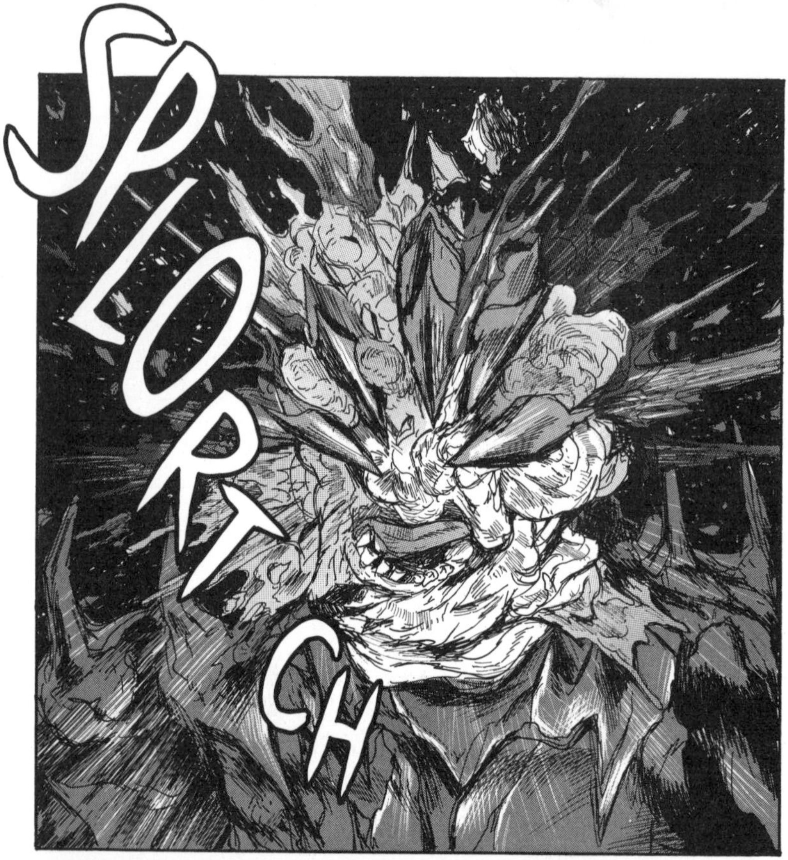
SPLORTCH

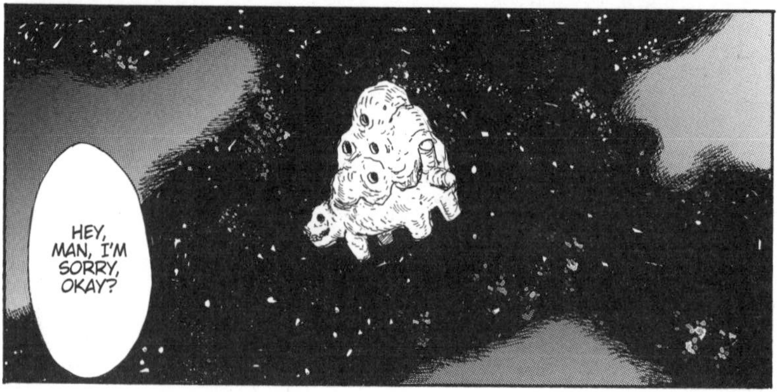
HEY, MAN, I'M SORRY, OKAY?

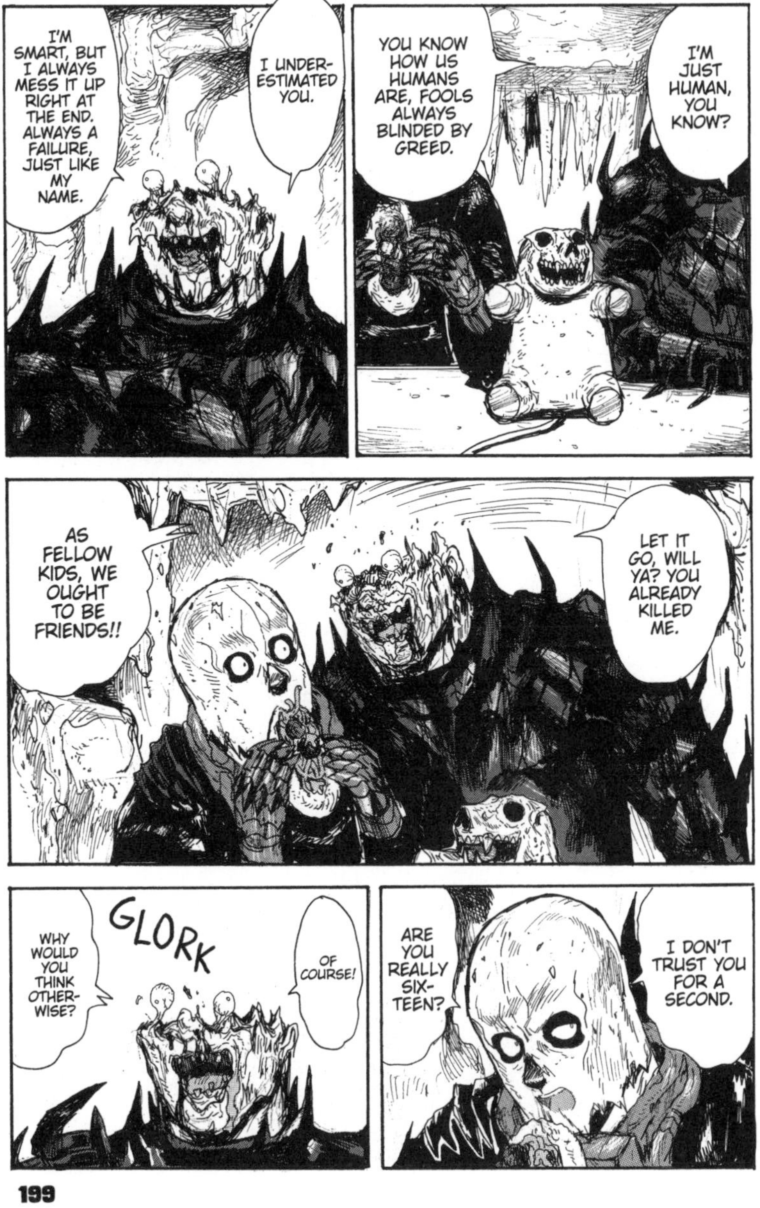
I'M JUST HUMAN, YOU KNOW?
YOU KNOW HOW US HUMANS ARE, FOOLS ALWAYS BLINDED BY GREED.
I UNDER-ESTIMATED YOU.
I'M SMART, BUT I ALWAYS MESS IT UP RIGHT AT THE END. ALWAYS A FAILURE, JUST LIKE MY NAME.
LET IT GO, WILL YA? YOU ALREADY KILLED ME.
AS FELLOW KIDS, WE OUGHT TO BE FRIENDS!!
I DON'T TRUST YOU FOR A SECOND.
ARE YOU REALLY SIX-TEEN?
OF COURSE!
GLORK
WHY WOULD YOU THINK OTHER-WISE?

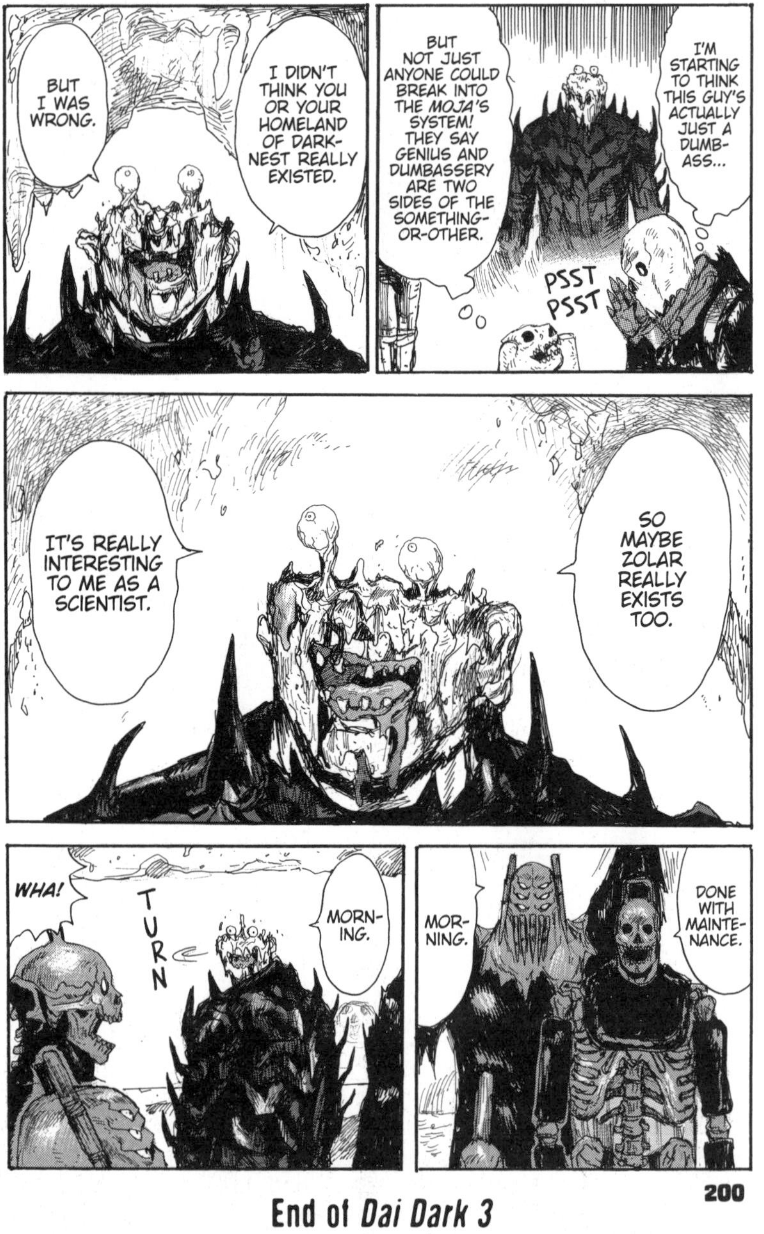
I'M STARTING TO THINK THIS GUY'S ACTUALLY JUST A DUMB-ASS...
BUT NOT JUST ANYONE COULD BREAK INTO THE *MOJA'S* SYSTEM! THEY SAY GENIUS AND DUMBASSERY ARE TWO SIDES OF THE SOMETHING-OR-OTHER.
PSST PSST
I DIDN'T THINK YOU OR YOUR HOMELAND OF DARK-NEST REALLY EXISTED.
BUT I WAS WRONG.
SO MAYBE ZOLAR REALLY EXISTS TOO.
IT'S REALLY INTERESTING TO ME AS A SCIENTIST.
DONE WITH MAINTE-NANCE.
MOR-NING.
MORN-ING.
TURN
WHA!

End of *Dai Dark 3*

DAI DARK

DAI DARK

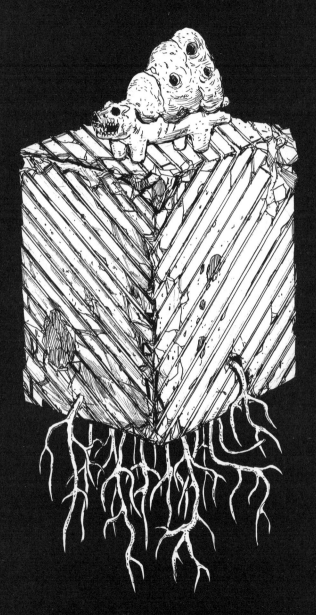

Bonus Bone

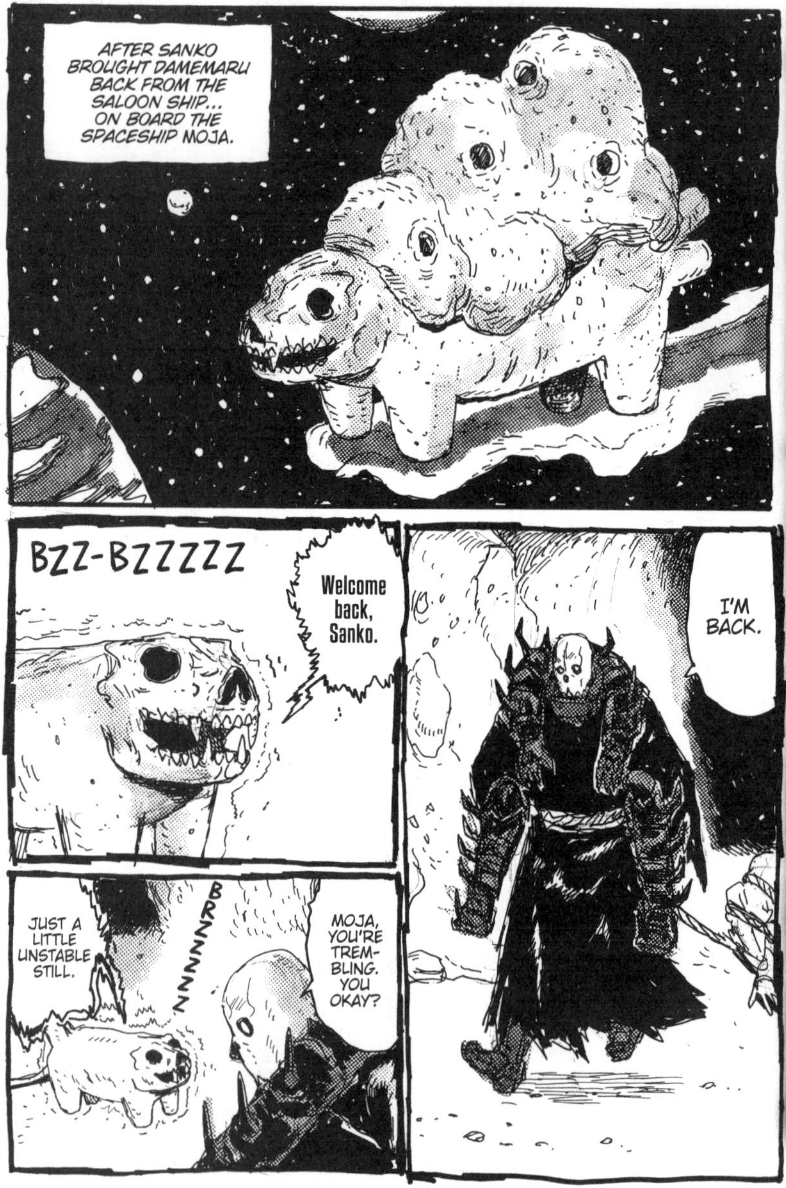
AFTER SANKO BROUGHT DAMEMARU BACK FROM THE SALOON SHIP... ON BOARD THE SPACESHIP MOJA.
I'M BACK.
BZZ-BZZZZZ
Welcome back, Sanko.
MOJA, YOU'RE TREM-BLING. YOU OKAY?
BRNNNNNN
JUST A LITTLE UNSTABLE STILL.

A fight between kids is followed by a return home with a headless corpse. What a day!!

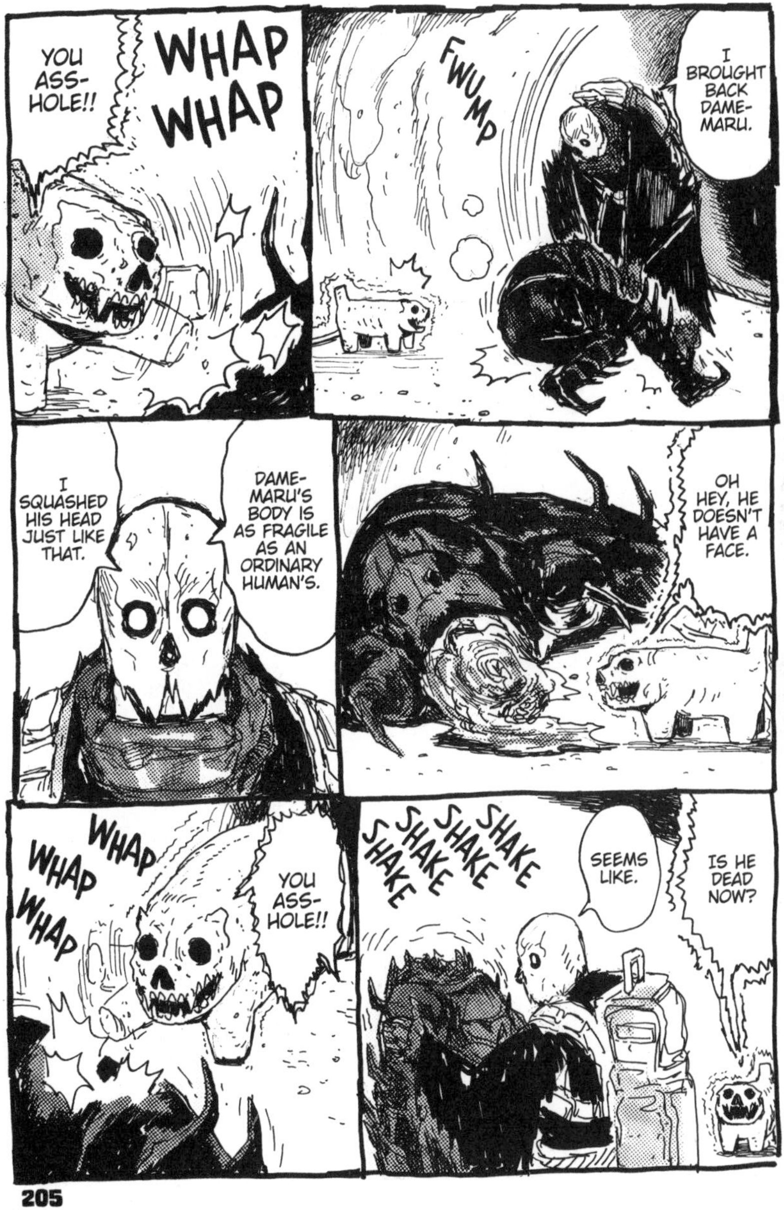
I BROUGHT BACK DAME-MARU.
FWUMP
WHAP WHAP
YOU ASS-HOLE!!
OH HEY, HE DOESN'T HAVE A FACE.
DAME-MARU'S BODY IS AS FRAGILE AS AN ORDINARY HUMAN'S.
I SQUASHED HIS HEAD JUST LIKE THAT.
IS HE DEAD NOW?
SEEMS LIKE.
SHAKE SHAKE SHAKE SHAKE
YOU ASS-HOLE!!
WHAP WHAP WHAP

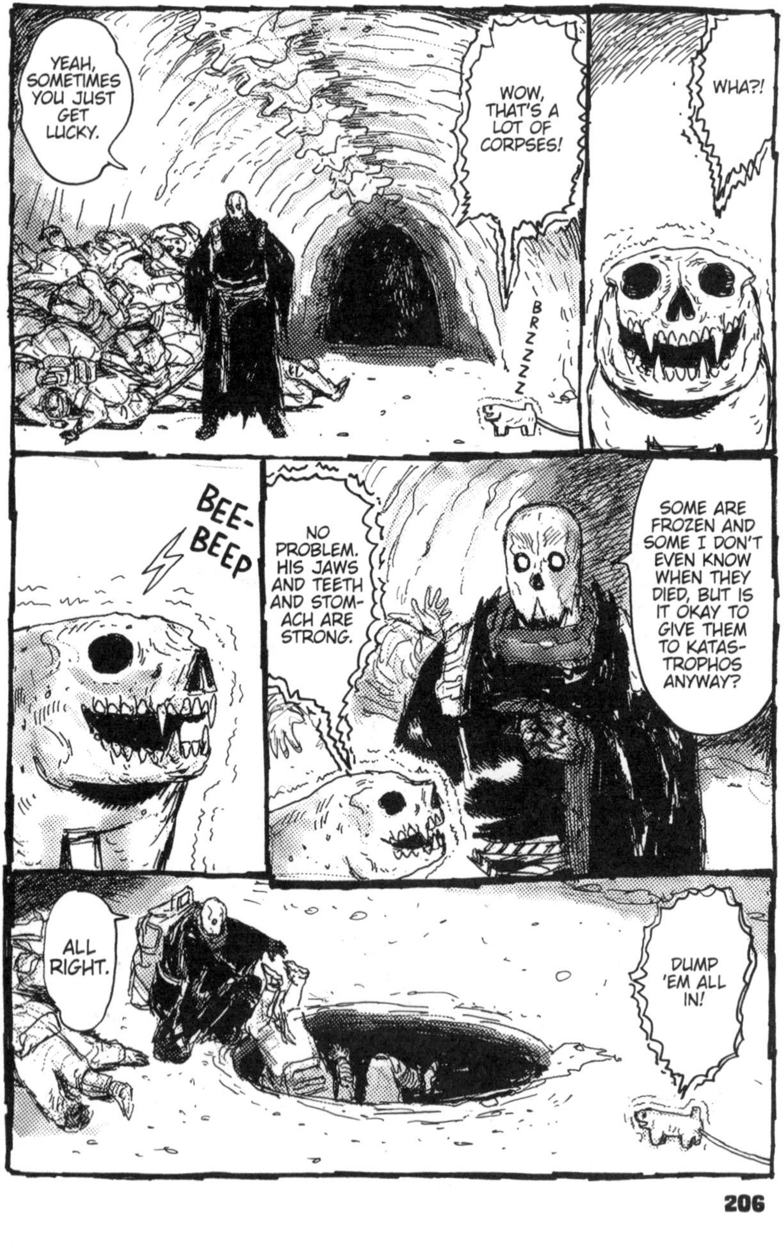
WHA?!
WOW, THAT'S A LOT OF CORPSES!
BRZZZZZ
YEAH, SOMETIMES YOU JUST GET LUCKY.
SOME ARE FROZEN AND SOME I DON'T EVEN KNOW WHEN THEY DIED, BUT IS IT OKAY TO GIVE THEM TO KATASTROPHOS ANYWAY?
NO PROBLEM. HIS JAWS AND TEETH AND STOMACH ARE STRONG.
BEE-BEEP
DUMP 'EM ALL IN!
ALL RIGHT.

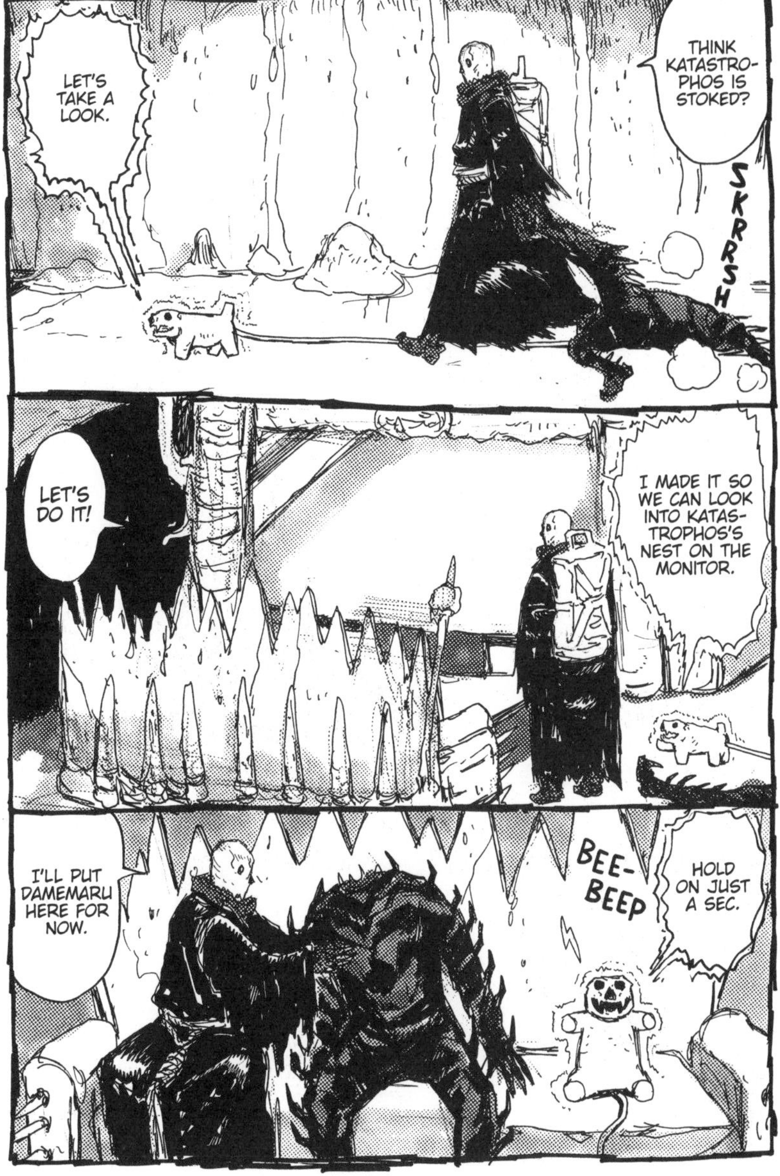
THINK KATASTROPHOS IS STOKED?
SKRRSH
LET'S TAKE A LOOK.
I MADE IT SO WE CAN LOOK INTO KATASTROPHOS'S NEST ON THE MONITOR.
LET'S DO IT!
HOLD ON JUST A SEC.
BEE-BEEP
I'LL PUT DAMEMARU HERE FOR NOW.

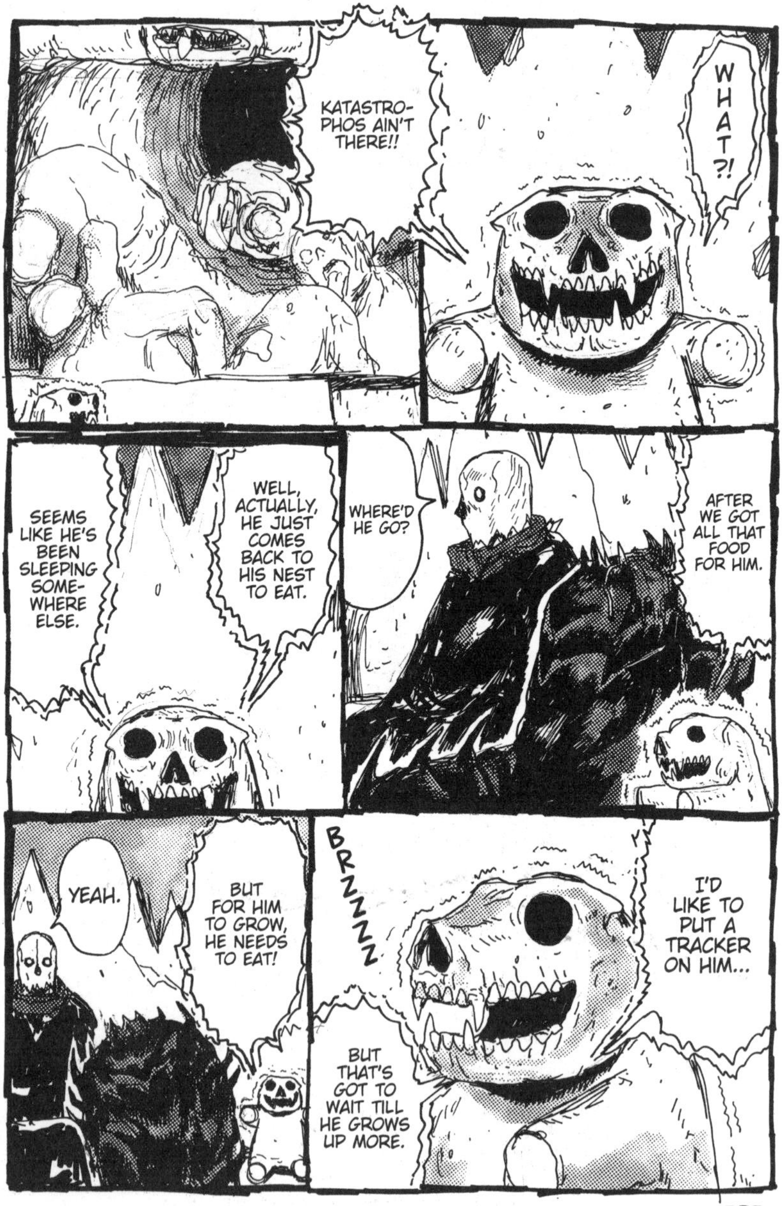
KATASTROPHOS AIN'T THERE!!
WHAT?!
AFTER WE GOT ALL THAT FOOD FOR HIM.
WHERE'D HE GO?
WELL, ACTUALLY, HE JUST COMES BACK TO HIS NEST TO EAT.
SEEMS LIKE HE'S BEEN SLEEPING SOMEWHERE ELSE.
BRZZZZZ
I'D LIKE TO PUT A TRACKER ON HIM...
BUT THAT'S GOT TO WAIT TILL HE GROWS UP MORE.
BUT FOR HIM TO GROW, HE NEEDS TO EAT!
YEAH.

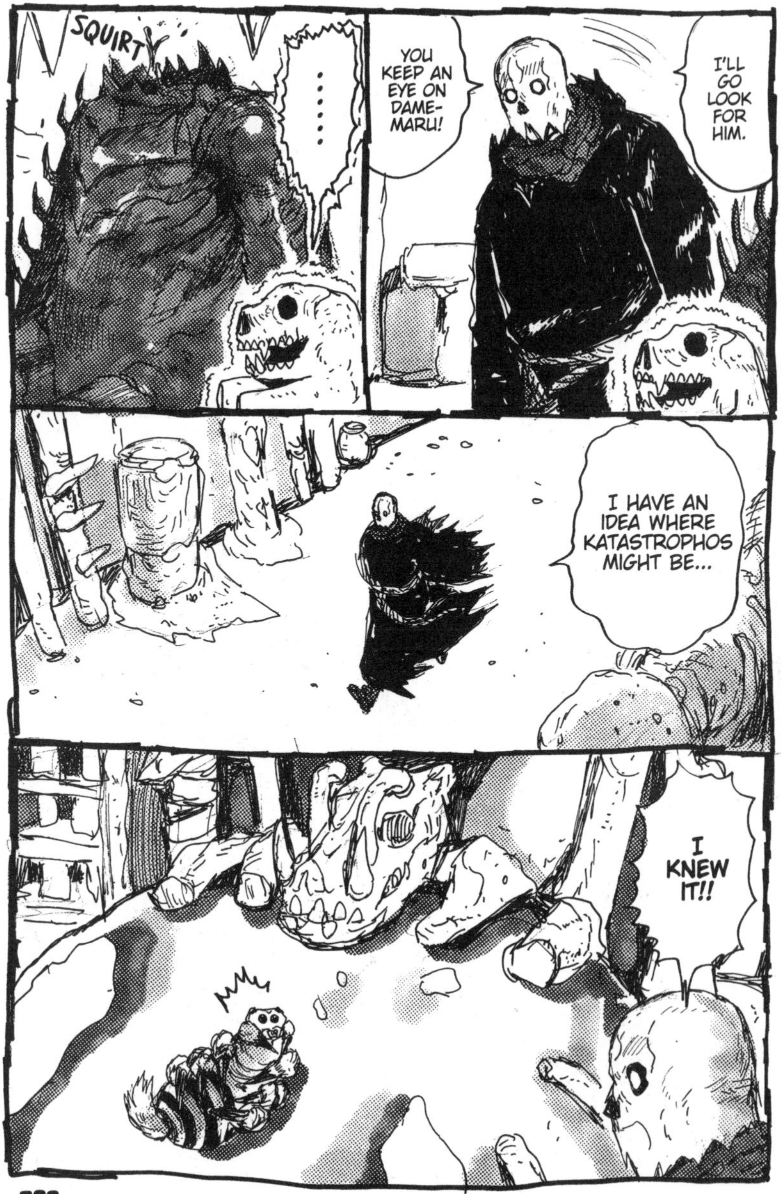
I'LL GO LOOK FOR HIM.
YOU KEEP AN EYE ON DAME-MARU!
SQUIRT
......
I HAVE AN IDEA WHERE KATASTROPHOS MIGHT BE...
I KNEW IT!!

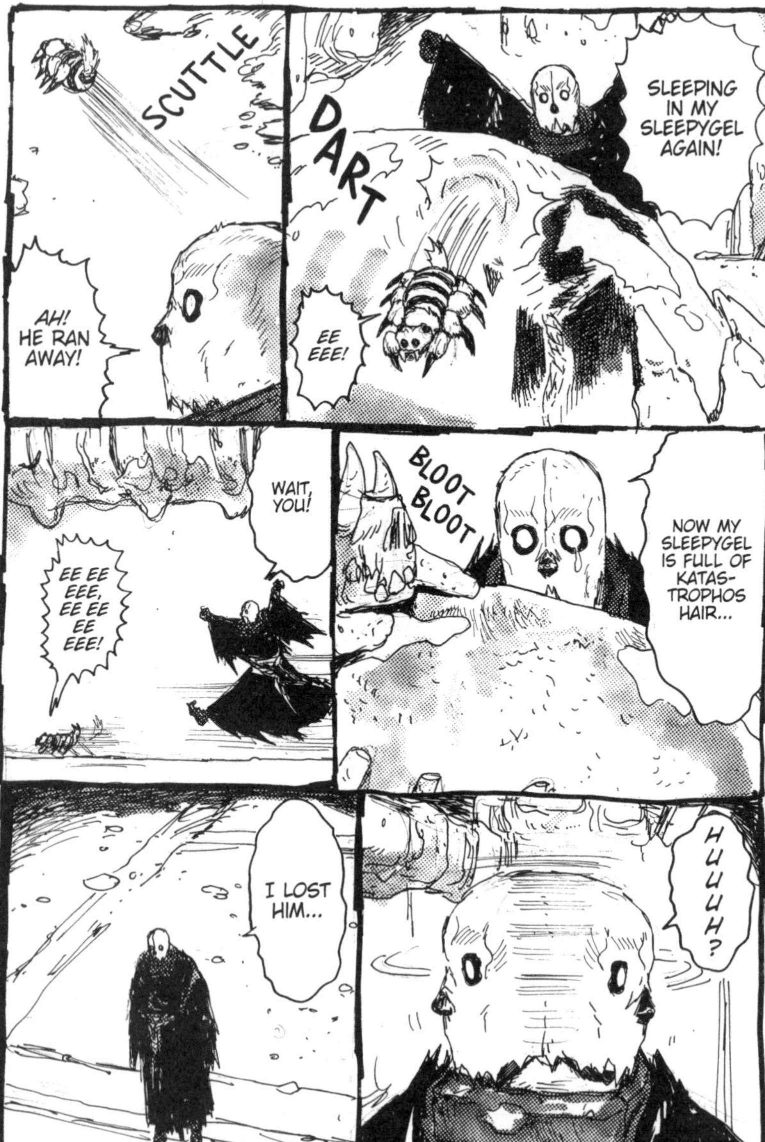
SLEEPING IN MY SLEEPYGEL AGAIN!
DART
EE EEE!
SCUTTLE
AH! HE RAN AWAY!
NOW MY SLEEPYGEL IS FULL OF KATAS-TROPHOS HAIR...
BLOOT BLOOT
WAIT, YOU!
EE EE EEE, EE EE EE EEE!
HUUUH?
I LOST HIM...

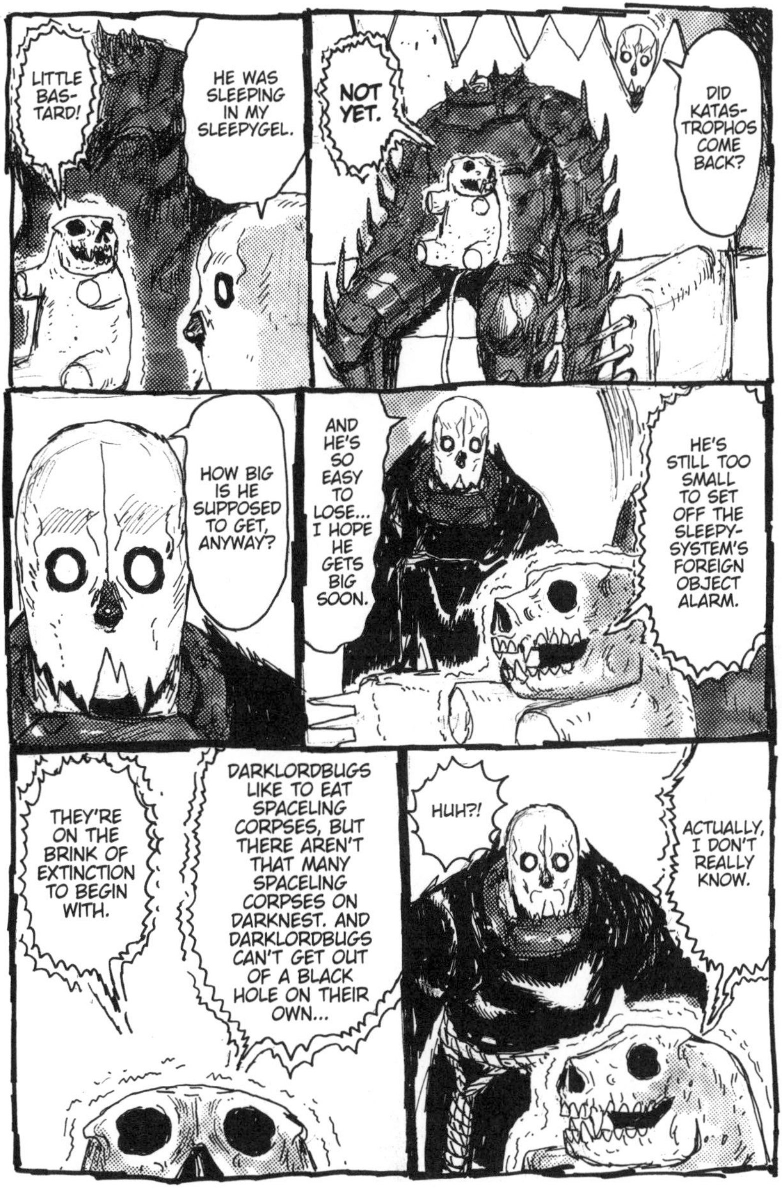

DID KATAS-TROPHOS COME BACK?
NOT YET.
HE WAS SLEEPING IN MY SLEEPYGEL.
LITTLE BAS-TARD!
HE'S STILL TOO SMALL TO SET OFF THE SLEEPY-SYSTEM'S FOREIGN OBJECT ALARM.
AND HE'S SO EASY TO LOSE... I HOPE HE GETS BIG SOON.
HOW BIG IS HE SUPPOSED TO GET, ANYWAY?
ACTUALLY, I DON'T REALLY KNOW.
HUH?!
DARKLORDBUGS LIKE TO EAT SPACELING CORPSES, BUT THERE AREN'T THAT MANY SPACELING CORPSES ON DARKNEST. AND DARKLORDBUGS CAN'T GET OUT OF A BLACK HOLE ON THEIR OWN...
THEY'RE ON THE BRINK OF EXTINCTION TO BEGIN WITH.

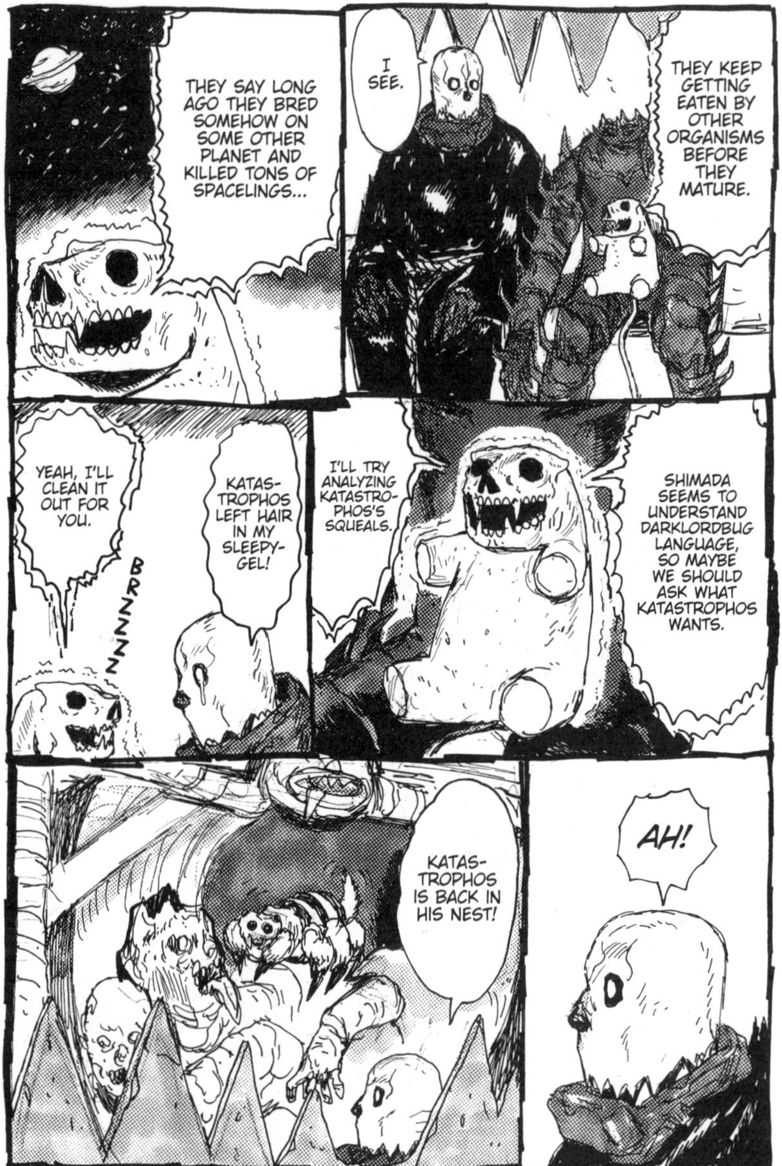
THEY KEEP GETTING EATEN BY OTHER ORGANISMS BEFORE THEY MATURE.
I SEE.
THEY SAY LONG AGO THEY BRED SOMEHOW ON SOME OTHER PLANET AND KILLED TONS OF SPACELINGS...
SHIMADA SEEMS TO UNDERSTAND DARKLORDBUG LANGUAGE, SO MAYBE WE SHOULD ASK WHAT KATASTROPHOS WANTS.
I'LL TRY ANALYZING KATASTROPHOS'S SQUEALS.
KATASTROPHOS LEFT HAIR IN MY SLEEPYGEL!
YEAH, I'LL CLEAN IT OUT FOR YOU.
BRZZZZ
AH!
KATASTROPHOS IS BACK IN HIS NEST!

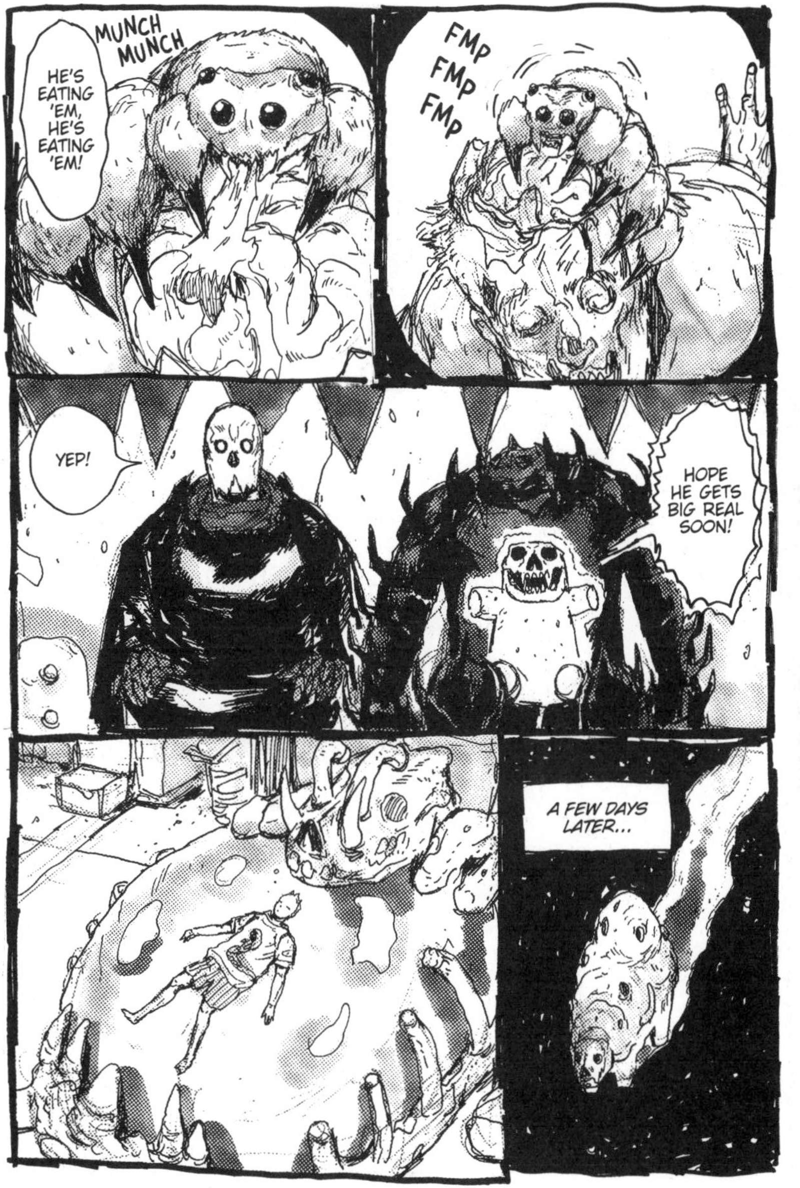
FMP
FMP
FMP
MUNCH
MUNCH
HE'S EATING 'EM, HE'S EATING 'EM!
HOPE HE GETS BIG REAL SOON!
YEP!
A FEW DAYS LATER...

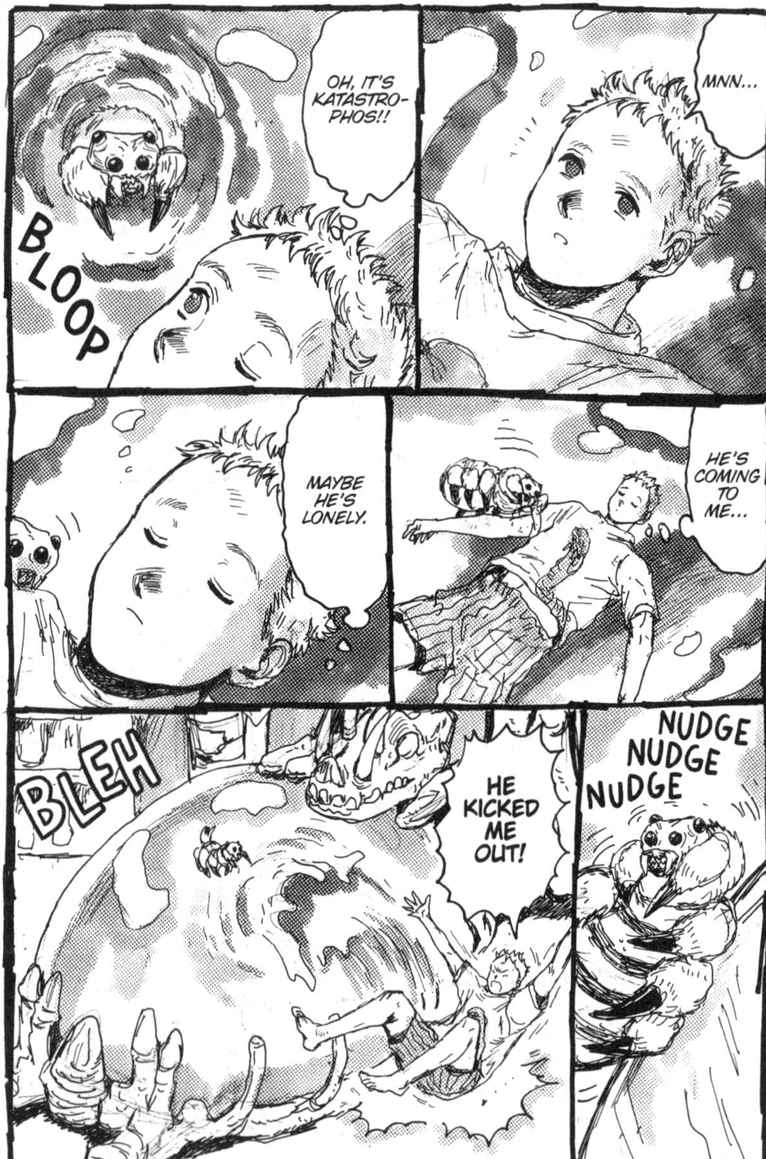
MNN...
OH, IT'S KATASTROPHOS!!
BLOOP
HE'S COMING TO ME...
MAYBE HE'S LONELY.
NUDGE NUDGE NUDGE
HE KICKED ME OUT!
BLEH

Life in space has no luxury like a good sleep in sleepygel. It's a must!

★ The true face of Hajime Damemaru

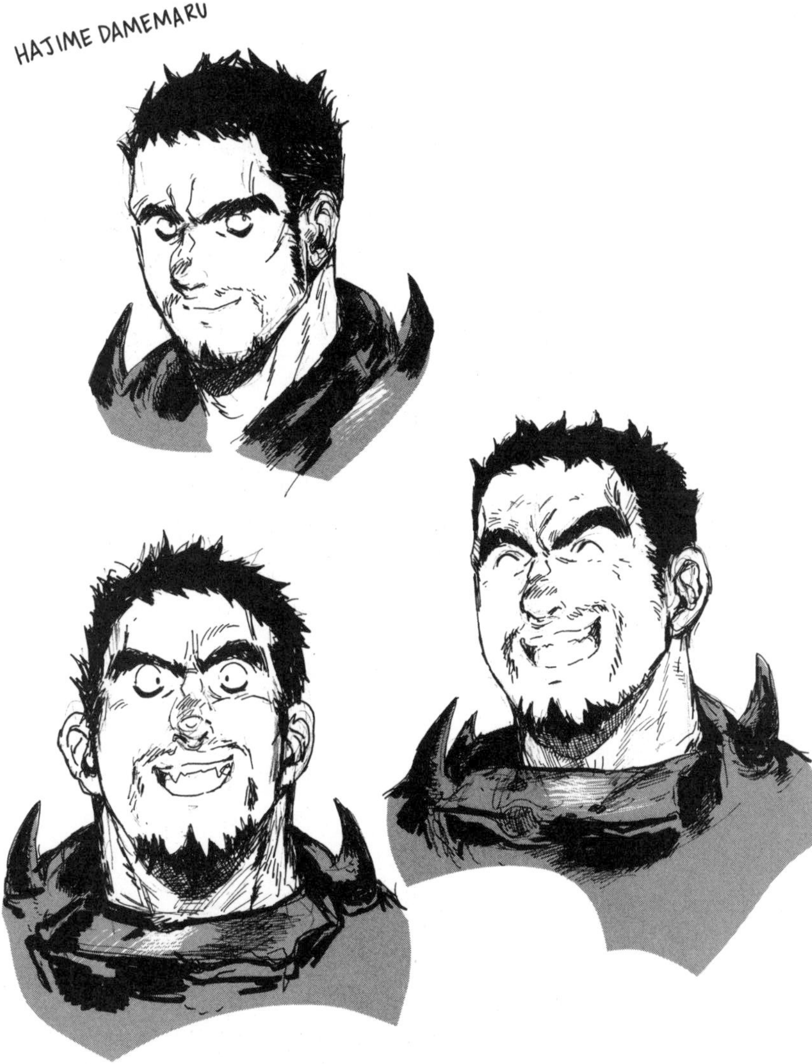
HAJIME DAMEMARU

SUPER-FUN CROSSWORD PUZZLE

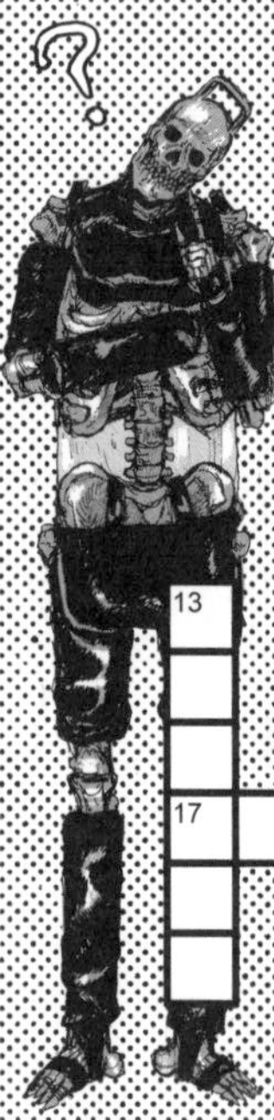

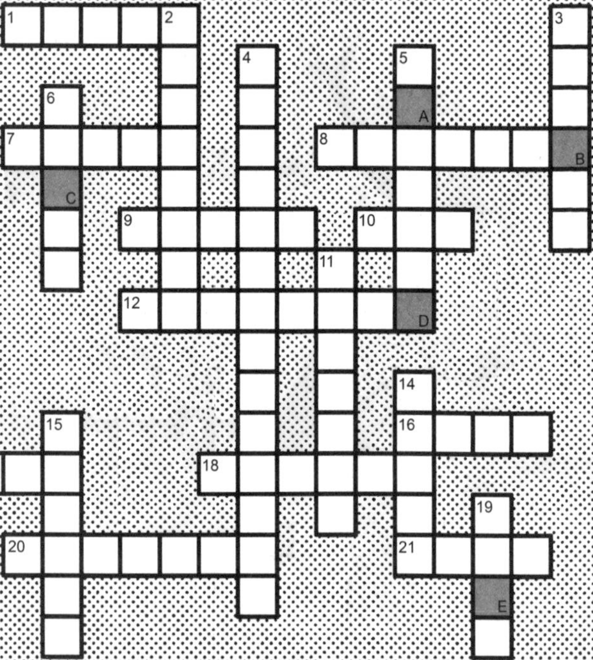
1
2
3
4
5
6
7
8
9
10
11
12
13
14
15
16
17
18
19
20
21
A
B
C
D
E

And in volume 4...we meet the

A B C D E!

ACROSS

1. Translucent mollusk. Has ten legs and squirts ink.

7. _____ and punishment.

8. A parasite that devours its spaceling host in order to grow bigger and bigger.

9. Espresso and milk make a caffe _____.

10. Silence. _____ it.

12. A really important member of the Lighthead Order.

16. Pink wine named after a flower.

17. Flat-shaped crustacean. Walks fast sideways and blows bubbles.

18. Shoot the shit at the main _____.

20. You don't need this, but it's worth having.

21. Like (17 Across), but not.

DOWN

2. One of the Four Little Shits. Actually a mere human of sixteen.

3. Long electrical weapon. Light _____.

4. Annual docking with the supply ship _____.

5. To correct that which is amiss.

6. Common description of the air outside.

11. A very good idea considering who knows what you might catch in space.

13. The *Moja's* interior is decorated with spacelings on _____.

14. *Su-pa-pi-ro-pe-ra-pi-ro...* It's _____ to me.

15. To steal someone away.

19. (2 Down) longs for a new one.

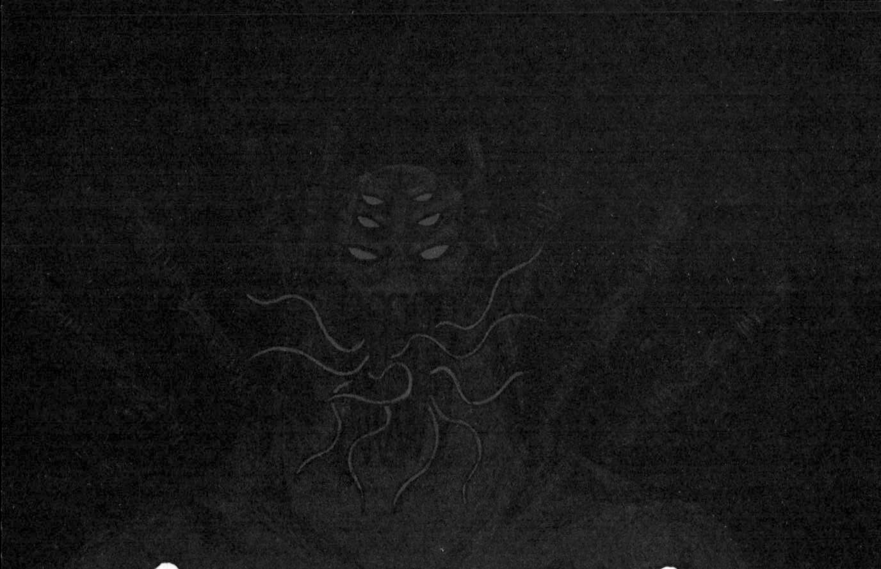

Dai Dark ② CROSSWORD PUZZLE ANSWER KEY

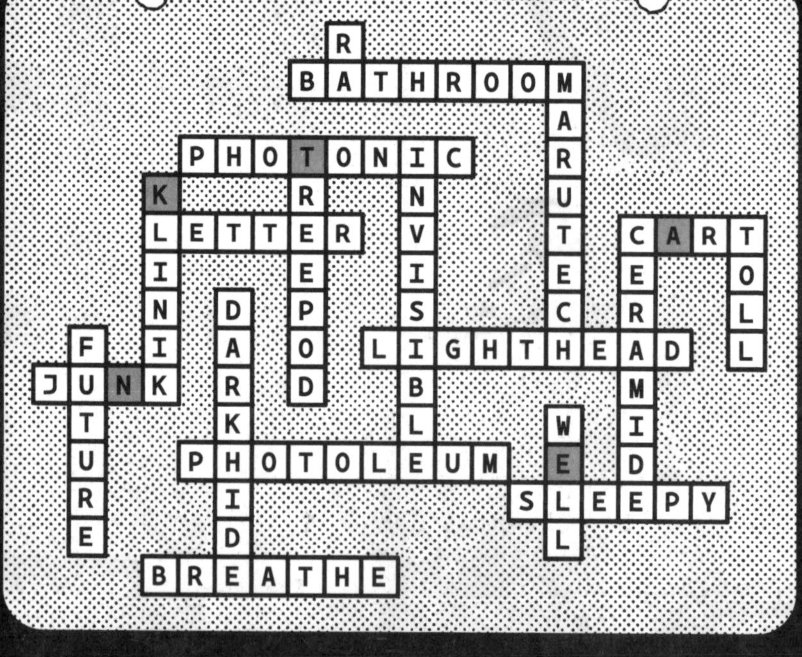

BATHROOM
MARUTECH
PHOTONIC
TREEPOD
KLINIK
LETTER
INVISIBL
CART
TOLL
CERAMID
DARKHID
FUTURE
JUNK
LIGHTHEAD
PHOTOLEUM
WELL
SLEEPY
BREATHE

DAI DARK

DAI DARK